NEW DIRECTIONS IN GERMAN STUDIES
Vol. 10

Series Editor:

Imke Meyer
Director, School of Literatures, Cultural Studies and Linguistics, and Professor of Germanic Studies, University of Illinois at Chicago

Editorial Board:

Katherine Arens
Professor of German, University of Texas at Austin

Roswitha Burwick
Distinguished Chair of Modern Foreign Languages Emerita, Scripps College

Richard Eldridge
Charles and Harriett Cox McDowell Professor of Philosophy, Swarthmore College

Erika Fischer-Lichte
Professor of Theater Studies, Freie Universität Berlin

Catriona MacLeod
Edmund J. and Louise W. Kahn Term Professor in the Humanities and Professor of German, University of Pennsylvania

Stephan Schindler
Professor of German and Chair, University of South Florida

Heidi Schlipphacke
Associate Professor of Germanic Studies, University of Illinois at Chicago

Ulrich Schönherr
Professor of German and Comparative Literature, Haverford College

James A. Schultz
Professor of German and Chair, University of California, Los Angeles

Silke-Maria Weineck
Professor of German and Chair of Comparative Literature, University of Michigan

David Wellbery
LeRoy T. and Margaret Deffenbaugh Carlson University Professor, University of Chicago

Sabine Wilke
Professor of German, University of Washington

John Zilcosky
Professor of German and Comparative Literature, University of Toronto

Volumes in the series:

Vol. 1. *Improvisation as Art: Conceptual Challenges, Historical Perspectives*
by Edgar Landgraf

Vol. 2. *The German Pícaro and Modernity: Between Underdog and Shape-Shifter*
by Bernhard Malkmus

Vol. 3. *Citation and Precedent: Conjunctions and Disjunctions of German Law and Literature*
by Thomas O. Beebee

Vol. 4. *Beyond Discontent: 'Sublimation' from Goethe to Lacan*
by Eckart Goebel

Vol. 5. *From Kafka to Sebald: Modernism and Narrative Form*
edited by Sabine Wilke

Vol. 6. *Image in Outline: Reading Lou Andreas-Salomé*
by Gisela Brinker-Gabler

Vol. 7. *Out of Place: German Realism, Displacement, and Modernity*
by John B. Lyon

Vol. 8. *Thomas Mann in English: A Study in Literary Translation*
by David Horton

Vol. 9. *The Tragedy of Fatherhood: King Laius and the Politics of Paternity in the West*
by Silke-Maria Weineck

Vol. 10. *The Poet as Phenomenologist: Rilke and the* New Poems
by Luke Fischer

Vol. 11. *The Laughter of the Thracian Woman: A Protohistory of Theory*
by Hans Blumenberg, translated by Spencer Hawkins

Vol. 12. *Roma Voices in the German-Speaking World*
by Lorely French

Vol. 13. *Vienna's Dreams of Europe: Culture and Identity beyond the Nation-State*
by Katherine Arens

Vol. 14. *Thomas Mann and Shakespeare: Something Rich and Strange*
edited by Tobias Döring and Ewan Fernie

Vol. 15. *Goethe's Families of the Heart*
by Susan Gustafson

Vol. 16. *German Aesthetics: Fundamental Concepts from Baumgarten to Adorno*
edited by J.D. Mininger and Jason Michael Peck

The Poet as Phenomenologist

Rilke and the New Poems

Luke Fischer

Bloomsbury Academic
An imprint of Bloomsbury Publishing Inc

B L O O M S B U R Y
NEW YORK • LONDON • OXFORD • NEW DELHI • SYDNEY

Bloomsbury Academic
An imprint of Bloomsbury Publishing Inc

1385 Broadway	50 Bedford Square
New York	London
NY 10018	WC1B 3DP
USA	UK

www.bloomsbury.com

BLOOMSBURY and the Diana logo are trademarks of Bloomsbury Publishing Plc

First published 2015
First published in paperback 2016

© Luke Fischer, 2015, 2016

All rights reserved. No part of this publication may be reproduced or transmitted in any form or by any means, electronic or mechanical, including photocopying, recording, or any information storage or retrieval system, without prior permission in writing from the publishers.

No responsibility for loss caused to any individual or organization acting on or refraining from action as a result of the material in this publication can be accepted by Bloomsbury or the author.

Library of Congress Cataloging-in-Publication Data
Fischer, Luke.
The poet as phenomenologist : Rilke and the new poems / Luke Fischer.
 pages cm. -- (New directions in German studies)
 Summary: "A groundbreaking contribution to Rilke scholarship that significantly expands the existing debate concerning the relation between Rilke's poetry and phenomenological philosophy"-- Provided by publisher.
 Includes bibliographical references and index.
 ISBN 978-1-62892-543-2 (hardback)
 1. Rilke, Rainer Maria, 1875-1926--Criticism and interpretation. 2. Rilke, Rainer Maria, 1875-1926--Aesthetics. 3. Phenomenology and literature. 4. Literature--Philosophy. I. Title. II. Title: Rilke and the new poems.
 PT2635.I65Z7189 2015
 831'.912--dc23
 2014039940

ISBN: HB: 978-1-6289-2543-2
 PB: 978-1-5013-2603-5
 ePub: 978-1-6289-2544-9
 ePDF: 978-1-6289-2545-6

Series: New Directions in German Studies

Cover design: Andrea F. Bucsi
Cover image: Rainer Maria Rilke, 1906 © Bettmann/CORBIS

Typeset by Fakenham Prepress Solutions, Fakenham, Norfolk NR21 8NN

To Jakob Ziguras and the art of poetic thinking

We speak of "inspiration," and the word should be taken literally. There really is inspiration and expiration of Being, respiration in Being, action and passion so slightly discernible that it becomes impossible to distinguish between who sees and who is seen, who paints and what is painted …
—Maurice Merleau-Ponty

And twofold Always. May God us keep
From Single vision and Newton's sleep.
—William Blake

Contents

Acknowledgments	ix
Preface	xi
Note on the German and English	xiii
List of Abbreviations	xv

Introduction 1
   Poetry and the Crisis of Philosophy 1
   Rilke and Phenomenology 8
   The Structure of the Work 10

1 Phenomenology and the Problem of Dualism 15
   The Problem of Dualism 15
      Dualism as an Existential Condition 18
      The Inadequacy of Metaphysical Dualism 22
      Materialist Monism 23
      Idealist Monism 24
      The Privileged Status of Phenomenology 25
   The Twofold Seeing of the Human Other 40
      Elementary Reflections on the Perception of the Other 44
      The Genesis of the Sense of an Individual Character 60
   Conclusion of Chapter 65

2 Learning to See: Rilke and the Visual Arts 69
   Rilke's Formulation of the Problem of Dualism 75
   Rilke's Developmental Conception of the Dualistic Condition 78
   Rilke and Romanticism 90
   Rilke's Engagement with Rodin and Cézanne: The
     Formulation of "das Werk des Gesichts" 96
      The Disposition of the Artist 100
      Rodin's Physiognomic Vision 115

	From *Ding* to *Kunst-Ding:* The Translation of Vision into the Sculptural Work of Art	123
	Cézanne's Participative Vision	141
	The Task of *Réalisation* and Cézanne's *Sachliches Sagen*	150
	Conclusion of Chapter	169
3	**Rilke as Seer: A Twofold Vision of Nature**	**171**
	Rilke's Seeing	177
	From the Middle Rilke to the Later Rilke	198
	Rilke's *Sachliches Sagen*	207
	Conclusion of Chapter	211
4	**The *Neue Gedichte* as a Twofold Imagining of Things**	**215**
	Introduction	215
	The Phenomenological Character of the *Neue Gedichte*	216
	Poetry as the Language of Imagination	221
	Rilke's *Dinggedichte*	227
	Nature as Poetically Disclosed	231
	Animal Poems	231
	Flower Poems	253
	Other Aspects of Nature	267
	Conclusion of Section	275
	Other *Dinggedichte*	275
	Conclusion of Chapter	297
Conclusion		**299**
Epilogue		**305**
Bibliography		307
Index		319

Acknowledgments

First and foremost I would like to thank my wife, Dalia Nassar, for her constant support, constructive comments, and engaging conversations over the many years in which I have worked on this project. I would like to thank Christoph Jamme for his keen interest in this interdisciplinary research from its early stages up until the present and for his invaluable comments on drafts of this manuscript. I am also grateful for the DAAD Post-Doctoral Research Grant that I received in 2009 in order to work on this book under the sponsorship of Christoph Jamme at Leuphana University. I would like to thank the Rilke scholar, Manfred Engel, and the philosophers, Anthony Steinbock and Richard Eldridge, for their interest in this project and their helpful comments on drafts of this manuscript. I am also grateful to John Grumley for his feedback on an early draft of the book. Much of the initial research for this book was undertaken in Tübingen, Germany, and part of my time in Tübingen was supported by a DAAD Research Grant. I am grateful to Manfred Frank for sponsoring this grant and to the conducive intellectual community I found in Tübingen. I would like to thank my friend Jakob Ziguras for many years of stimulating conversations about the relation between poetry and philosophy, and Lutz Näfelt for his friendship and illuminating discussions of Rilke's poems. I am also grateful to David Macauley for fruitful conversations about environmental philosophy and poetry. Many friends, family members, and academics have assisted this project in diverse ways; while I will not name them all here, I am immensely grateful for their support.

Preface

The central argument as well as much of the research for this book were completed as early as 2007 (a hundred years after the first of volume of Rilke's *Neue Gedichte* [*New Poems*] was published). The overall project had assumed written form by 2008 (the centenary of the second volume of *New Poems*). Since then I have undertaken further research and both revised and polished the monograph a number of times. Nevertheless, the fundamental argument and thoughts remain unchanged, and I had originally planned to publish *The Poet as Phenomenologist: Rilke and the New Poems* earlier than 2015. Why do I mention this?

For many years I have seriously pursued both philosophy and the creative writing of poetry (as well as academic literary studies). These two pursuits have both benefited and conflicted with each other. It had been my aim to publish the present work and subsequently to publish my first collection of poems. There were two reasons behind this aim (in addition to my love of writing poetry). First, one of the main conclusions of *The Poet as Phenomenologist* is that the art of poetry can address certain philosophical problems more adequately than philosophy itself. In other words, the present work provides a philosophical justification for the writing of poetry. Second, there is an intimate connection between my interpretation of Rilke's *New Poems* and central features of my poetry collection *Paths of Flight* (North Fitzroy, VIC: Black Pepper, 2013). The poetry collection creatively explores and expands on some of the key concerns of the present work. In short, I wanted to publish *The Poet as Phenomenologist* prior to *Paths of Flight*, as this order reflects the chronology of my own development and the former, in significant respects, provides a hermeneutic, critical, and philosophical horizon for the latter.

It is likely that the above aim was limited by a one-sidedly philosophical orientation. Poems mediate their own background and message, even if they do not conceptualize them. Nevertheless, I am glad that both *The Poet as Phenomenologist* and *Paths of Flight* are now in print.

In addition to the theme of dualism, a central theme of *The Poet as Phenomenologist* is Rilke's poetic vision of the natural world. In recent years my knowledge of ecocriticism and environmental philosophy has deepened significantly. While I have made some references to scholarship in these areas, it did not seem necessary or advantageous to the main argument of the present work to reframe the consideration of nature in light of scholarship in the environmental humanities. Nevertheless, there are numerous ways in which my approach to Rilke could contribute to current debates in these areas. I have published some articles that contribute to these debates, and plan to make further contributions to scholarship in ecopoetics and environmental philosophy.

In *The Poet as Phenomenologist* I have generally sought to discuss phenomenology and Rilke in a way that is intelligible to readers who have not previously specialized in either or both of these areas. Nevertheless, some of the more philosophical parts of this work may be challenging to those with little background in philosophy or theory. While philosophical issues are discussed throughout the text, Chapter 1 is exclusively philosophical in nature. This chapter is crucial to the development of the argument that runs through the book. However, should certain readers (without a background in philosophy or theory) share an interest in Rilke but find Chapter 1 (and parts of the Introduction) too challenging, they may still find it valuable to read the book from Chapter 2 onward, which is where the focus on Rilke begins.

Note on the German and English

The Poet as Phenomenologist draws on many German sources—German philosophy, literary criticism, prose, and poetry. However, I wanted to make the text accessible to readers without German. Due to the many quotations from German sources I was faced with the dilemma of how to render English translations without sacrificing dimensions of meaning that are inevitably lost in translation. The compromise I reached was to substitute English translations for the excerpts from German prose (philosophical, critical, and literary prose); however, due to the untranslatability of poetry I have provided quotations from German poems in their original form and English translations in the footnotes.[1] The reader without German can, thereby, still follow the discussion of the poems.

In many cases I have provided my own translations of the German sources. Whenever there is no indication of an English source and the translations have not been attributed to others, the translations are my own. In other cases I have drawn on existing translations—sometimes modifying and sometimes maintaining them. In all cases (excluding my own translations) the sources have been referenced in the footnotes. In my translation of poems from the *Neue Gedichte* I consulted the translation by Edward Snow.[2] I would like to thank Lutz Näfelt for his co-translation of a number of the poems and for his feedback on other translations.

---

1 For a discussion of the specific difficulties of translating Rilke's *Neue Gedichte* see Luke Fischer, "Understanding through Translation: Rilke's *New Poems*," in *Perspectives on Literature and Translation: Creation, Circulation, Reception*, ed. Brigid Maher and Brian Nelson (New York: Routledge, 2013), 56–72.
2 Rilke, *New Poems: A Revised Bilingual Edition*, trans. Edward Snow (New York: North Point Press, 2001).

List of Abbreviations

KA 1–4	Rilke, Rainer Maria. *Werke: Kommentierte Ausgabe in vier Bänden.* Edited by Manfred Engel, Ulrich Fülleborn, Horst Nalewski, and August Stahl. Frankfurt am Main: Insel Verlag, 1996.
KA 5	Rilke, Rainer Maria. *Werke: Kommentierte Ausgabe. Supplementband: Gedichte in französischer Sprache. Mit deutschen Prosafassungen.* Edited by Manfred Engel and Dorothea Lauterbach. Frankfurt am Main: Insel Verlag, 2003.
AR dt	Rilke, Rainer Maria and Auguste Rodin. *Der Briefwechsel und andere Dokumente zu Rilkes Begegnung mit Rodin.* Edited by Rätus Luck. Frankfurt am Main: Insel Verlag, 2001.
Ben	Rilke, Rainer Maria. *Briefwechsel mit Magda von Hattingberg "Benvenuta."* Edited by Ingeborg Schnack and Renate Scharffenberg. Frankfurt am Main: Insel Verlag, 2000.
AR	Rilke, Rainer Maria. *Auguste Rodin.* Translated by G. Craig Houston. Mineola, NY: Dover Publications, 2006.
LC	Rilke, Rainer Maria. *Letters on Cézanne.* Translated by Joel Agee. Foreword by Heinrich Wiegand Petzet. New York: Fromm International Publishing Corporation, 1985.

Introduction

Poetry and the Crisis of Philosophy

Modern philosophy is in a time of crisis. Not only has the "end of metaphysics" been announced but also the "end of philosophy." No one who advocates these "ends" means that there is no longer a *need and task of thinking*. Rather, "metaphysical" or traditional forms of philosophical conceptualization are no longer regarded as adequate or satisfying. What was and is metaphysics and philosophy is called to transform itself into something else which might no longer bear the name "philosophy."

The Poet as Phenomenologist: Rilke and the New Poems offers a unique response to this crisis of philosophy. It addresses a traditional metaphysical problem—the problem of dualism—but in an unconventional manner. After demonstrating the necessity of a phenomenological approach to the problem of dualism, I articulate a phenomenology of poetic vision as an exceptional overcoming of dualism. In particular, the poetry of Rainer Maria Rilke (1875–1926) is explicated as a distinctive and significant response to this problem. Rilke was one of the greatest poets of the twentieth century, and the transcendence of the dualism between the visible and the invisible, the inner and the outer, was one of his primary concerns. Moreover, as certain critics have argued, his poetry is implicitly phenomenological (see below).

This book takes a traditional metaphysical problem, that of dualism, and argues that it is more adequately addressed through turning to poetic vision and poetic language. In this way it places philosophy into question and shows that poetry can extend the horizons of "philosophical" understanding. It argues that in certain respects poetry can address a philosophical problem better than philosophy itself. The individual chapters challenge philosophy and metaphysics in various ways. Chapter 1 draws attention to essential limitations of metaphysical thought in a way that is directly related to Husserl's phenomenological critique of traditional metaphysics, and also positively illustrates the manner in which a phenomenological approach is better able

2 The Poet as Phenomenologist

to address the problem of dualism than metaphysical approaches. Chapter 1 provides the foundation and background for the most significant contributions, which are made in Chapters 2, 3, and 4. Chapters 2 and 3 draw on Rilke in order to articulate an artistic and poetic vision of the world (with a special focus on Nature), which transcends the horizon of everyday and scientific perception as well as philosophical reflections on perception. Chapter 4 illustrates the manner in which poetic language exceeds the language of the concept—the traditional language of philosophy. In these ways the present work places philosophy into question and offers a response to the crisis of philosophy and metaphysics. As should already be clear, the turn to poetic vision and poetry is not motivated by purely literary and aesthetic concerns, although these play an essential role in my interpretation of Rilke. Rather, it is primarily motivated by the conviction that poetry can reveal insights that "answer" metaphysical and philosophical questions in a more adequate way than philosophy itself. While an extensive answer to the question as to how *philosophy* might transform itself is not provided, the book contributes to the philosophical tradition (of which Martin Heidegger is the most prominent exponent) which finds in poetry food for thought, and shows that a poetic way of being, poetic vision, and poetic language, facilitate insights which are philosophically significant.

In order to specify how I seek to respond to the crisis of metaphysics, it is important to give further consideration to the meaning of the expression, the "end of metaphysics." The dictum of the "end of metaphysics" (like the "end of art" and the "end of history") is a view much older than twentieth- and twenty-first-century philosophy. Hume, Kant, and Nietzsche are just a few earlier thinkers who in distinctive ways announced the "end of metaphysics." In the twentieth century Heidegger, and later Derrida, also spoke of such an "end." However, each of these thinkers means something different by "end" and "metaphysics." For this reason when this expression is used in contemporary philosophy it is often ambiguous; a polyvocal history resonates in it. If the expression is to acquire any clarity it requires specific consideration. While there are surely points of connection between Kant's and Heidegger's understandings of the "end of metaphysics," there are also important differences. As Kant and Heidegger exemplify paradigmatic and influential ways in which the "end of metaphysics" has been thought, what I mean by the "end of metaphysics" will be articulated in relation to their views.[1]

---

1 For a consideration of the end of metaphysics in Heidegger and phenomenology, see John Sallis, *Delimitations: Phenomenology and the End of Metaphysics* (Bloomington, IN: Indiana University Press, 1995 [2nd edn]). On the connections

Introduction 3

As it has already been indicated that the present work aims to address a metaphysical question while seeking a non-metaphysical solution, it is clear that I do not regard the "end of metaphysics" as implying that it is no longer relevant to contemplate the great *metaphysical questions*. The questions of freedom, Being, God, death, immortality, dualism, etc. are questions central to human existence. Were the "end of metaphysics" to mean the cessation of the attempt to *thoughtfully* address these questions then nothing should be more vigorously rejected than the "end of metaphysics." The "end of metaphysics" would then, in renouncing such essential human questions, conceal, perhaps behind a harmless façade, a telos of barbarism. A renunciation of these questions implies nothing less than the relinquishment of the genuine attempt to orient ourselves as human beings in the world or cosmos. These questions have a bearing on us whether we explicitly ask them or not, and to ignore them is a passive, inauthentic, and confused response to them.

While Kant was clearly concerned with metaphysical questions, the limitations that he placed on human reason (metaphysics) and the rigid boundary he set up (a boundary already present in a less rigid way in Scholastic thought) between reason and faith, ultimately relegating such questions to the realm of faith, contributed to an "effective history" which has in many respects led to a philosophical agnosticism and the renunciation of the aspiration to resolve metaphysical questions. No doubt, the Humean variety of this "end" and all strains of reductive, scientific, and skeptical thought have also contributed to this state of affairs.

While in Heidegger and Kant a shared emphasis on human finitude is perceptible, there are central differences between them.[2] For Kant "metaphysics" is the attempt to determine rationally the reality of God, freedom, immortality, etc. The Kantian "end of metaphysics" is the judgment that human reason is essentially incapable of determining these realities. The critique of reason is the illustration of the impotence of reason and the lack of intellectual intuition, which would be required to grant reality to reason's ideas. For Heidegger "metaphysics" means

---

between Heidegger's path beyond "philosophy" and mystical thought, see John D. Caputo, *The Mystical Element in Heidegger's Thought* (New York: Fordham University Press, 1986). For a recent discussion of the "end of philosophy" in the context of German Idealism, see Eckart Förster, *Die 25 Jahre der Philosophie: Eine systematische Rekonstruktion* (Frankfurt am Main: Vittorio Klostermann, 2011).

2 See n. 6. For Heidegger's particular interpretation of the "finitude" of human knowing in Kant, see Martin Heidegger, *Kant und das Problem der Metaphysik*, *Gesamtausgabe* [henceforth *GA*] 3 (Frankfurt am Main: Vittorio Klostermann, 1991 [1929]).

4 The Poet as Phenomenologist

the history of philosophy beginning with Plato (the end of Pre-Socratic thought) which is founded on an inadequate understanding of Being. The "end of metaphysics" implies the need to think Being differently and the historical "completion" of metaphysics in the technological world-disclosure.[3] The "end of metaphysics" in Heidegger certainly does not mean the renunciation of "metaphysical" questions, while it does involve their reformulation and a new kind of response. "Being" is, after all, the central metaphysical concern; the "end of metaphysics" does not involve abandoning the question of Being but thinking Being more radically. A similar point can be made in relation to the place of the divine ("God," "gods," "the Holy") in Heidegger's later thought. As in metaphysical thought the divine and its relation to the human are a central question. However, Heidegger is no longer satisfied with the God of traditional metaphysics; he renounces this God, the God understood as *causa sui* and articulated in "onto-theo-logical" terms—God thought on the basis of the failure to properly think the "ontological difference."[4] Drawing on Hölderlin, Heidegger regards the absence of the divine in the modern world—in other words nihilism—as bearing historical and ontological significance. This absence is conceived as an ontological deprivation, and discerned in relation to a possible *self-showing* or *self-revelation* of the divine or "the Holy."[5] In that the divine is thought "phenomenologically," there are also significant respects in which Heidegger's thought here transcends the "Kantian limits" but within a different horizon of thought. The only thing that could enable a self-showing of the divine in Kant is intellectual intuition, which Kant rules out. In short, Heidegger's "end of metaphysics" does not involve a renunciation of fundamental metaphysical questions on the part of thought; it involves

---

3 See, for instance, Heidegger, "Die Frage nach der Technik," in *GA* 7 (2000 [1953]), 7–36; "The Question Concerning Technology," in *Basic Writings*, ed. David Farrell Krell (London: Routledge, 1978).
4 Heidegger, "Die Onto-theo-logische Verfassung der Metaphysik," in *Identity and Difference*, trans. Joan Stambaugh (Chicago: University of Chicago Press, 2002), 107–43. [*Identity and Difference* is a bilingual publication of two texts—"Die Onto-theo-logische Verfassung der Metaphysik" and "Der Satz der Identität." The reference here is to the German.]
5 See, for instance, Heidegger, "Wozu Dichter?," in *GA* 5 (1977 [1946]), 269–320; "What Are Poets For?," in *Poetry, Language, Thought*, trans. Albert Hofstadter (New York: Harper & Row, 1971), 91–142. With regard to the phenomenological character of Heidegger's later thought, see Heidegger, "Seminar in Zähringen 1973," in *GA* 15 (1986), 372–407; "Die Herkunft der Kunst und die Bestimmung des Denkens," in *Denkerfahrungen 1910–1976*, ed. Hermann Heidegger (Frankfurt am Main: Vittorio Klostermann, 1983), 135–49. Cf. Yoshihiro Nitta, "Der Weg zu einer Phänomenologie des Unscheinbaren," in *Zur philosophischen Aktualität Heideggers*, vol. 2, ed. Dietrich Papenfuss and Otto Pöggeler (Frankfurt am Main: Vittorio Klostermann, 1990), 43–54.

the attempt and the need to address and formulate them *otherwise*.[6] If *The Poet as Phenomenologist* has a bearing on the "end of metaphysics" it is in the latter sense. This work shares a close affinity to Heidegger in that it places "philosophy" and "metaphysics" into question, and does *not* relinquish central philosophical or metaphysical questions, but regards them as better addressed when approached in an unconventional way.

Turning to poetry for "philosophical" reasons also places the present project in proximity to Heidegger's thought. However, Heidegger was not the first thinker to see philosophical significance in poetry. Though working within a very different philosophical milieu the early German Romantics, to take an exemplary case, saw the origin and telos of philosophy and the sciences in poetry. Moreover, irrespective of any specific philosophical tradition, philosophy (including analytic philosophy), even when it does not explicitly reflect on poetry, is in its essence determined by a relation to poetry, at least, in the broad sense of the word. Philosophy and poetry both share an intrinsic relation to language. However, the original poetry of *mythology* is *older* than philosophical thought. The world is first understood and articulated in the language of mythology. Philosophy, beginning with the Pre-Socratics, inherits this older language and thinking, and involves the gradual internal transformation of mythic thinking and language into conceptual thinking and language. Philosophy is the daughter of mythology and its transformation. Of course, poetry in the modern age

---

6 This is, at least, what I regard to be Heidegger's most significant contribution. Nevertheless, there are aspects, as suggested above, in which Heidegger's emphasis on human finitude is close to Kant. While the emphasis on finitude and temporality in hermeneutic phenomenology (Heidegger and Gadamer) is important in that it brings to awareness the concrete situatedness of all human endeavors, I am also of the view that in certain respects contemporary thought is characterized by a one-sided emphasis on finitude. The concrete situatedness of human existence does involve boundaries or horizons that might be thought of as "limits." However, it is problematic if these limits are regarded as rigid and as absolute, which is often the case (the Kantian limitations of knowledge, for instance). Human existence is equally characterized by a capacity of self-transcendence—the ability to transcend existing horizons—and thus it is problematic to delineate absolute limits of human understanding. As Heraclitus already remarked, "You would not find the limits of the soul although you travel all the path—so deep is its account [logos] (B 45)" and the "soul has a self-increasing account [logos] (B 115)," *Early Greek Philosophy*, trans. Jonathan Barnes (New York: Penguin, 1987). Romantic irony is another earlier (though modern) historical conception which acknowledges the interrelationship of finitude and what might be called "infinitude." The contemporary emphasis on finitude to my mind needs to be complemented with such an acknowledgment of infinitude. However, an extensive discussion of this matter is beyond the scope of the present work.

differs from the original poetry of mythology. However, modern poetry still bears a closer relationship to the mythological, in its *imaginative* portrayal of the world and appropriation of mythical topoi, than the other offspring of mythology, philosophy.

In the course of philosophy's history, poetry sometimes appears as a friend and leader, and sometimes as an opponent of philosophy. Mytho-poetic elements still abound in the thought of the Pre-Socratics. The mythological persists in Plato's thought but it is situated within, one might say "tamed" by, a larger rational context, and Plato famously sets the philosopher against the poet. The poets lack the critical awareness of philosophers in that they are unable to articulate reflectively the meaning of their works. Aristotle, in contrast to Plato, sees a philosophical significance in poetry, placing it above history as it presents circumstances in their essence and necessity rather than being bound to contingent events. However, philosophy is still clearly ranked above poetry, and the works of Aristotle bequeathed to us are far from poetic in style. In modern German philosophy we find in Schiller the view that the poet is representative of the true human being, and that beauty announces new insights ahead of reason. As aforementioned, the early German Romantics saw the culmination of philosophy and the sciences in poetry. Hegel, in contrast, while acknowledging poetry as the highest of the arts and the highest artistic mediation of the truth, regards it as the point of transition between art and philosophy. Art is finally "sublated" or *aufgehoben* in the self-transparency of conceptual thought. In the twentieth century we find in Heidegger a kind of reversal of the Hegelian priorities, which shows a certain kinship between Heidegger and German Romanticism, though Heidegger's thought differs in central respects from German Romanticism and Idealism. Heidegger nevertheless turns primarily to a poet of this period (though little recognized then), finding in Hölderlin a poetry which addresses us out of the future, meaning that it speaks from and to a kind of thinking *beyond* and *after* metaphysics. In Heidegger, Nietzsche, and more recent French thought one also notes a *stylistic* kinship between philosophy and poetry in that the boundary between philosophical prose and literature is no longer clear. At the other end of the spectrum are all forms of scientistic philosophy and reductionism which see in poetry nothing more than "fiction" and the subjective "expression of feelings." These scant considerations will suffice as a few pointers to some of the diverse relationships between philosophy and poetry in their intertwined history.[7]

---

7 I have focused on the relationship between philosophy and poetry from the side of philosophy, rather than the attitude of poets toward philosophy, as the former is the main emphasis of the present work. One well-known and pertinent example of the latter is Paul Celan's engagement with Heidegger's thought.

The present work stands in close proximity to those directions of thought that see in poetry a significance which in important respects *surpasses* philosophy. As my approach is phenomenological in nature and draws on central aspects and motifs of Heidegger's thought, I would like to make a few further comments on similarities and differences between this project and Heidegger's thinking, as well as on its relation to phenomenology more broadly.

While Heidegger's thought plays a significant role, this monograph does not follow a Heideggerian trajectory. It sets forth an independent argument and the work of other phenomenologists, particularly Maurice Merleau-Ponty, is also of central importance. Heidegger's critique of metaphysics, and his thought as a whole, revolves around the question of Being. While I do discuss Being and the relation between thinking and Being, Being is not my central theme. It is dualism and its many facets that are the central concern; the opposition between Being and thinking is addressed as one member of a whole list of related dichotomies—visible/invisible, outer/inner, sensible/spiritual, passivity/activity—which must be transcended if a solution to the problem of dualism is to be found. This said, I adhere to the Heideggerian conception of "truth" as unconcealment, and in so far as this conception is based on the view that the event of truth involves a kind of coincidence of Being and thinking, my thought relates to Heidegger's understanding of Being more generally. The concept of "experience" along with other concepts that play an important part in much phenomenology (Husserl, Merleau-Ponty), but a less significant role in Heidegger's thought, are also central to this work. The thematization of perception in Chapter 1 and poetic vision in Chapters 2 and 3 is closer to Merleau-Ponty's "chiasmic phenomenology" than Heidegger's thought. However, in so far as I address themes such as the holy, the divine, poetic epiphany, and mysticism, it is again closer to motifs in Heidegger's oeuvre than the more agnostic thought of Merleau-Ponty. Merleau-Ponty's meditations on art primarily focus on *painting*. This is in keeping with the centrality of perception in all of his writings. Heidegger in contrast devotes more attention to poetry, which directly relates to the centrality of language in his thought. In this sense, my presentation is again closer to Heidegger. However, the visual arts were absolutely central to Rilke's poetic endeavors and Rilke's writings on Auguste Rodin and Paul Cézanne bear much in common with Merleau-Ponty's thought. Moreover, Heidegger, Merleau-Ponty, and Rilke all share in common a veneration and supreme estimation of the significance of Cézanne.[8]

---

8 This is discussed in Chapter 2.

8   The Poet as Phenomenologist

Rilke and Phenomenology

Heidegger was certainly influenced by Rilke but his explicit engagement with Rilke's poetry mostly consists in scattered remarks, often insisting on important differences between his thought and Rilke's poetry even where the language is on the surface the same—"das Offene" is, for instance, a key word in Rilke's poetry, a word which is also central to Heidegger but understood differently.[9] Heidegger's only detailed reflection on the significance of Rilke's poetry is in his well-known essay "Wozu Dichter?"[10] This piece was first delivered as a lecture to a small audience to commemorate the twentieth anniversary of Rilke's death.[11] While I am sympathetic to some aspects of Heidegger's reading of Rilke there are also points of disagreement. A comprehensive consideration of Heidegger's reading of Rilke is beyond the scope of the present work; however, I do articulate certain differences at various points. Heidegger's remarks on Rilke are also mostly limited to Rilke's late works, *Duineser Elegien* (*Duino Elegies*) and *Die Sonette an Orpheus* (*The Sonnets to Orpheus*), as well as other late fragments and poems.[12]

---

9   See Heidegger, *Parmenides*, GA 54 (1992 [1942/43]); *Parmenides*, trans. André Schuwer and Richard Rojcewicz (Bloomington, IN: Indiana University Press, 1992), 151ff.; Luke Fischer, "Animalising Art: Rainer Maria Rilke and Franz Marc," *Australasian Journal of Ecocriticism and Cultural Ecology* 3 (2013): 54ff., n. 7; Giorgio Agamben, *The Open: Man and Animal*, trans. Kevin Attell (Stanford, CA: Stanford University Press, 2004), 57ff.

10 See n. 5.

11 Rilke died on December 19, 1926.

12 In "Wozu Dichter?" Heidegger refers to these two late works, for which Rilke is most renowned, as Rilke's "gültiges Gedicht" or "valid poetry," meaning that in these poems Rilke presents an authentic and significant poetic response to the situation of nihilism or the time of the "world's night." Heidegger, "Wozu Dichter?," 274; "What Are Poets For?," 96. In Chapter 2 I argue that a proper appreciation of Rilke's late work must pass through his writings of the middle period. This claim already differs from Heidegger's sharper division between Rilke's later and earlier work. I do not explicitly address the theme of the significance of Rilke's writings of the middle period for the predicament of nihilism and it can be said that Rilke's middle writings do not have the same kind of "philosophical" scope as, for instance, the *Duineser Elegien*. Nevertheless, in Chapter 2 I point out aspects in which Rilke's middle work surpasses his later poetry and I leave it to the reader to decide the extent to which my explication of the middle Rilke offers a significant response to the situation of nihilism. Gadamer was also a sincere admirer of Rilke's poetry, as is already indicated by the posthumously published poem by Rilke that provides the epigraph to his magnum opus, *Wahrheit und Methode* (*Truth and Method*). However, like Heidegger, Gadamer primarily engaged with Rilke's late work (though in Chapter 4 I indicate mutually illuminating connections between Rilke's middle poetry and Gadamer's thought). For an overview of Gadamer's interpretations of Rilke, see Christoph Jamme, "'Doppelbotschaft

This book, in contrast, focuses on the "middle Rilke," in particular the *Neue Gedichte* (*New Poems*) and their background.

The Poet as Phenomenologist makes a distinctive contribution to the phenomenological tradition, a contribution that shares much in common with Heidegger's and Merleau-Ponty's views, without being identifiable with them. My approach is guided both by independent phenomenological investigations and the attempt to find an adequate way of articulating Rilke's "philosophical," and more specifically phenomenological, significance.

Although Rilke did not have any explicit ties to phenomenological philosophy, it is my conviction that his philosophical significance can be best understood from a phenomenological perspective. This inherent affinity between Rilke and phenomenology has been investigated by a number of literary critics. Most notably, Käte Hamburger argues for a Husserlian phenomenological interpretation of Rilke in her essay "Die Phänomenologische Struktur der Dichtung Rilkes."[13] More recently, Wolfgang Müller has objected to Hamburger's identification of Rilke and Husserl, although he does acknowledge certain respects in which Rilke is implicitly phenomenological.[14] In Chapter 4 I contribute a new point of view to this debate. One of the key shortcomings in this discussion of Rilke and phenomenology is the limitation of phenomenology to its Husserlian form. In contrast, I situate Rilke in a broader phenomenological context and regard him as sharing more in common with aspects of Heidegger's and Merleau-Ponty's thought.

There are two main ways in which the projects of Rilke's middle period (1902–10), offer a distinctive phenomenological and poetic response to the problem of dualism. First, inspired by the example of visual artists (most importantly Rodin and Cézanne), Rilke devoted his attention to the world and activity of perception. Rilke's praxis of perception led to a privileged disclosure of things, in which inner and outer, the invisible and the visible, activity and passivity, are revealed as two aspects of a single whole. This integrated or non-dualistic vision, which I call a twofold seeing, bears much in common with Merleau-Ponty's phenomenology of perception and his characterization of the

---

vom wirklichen Liebenkönnen und vom Sterbenmüssen': Gadamer und Rilke," in *Wege zur Wahrheit: Festschrift für Otto Pöggeler zum 80. Geburtstag*, ed. Annemarie Gethmann-Siefert and Elisabeth Weisser-Lohmann (Munich: Fink, 2009), 145–56.

13 Käte Hamburger, "Die phänomenologische Struktur der Dichtung Rilkes," in *Philosophie der Dichter: Novalis, Schiller, Rilke* (Stuttgart: W. Kohlhammer Verlag, 1966), 172–275.

14 Wolfgang Müller, "Rilke und die Dinglyrik der Moderne," in *Rilke und die Weltliteratur*, ed. Manfred Engel and Dieter Lamping (Düsseldorf: Artemis und Winkler, 1999), 214–35.

perception of visual artists. In a discussion of the inspired perception of painters, Merleau-Ponty states the following, which is equally applicable to the "inspiration" of Rilke's poetry, particularly the *Neue Gedichte*:[15]

> We speak of "inspiration," and the word should be taken literally. There really is inspiration and expiration of Being, respiration in Being, action and passion so slightly discernible that it becomes impossible to distinguish between who sees and who is seen, who paints and what is painted. We say that a human being is born the moment when something that was only virtually visible within the mother's body becomes at once visible for us and for itself. The painter's vision is an ongoing birth.[16]

Chapters 2 and 3 articulate Rilke's inspired seeing as a non-dualistic vision, with a special focus on his vision of Nature. While Rilke's vision is very close to Merleau-Ponty's phenomenology of perception, a point noted by Edward Snow and discussed by Jennifer Anna Gosetti-Ferencei,[17] I also articulate slight differences between their views.

Second, Rilke sought to translate his twofold vision into his poetry, and many of his *Neue Gedichte*, particularly the so-called *Dinggedichte* ("thing-poems"), facilitate a twofold disclosure of things for the reader's *imagination*. Chapter 4 closely considers a number of Rilke's *Neue Gedichte* and explicates how his *poetic language* is able to transcend dualism in ways that are not possible for traditional *philosophical language*, namely the language of conceptual thought. Rilke's vision and poetry are thus able to reveal phenomena in a non-dualistic manner and to transcend the dualism or opposition between the visible and the invisible, the outer and the inner.

The Structure of the Work

Chapter 1 is divided into two main sections and provides the necessary philosophical background for the approach to Rilke. The first section introduces the philosophical problem of dualism and the shortcomings

---

15 See Luke Fischer, "Perception as Inspiration: Rilke's *New Poems*," *Agenda* (Special Rilke Issue) 42, nos. 3–4 (2007): 170–83.
16 Maurice Merleau-Ponty, "Eye and Mind," in *The Merleau-Ponty Aesthetics Reader: Philosophy and Painting*, ed. Galen A. Johnson and Michael B. Smith (Evanston, IL: Northwestern University Press, 1993 [1961]), 129.
17 Edward Snow, "Introduction," in Rilke, *New Poems: A Revised Bilingual Edition*, trans. Edward Snow (New York: North Point Press, 2001), 5–6; Jennifer Anna Gosetti-Ferencei, *The Ecstatic Quotidian: Phenomenological Sightings in Modern Literature and Art* (University Park, PA: The Pennsylvania State University Press, 2007), 156ff.

Introduction 11

of traditional philosophical responses to this problem. Conventional "solutions" to the problem of dualism are shown to suffer from a deficiency at the level of experience. While materialist monism and idealist monism claim to overcome dualism, I demonstrate that as long as they fail to address the *experiential* dimension of dualism, they do not succeed in their goal. In short, a dualism remains between the *experience* of reality and what is *posited* as the *unifying ground* of reality. Hence, dualism must be addressed as an experiential problem. However, this conclusion entails another difficulty, namely the question as to what is the most adequate way of articulating experience. I demonstrate that only a phenomenological approach can adequately articulate the structure of experience. Thus, the present work does not take a phenomenological horizon for granted; rather, it illustrates that the attempt to overcome dualism in a satisfying manner calls for a phenomenological approach.

The second section of Chapter 1 provides a bridge between phenomenological philosophy and the subsequent interpretation of Rilke. It is devoted to a phenomenological analysis of the perception of the human Other and serves a number of related purposes. Most importantly, the phenomenological inquiry serves to articulate the *structure of a non-dualistic vision* that is implicit to our everyday perception of the Other. While Chapters 2 and 3 argue that Rilke's vision of Nature transcends a quotidian perception of the world (as well as a phenomenology of the everyday[18]), this section of Chapter 1 serves to delineate and introduce a structure of non-dualistic seeing that is deepened in the interpretation of Rilke. Put simply, Rilke's vision of Nature is in many ways analogous in structure to our everyday perception of the human Other. In addition, Chapter 1 performs the important function of discarding, on the basis of phenomenological analyses, certain prejudices that hinder the recognition of a non-dualistic or twofold vision. In relation to our perception of human Others, for instance, there is a widespread prejudice that we perceive the bodies of Others directly while the *interiority of Others* is mediated by a kind of *projection* or *introjection*. Even Husserl's view of the givenness of Others in the *Cartesian Meditations* in significant respects conforms to this common view. In contrast, I present an independent phenomenological investigation, which builds on aspects of Heidegger's and Merleau-Ponty's work and shows that Others are revealed as *unique* characters. I, in each case, do not understand the Other through introjecting my own internal qualities into him or her; rather, the Other is revealed as a distinctive

---

18 Much phenomenology has thematized the *life-world* in its *everydayness*. Husserl's phenomenological analysis of the "natural attitude" and Heidegger's articulation of *Dasein* in its everydayness are two of the best-known cases.

sensible-spiritual or twofold unity. These considerations serve to correct common dualistic misconceptions about the nature of experience and thus open the way for the more radical approach to the problem of dualism undertaken in relation to Rilke. Chapter 3, for instance, argues that Rilke cultivated a twofold seeing of animals that enabled a distinctive revelation of the animals themselves. While our usual conceptions of the human Other are dualistic, widespread views about the perception of animal Others are even more dualistic. By clearing up misconceptions about the perception of human Others, the way is paved for the more radical claims that are made about Rilke's perception.

Chapter 1 leads from the attempt to address the philosophical problem of dualism, to the unique prospects revealed by Rilke's poetic overcoming of dualism. Chapters 2 and 3 draw on Rilke's letters, essays, short stories, poems, and his novel *Die Aufzeichnungen des Malte Laurids Brigge* (*The Notebooks of Malte Laurids Brigge*), in the argument that his vision of the world transcends the horizon of everyday perception and differs from an ordinary philosophical approach to dualism. While Merleau-Ponty is probably the philosopher and phenomenologist who came closest to "philosophizing" like a painter—in his close attention to the perceptual world and serious engagement with visual art—philosophers generally devote more attention to *reflection* and *thought* than to *perception*, even if perception is the theme under consideration. Chapters 2 and 3 argue that, and explicate how, Rilke's *praxis* of perceiving the world in a similar manner to visual artists who paint *en plein air* led to a non-dualistic disclosure of phenomena that cannot be attained by other means. Chapter 2 focuses in particular on Rilke's formulation of the problem of dualism and his engagement with the visual arts, while Chapter 3 provides a culmination to these considerations by focusing more exclusively on Rilke's praxis of seeing.

Chapter 4, as previously mentioned, explicates the way in which various poems in the *Neue Gedichte* mediate a twofold vision for the reader's imagination that surpasses the conceptual and abstract language of traditional philosophy. The central thesis of the present work is that Rilke's vision (the focus of Chapters 2 and 3) and poetry (the focus of Chapter 4) reveal an exceptional overcoming of dualism.[19]

While *The Poet as Phenomenologist* makes a significant contribution to phenomenological thought and Rilke scholarship, I am also aware of

---

19 What I later elaborate as a "phenomenology of the exceptional" may in some ways be compared to Heidegger's characterization of his later thought as being concerned with a "phänomenologie des Unscheinbaren [phenomenology of the unapparent]"; however, my approach to perception does not repeat a Heideggerian path of thought, and has more in common with Merleau-Ponty. See n. 5.

its limits. By no means does it address the full extent and every facet of the problem of dualism. Nevertheless, it reveals the importance of an *experiential* approach to the problem of dualism and demonstrates the value of a continuing dialogue between poetry and thought, "Dichten und Denken." More broadly speaking, it elaborates the "philosophical" import of a poetic way of being, seeing, thinking, and speaking.

One Phenomenology and the Problem of Dualism

The Problem of Dualism

The problem of dualism has been a central and recurring issue in the history of philosophy. The attempts to address dualism have differed in relation to specific historical and intellectual contexts. Most recently, it has become evident that the metaphysics of dualism needs to be overcome in order to facilitate a more sustainable relationship between humanity and the natural environment, and for this reason environmental philosophers have challenged dualistic modes of thought and sought to reconceive the human/nature and mind/body relation in a variety of ways.[1]

The problem of dualism is a conceptual, metaphysical, and experiential/existential problem. It is a conceptual problem in that oppositional concepts are operative in various realms of discourse (academic and everyday discourse). This generally involves the operation and assumption of a metaphysics that determines a conceptualization of the world without being explicitly thematized. The virtue of metaphysics lies in the fact that it explicitly thematizes the problem of dualism and seeks to articulate a solution. However, a failing of metaphysics lies in the fact that it more often than not regards the problem of dualism as a merely *theoretical* problem. Metaphysics seeks to solve the problem of dualism through a certain conceptualization of the fundamental nature of reality or Being (as matter, spirit, or both). However, the problem of dualism is more than a merely theoretical problem. It is also an experiential or existential condition.

---

1 See, for instance, Val Plumwood's insightful discussion of the problem of dualism in *Feminism and the Mastery of Nature* (London: Routledge, 1993). See also Arne Naess, "The Shallow and the Deep, Long-range Ecology Movement," *Inquiry* 16 (1973): 95–100. My approach to Rilke in Chapters 2, 3, and 4 also makes contributions toward overcoming human/nature dualism that are significant for environmental philosophy, ecophenomenology, and ecocriticism.

The subsequent considerations illustrate the experiential deficiency in metaphysical responses to the problem of dualism.

The word "metaphysics" has become so multivalent over the last few hundred years that one is faced with doubt as to whether the word has any coherent meaning when uttered by a philosopher. When so many philosophers from Hume to Kant, from Nietzsche to Heidegger to Derrida, have announced the "end of metaphysics," and each philosopher means something quite different by "metaphysics" and "end," the use of the word "metaphysics" is ambiguous and confused if one does not specifically articulate what one means by the word.

In the present chapter, "metaphysics" is used in reference to endeavors to conceptualize the fundamental nature of reality. By "metaphysics," I mean ontology of a certain sort, namely those philosophical conceptions that articulate the whole of reality as being fundamentally "material," "ideal," or as including two substances— "material" and "ideal." These basic conceptions appear in various forms but can be broadly designated as materialist monism, idealist monism, and metaphysical dualism. Due to the fact that metaphysics has primarily been concerned with the *theoretical* articulation of the fundamental character of reality, it has generally suffered from an experiential deficiency. This deficiency can be gleaned in the difference between the manner in which the metaphysician and the mystic talk about God. Within metaphysical discourse "God" functions as a postulate. For the mystic "God" contains a reference to an experiential content, a *revealed* or *experienced* God. The former is like a person who talks about roses but has never seen a rose, whereas the latter is analogous to someone who knows roses from first-hand experience. It is due to this deficiency in experience that metaphysics shows itself as incapable of providing an *experiential* overcoming of dualism. However, it is important to qualify that different "metaphysical systems" vary with regard to the place they make for experience (and some theories that are commonly designated as "metaphysical" may not fit within the boundaries of the concept as delimited here). The notion of *intellektuelle Anschauung* (intellectual intuition) in German Idealism, for instance, in that it refers to an *experience* (*intellectual* experience) of the point of identity between matter and spirit, the finite and the infinite, etc. could possibly be articulated as a phenomenological or experiential moment of non-dualism (such an inquiry is, of course, beyond the scope of this work).[2] However, even in the case of an Idealist such as Schelling,

---

2 It should perhaps be said that I am using the word "experience" in the broadest sense possible, meaning anything of which I can become conscious. This includes the German *Erlebnis* as well as *Erfahrung* (i.e., *hermeneutische Erfahrung*).

a tension is evident between the foundational role of intellectual intuition and systematic theoretical aims.³

What I mean by metaphysics could be defined further as a kind of *objectifying* thought, which is another way of saying that it is a theorizing that does not translate into experience or intuitive givenness. When the metaphysician speaks of God or matter he/she speaks of an in-itself, a reality that is supposed to exist independently of the knower. Any notion of an in-itself that is incapable of attaining the status of a for-itself cannot possibly achieve a solution to the problem of dualism; such a notion sets up an ultimate rift between being and knowing. Moreover, the very notion of an in-itself, or to be more specific, a *Ding an sich*, whether it be conceived as material or spiritual or both, is problematic. This is due to the fact that the only content that the notion of a thing in itself can acquire derives from *my representation of it*. However, the metaphysician assumes that the "thing in itself" refers to something *objective* that cannot come to any subjective givenness. What the metaphysician fails to see is that the *Ding an sich* is a phantom of the metaphysician's own making. It derives all its content from the subject. This content is then *objectified* into a realm of absolute transcendence. The very notion is, thereby, also deficient in content, because it cannot attain to any intuitive givenness—neither sensible nor intellectual intuition. For this reason metaphysical habits of thought tend to be the most *subjectivistic* and *objectivistic* at the same time. Whatever is ascribed the status of a for-itself is interpreted as *subjective*, while the genuine ground of reality is *objectified* as a pure in-itself. In this light, although Kant sought to put an end to metaphysics, his actual manner of thinking executes the epitome of a metaphysical direction of thought. It combines the most extreme objectivism with the most extreme subjectivism, albeit *transcendental* subjectivism. In so far as what fundamentally exists—*das Ding an sich*—is defined as completely transcendent, and all appearances or phenomena are defined as subjective (transcendentally subjective), Kant's first critics (Maimon, Schulze, Jacobi, and others) were right in seeing that his thought is ultimately a kind of skepticism. There is a complete rift between being and knowing such that there is no way in which knowing can ever gain access to what is. For the present purposes, it can be said that an extreme dualism is at work here, despite Kant's efforts to bridge

---

3 The most problematic aspect of intellectual intuition within the German Idealist project relates to the fact that it offers an immediate and unconditioned ground for a system of knowledge that is otherwise based on deduction. See Manfred Frank's discussion of the early critics of Fichte and Schelling's view of an unconditioned first principle in *Unendliche Annäherung: Die Anfänge der philosophischen Frühromantik* (Frankfurt am Main: Suhrkamp, 1997).

this gap in the third *Critique*.[4] The metaphysical characteristic of this thought lies in the fact that it represents the fundamental ground, or *Being*, as totally transcendent, as incapable of attaining to any intuitive givenness. It is an *objectifying* thought. Following the above considerations, metaphysics can be preliminarily defined as the *theoretical* endeavor to define *Being* in *objectifying* terms.

An inquiry into the specificities of different metaphysical views is beyond the scope of this chapter and book. My aim then, is not to provide an exhaustive critique of everything that goes under the name of metaphysics. Rather, I set forth typifying directions and tendencies within metaphysical conceptions. As typifying, these characterizations and criticisms are broadly applicable to much metaphysical thought.

Dualism as an Existential Condition

Dualistic ways of thinking are pervasive both in everyday and academic discourse. We employ binary concepts such as inner/outer, spiritual/sensible, mind/matter, thinking/perception, internal/external, knowing/being, activity/passivity, etc. in an oppositional manner. Although each of these dichotomies is nuanced in its meaning, and scientific and everyday conceptions are multifarious, there is a general tendency to conceive the concepts on the left in subjective terms and those on the right in objective terms. Feelings and thoughts—"inner phenomena"—for instance, are broadly regarded as having a subjective status, whereas the chair or the tree before me—the "material" world—is regarded as objective or as referring to an "external" reality. Reality is more or less conceived as divided into two sides, with some sort of abyss separating the two. Even if in most scientific (*wissenschaftlich*) discourse these dichotomies are not thematized with regard to metaphysics, there is a kind of implicit metaphysics or ontology at work in the oppositional use of such concepts. With respect to natural-scientific discourse, Husserl clearly illustrates the tendency to conceive the reference of scientific claims as an objective being totally independent of the subject; a dualism between objective being and subjective experience is thereby assumed.[5] In the chapters on Rilke it

---

4 Kant himself acknowledges that his "transcendental idealism" is ultimately a form of dualism, due to its conception of all experience as subjectively conditioned appearances, in contrast to reality in itself. Immanuel Kant, *Critique of Pure Reason*, trans. Norman Kemp Smith (London: Macmillan Press, 1929), A 370. See also Immanuel Kant, *Critique of Judgment*, trans. Werner Pluhar (Indianapolis, IN: Hackett, 1984), 14–15.

5 In Husserl's major works he repeatedly thematizes the objectifying character of the scientific attitude. The scientist takes the life-world, the world of experience, for granted and believes that science concerns itself with a reality-in-itself. Science conceives the subjective and objective in opposition. Husserl, thus

will be shown that a similar metaphysics is often at work in the human sciences, with specific regard to literary criticism or *Literaturwissenschaft* (literary-science). A kind of dualist metaphysics is operative in various realms of discourse without being explicitly thematized. It unconsciously determines habits and horizons of thought. The significance of metaphysical inquiry lies in the fact that it directly and consciously addresses dualism.

This implicit metaphysical dualism is clearly a cultural-historical phenomenon.[6] The Pre-Socratics certainly did not conceive the world in such a dualistic manner. Much of medieval Christian thought was dualistic but this dualism differed from modern varieties; the dualism of the Middle Ages referred primarily to an opposition between the worldly and the divine rather than to a distinction between the interiority of the subject and an independently existing external or material world. However, the present concern is not to elaborate the historicity of metaphysics but to demonstrate that modern dualistic conceptions

---

makes the following characteristic remark, in *The Crisis of European Sciences and Transcendental Phenomenology*: "It is, of course, the one world of experience, common to all, that Einstein and every other researcher knows he is in as a human being, even throughout all his activity of research. [But] precisely this world and everything that happens in it, used as needed for scientific and other ends, bears, on the other hand, for every natural scientist in his thematic orientation towards its 'objective truth,' the stamp 'merely subjective and relative.' The contrast to this determines, as we said, the sense of the 'objective' task. This 'subjective-relative' is supposed to be 'overcome'; one can and should correlate with it a hypothetical being-in-itself, a substrate for logical-mathematical 'truths-in-themselves' ..." This is, of course, the scientist's own naïve relationship to scientific practice; it is a kind of forgetting of the fact that the scientist and the world of experience are inextricably involved in the generation and meaning of scientific claims; a recognition of this fact at the same time undermines the objectifying conception of being that is operative in the scientific attitude. Thus Husserl continues: "This is one side. But while the natural scientist is thus interested in the objective and is involved in this activity, the subjective-relative is on the other hand still functioning for him, not as something irrelevant that must be passed through but as that which ultimately grounds the theoretical-logical ontic validity for all objective verification, i.e., as the source of self-evidence, the source of verification ..." Husserl, *The Crisis of European Sciences and Transcendental Phenomenology*, trans. David Carr (Evanston, IL: Northwestern University Press, 1970 [1936]), 126. From now on I will refer to this book as *Crisis*.

6 For discussions of the cultural-historical dimensions of dualism and the emergence of modern dualism and its problems, see Carolyn Merchant, *The Death of Nature: Women, Ecology, and the Scientific Revolution* (San Francisco, CA: HarperCollins, 1983 [1980]); Owen Barfield, *Saving the Appearances: A Study in Idolatry* (Middletown, CT: Wesleyan University Press, 1988 [1957]); Val Plumwood, *Feminism and the Mastery of Nature*.

find a certain degree of legitimacy in the way in which we *experience* the world. This dualism has more than a merely theoretical status and concerns more than simply the history of ideas considered in abstraction from human experience. It has an experiential or existential dimension.

My very experiencing of the world seems to support and validate, at least to a certain extent, a dualistic manner of conceiving the world. One can, for instance, contrast the experienced character of thought with that of perception. My thoughts appear to me as a purely private affair. I can articulate them in a conversation and make them accessible to others but the thoughts appear to me as my own. There is a clear difference between my perception of a tree and my awareness of my own thoughts. With regard to my thoughts, I feel myself to be present at their birth or origin, to be bringing them forth through my own inner activity. My thoughts thus appear to me as transparent (*durchsichtig*), as penetrated by my own activity. The tree before me, in contrast, strikes my gaze with a sense of brute givenness. I can think or imagine what I like, but the tree, via my sense of sight, seems to impose itself on me and seems opaque in contrast to my thoughts. In such basic observations an *experienced dualism* becomes evident. To a certain extent I experience my own thoughts as subjective and the tree as objectively there, my thoughts as something that I bring about, the tree as something that is there independently of me. To conceive the world in certain categories is a historical, cultural development but it is also synchronized with a development in our manner of *experiencing* the world (the question concerning the human experience of the world in previous cultural, historical epochs need not concern us here[7]).

In the above example an existential rift between our inner experience and our experience of the "outer" world is made evident. I say "existential" because it is more than simply a matter of thought. I can, for instance, propose to myself that the whole world is actually spirit or mind; however, this thought alone will not change my experience that the tree standing before me confronts my gaze with an opaqueness that contrasts with the transparency of my own thoughts. I can alternatively propose to myself that the whole world is matter (including myself) but this will not make all my thoughts opaque and turn me into a non-conscious being.

The conceptual dichotomies mentioned thus show themselves as more than just a theoretical articulation of the nature of reality; these distinctions seem to be supported by our very experience of the world and ourselves. These conceptual dichotomies evince an experienced opposition or dualism between world and mind. This recognition can

---

7 See Owen Barfield, *Saving the Appearances*.

give rise to a number of questions. Does this opposition, this experienced dualism, reflect the fundamental nature of reality? Are mind and world fundamentally (ontologically) different from one another and do we, for this reason, experience the world in such a way? Or, do such experiences pertain to an impoverished disclosure of things that might be remedied? Is a disclosure of reality possible where mind and world would no longer appear in opposition to one another, but as two sides of a single whole? In short, is this existential dualism surmountable?

As an anticipation of the later direction of this inquiry, I would like to turn to a suggestive fragment of poetry by Rilke that affirms the surmountability of this predicament. The fragment thematizes the experience of the division between mind and cosmos and proceeds to intimate a transformation of the human interior such that it would reveal itself as the interior revelation of the world, rather than as merely subjective.

> Ach, nicht getrennt sein,
> nicht durch so wenig Wandung,
> ausgeschlossen vom Sternen-Maß.
> Innres, was ists?
> Wenn nicht gesteigerter Himmel,
> durchworfen mit Vögeln und tief
> von Winden der Heimkehr.[8]

At this juncture it is instructive to consider the following question: What, in the broadest terms, would an experiential or existential overcoming of dualism look like? What sort of disclosure or experience of the world would be necessary for such an overcoming of dualism? *Percept and concept, thinking and perception, meaning and appearance, inner and outer, would have to show themselves as two sides of the revelation of a single phenomenon.* Such a disclosure of things would find its formulation in expressions like the following: *The world thinks itself in me; Nature thinks in me; what appears within me is a revelation of another aspect of what is partially revealed outside; the intelligible is the other side of the sensible; the sensible is the other side of the intelligible; what comes to*

---

8 "Oh, not to be divided,/ not through such a thin partition,/ to be excluded from the stars' measure./ Inwardness, what is it?/ If not intensified sky,/ thrown-through with birds and deep/ with winds of homecoming." Rainer Maria Rilke, *Werke: Kommentierte Ausgabe in vier Bänden*, ed. Manfred Engel, Ulrich Fülleborn, Horst Nalewski, August Stahl, vol. 2 (Frankfurt am Main: Insel Verlag, 1996), 392. Henceforth this edition of Rilke's works will be referred to as *KA 1*, *KA 2*, etc. for vol. 1, vol. 2, etc.

expression in my thoughts and feelings is a revelation of the things themselves; knowing and being are the same, etc.

Although philosophical metaphysics directly engages with the question of dualism, its treatment of dualism is one-sidedly theoretical and experientially deficient. This will be illustrated through a brief examination of some of the fundamental directions of metaphysical thought.

The Inadequacy of Metaphysical Dualism

Metaphysical dualism does not regard dualism as a problem. Rather, it grants an absolute status to oppositional concepts. When we speak of mind and matter, invisible and visible, etc. we are ultimately referring to two completely different *substances*. This form of dualism—represented by Descartes, for instance, under the concepts of *res extensa* and *res cogitans*—has for good reasons often been criticized and regarded as unsatisfactory. Even though we previously pointed to experiences that support dualistic conceptions, simple observations and intellectual considerations problematize such a position. Despite a sensed opposition between the sensible and the intelligible, the most simple sense perception involves an intertwining of the sensible and the mental, such that it is impossible to conceive the two terms as radically opposed to one another in the manner of metaphysical dualism. To look at something, for instance, involves an intentional act (mental act) that is at the same time a movement of my eyes, and this act taken as a whole enables the sensible object to appear for me, to come into focus.[9] How could there be such a complex intertwining of the material and the spiritual, the conscious and the non-conscious, the invisible and the visible, if they are ultimately two completely different substances, or if there is not a third term which encompasses the difference? Metaphysical dualism cannot provide a satisfying answer to this question.

A more purely theoretical objection to metaphysical dualism is readily available upon considering the concept of *Being*. This insight is, of course, first to be found in Parmenides' argument that *Being* can only be *one* and not *two*. If we conceive of two fundamental *beings* or *substances* then in the notion that they both *are*, both *exist*, we already have a term that is more encompassing than their difference. In that both *res extensa* and *res cogitans* are, *Being* encompasses both of them,

---

9 Within the phenomenological tradition, Merleau-Ponty has executed the most exhaustive analyses of perception in this regard, which ultimately led to the articulation of his ontology of the "flesh." See Merleau-Ponty, *The Visible and the Invisible*, trans. Alphonso Lingis (Evanston, IL: Northwestern University Press, 1968 [1964]), 130ff.

and indicates that their separateness is not absolute.[10] This applies, of course, to any plurality of *beings*; what unites them is that they *are—Being*.

Materialist Monism

Materialist monism is unsatisfied with the division of reality into *two substances* or *two beings*. Rather than absolutizing the oppositional terms (spiritual/material, etc.) it seeks to reduce one term to the other. In the case of *materialist* monism the spiritual is reduced to the material. There is ultimately only one ground of the whole of reality, and this ground is matter. Whatever goes under the name of the religious, spiritual, psychological, consciousness, thinking, etc. has only a secondary status, it does not have any ultimate ontological status; fundamentally it is *not*.

The problem with materialist or physicalist monism is that it can only ever be a *posited* or *postulated* monism. It is an *objectifying* thought. Matter is understood as what is *inanimate, material, non-conscious*, etc. It is the "object" of the physical sciences (in the narrowest sense)—the object of physics and chemistry—or the "reference" of some alternative definition of matter. The difficulty is that at the *experiential* level the materialist (the philosopher) *is not* what is posited as the fundamental ground. This is the case for numerous, though related, reasons.[11]

Materialism is a certain system of thought, or way of thinking. Thought is something *experienced* by the thinker. However, the thought of materialism can never be experientially reduced to what it posits as the fundamental ground. Thought is, in principle, something *conscious*, something *experienced*. However, what the materialist posits as the most fundamental ground is *non-conscious* and, in principle, incapable of self-experience. An abyss thereby opens up between the materialist's self-experience and what he/she posits as the fundamental ground—between the conscious and the non-conscious. Materialism ends up

---

10 Of course, the big question, as Heidegger recognized, is: *what, then, is the meaning of Being?* However, this is not something we need to consider here. The point is simply to present a theoretical consideration that undermines metaphysical dualism.

11 In a well-known essay, the analytic philosopher Frank Jackson, *in part*, makes this point, arguing that physicalist descriptions are deficient with regard to the *experience* of things or "qualia" ("Epiphenomenal Qualia," *Philosophical Quarterly* 32 [1982]: 127–36). However, my objections are far more encompassing than those offered by Jackson. Jackson sees that something is gained in experience which is not contained already within physicalist theory (the actual *perception* of color is not given in physicalist theory); however, he does not see that *theorizing* is itself a mode of *experiencing* and that physicalism *objectifies* its own terms and forgets the irreducible place and role of the *knower* in the world.

with an implicit dualism between what it conceives as the ground and its own character as something thought, between a non-conscious in-itself and a conscious for-itself. The materialist can *entertain* the thought that all conscious life is reducible to matter, but this reduction cannot be carried out *in fact*. In order for it to be true in fact the materialist would have to become a non-conscious, material process. This never occurs so long as the materialist thinks and experiences.

Materialism is a form of *reductionism*. As such it implicitly undermines its own view. To reduce one thing to another thing is to think the reduced thing *inadequately* or *improperly*. To think something adequately means not to reduce it to something else, but to understand it in its own terms, in an *adequate* or *appropriate* (*angemessen*) way. Reductionism is in this sense always problematic because it begins with an injustice to certain phenomena, with a kind of denial of certain phenomena. In the case of materialism there is an injustice to all phenomena that fall under the category of the *mental* or *spiritual* or *experiential*, etc.[12]

Materialist monism is *metaphysical* in the critical sense that has been articulated. What it posits as the fundamental or encompassing ground lies outside all possible experience. There is thus a complete abyss or dualism between the *in-itself* (matter) and the *for-itself* (conscious experience). Materialist monism is a kind of *metaphysical* monism and for this reason it shows itself in truth to be a kind of *dualism*. The terms material/spiritual, sensible/intelligible, etc. find no proper reconciliation in its thinking.

Idealist Monism

Monistic idealism fares better than materialism in that it has no need to reduce conscious life to something that is non-conscious. It ascribes a fundamental priority to the mental. However, many forms of monistic idealism run into problems.

Idealism acknowledges the fundamental ground of *beings* as mental, spiritual, or ideal. Idealism, in contrast to materialism, is generally religious. The fundamental ground of all things is often postulated as God; this is what Heidegger refers to as the onto-theo-logical constitution of metaphysics.[13] However, if this unifying ground is conceived as transcending all possible human experience then idealism shows itself to be *metaphysical* in the sense elaborated with regard to materialism. An abyss in this case opens up between human consciousness and God as the ultimate ground. This is again not an overcoming

---

12   For further implications of materialism as a form of reductionism, see Val Plumwood, *Feminism and the Mastery of Nature*, 122–5.
13   Heidegger, "Die Onto-theo-logische Verfassung der Metaphysik," in *Identity and Difference*, 107–43.

of dualism *in fact*. There is in this case a dualism between human consciousness and the divine ground.

Another form of idealism that reveals itself as inadequate is one in which everything is ultimately understood in terms of ordinary human thought and consciousness. This might be formulated in the words that, "everything is ultimately of the nature of thought," and by "thought," ordinary human thought is meant. This equally runs into problems at the experiential level. One of the characteristics of thought, as already mentioned, is transparency or *Durchsichtigkeit*. However, in perceiving a table, for instance, I am confronted with something that contrasts with the self-transparency of thought. The material or sensible presence of the table seems to present a resistance or opacity in contrast to the transparency of thought. To say that everything is thought thus also involves a kind of reductionism, a reductionism in the reverse direction of materialism. If materialism seeks to reduce the transparency of thought to the opacity of matter, this form of idealism seeks to reduce the felt opacity of matter to the transparency of thought. However, this opacity is not actually overcome by such idealism.

These basic metaphysical positions, despite their own claims, are incapable of adequately solving dualism. They fail to solve the problem of dualism at the existential or experiential level. As I have not represented any specific forms of metaphysical thought at any length—whether dualist, materialist, or idealist—the reader might object that the views presented do not correspond to any specific metaphysical system. However, such an objection would not undermine the presentation. This is due to the fact that even if there is no specific metaphysics that corresponds totally to the presented views, many forms of metaphysics face the described problem concerning the need for an *experiential* overcoming of dualism. The above discussion serves to typify particular directions of thought and thus makes visible certain basic problems, which find innumerable variations within the history of philosophy.

The pressing question at this point is: Where and how can a more adequate, *experiential* overcoming of dualism be discovered and articulated?

The Privileged Status of Phenomenology

A more adequate overcoming of dualism requires a non-dualistic disclosure or experience of things.[14] Why does phenomenology merit a

---

14 By experience I do not mean something psychologistic. A solution to the problem of dualism cannot have a merely psychologistic status for then it would in principle have a merely subjective status and not a non-dualistic status. The experience must be a disclosure—an unconcealment of Being.

privileged status (as the title of this sub-section suggests) with regard to the task of explicating an *experiential* overcoming of dualism? While the concept of experience is central to phenomenology, experience also plays an important role in other philosophical traditions such as Empiricism. In the transcendental idealist tradition—in Kant, for instance—one can also find an articulation of the character of experience. Why privilege phenomenology?

The first and most significant answer to this question is that only a phenomenological approach can properly articulate experience. The second and less fundamental reason is that many fruitful non-metaphysical approaches to the problem of dualism have been developed within the tradition of phenomenological thought. These two reasons will be respectively elaborated.

The fact that Empiricism does not attain to an adequate articulation of experience qua experience is demonstrated most clearly by its doctrine of sensationism. Locke, for instance, regards the most primordial perception of the world as involving the passive reception of discrete sensations. It is not necessary to repeat here the phenomenological analyses of perception which make clear that nothing could be further from the truth of perception than this doctrine. Many phenomenologists have completely undermined this doctrine and Merleau-Ponty has probably offered the most exhaustive criticisms of this view.[15] Empiricism understands itself as a philosophy of experience. However, its conception of experience does not match experience itself. The reason for its analytic conception of the character of perceptual experience is to be found in its adoption of scientific—primarily from the realm of physics—representations of the world. The physics of the time of Locke represented reality as being fundamentally made up of atoms or small interacting particles. This preference for accounting for the whole in terms of a combination of parts—the view that discrete parts are more fundamental—determined the Empiricist conception of perception. In addition, scientific perception begins with the procedure of analyzing a thing into its parts. Scientific representations and scientific procedure determined Empiricism to regard discrete sensations as the fundamental "data" of perception. Such representations of perception are still to be found in contemporary scientific discourses (physiological and neurological accounts of perception, for instance).

There are two naïvetés in this view of perception. The first is that the scientific perception and representation of the world presuppose the pregivenness of things and the world.[16] This view of the primacy

---

15 See, for instance, Merleau-Ponty, *Phenomenology of Perception*, trans. Colin Smith (London: Routledge Classics, 2002 [1945]), 3ff.
16 "It [the life-world] belongs to what is taken for granted, prior to all scientific thought and all philosophical questioning, that the world is ... Objective

of sensation takes scientific analysis as primary rather than secondary. The second naïveté is based on the first. After taking the pregivenness of the world—the world as life-world or *Lebenswelt*—for granted, it proceeds to represent the givenness of the world in experience in accordance with a scientific model. It thereby never attains to a proper thematization of experience. It takes the pre-scientific *Lebenswelt* for granted, and then represents the primary givenness of the world according to a scientific picture of the world.

However, the *Lebenswelt* has its own integrity (even though there are many ways in which it is influenced by science) and this scientific reconstruction of primary experience replaces the primary givenness of the world only in the space of the philosopher's reflections. As soon as the philosopher "steps outside," the unthematized life-world implicitly defies this reconstruction of experience. Scientific understanding is secondary and it never entirely replaces the primary givenness of things. No matter how hard I try to conceive the world in terms of atoms or sub-atomic particles or see the world in isolated sensations, what I actually see are irreducible perceptual wholes or *Gestalten* ("things") within a perceptual horizon. Even when I perceptually analyze the color of a certain thing, attend specifically to its color, the wholeness of the form does not fall to pieces; I see the color as part of the integral whole or *Gestalt*, i.e., the green of a tree's leaves comes into focus, as part of the whole appearance of "this tree," and not as an isolated sensation.[17] Empiricism fails to bring actual experience into the sphere of its reflections as it reconstructs experience on the basis of scientific and metaphysical conceptions. The *Lebenswelt* is completely overlooked by this kind of philosophizing.

The phenomenological articulation of the structure and character of experience must also be distinguished from the Kantian articulation of the "conditions of the possibility of experience." While Husserl is often close to Kant's "transcendental idealism," Husserl made important advances over Kant. Moreover, later phenomenologists (as well as Husserl's contemporary, Max Scheler) distanced themselves more and more from Kantian presuppositions.[18] Many presuppositions determine Kant's account of the "conditions of the possibility of experience"—the opposition between transcendental subjectivity

---

science, too, asks questions only on the ground of this world's existing in advance through prescientific life. Like all praxis, objective science presupposes the being of this world, but it sets itself the task of transposing knowledge which is imperfect and prescientific in respect of scope and constancy into perfect knowledge." Husserl, *Crisis*, 110.

17 Here I am simply drawing on elementary observations made by Husserl and Merleau-Ponty.
18 Specific differences are elaborated in the further course of this book.

and *das Ding an sich*, the opposition between concept and intuition, the attempt to prove the validity of synthetic a priori judgments—and most significantly, Kant's *approach* differs in fundamental respects from Husserl's. Husserl, like Kant, emphasizes *possibility* as central in accounting for *essential* and *universal* structures of experience; however, his description of experience is based on a far more concrete articulation of experience itself. Although phenomenology privileges possibility over actuality, this is not in the sense of conditions of possibility thought prior to an investigation of experience itself, but in the sense that any actual experience can be regarded as the instance and exemplification of a possible experience. This explication of the actual in its possibility allows for the grasping of universal structures of experience. This grasping of universal structures is facilitated by "imaginative variation."[19] Thus Husserl writes (offering "perception" as an example),

> Starting with this table-perception as an example, we vary the perceptual object, table, with a completely free optionalness, yet in such a manner that we keep perception fixed as a perception of something, no matter what ... We, so to speak, shift the actual perception into the realm of non-actualities, the realm of the as-if, which supplies us with "pure" possibilities, pure of everything that restricts to this fact or any fact whatever. As regards the latter point, we keep the aforesaid possibilities, not as restricted even to the co-posited de facto ego, but just as a completely free "imaginableness" of phantasy ... Perception, the universal type thus acquired, floats in the air, so to speak – in the atmosphere of pure phantasiableness. Thus removed from all factualness, it has become the pure *"eidos"* perception whose *"ideal"* extension is made up of all ideally possible perceptions, as pure phantasiable processes.[20]

Phenomenology is not concerned with possibility in the sense of accounting for the manner in which the structure of experience enables a priori synthetic judgments. It is concerned with uncovering universal types of experience through seeing any factual experience as the exhibition of a more general type or essence which is grasped through imaginative variation. It thus moves beyond a description of the

---

19 See Richard Kearney's good discussion of the role of imagination in Husserl's phenomenology, in Richard Kearney, *Poetics of Imagining: Modern to Post-modern* (New York: Fordham University Press, 1998), 13–45.
20 Husserl, *Cartesian Meditations*, trans. Dorion Cairns (The Hague: Martinus Nijhoff, 1960 [1931]), 70.

contingent, to that of the universal, through grasping the contingent as the realization of a general possibility and type, and understanding it as an exemplification of the latter. Husserl was sympathetic to Kant's recognition of the role of knowing subjectivity in the constitution of all experience.[21] However, he criticized Kant's method of regressive argument which fails to exhibit the actual constitution of experience.[22] Merleau-Ponty offers the clearest formulation of the difference between the Kantian and Husserlian approaches.

> Analytical reflection starts from our experience of the world and goes back to the subject as to a condition of possibility distinct from that experience, revealing the all-embracing synthesis as that without which there would be no world. To this extent it ceases to remain part of our experience and offers, in place of an account, a reconstruction. It is understandable, in view of this, that Husserl, having accused Kant of a 'faculty psychologism', should have urged, in place of a noetic analysis which bases the world on the synthesizing activity of the subject, his own 'noematic reflection' which remains within the object and, instead of begetting it, brings to light its fundamental unity.[23]

---

21 Husserl, *Crisis*, 99. Husserl became more and more sympathetic to Kant; in his last great work, *Crisis*, he places his own phenomenology as transcendental idealism in direct lineage with Kantian idealism while nevertheless making important criticisms of Kant's philosophy. I regard, however, many of the points where Husserl comes closest to Kant as the most problematic aspects of his philosophy. Some of these points are discussed later in this chapter. For the purposes of clarity I do not enter into these matters in any detail in the present chapter. Even though our presentation will move in the direction of a *chiasmic* phenomenology rather than Husserl's form of transcendental idealism, for the present purposes it is important to distinguish where phenomenology, in its very beginning (Husserl), departs in important respects from Kant's transcendental philosophy. The most important difference, to characterize it at a far too general level, is the greater *concreteness* in Husserl's approach. Phenomenologists after Husserl, however, such as Heidegger and Merleau-Ponty, achieved a *concreteness* in their explication of the *Lebenswelt* which shows Husserl to have been still largely determined by various unquestioned scientific prejudices. Thus, Heidegger reveals that the "things" of the *Lebenswelt*—as disclosed to *Dasein* as *In-der-Welt-sein*—are *Zeuge* which are disclosed in their *Zuhandenheit* and not merely as "perceptual objects" which are *vorhanden* or present-at-hand etc. Similarly, while Husserl points to aspects of the expressive body, Merleau-Ponty reveals the character of the living body and its relation to the whole world of perception in a far richer way than Husserl. Hence, in the development of phenomenology one might speak of an evolution toward greater *concreteness*, to stick, for the present purposes, to this insufficient term.
22 Husserl, *Crisis*, 103–4.
23 Merleau-Ponty, *Phenomenology of Perception*, x.

Kant's attempt to determine the necessary conditions for the possibility of experience, involves, as much as Locke's philosophy, a *representation* or *reconstruction* of the character of experience, rather than an *inquiry* into the structure and character of *experience itself*. Kant assumes the fact of experience and then attempts to reconstruct what is necessary for such a fact to be possible. However, this assumes that we already have thematic and explicit access to the character of experience.[24] For Kant, the question is: What makes experience possible? Phenomenology in contrast opens up the question: What *is* experience as experience?[25] Experience is a question for it, a proper theme of investigation. We are always experiencing but we do not have an explicit, thematic grasp of the "who," "how," and "what" of experiencing. We cannot simply *reconstruct* experience through an inquiry into the elements required to make experience possible—the forms of space and time, the categories of the understanding, etc. This is due to the simple fact that we do not yet explicitly know what *experience* is. It is experience, the *Lebenswelt* itself, that must be interrogated. This does not involve a consideration of the subjective conditions of the possibility of experience in abstraction from all experience but a reflection on the very manner in which "things" appear in experience, a "noematic-reflection." Kant, as little as Locke, discovers the problematic and actuality of the life-world.

In addition to overlooking the genuine character of experience, Empiricism and transcendental subjectivism (of the Kantian sort) do not allow for the possibility of a non-dualistic disclosure of things. For Locke, the mind is completely passive in perception. What it registers are, moreover, purely exterior qualities. There is no awareness of the "operative intentionality" (*fungierende Intentionalität*) or understanding involved in all perceptual experience, and the division of the world into "outer sense" and "inner sense" is clearly dualistic. While Kant, with his "Copernican revolution," recognized the active role of the mind in the constitution of experience, this is in the form of his extreme transcendental subjectivism and what might be called a kind of transcendental nominalism. The only thing that comes from an objective source in perception is sensation. This is then organized by the forms of intuition (sensible intuition) and the categories of understanding. However, these forms and categories have a merely subjective status. They are not the essences of the things themselves, but merely play the role of structuring experience; they make experience possible but are not a revelation of the essence of things themselves; this is

---

24 Husserl regards Kant as taking the *Lebenswelt* for granted without explicating or exhibiting its character. See Husserl, *Crisis*, 111ff.
25 As Merleau-Ponty states, phenomenology "tries to give a direct description of our experience as it is." *Phenomenology of Perception*, vii.

Kant's nominalism. All experience thereby bears the stamp of subjectivity. There is no way in which experience can involve a revelation of the things themselves; the transcendental subject, in a sense, simply finds itself in everything.

In short, Empiricism and Kantianism do not uncover the problematic of the life-world. Therefore, they do not uncover experience as it is, experience in its actual structure. Furthermore, an experiential overcoming of dualism cannot be envisaged in the terms of their views. These two traditions, which in many respects represent fundamentally opposing perspectives, are equally incapable of solving the problem of dualism at an experiential level.

Access to the life-world as experienced requires a methodology that Husserl reiterates in various ways. Following Husserl, I will use the terms "phenomenological epoché" and "phenomenological reduction" to refer to this methodology. In order to uncover the *Lebenswelt* as a theme of philosophical investigation a phenomenological epoché must be executed. Husserl explains the epoché as follows: "Clearly required before everything else is the epoché in respect to all objective sciences … What is meant is … an epoché of all participation in the cognitions of the objective sciences, an epoché of any critical position-taking which is interested in their truth or falsity …"[26]

As previously illustrated, scientific representations and claims concerning the status of objective reality overlook and obscure the character of the life-world. Only if we suspend received scientific and metaphysical conceptions and seek to reflect in an unprejudiced manner on experience will our actual experience of the world come into view. Over and above this, any views that we might hold in everyday life about the nature of reality must also be suspended. Thus Husserl writes:

> *We put out of action the general positing which belongs to the essence of the natural attitude*; we parenthesize everything which that positing encompasses with respect to being: *thus the whole natural world* which is continually "there for us," "on hand," and which will always remain there according to consciousness as an "actuality" even if we choose to parenthesize it.[27]

This involves the suspension of the naïve ontology or metaphysics implicit to the "natural attitude." In everyday existence I take chairs,

---

26 Husserl, *Crisis*, 135.
27 Husserl, *Ideas Pertaining to a Pure Phenomenology and to a Phenomenological Philosophy—First Book: General Introduction to a Pure Phenomenology*, trans. F. Kersten (The Hague: Martinus Nijhoff, 1982 [1913]), 61–2.

tables, others, as objectively existing beings, as being there independently of me. An *objectifying* ontology or metaphysics is at work here. Metaphysics, as we have seen, also seeks to determine the nature of reality as something independent of human experience. Being is thought in *objectifying* terms, is projected into a realm independent of human thought and experience. The phenomenological reduction involves a suspension of this *metaphysical* stance that is implicit to the "natural attitude." Husserl often compared this procedure of suspending "positings" concerning objective being to that of Descartes' method of doubt. However, phenomenological epoché does not go as far as to doubt the existence of the world. It *suspends* rather than *doubts* given conceptions of reality in order to bring the world into view as a *phenomenon*. This difference can be made clear by way of an example. If I reflect on my current situation, sitting in a café, I assume that the tables, the chairs, the coffee cup, and the person behind the counter all *exist*. Cartesian doubt would involve doubting whether all these "things" actually exist; perhaps this is all a dream? In contrast, the phenomenological reduction does not lead me to doubt whether all these things exist; it simply converts the belief and sense that all these things exist, into an appearance. I do actually *know* that I am awake, I can tell that I am not in a dream, all these things *do* strike me as existing. I no longer simply accept that all these things exist, nor do I doubt that they exist; I merely bring into view this state of affairs as a phenomenon. The naïve acceptance of *existence* is converted into the *sense* of existence, such that this state of affairs is reduced to the phenomenon of *appearing* to exist. As a phenomenon the state of affairs becomes a matter to be investigated rather than a naïvely accepted reality. The question is raised as to how this sense comes to be constituted.

The phenomenological reduction reduces the world to the status of an *experienced phenomenon* rather than maintaining the naïve realism of the "natural attitude" (*natürliche Einstellung*). It thereby brings into view the world as *experienced* while the phenomenological analyses seek to articulate the structure and character of this experience—its constitution. The phenomenological reduction does not involve doubting the existence of the world; such a procedure is rejected by phenomenology because the evidence of the world is never replaced by an evidence which actually suffices to throw such a belief into doubt. I follow Descartes' line of reasoning but as soon as I step out of my study the world is disclosed to me with a sense of reality much more compelling than the evidence of Descartes' arguments. In everyday life I have no doubt as to the existence of the world. Cartesian doubt is genuinely hyperbolic; it is an exaggeration. I might actually *entertain* the doubt with Descartes that the world does not exist. However, I am never in the long run convinced. I play with the idea but the world's sense of existing is more convincing than Descartes' argument. The world is given with a sense of evidence that is foolish to doubt. However, the everyday attitude or "natural attitude" is naïve, it does not grasp itself explicitly, it does not see that the world as experienced is fundamentally a *meaningful* world and that the subject living-in-the-world is involved in the genesis of its appearance and sense. Phenomenological investigation aims to lead the "natural attitude" to its genuine sense, articulate the *Lebenswelt* in its true meaning, free it from naïveté.

A theme that is sometimes a point of confusion with regard to phenomenological procedure is the relationship between phenomenology and ontology. The phenomenological epoché, in its requirement that one suspend one's belief in the existence of the world and reduce the world to the status of a phenomenon, might appear to involve the avoidance of any ontological considerations. Were this the case, phenomenology would not be anything more than a type of "descriptive psychology." However, this is not the case. While phenomenology rejects objectifying metaphysics it does not involve, as is sometimes thought, the avoidance of all questions concerning true or genuine Being.[28] The ultimate aim of phenomenology is to articulate a more adequate ontology.[29] In the "natural attitude" I assume that the things I encounter in the world are there independently of me. It is true that this naïve realism, this naïve ontology, is suspended and ultimately rejected by the phenomenologist. However, this is due to the fact that within the "natural attitude" as well as what we might call the "metaphysical attitude," we assume that reality is an *objectivity* independent of any meaningful constitution, a pure in-itself. In contrast, the "phenomenological attitude" reveals that an operative intentionality is involved in the appearing of the world and things. This recognition reveals that the naïve realism of the "natural attitude" is, in truth, a way of *understanding* or constituting the meaning of the world, without which there would be no *appearance* and no "world." The "natural attitude" does not see that this is the case. The "phenomenological reduction" allows this to come into view. The phenomenologist rejects the naïve realism of the "natural attitude" not because the project of an ontology is rejected altogether but because the *naïve* ontology of the "natural attitude" fails to grasp its own character reflectively. An ontology has to

---

28 See Dan Zahavi's very good essay on this theme. Dan Zahavi, "Phenomenology and Metaphysics," in *Metaphysics, Facticity, Interpretation: Phenomenology in the Nordic Countries* (Dordrecht: Kluwer Academic Publishers, 2003), 3–22.

29 This is not only the case in Heidegger but also in Husserl as we will see. For a complex discussion of the relation between ontology and phenomenology in Husserl and Heidegger, see Jean-Luc Marion, *Reduction and Givenness*, trans. Thomas A. Carlson (Evanston, IL: Northwestern University Press, 1998).

take into account the fact that the world is a meaningful world and that I am involved in the constitution of its meaning, and this involvement must be included within any articulation of the meaning of Being.

Although certain aspects of Husserl's transcendental subjectivism will be criticized later in the present work, I want to draw attention to the following statement by Husserl in *Crisis*, simply to illustrate his view that phenomenology does not involve the avoidance of ontology but enables the articulation of a more adequate and more fundamental ontology:

> Are we not establishing truths about true being? ... The answer, of course, is as follows: it is precisely the result of inquiry within the epoché ... that the natural, objective world-life is only a particular mode of the transcendental life which forever constitutes the world, [but] in such a way that transcendental subjectivity, while living on in this mode, has not become conscious of the constituting horizons and never can become aware of them. It lives in "infatuation," so to speak, with the poles of unity without being aware of the constituting multiplicities belonging essentially to them ...[30]

Phenomenology does not reject ontology; it is concerned with "true being." Phenomenology demonstrates the problems with naïve and objectifying ontologies (metaphysics) and articulates an ontology in which the "knower" or "experiencer" is taken into account. Since a clear argument has been presented for the privileged status of phenomenology with regard to the articulation of experience, we can now elaborate the second reason for turning to phenomenology.

Within the phenomenological tradition much work has been done that implicitly and explicitly contributes toward a phenomenological or experiential approach to the problem of dualism. Heidegger's conception of truth has a non-dualistic character.[31] Truth is not a correspondence between a statement and reality but at the most fundamental level the happening of the disclosure of Being. It is the event in which something shows itself as Being. The event of unconcealment is neither a subjective event nor an objective state of affairs; it transcends

---

30 Husserl, *Crisis*, 175–6.
31 For one of Heidegger's clearest elaborations of his understanding of truth, see "Vom Wesen der Wahrheit," in *GA* 9 (1976 [1930]), 177–202. Heidegger's concept of "truth" evolved with time; there is, nevertheless, a clear continuity in his thought from *Sein und Zeit* (1927) to "Vom Wesen der Wahrheit" (first given as a lecture in 1930) to "Das Ende der Philosophie und die Aufgabe des Denkens" (1966). While Heidegger's focus shifts from *Dasein* to Being as such he maintains his view of truth as an event of unconcealment.

these terms. The subjective and objective presuppose unconcealment rather than unconcealment requiring them. *Aletheia* or truth as unconcealment is what first allows for something to *be there* for me. Of course, there is never total unconcealment: unconcealment always presupposes concealment—what is not revealed. However, we need not enter into a detailed elaboration of Heidegger's conception of truth here. It suffices to indicate its non-dualistic or pre-dualistic character.

Heidegger also offers a critique of the history of philosophy which has a bearing on the problem of dualism. For the Pre-Socratics there can be no talk of dualism in the modern sense.[32] *Aletheia* is the self-unconcealment of *physis*, and does not involve anything even closely approximating a modern opposition between subject and object. The fateful division between two realms of Being decisively occurs with Plato, in the division between a sensible order which is illusory and an intelligible order of true Being. Heidegger looks to the Pre-Socratics for the articulation of a disclosure of Being that is prior to any dualism between essence and existence, whatness and thatness.[33] He looks for a belonging together of Being and thinking that is prior to their separation.[34] In his critique of modern subjectivity (which, according to Heidegger, achieves its most pronounced philosophical form in Nietzsche's doctrine of the "will to power"), he articulates an alternative to the modern dominating subject, which reduces Being to the determination of the subject. The essential gesture of understanding or knowing is not to be found in an activity that dominates, but in an activity of *letting-be*, in a disposition of *Gelassenheit*. The event of unconcealment, which always, of course, presupposes mystery and concealment, transcends the opposition between activity and passivity. Although *Dasein* as the "shepherd of Being" is directly implicated in the unconcealment of Being, unconcealment cannot be willed by the subject. The event of unconcealment is as much an act of reception as a being-there of the self; it is an *Ereignis* understood as a mutual corresponding of Being and human being. Unconcealment is in a sense granted; it is not something that can be willed, hence the significance of *Gelassenheit*.[35] True thinking, poetic, or meditative thinking (as opposed

---

32 For a good introduction to Heidegger's account of the "history of Being" see Heidegger, *Einführung in die Metaphysik*, GA 40 (1985 [1935]); *Introduction to Metaphysics*, trans. Gregory Fried and Richard Polt (New Haven, CT: Yale University Press, 2000).
33 See, for instance, Heidegger, *Parmenides*, GA 54 (1992 [1942/43]); *Parmenides*, trans. André Schuwer and Richard Rojcewicz (Indianapolis, IN: Indiana University Press, 1992).
34 See Heidegger, "Der Satz der Identität," in *Identity and Difference*, 85–106.
35 See Heidegger, "Zur Erörterung der Gelassenheit: Aus einem Feldweggespräch über das Denken," in *GA* 13 (1983 [1944/45]), 37–74.

to calculative thinking and instrumentalist reason), is, for this reason, a "thinking as thanking"—"Denken als Danken."[36] These conceptions obviously have a direct bearing on the question of dualism.

Max Scheler's conception of love includes ideas that are not unrelated to the direction that Heidegger pursued after him. Love is clearly a form of non-dominating intentionality, a form of active-passivity. It suffices to turn to the following passage from *The Nature of Sympathy* (*Wesen und Formen der Sympathie*, 1923):[37] "*love itself, in the course of its movement, is what brings about the continuous emergence of ever-higher value in the object—just as if it was streaming out from the object of its own accord, without any sort of exertion (even of wishing) on the part of the lover.*"[38]

Scheler also illustrates that the most basic perception of other persons and natural things is not of discrete sensations or merely sensible appearances, but of expressive wholes that do not yet involve a distinction between the psychological and the physical; the most basic perceptions are pre-dualistic. In addition, he demonstrates the cognitive dimension of feeling and regards it as ontologically the case that two or more people can partake in *one* feeling.[39] This is just to indicate a few of the many directions of Scheler's thought which relate to the problem of dualism.[40]

In the work of Merleau-Ponty the most explicit response to the problem of dualism is to be found. The basic direction of his philosophizing is guided by an attempt to overcome dualism. In the *Phenomenology of Perception* (*Phénoménologie de la perception*, 1945) he seeks a middle position between intellectualism and empiricism. In his attentiveness to expressive phenomena, from the living body (*Leib*) to the character of language in its living articulation, he explicates essences that cannot be regarded as merely subjective or as the opposite of the sensible or visible. The work of art is a distinctive example in that it institutes a meaning by virtue of its sensible form,

---

36 See, for instance, Heidegger, "Der Weg zur Sprache," in *GA* 12 (1985 [1959]), 227–57; "The Way to Language," in *Basic Writings*, trans. David Farrell Krell (San Francisco: Harper, 1993), 425.
37 See also Scheler's essay, "Liebe und Erkenntnis," in *Liebe und Erkenntnis* (Munich: Lehnen Verlag, 1955), 5–28.
38 Max Scheler, *The Nature of Sympathy* [*Wesen und Formen der Sympathie*], trans. Peter Heath (London: Routledge and Kegan Paul, 1954), 157.
39 Scheler, *The Nature of Sympathy*, 18ff.
40 For a more detailed discussion of Scheler's thought as a whole, in relation to the question of dualism, see Arthur R. Luther, "The Articulated Unity of Being in Scheler's Phenomenology: Basic Drive and Spirit," in *Max Scheler (1874–1928): Centennial Essays*, ed. Manfred S. Frings (The Hague: Martinus Nijhoff, 1974), 1–42.

a meaning which therefore cannot be regarded as the opposite of the sensible. These ideas, already to be found in the *Phenomenology of Perception*, undergo an ontologization in his later thought. He comes to acknowledge an ontological deficiency in his earlier philosophy. In his late unfinished work *The Visible and the Invisible* (*Le visible et l'invisible*, 1964) he seeks to articulate a non-dualistic ontology of the "flesh" which recognizes an ontological community between the perceiver and the perceived, the sensing and the sensed, the intelligible and the sensible. Along these lines he articulates the notion of sensible-ideas, or non-Platonic ideas.[41] These immanent ideas are not understood in abstraction from sensible appearances but are "received" along with sensible appearings. The musical work of art is a clear example of such an idea in that the meaning of a piece of music is only generated through listening to the *music itself*. Merleau-Ponty comes to regard the whole sensible world along these lines. The genesis of such ideas lies in an active-passivity, a reception of the sensible. In his late lecture courses, *Nature* (1952–60) we see the attempt to conceive a fundamental continuity between organic life and higher cultural practices.[42] The way in which the embryo comes into being is analogous to the manner in which a painter builds up a canvas; there is a fundamental continuity of life. In his late work he sketches an ontology that is neither idealist nor mechanistic. The organism, for him, is a kind of incarnate, non-Platonic idea or "flesh."

Of course, it is Husserl's methodology that first opens up the phenomenological tradition of thought. Although I consider Husserl's form of transcendental idealism as a less adequate response to the problem of dualism than some of the phenomenological philosophies that succeeded him, Husserl made important steps toward addressing the problem of dualism. This can be seen most clearly in his institution of a concrete manner of philosophizing in his discovery of the world of the "natural attitude" and the *Lebenswelt* as a theme of philosophical investigation; most important here is the recognition of the problem of *constitution*.[43] Although Husserl maintains a certain continuity with the tradition of transcendental idealism that begins with Kant, this

---

41 Merleau-Ponty, *The Visible and the Invisible*, 130ff.
42 Merleau-Ponty, *Nature: Course Notes from the Collège de France*, trans. Robert Vallier (Evanston, IL: Northwestern University Press, 2003 [1995]), 139ff.
43 Husserl introduced the concept of the *Lebenswelt* in his last major work, *Crisis*. Although the problematic of the *Lebenswelt* introduces elements that are lacking in his earlier writings, in particular, a deepened *historical* reflection, the notion is continuous with Husserl's earlier notion of the world of the "natural attitude" (*natürliche Einstellung*). For our purposes a detailed consideration of the similarities and differences between Husserl's earlier and later conception is unnecessary.

concrete problematic of the life-world, as has been already illustrated, must be distinguished from Kant's deductive method.[44] Kant's method starts with the assumption of the for-itself as the condition of the possibility of experience; it begins with the idea of an ego abstracted from embodiment and situatedness and seeks to explain all experience on this basis. However, this abstracted self is not the self operative in the situated living present. In contrast to Kant's abstract starting point, Husserl's analyses seek to understand constitution from within the thick of experiencing. When Merleau-Ponty states the following he is also clearly referring to the approach developed by Husserl: "We must discover the origin of the object at the very centre of our experience; we must describe the emergence of being and we must understand how, paradoxically, there is *for us* an *in itself*."[45]

Husserl's rehabilitation, following Franz Brentano, of the concept of intentionality, which is always structured as a "consciousness-of," allowed for an articulation of the interrelation of consciousness and world, rather than explaining the appearance of the world starting from consciousness—Kant's subjective forms of space and time, the categories of the understanding, etc. With this concrete problematic of constitution Husserl made a decisive advance from Kant's form of transcendental subjectivism. Kant did not uncover the problematic of the constitution of the experience of the world in its living-presentness. Through explications of the *relationality* of world and consciousness Husserl made an important contribution toward overcoming dualism. However, Husserl's transcendental idealism shares certain characteristics with Kant's, which do not enable a satisfactory solution to the problem of dualism. He shares, for instance, the Kantian (and Cartesian) trait of tracing all constitution and meaning back to the acts of transcendental subjectivity.[46]

Due to the fact that phenomenological methodology is especially suited to bring into view experience as experience, and that the phenomenological tradition has opened up many fruitful (and non-metaphysical) responses to the problem of dualism, phenomenology has been accorded a privileged status for the present inquiry.

As is often stated, phenomenology does not stand for a certain body of thought but for a *methodological conception*. Thus a genuinely phenomenological approach to the problem of dualism cannot consist in simply repeating the thought of one of the many respected phenomenologists. Therefore, in the following I undertake phenomenological explications with "fresh eyes" (while, of course, building on the work

---

44 Husserl, *Crisis*, 91ff.
45 Merleau-Ponty, *Phenomenology of Perception*, 82–3.
46 See, for instance, Husserl, *Cartesian Meditations*.

of other phenomenologists) and communicate insights that are legitimated by an intuitive givenness or disclosure.[47]

Rather than leaping to the "phenomenology of the exceptional" or "epiphanic phenomenology" that is pursued through the engagement with Rilke in Chapters 2, 3, and 4, the following section seeks to answer the proximate question: Is it possible to find a non-dualistic disclosure of things operative in the *Lebenswelt* in the mode of *everydayness*? That this can be answered to a great extent affirmatively is demonstrated by much of Merleau-Ponty's work. To my mind there is one aspect of the *Lebenswelt* that most clearly demonstrates a non-dualistic disclosure and this is the disclosedness of the human Other, which is the theme of the next section.

Before proceeding, a few qualifications about my approach to the problem of dualism are worth mentioning. A reader might object that many different kinds of dualism have been mentioned or implied and each kind of dualism actually presents a different problem. In other words, it could be objected that the present treatment of dualism is lacking in specificity and there is little in common between the dichotomies: self/other, mind/nature, sensible/spiritual, being/knowing. While it is true that there are many different kinds of dualism, it is false (and even dualistic) to believe that these "dualisms" are unrelated. For instance, the way in which one conceives the relation between the sensible and the spiritual has a bearing on the relation between the mind and nature. If one, for instance, views the sensible world as a manifestation of the spirit, nature will be understood as bearing a relationship to the spiritual. This view of mind (spirit) and nature, the sensible and the spiritual, will also differ from the corresponding views of the materialist. To offer another example, as Val Plumwood has rigorously demonstrated, mind/body dualism has a bearing on human/nature dualism (and in the case of Descartes they are virtually identical).[48] Thus, while there are different kinds of dualism the *relationship* between different dualisms warrants a unified consideration. However, my treatment of dualism is certainly not exhaustive, and this experiential and phenomenological approach by no means addresses every aspect of dualism. Rather, I believe that the present work addresses a *central aspect*—the experiential dimension—of dualism that is often overlooked.

---

47 This is in keeping with Husserl's "principle of principles" and the variations of this principle in the work of other phenomenologists. See Husserl, *Ideas Pertaining to a Pure Phenomenology and to a Phenomenological Philosophy, First Book*, 44.
48 Val Plumwood, *Feminism and the Mastery of Nature*, 120ff.

The Twofold Seeing of the Human Other

Much phenomenology has given attention to a "phenomenology of the everyday." Husserl's phenomenological explications of the "natural attitude" and Heidegger's phenomenology of *Dasein* (existence/being-there) in its "everydayness" (*Alltäglichkeit*) are the two most notable examples. The theme of this section is also a phenomenology of the life-world in the mode of everydayness. The advantage of a "phenomenology of the everyday" is that the phenomena considered are, in principle, accessible to everyone. Thus, anyone who is capable of adopting a phenomenological attitude or approach can repeat the phenomenological analyses on the basis of his or her own *experiences*.

While phenomenologists have offered many analyses of the everyday, this does not mean that these analyses and phenomenological insights are themselves everyday or common. Rather, in the "natural attitude" consciousness does not achieve a genuine self-understanding. Thus Husserl writes,

> Daily practical living is naïve. It is immersion in the already-given world, whether it be experiencing, or thinking, or valuing, or acting. Meanwhile all those productive intentional functions of experiencing, because of which physical things are simply there, go on anonymously. The experiencer knows nothing about them, and likewise nothing about his productive thinking.[49]

The phenomenological structure of the "natural attitude" is thus unknown to the consciousness that is immersed in the natural attitude. A similar relationship is evident in Heidegger's distinction between the "ontic" and the "ontological" in *Sein und Zeit (Being and Time)*.

However, phenomenological structures that are uncovered through a phenomenology of the everyday are to a certain extent specific to the everyday. A phenomenological analysis of a cup, for instance, as "ready-to-hand" (*zuhanden*) and as implicated in a network of relationships to other "ready-to-hand" things (water, table, cupboard, etc.) is very different from a phenomenology of *mystical experience*.[50] Everyone knows to some extent what a cup is but not everyone has had first-hand mystical experiences, and a phenomenology of mystical experience will reveal *phenomenological structures* that differ from those that are revealed through a phenomenology of the everyday. Due to

---

49 *Cartesian Meditations*, 152–3.
50 See Heidegger, *Sein und Zeit*, GA 2 (1977 [1927]), 68ff. For a phenomenological approach to mystical experience, see Anthony J. Steinbock, *Phenomenology and Mysticism: The Verticality of Religious Experience* (Bloomington, IN: Indiana University Press, 2007).

Phenomenology and the Problem of Dualism   41

this difference I have chosen in this work to distinguish a "phenomenology of the everyday" from a "phenomenology of the exceptional"; I would, for instance, refer to a phenomenology of mystical experience as a phenomenology of the exceptional. Likewise, in Chapters 2 and 3, I uncover in Rilke's epiphanic vision (particularly of Nature) a phenomenology of the exceptional, and argue that this exceptional phenomenology involves a deeper overcoming of dualism than is implicit to everyday perception. More specifically, Rilke consciously devoted himself to a *praxis* of seeing that enabled a privileged disclosure of things. Neither this praxis nor its correlative disclosure are part and parcel of daily life.

As the standpoint of the phenomenologist is always an exceptional one relative to everyday existence, a few more words should be said about the difference between what could be called the "exceptionality of phenomenology" and the "phenomenology of the exceptional" that is later executed in relation to Rilke. Phenomenological philosophy like all philosophy primarily proceeds by way of *thinking* and *reflection*. As mentioned in the Introduction, while the nature of perception is a widely treated theme of philosophical investigation, it does not belong to conventional philosophical methodology to immerse one's gaze in a landscape in the manner of a painter such as Cézanne as he paints *en plein air*. This said, Merleau-Ponty's phenomenological concern with perception could be described as closely approximating a *painterly* philosophy. However, Merleau-Ponty's approach is far from the more common procedures of philosophy and, for the most part, a philosophical examination of perception involves a *reflection* on perception (even if it attempts to reflect on the very act of perceiving) more than an immersion in the act of perceiving. Of course, this difference between the praxis of the philosopher and the praxis of the painter may be more a matter of degree than kind; the philosopher also *perceives* and the painter *reflects*. Nevertheless, the painter is more intensely involved in the *art* and *praxis* of perceiving. Moreover, and this pertains to one of the main theses of the present work, this immersion in perception can lead to an exceptional and richer disclosure of phenomena than is implicit to everyday perception and that also differs from the insights gained by way of a philosophical reflection. It is in this sense that Rilke's vision is later interpreted as a "phenomenology of the exceptional." What then is the purpose of the phenomenology of the everyday executed below?

A particular problem emerges in approaching a phenomenology of the exceptional, namely that the *phenomena* considered are not readily accessible to reflection. Thus a discussion of *exceptional* or *uncommon* phenomena can appear as ungrounded speculation. This is, of course, a major source of the implicit or explicit disagreement between an atheist and a mystic. The atheist claims that the mystic imagines things that do not in reality exist, whereas the mystic claims that she knows from first-hand experience that there is a divine world, just as we all know from first-hand experience that cups exist. While mysticism is not the main theme of this work (although mystical aspects of Rilke's poetic vision are discussed), the purpose of the present section is to bridge a divide between the everyday and the exceptional. I aim to illustrate a structure of understanding and perception that is implicit to everyday experience and is structurally similar to Rilke's exceptional vision. However, this does not mean that this phenomenology of the everyday already includes the phenomenology of Rilke's poetic vision; if this were the case, then turning to Rilke would be unnecessary. Rather, this phenomenology of the everyday will bring us *closer* to the phenomenology of the exceptional that is subsequently elaborated. In other words, it makes the latter more feasible by placing it in continuity with more readily discernible phenomenological structures.

There is a continuity between the everyday and the exceptional and they could be regarded as parts of a spectrum. For example, as I make my way home from work I might be suddenly struck by the immense beauty of the sunset over the horizon. This phenomenon might be called an exceptional experience in the midst of the everyday. However, for conceptual purposes it makes sense to distinguish the exceptional from the everyday, just as it makes sense to distinguish blue from green although there are shades of turquoise that are difficult to place, and the colors form an unbroken continuum.

It is worthwhile mentioning one more point before proceeding to the central theme of this section. The distinction between the exceptional and the everyday might be regarded as suggesting some kind of problematic elitism. This charge is invalid for a few reasons. First, exceptional phenomena are no more elite than the phenomena only known to those with a high-level understanding of mathematics (or philosophy). High-level mathematics is only known to those who devote their lives to the study of mathematics but this does not make it problematically elitist. Second, phenomenology must aim to do justice to all kinds of phenomena and thus should not be (and *has not* been) limited to the everyday.[51] Third, as aforementioned, there is a degree of continuity between the everyday and the exceptional.

The focus of the present phenomenological investigation is the individual human Other. The reason for choosing to focus on the disclosedness of the human Other in the life-world lies in the fact that

---

51 The "everyday" and the "natural attitude" are only one theme of phenomenological investigation and as a methodology phenomenology involves an exceptional standpoint (as aforementioned) and can be applied to any phenomena. See also Introduction, n. 5 and n. 19.

it offers a clear example of a non-dualistic disclosure that is operative in our everyday being-in-the-world, and reveals a phenomenological structure that will be deepened in our subsequent considerations of Rilke. In particular, this consideration of the Other will reveal a kind of disclosure in which the sensible and the intelligible form two aspects of a single reality, rather than being opposed to one another.

The theme of the Other played a significant role in the development of twentieth-century philosophy, from Scheler's considerations of sympathy, to Husserl's account of the constitution of the "other ego" in his *Cartesian Meditations* (Fifth Meditation), to Heidegger's articulation of *Mitsein* in *Sein und Zeit*, to Merleau-Ponty's descriptions of the perception of the expressive Other as *Leib* (animate-body), to Levinas's ethical philosophy of the Other, through to the focus on the Other and difference in Derrida, and continues to be a pertinent theme in contemporary philosophical discourse. In some respects the main developments of the last hundred years of philosophy might be seen as a movement from privileging the self (in Husserl) or the "same" to privileging the Other and the different (post-modernism).[52] I do not wish to consider the course of this intellectual history in any detail. My aim is not a historical-conceptual exegesis (a historical overview would require a separate monograph), but a phenomenological explication. My explication will naturally draw on elements from this rich history but only in so far as they illuminate pertinent phenomenological facts. Nevertheless, my approach will naturally be aligned with particular tendencies concerning the problem of the Other.

According to my knowledge, there are no thinkers within the phenomenological tradition who have denied the existence of a *plurality* of human selves. The question, however, is whether these selves ("we") are many islands cut off from one another, or whether there is a distinctive revelation of the Other, and *dialogue*, in the strong sense of the word, *between* selves.[53] In arguing for the latter I will draw on Scheler, Heidegger, and Merleau-Ponty, but the primary aim is to offer a self-transparent phenomenological explication. The specific focus will be the *perception of the individual character of the human Other* and the analysis aims to demonstrate the following:

1   A way of seeing that involves a close intertwining of the sensible and the intelligible.

---

52 See Brian Treanor, *Aspects of Alterity: Levinas, Marcel, and the Contemporary Debate* (New York: Fordham University Press, 2006).
53 Cf. Bernhard Waldenfels, *Das Zwischenreich des Dialogs: Sozialphilosophische Untersuchungen im Anschluss an Edmund Husserl* (Den Haag: Martinus Nijhoff, 1971).

44 The Poet as Phenomenologist

2 An "active-passivity" that transcends the opposition between the active (thought as *subjective*) and the passive (thought as *objective*).
3 A genuine disclosure of the individual Other which illustrates that the Other is *not* entirely transcendent and the Self is *not* solipsistic.

I call this way of seeing that involves a marriage (rather than an opposition) of sense perception and understanding a "twofold seeing." My hermeneutic-phenomenological account of the givenness of the individual Other is divided into two sub-sections. The first sub-section serves to undermine dualistic conceptions of the phenomenality of the Other on the basis of diverse phenomenological observations. These observations also provide the necessary elements for the more comprehensive genetic account of the sense of individual character that is undertaken in the second sub-section.

Elementary Reflections on the Perception of the Other
In the life-world it is common for two people to discuss the character of an Other. Let us assume, for instance, two people are discussing the character of a third person, whom they both *know* well. What do these two people *have in mind* when they discuss the character or personality of an Other? The third person is obviously not sensibly present in their minds. However, the other person is quasi-present in the sense of being the "intentional correlate" or "matter" (*Sache*) of the conversation. The conversation intends the "character of the specific third person." The third person is described with familiar adjectives; for instance, as "friendly," "generous," a bit "odd," etc. These adjectives are generic; they can be applied to many people and things. However, what is it that such ascriptions seek to attain? They seek to bring into view *the specific character of the person herself*. The conversation aims to bring this personality to its self-disclosure. A genuine conversation has the character of a questioning inquiry. The answer to this questioning inquiry is not revealed outside of the conversation but within the space of the conversation. What is to be revealed is the character of the person herself, but as the partners in conversation both know the person well, the conversation does not have the status of a first revealment of the third person, but has the status of a further explication and clarification of the individuated "who" of the third person. As it is the individuated and holistic character of the third person that is sought, all the ascriptions have a merely *approximating* character. If one inquires into the givenness of another person whom one knows well, one finds an individuated sense (a haecceity). Although there are all sorts of generic descriptions that are employed in describing a person—one person is "shy" and "introverted," another is "gregarious," "outgoing," and "confident," etc.—a singular sense is intended and disclosed, which

cannot be reduced to generic predicates. However, how is it possible for the conversation to facilitate a revelation of the Other's haecceity if the terms of language are limited to generic senses? Furthermore, when I have already pointed out that terms such as "kind," "friendly," and "light-hearted" are generally applicable, how can it be maintained that within the conversation it is the specific or individuated Other who comes to disclosure? There are two factors that must be brought to mind in order to understand the entirety of this situation. However, it should be qualified that there is no logical proof that such an individuated sense or haecceity exists. The only way in which it can come into view is through a phenomenological reflection that shows it to be a phenomenological fact.

The two factors that must be brought into mind in order to understand the entire situation of the individuated disclosure of the Other are, 1) that the Other, in the present example, is already known and, 2) that the significance of language does not find its end or *fulfillment* at the level of the general but rather in the "sense of the things themselves" (in this case the haecceity of the Other). These two points are interrelated. That the Other is already known allows for the *fulfillment* of the language in this individuated sense. The parallel with works of art is illuminating here. The difficulty of conveying the sense of a musical work in language is well known. However, if one has *experienced* the musical work then the linguistic characterization assumes a specificity that it lacks for the one who has not experienced the work. One might speak of the "gaiety" of a work by Mozart; however, the "joy" or "lightness" which expresses itself in much of Mozart's music has a specific quality; one might say that a certain "depth" is intrinsic to this sense of joy. The "gaiety" in a piece by Mozart is not the same as the "gaiety" in "Jingle Bells." Such characterizations are *approximations* but someone who knows Mozart's music will understand the enigmatic sense of the music that these characterizations are trying to *get at*.[54] Hence, language seems to be stuck at the level of generalities; however, it finds its true *fulfillment* and end in passing beyond this level such that the "thing itself" becomes its own irreducible *word*.[55]

There is then, in this conversation between two interlocutors about a third person, the intentional correlate of the individuated sense of

---

54 Language in its full phenomenality is actually *not* generic as through *style* an individual sense is suggested. In addition, the meaning of an utterance is specified by its hermeneutic context.
55 This statement obviously recalls Gadamer's statement that "Being that can be understood is language." Hans-Georg Gadamer, *Wahrheit und Methode* (Tübingen: J. C. B. Mohr [Paul Siebeck], 1990 [1960]), 478; *Truth and Method*, translation revised by Joel Weinsheimer and Donald G. Marshall (New York: Continuum, 1999), 470.

the third. It is the *specific* character of a *singular* person that the interlocutors *have in mind* and that *comes into the light* of the conversation. However, this haecceity should not be regarded as an absolute or *complete* givenness of the Other. As Husserl repeatedly illustrates, a complete givenness of a "spatial object" is out of the question, let alone that of another person.[56] Moreover, the two people may disagree in certain respects concerning the third person's character. One person states, for instance, "she can sometimes be a bit unfriendly," while the other states, "I don't think that's true." Such differences involve *differences of interpretation*. The character of the Other is not a brute given, but a hermeneutic given. Thus, it is open to differences of interpretation. This does not discredit, however, the aforementioned "individuated sense." If two people know a third person well there will be a certain degree of accord in the *interpretations*. It is also important to point out that although this meaning tends toward a haecceity, and it is perhaps only as correlative to the intentionality of love that the most extreme haecceity is attained, this haecceity is *universal*. However, this is not the universality that is present in an adjective such as "nice" when considered abstractly. The adjective "nice" can be ascribed to innumerable people and things, whereas the "individuated sense" has an irreducible *thisness*; it is the meaning of a singular person and no one else; a person's phenomenality is its own irreducible and irreplaceable *word*. The universality of this phenomenality lies in the fact that two people can to a certain extent be in accord with one another concerning the specific character of a third person. There is an *intersubjective* opening onto the specific character of another individual.

The above serves as a preliminary consideration of the givenness of the character of a person. However, much has been presupposed. It was presupposed that two people already *know* a third person. It was this "knowledge" that allowed the language of the conversation to attain to an individuated *fulfillment*. Knowing an Other in the life-world presupposes a history of interaction with a person, the biography of a *relationship*. It is out of shared *experiences* with another person that a sense of the person's character gradually emerges. Such experiences involve at the very least a *perceiving* of the Other. Such a perceiving, like all perceiving, is situated. If we are to trace the genesis of the sense

---

56 I only see one side of an object at a time. I see one side of the cup now and in the next moment another side. I can observe the cup from innumerable perspectives and innumerable features are potentially noticeable—shapes, colors, form, etc. The "spatial object" is, in this sense, inexhaustible. The essential incompleteness of a perception of an object and the role of appresentation are themes to which Husserl often returns. For a discussion of these themes in *Cartesian Meditations*, see 39ff.

of the character of an Other it must first be articulated how the Other, now as second person, is *perceived* and *encountered* in the life-world.

There are two widespread interrelated prejudices concerning the givenness of the Other. The first prejudice is that when it comes to perceiving the Other the only datum that I am, in some sense, directly given is the Other's *body*. When it comes to myself I am directly aware of my own psychic states—I directly experience my feelings, desires, thoughts, but when it comes to the Other I am fundamentally given their body but not their psyche. The second prejudice, intrinsically related to this first prejudice, is that my means of "knowing" about another's *internal* states is *empathy*. The view is that while the Other's body is *presented* to me the Other's states of mind must be *appresented*; they must, in a specific sense, be *introjected* by me. Whereas the Other's body is *presented directly*, the Other's soul is *presented indirectly* by way of the more originary presentation of the body, and myself as a *psychophysical subject*. While Husserl in other places presents a more nuanced perspective and his late "generative phenomenology" may be able to offer a deeper *relational* account of the constitution of the Other,[57] in the *Cartesian Meditations* (Husserl's most well-known discussion of the phenomenological constitution of the Other) he appears to subscribe to both of these views and writes the following: "If I reduce *other* men to what is included in my ownness, I get *bodies* included therein; if I reduce *myself* as a man, I get *'my animate organism'* and *'my psyche'*, or myself as a *psychophysical unity – in the latter my personal Ego* ..."[58]

There is certainly a key difference between myself and the Other, which is evident in the fact that I *inhabit* my own body but do not

---

57 See, for instance, Husserl, *Analyses Concerning Passive and Active Synthesis: Lectures on Transcendental Logic*, trans. Anthony J. Steinbock (Dordrecht: Kluwer Academic Publishers, 2001 [1966]), 221ff. See also Steinbock's discussion of "affective force" and the notion of a "constitutive duet" in the Translator's Introduction to the same volume (xlixff.). In his essay "Spirit and Generativity: The Role and Contribution of the Phenomenologist in Hegel and Husserl," Steinbock distinguishes Husserl's generative phenomenology from the *Cartesian Meditations* in the following way: "Unlike the Fifth Cartesian Meditation where the alter ego was founded in the ego, the intersubjective structure of home and alien is co-original in the sense of being mututally co-foundational. It is through their intertwining that there is not simply a *genesis* of individual sense, but a *generation* of historically normative and intersubjective sense: generativity." Steinbock, "Spirit and Generativity: The Role and Contribution of the Phenomenologist in Hegel and Husserl," in *Alterity and Facticity: New Perspectives on Husserl*, ed. Natalie Depraz and Dan Zahavi (Dordrecht: Kluwer Academic Publishers, 1998), 182. Steinbock's view contrasts with Waldenfels' earlier argument that throughout his writings Husserl maintains a position of "transcendental solipsism." See Waldenfels, *Das Zwischenreich des Dialogs*, 1ff.
58 *Cartesian Meditations*, 97.

inhabit the bodies of Others, and in this respect Husserl's distinction is warranted. However, I believe that Husserl here distinguishes *too sharply* between the interiority of the Self and the interiority of the Other. Husserl is of the view that only the *body* of the Other is directly given to me, is immanent to my consciousness. If I am to acquire the sense that there is a psyche and not merely a body before me, then an *apperception* is required that is founded on the more original *perception* of the Other's body. Such an apperception is involved in my first becoming aware of the Other as an animate organism "like myself" and also involved in more specific acts of "empathy" with the psychological states of the Other. Thus Husserl writes,

> Since ... my animate organism is the only body that is or can be constituted originally as an animate organism (a functioning organ), the body over there, which is nevertheless apprehended as an organism, must have derived this sense by an *apperceptive transfer from my animate organism* ...[59]

A little later Husserl writes,

> The *first determinate content* obviously must be formed by the understanding of the other's organism and specifically organismal conduct ... With this the Ego at first is determined only as governing thus somatically ... It is quite comprehensible that, *as a further consequence*, an "empathizing" of definite contents belonging to the *"higher psychic sphere"* arises. Such contents too are indicated somatically and in the conduct of the organism toward the outside world – for example: as the outward conduct of someone who is angry or cheerful, which I easily understand from my own conduct under similar circumstances.[60]

While it is true that my own organism is the only one that is an *organ* for me and I never perceive the world with, for instance, an Other's eyes, or move an Other's body as I move my own, we will see that the Other is not originarily and more immediately given to me as body nor is it the case that the only way in which I can become aware of the Other as *psyche* is by way of an indirect appresentation on the basis of the direct givenness of the Other's body.

The widespread view that I am presented with the Other's body and must appresent psychological phenomena can be traced back to certain metaphysical assumptions. It is assumed that the Other can

---

59 Ibid., 111.
60 Ibid., 118–19.

only be presented to my senses, and as my senses can necessarily only receive "physical sensations" as data the only aspect of the Other that can be given to me originarily is his or her body. A related metaphysical assumption is that an intuition of the Other's inner states is out of the question. Any content that is not "purely sensible" is intelligible but this intelligibility or meaning must come from me and cannot involve a givenness of the Other's state of mind with the originariness in which the Other's body is given. It is clear that a whole metaphysics of the relation between mind and body, and the relation between one self and another self, motivates the assumptions that only the body is genuinely given, and selves are incapable of participating in one another. As a phenomenologist one might *in the end* support such conclusions on phenomenological grounds. However, by way of principle, a phenomenological investigation must turn to the phenomena themselves with the suspension, as far as is possible, of any metaphysical assumptions. To my mind, Husserl's account in the *Cartesian Meditations* is not phenomenological enough; it is determined by certain uninterrogated, metaphysical presuppositions.

While these assumptions concerning the priority of the givenness of the Other's body and the indirect givenness of the Other's psyche will be undermined, some nuanced qualifications need to be made. First, these assumptions are not simply false. They are perhaps correct when it comes to certain modes in which the Other is given. In a medical examination, for instance, or when a person is "objectified" as a "sexual object" the Other is primarily given as a body (though there are important differences in these two examples). However, while this might be the case, it is not true of all modes of givenness of the Other and, moreover, it is distinctive of an *impoverished mode of givenness*. Jean-Luc Marion and Bernhard Waldenfels have rightly pointed out Husserl's prioritization of the givenness of the "object."[61] In Husserl's consideration of the Other he prioritizes a "passive synthesis" of the spatial "object."[62] According to Husserl, in perception I am primordially given the sensible aspects of an object correlated to my point of view. I appresent the sides of the object not yet given but these sides are always potentially given or presented rather than appresented, although every side of an object is never given at once. On this founding stratum, of the Other constituted as object, further aspects are appresented—for instance, that a psyche is operative "there."

---

61 Jean-Luc Marion, *Reduction and Givenness*, 1ff.; Jean-Luc Marion, *Being Given: Toward a Phenomenology of Givenness*, trans. Jeffrey L. Kosky (Stanford, CA: Stanford University Press, 2002), 27ff.; Bernhard Waldenfels, *Das Zwischenreich des Dialogs*, 44ff.
62 Husserl, *Cartesian Meditations*, 78ff.

This appresentation of the psychological, however, can never attain to the original givenness of a percept. In this way, the givenness of the "object" is prioritized. I will contend, in contrast, that while this might sometimes be the case, there are other cases in which psychological and spiritual levels of givenness must be prioritized and cannot be understood as mere "appresentation"; they are, at least, as originary as any sensible givenness.

My second objection to Husserl's description in *Cartesian Meditations* concerns the fact that it does not actually elaborate the phenomenon that I have called "knowing the individuated character of an Other." If I perceive someone stamping his fist on the table and yelling, then I perceive that the person is "angry." However, anger is merely a generic trait. The same holds for any structurally similar phenomenon. If I perceive a smile as "friendliness" then this is equally generic. This is not yet an individuated givenness. In other words this kind of empathic appresentation would only ever allow for the givenness of a generic Other, and not for the givenness of an *individuated* person, whom I address as "you" or with a first name. Rudolf Makkreel provides a good discussion of the limitations of Husserl's account in this sense. Husserl's account of empathy only allows me to recognize in the Other what I know from myself.[63] At one point Makkreel contrasts Husserl's view of empathy with Schleiermacher's notion of "divination." Schleiermacher's "divination" occupies, in some respects, the same place as Husserl's empathy but it allows for a givenness of the *individuated* Other. "Divination" is a mode of understanding that enables me to grasp the individual Other in her uniqueness or individuality. Although Makkreel does not discuss this difference in any detail the following passage is relevant to our concerns:

> Schleiermacher speaks of the divinatory method as one by which "one transforms oneself, as it were, into the other and seeks to grasp individuality immediately." ... To be sure, insofar as divination posits something, however minimal, that I share with someone else, whoever he or she may be, it would seem to be like empathy. But whereas empathy projects primarily from the self to others, divination seems to make room for the reverse way in which others allow me to find a plurality of selves in myself. The receptivity for all other human beings claimed by Schleiermacher thus overcomes the problem that we noted earlier about empathy,

---

63 This is also Scheler's critique of "empathy" and his reason for privileging "sympathy" over empathy. Scheler, *The Nature of Sympathy*, 242.

namely, its tendency merely to find the self replicated in the other.[64]

Although I do not wish to enter into a discussion of Schleiermacher's hermeneutics the difference that Makkreel draws between Husserl's understanding of empathy and Schleiermacher's "divination" is pertinent to the analyses below; I will explicate an understanding of the Other that is more immediate and specified than Husserl's account allows.

My third objection is not unrelated to the second one. Husserl's view of empathy is modeled on the standard of self-perception. As I can perceive my own mental states directly but not the Other's I must appresent the Other's mental states in association with the more direct givenness of his/her bodily appearance. In this way I "perceive" in the Other something analogous to my self-perception or self-presentation. Self-presentation is matched with Other-appresentation. However, this view can only account for knowledge of myself or an Other to a very limited extent. To know myself in a richer sense does not mean merely to *perceive* my mental states. It is a question that accompanies me throughout my life and a progressive complex affair that involves my *relationship* to Others. As a free being, or potentially free being, there is also no final terminus to self-knowledge because the self can always realize new, unforeseen possibilities, etc. Hence, although self-perception may play a role in self-knowledge, and count as a certain kind and aspect of self-knowledge, it is not equivalent to self-knowledge and does not suffice as a general standard for knowledge. Likewise, the analogous ap*presentation* of the other self can only count as knowledge of the Other in the limited sense of knowing the Other's mental states in a given situation. Hence, the question of individual character leads beyond the horizon and framework of the *Cartesian Meditations*.

The final thesis I would like to put forth concerning the present issue is that the prioritization of a particular kind of givenness is to a certain extent misguided.[65] Whatever is given to perception is a hermeneutic matter. It is a mistake to believe in a basic non-hermeneutic datum. There is no simple given. The "given" is always hermeneutically

---

64 Rudolf Makkreel, "How is Empathy Related to Understanding?," in *Issues in Husserl's Ideas II*, ed. Thomas Nenon and Lester Embree (Dordrecht: Kluwer Academic Publishers, 1996), 207.

65 I say to a "certain extent" misguided because the idea of "prioritization" does have some degree of validity. We have, for instance, already supported the phenomenological *prioritization* of the life-world and there are certain disclosures that must be *prioritized* in terms of being irreducible and irreplaceable.

"mediated," disclosed correlative to a way of *understanding*. It must be asserted, however, that "hermeneutic" does not mean "subjective." Understanding is, in principle, always *intersubjective* and *universal*; I understand the *world* or *universe* and what I have understood can always, in principle, be understood by another.

The following scenarios *typify* certain kinds of perception of the Other and illustrate the hermeneutic character of perception:

1. A painter seeks to catch the exact color of his model's skin on the canvas. He looks at the surface of the skin and discerns a complexity of individual hues.
2. A dentist examines a patient's teeth for cavities.
3. A father in a park sees his child running in a state of joy.
4. A lover sees in the beloved a manifestation, a presencing, of the ineffable, which appears as irreplaceable and even holy.

It is the correlation "seeing-seen" that must be acknowledged as the fundamental fact in each of the examples. Each perception is oriented by a hermeneutic horizon. The painter's vision is guided by the task of painting. The dentist's vision is guided by her dental knowledge that is operative in what she is looking for.[66] Each perception is also spatio-temporally as well as hermeneutically situated. The father's vision is within the horizon of "being-in-the-park-so-his-child-can-play." The lover is situated in a particular place and in the meaningful and intimate context of a "dialogue" between lover and beloved. Moreover, it is only in scenarios 1 and 2 that one might speak of the noema or content of the perception as focused on sensible properties. However, even these perceptions cannot in the first place be severed from the overall hermeneutic context—they are not brute givens. Furthermore, they cannot be separated from a highly specified intentionality or understanding. It is quite an act to manage to perceive the precise colors of a perceptible surface. The painter's vision becomes more and more refined through her artistic training, in contrast to which the non-painter possesses a very vague and generic color-perception. This precise color-perception of the painter is perhaps the *closest* thing to the Empiricist's notion of the givenness of distinct sensations. However, such a perception is the furthest thing possible from a passive reception

---

66. The hermeneutic-phenomenological approach to perception undertaken in this chapter could be related to the view of the "theory-ladenness" of observation in analytic philosophy. See Norwood Russell Hanson, *Patterns of Discovery: An Inquiry into the Conceptual Foundations of Science* (Cambridge: Cambridge University Press, 1958). Cf. Ludwig Wittgenstein, *Philosophische Untersuchungen*, ed. Joachim Schulte (Frankfurt am Main: Suhrkamp, 2001), 1025ff.

of discrete sensations. It is a complex hermeneutic act. The meanings, "body," "skin," and the specific hues that are seen but lack specific names, are operative meanings within the perceiving. It is only within the spontaneous intentional activity that these meanings, and thereby the appearances, first crystallize. Examples 3 and 4 are no more nor less indirect or direct. What appears is correlative to the hermeneutic horizon and noesis or intentional act operative in perceiving. However, this does not mean that all appearances are correlative to mere "subjective interpretations." Outside an intentional horizon nothing appears. There is no brute givenness. The intentional horizon *enables* the appearing. In this sense, what appears is always in accordance with a certain meaning, and for this reason it is problematic to speak of the more direct or less direct. These considerations positively demonstrate the fact that the prioritization of a certain givenness of the Other is to a certain extent misguided; the Other is "hermeneutically given" according to different hermeneutic possibilities.

If one is to give any meaning to the notion of a "priority" of certain manners of appearing then this is in no sense the "priority" imagined by Empiricism and materialism. Within developmental psychology as well as historically, the Other is first, and for the most part, perceived as a pre-dualistic psycho-physical unity—a unity not yet divided into the two terms "psyche" and "body." Genetically considered, we do not begin with the "body" and then add "soul" to it. We begin with an as yet undifferentiated unity that is later *divided* into "body" and "soul." This point, in its phylogenetic (the history of the human race) and ontogenetic (the biography of the individual) aspects, is clearly demonstrated by Scheler and Ernst Cassirer as well as by many others.[67] The primary perception of Others, in so far as it is legitimate to speak of one, is neither of disembodied souls nor of inanimate bodies, but of expressive phenomena not yet divided into two terms. In this sense, example 3 is typical of the manner in which Others are for the most part perceived; the child is seen as an irreducible expressive whole, as "running-in-a-state-of-joy." The datum of seeing is an undivided psycho-physical-expressive-phenomenon.

Despite these facts, objections might still be made. One could agree that all perception is hermeneutic and grant that if there is any priority

---

67 Scheler, *The Nature of Sympathy*, 238ff.; Ernst Cassirer, *The Philosophy of Symbolic Forms: Vol. III: The Phenomenology of Knowledge*, trans. Ralph Manheim (New Haven, CT: Yale University Press, 1957), 45ff.; Merleau-Ponty, *Phenomenology of Perception*, 410ff.; Bruno Snell, *The Discovery of the Mind: in Greek Philosophy and Literature*, trans. T. G. Rosenmeyer (New York: Dover Publications, 1982), 1ff.; Owen Barfield, *Poetic Diction: A Study in Meaning* (Middletown, CT: Wesleyan University Press, 1973), 79ff. This is just to list a handful of authors who, in different ways, elaborate the view that a pre-dualistic vision is phylogenetically and/or ontogenetically *prior* to a perception of the merely bodily or physical.

then it is in pre-dualistic, sensible-spiritual wholes, but nevertheless object that in reflection we can divide this whole into psychological and physical components, and discern that, *in fact*, the former is correlative to intuition (sensible intuition) and, therefore, more directly given, whereas the latter must be appresented because there is no such thing as an immediate intuition of the states of an Other's mind. Scheler offers instructive critiques of this objection, which pertain to example 3 above:

> Our immediate perceptions of our fellow-men do not relate to their bodies (unless we happen to be engaged in a medical examination), nor yet to their 'selves' or 'souls'. What we perceive are integral wholes, whose *intuitive* content is not immediately resolved in terms of external or internal perception.[68]

Scheler here insists that the "intuitive content" is not yet divided; such perceptions are prior to a division of the inner and the outer, the sensible and the intelligible. To relegate the "intelligible" to the subjective is to distort the actual manner in which the phenomena offer themselves. What is *disclosed* to such perceptual understanding is neither a purely sensible nor purely psychological content but a prior wholeness that does not involve the distinction between two terms. The psychological content is just as fundamental as the physical content. Scheler offers other examples that further undermine the prejudice that the psychological states of Others can only be given indirectly or appresented. He states,

> two people may very well feel the same sorrow; a strictly identical, not just a similar one, even though the experience may be differently coloured in each case by differing organic sensations. Anyone who holds that mental events are only accessible to one person at a time will never be able to explain the exact meaning of phrases like: 'All ranks were fired with the same enthusiasm', 'The populace was seized with a common joy, a common grief, a common delight', and so on. Custom, language, myth, religion, the world of the tale and the saga—how can they be understood on the assumption that mental life is essentially private?[69]

The view of appresentation involves the idea that I "posit" the presence of the psychological along with the bodily appearance of the other, which is given more directly, or, in Husserl's terms, belongs to

---

68 Scheler, *Nature of Sympathy*, 261; my emphasis.
69 Ibid., 258.

my sphere of ownness. This positing assumes a direction of intentionality from the I-pole to the object-pole; the object-pole is in this case an object that is a subject. However, there are numerous phenomena pertaining to the perception of the Other where the reverse seems to be the case, the disclosure of the beloved before the lover as in example 4 being only one case in point. In this respect, it is fitting to quote once more Scheler's characterization of the phenomenality of love: "*love itself, in the course of its movement*, is what brings about the continuous emergence of ever-higher value in the object—just as if it was streaming out from the object of its own accord, without any sort of exertion (even of wishing) on the part of the lover."[70]

To the intentionality of love something like a reversal of directionality seems to take place in that meaning appears to emerge from the "object of its own accord." I say "something like a reversal" because it is clear that I do not simply become the "object-pole" while the Other becomes the "I-pole." However, the "object" becomes more verbal than substantive and the physical is absorbed into the psychic or personal. Within the intentionality of love I am not a subject that imposes a meaning onto a mere thing; rather, a process of unconcealment seems to unfold from the "correlate" of perception as a self-unveiling of the Other. Such a privileged disclosure is clearly far richer than the merely bodily disclosure of the Other or the Other as disclosed through "empathy."

There are various words employed in the life-world that document disclosures of the Other involving a reversal of intentional-directionality, words such as "impression," "charisma," "presence," etc. These words seem to indicate a spiritual, almost magical, influence starting from the Other, which involves a kind of reception on the part of the perceiver. The understanding at work here could be described as an "active receptivity." We speak of the "impression" we *received from* or *got from* someone or the impression *made* on us.[71] The movement here is not from myself to the Other but from the Other to myself. The "charisma" of a particular person can exercise a kind of spell over the perceiver or offer a kind of inspiration that cannot be separated from the actual presence and behavior of the Other. We speak of the "presence" of someone, of missing someone's presence, of enjoying someone's presence. It is truer to say that I "participate" in a person's presence than to say that I "introject" this presence. These terms and expressions point to situations where the encounter with the

---

70 Ibid., 157.
71 In his later account of "affective force" Husserl does give some attention to related phenomena. See Husserl, *Analyses Concerning Passive and Active Synthesis: Lectures on Transcendental Logic*, trans. Anthony J. Steinbock, 221ff.

Other enables a disclosure that is more psychological or spiritual than sensible, as though an *influence* proceeded from the Other, in an analogous manner to the way in which medieval astrologists thought of spiritual influences as proceeding from the stars.[72] These phenomena involve a "counter-intentionality" and present clear evidence against the privileging of the bodily givenness of the Other. The phenomenological *facts* then do not allow the prejudice that the Other is given primarily as body, while the soul of the Other must be appresented. In these cases there is a distinctive character or an influence from the Other that is not simply a categorical appresentation or matter of introjection; there is a specific content that I did not "put there" though I am involved in its manifestation. With such phenomena individuated aspects of the Other come into view.

For the most part the Other is revealed as an *expressive Leib* or *dynamic physiognomy*. I have chosen the German word *Leib*, as it suggests the animate-body or the embodied-soul in a manner which does not involve the separation of two terms. This manner of disclosedness is what Merleau-Ponty speaks of as the "objective spirit" that is overlooked by reductive Empiricism, "the anger or pain which I ... read in a face, the religion whose essence I seize in some hesitation or reticence, the city whose temper I recognize in the attitude of a policeman ..."[73] While it is also the individual's participation in a given culture which comes to disclosure in the *expressive Leib*, the present focus is the manner in which the individual qua individual manifests as *Leib* (the two are, of course, not in conflict with one another; an individual's participation in a culture belongs in a distinctive way to his or her identity).

The Other is always encountered as *acting* in the world—as speaking, as walking, as attending to a task, as doing something, etc. The *expressive Leib* is the focus of the Other's actions as disclosed to me. With regard to the *expressive Leib* of the Other, *how* something is done is as significant as *what* is done. It is not only *what* a person does that is revealing of "who they are" but the *manner* in which something is done; the "meaning" of someone's actions—what they reveal—is disclosed not only in "what they do" but also in "how they do it." It is not only significant that a person eats, walks, speaks, reads philosophy, etc. All these activities are generic (although their combination in one person does begin to reveal a more unique presence). The *specific sense* of these behaviors is communicated in their *how*. One person, for instance, walks in a *manner* that suggests pride and confidence, another in a *manner* that suggests timidity. A certain individual holds a

---

72 The origin of the word "influence" is actually astrological in this sense.
73 Merleau-Ponty, *Phenomenology of Perception*, 27.

coffee cup in a distinctive way, has a particular gait—a certain spring in her step—a characteristic tone of voice, a certain look in her eyes, a particular laugh, etc. These generic traits—drinking coffee, walking, speaking, looking, laughing—take on a specific sense in their *expressive how*. While the *expressive Leib* serves in disclosing that someone is "happy," "sad," "determined," or "depressed" it also enables a more specific revelation of the Other; it can assume an individuated sense. The following examples serve to elucidate the former. The gleam in a person's eyes and lightness in the person's step present a physiognomy of "happiness." Dull eyes and hunched shoulders can present a physiognomy of "sadness." A businessman walking upright and at a faster pace than others through a crowd displays a physiognomy of "determination." The slow monotone voice of an Other is a physiognomic aspect of her or his "depressed" state of mind. In these aspects of *Leiblichkeit* generic states of mind are disclosed. I see that someone is "happy," "sad," "determined," or "depressed," etc. While this is an important mode of the givenness of the Other, the *expressive Leib* can also enable a more distinctive disclosure of the individual.

The work of art offers another instance in which the expressivity of the *how* is at least as significant as that of the *what*. It is certainly significant that Cézanne painted Mont Sainte-Victoire, chose this as a theme, as a subject of his paintings. However, Mont Sainte-Victoire was painted by others prior to Cézanne. That Cézanne painted this mountain is not unique to him or his work. This is not to say that it is insignificant, as it is an impressive natural landscape that belongs to Cézanne's native region of Provence.[74] However, more individuating is the fact that while others had painted the mountain, no one had painted it in the same *manner* or *way* as Cézanne. What is most distinctive of Cézanne's paintings is the *how* in each case. Moreover, the *meaning* of the pictures cannot be separated from this *how*. That there is a kinship between the *how* of many paintings is what makes "Cézannes" generally, what we call Cézanne's *style*. This style unites Cézanne's paintings, makes them recognizable as parts of a single oeuvre. However, style is clearly not reducible to a universal concept or rule. Moreover, the *how* of each painting is that which most enables the picture to institute a sense that is specific to the individual work. The *how* of any work of art, the treatment of the material and the theme, enables a work of art, and ultimately an oeuvre, to "create its

---

74 Joachim Gasquet describes in detail Cézanne's identification with the landscape of Provence. Joachim Gasquet, *Joachim Gasquet's Cézanne: A Memoir with Conversations*, trans. Christopher Pemberton (London: Thames and Hudson, 1991).

audience" or transform its appreciators. A work of art is ultimately its own teaching.

What does this have to do with the *expressive Leib* of Others? As these considerations are close to the thought of Merleau-Ponty it is instructive to turn to the following passage from the *Phenomenology of Perception*:

> The body is to be compared, not to a physical object, but rather to a work of art. In a picture or a piece of music the idea is incommunicable by means other than the display of colours and sounds. Any analysis of Cézanne's work, if I have not seen his pictures, leaves me with a choice between several possible Cézannes, and it is the sight of the pictures which provides me with the only existing Cézanne, and therein the analyses find their full meaning. The same is true of a poem or a novel, although they are made up of words ... A novel, poem, picture or musical work are individuals, that is, beings in which the expression is indistinguishable from the thing expressed, their meaning accessible only through direct contact ...[75]

Merleau-Ponty also often uses the term "style" beyond the domain of works of art. Thus, for instance, he compares the style of the world to the character of a person (it is his description of the latter that is pertinent to the present considerations):

> This unity is comparable with that of an individual whom I recognize because he is recognizable in an unchallengeably self-evident way, before I ever succeed in stating the formula governing his character, because he retains the same style in everything he says and does, even though he may change his place or opinions. A style is a certain manner of dealing with situations, which I identify or understand in an individual ... even though I may be quite unable to define it: and in any case a definition, correct though it may be, never provides an exact equivalent, and is never of interest to any but those who have already had the experience ...[76]

The expressivity of another's actions is analogous to that of the work of art. The meaning of a work of art is disclosed in *how* it sensibly presents its theme. The meaning is not simply a universal concept. Likewise, the noetic comportment correlative to such an expressive sense is analogous

---

75 Merleau-Ponty, *Phenomenology of Perception*, 174–5.
76 Ibid., 381–2.

to *attending to* a work of art. The sense is not something imposed from the outside but rather emerges in an *attending to*, an understanding that gives itself over to the *how* of the expression. The sense emerges *chiasmically* or *in-relation*; it is neither contained in the understanding a priori, nor is it a mere sensible given. This sense does not emerge through an analogizing inference based on my own self-experience. This understanding is a *looking away from oneself*; the sense emerges in attending to the *how* of a physiognomically expressive behavior. Furthermore, I recognize someone's character in a manner analogous to the style of an artistic oeuvre. Particular instances of perceiving the Other can therefore be compared to grasping the sense of a single artistic performance while the understanding of someone's character is comparable to the style of an oeuvre. It is the *how* that remains particularly significant here; the "style" of someone's behavior "is a certain manner of dealing with situations." There is a very real analogy between the style of an artistic oeuvre and the character of an Other as disclosed through the person's expressive behavior in different circumstances. This analogy might also reveal an intimate connection between the style of an oeuvre and the individuality of the author (Schleiermacher), though an inquiry into this connection is beyond the scope of the present considerations.

The *expressive how* of an Other's behavior in different contextual situations has a *characteristic* sense. A certain person tends to walk with a lightness of step, to hold a cup in a delicate manner, to speak eloquently and with a tone that seems to echo the person's gait. Another person walks with a heavy gait, articulates things more slowly—his intonation has a reflective physiognomy and he proceeds with tasks at a measured pace, etc. In each case, a distinctive *how* is reflected in many variations across different forms of manifestation or *Leiblichkeit*. The attempt to *conceptualize* these phenomena inevitably remains to a certain extent generic. In the *Lebenswelt*, however, we often note that a person has a specific gesture or manner which is absolutely typifying and singular. The smallest gesture can manifest an especial *thisness* or *haecceity*. Across the various manifestations of behavior a *stylistic integrity* akin to the style of an oeuvre comes to manifestation. The sense of this *how* which is disclosed via various channels—sight, hearing, etc.—and in various social contexts plays a central role in the revelation of a person's character. The more we *get to know* a person and the more *individual* a person actually is—the less the person merely acts according to a culture's *das Man*[77]—the more the person's individual

---

[77] Heidegger, *Sein und Zeit*, 126ff; *Being and Time*, trans. John Macquarrie and Edward Robinson (Oxford: Blackwell Publishers, 1962 [1927]), H. 126ff ["H." refers to the original German pagination that is provided in the margins]. See Scheler, *The Nature of Sympathy*, 122.

character comes to be disclosed. In speaking of *knowing* someone's *character* we have returned to our original aim and theme, which following these elementary observations can now be elaborated in a consequential phenomenological account.

The Genesis of the Sense of an Individual Character
The process of getting to know an Other and the genesis of the sense of the Other's character begin with the first meeting or encounter. Any meeting with an Other is situated. I encounter an Other at a certain time in a certain place, in a certain country, the ultimate horizon being that of the world. The situatedness of place implies its own geographical (including the sense of nature or landscape), cultural, historical, and political senses. It is within such a horizon and its background senses that I encounter any Other. Furthermore, the specific situation of meeting carries a more determinate meaning. I meet someone on the street, in a café, at a performance or function—private or public; I encounter an Other within a certain pragmatic context. Heidegger describes this as follows: "When others are encountered ... they are encountered from out of the world ... even if others become themes for study, as it were, in their own Dasein, they are not encountered as Person-things present-at-hand: we meet them 'at work', that is, primarily in their Being-in-the-world."[78]

Others are encountered as being-in-the-world in a certain way; they are not encountered as "objects" standing over against me but as acting within a larger hermeneutic context within which I also understand myself. In any encounter with an Other I am also implicated. However, understanding transcends a mere dialectic between Self and Other. Understanding regards myself *and* others as agents within a larger situation. My self is distinguished by the sense of "I-ness" and the presence and character of my psycho-physicality, which opens up my perspective onto the scene from the "zero point" of my psycho-physical "here."[79] While my vision is to some extent restricted by my psycho-physical here (I cannot see everything and I see things from a particular angle), the limitations of my perspective are relativized by my understanding of the larger hermeneutic situation. (If I am at a performance, for instance, while my particular view onto the whole space is conditioned by my spatial position, I understand myself as "one member of the audience" and know that others see things from a different spatial point of view; my understanding is not reduced to

---

78 Heidegger, *Being and Time*, H. 119–20.
79 Husserl, *Ideas Pertaining to a Pure Phenomenology and a Phenomenological Philosophy*, Second Book, trans. Richard Rojcewicz and André Schuwer (Dordrecht: Kluwer Academic Publishers, 1989 [1952]), 166.

my particular sensible opening onto the scene.) As an actor within the scene, who both perceives and is perceptible to others, there is a dialectical involvement between my own actions and the actions of Others. There is no possibility here for inaction—my being-there, even if silently, is already an action and as an actuality has the status of an actualized *possibility*. I understand Others in relation to their response to a given situation which may include a response to my actions.

Within a certain situation, an Other, whom I had not previously known, appears. With this appearing the Other makes a *first impression* on me. The ways of seeing the Other previously elaborated—disclosures with the sense of presence, charisma, expressive significance (*expressive Leib*), etc.—are possibilities which might be constituted within the noesis. Anything I learn about the Other's biography naturally plays a significant role in coming to understand "who" the Other is (see the later discussion of language). Often there is a distinctive sense of the Other that arises in the very first moment of the encounter. This is naturally premature and subject to revision but the point is that the Other is not encountered as a mere body with a soul that I project onto it, but from the beginning (for the most part) as a physiognomic sense, which immediately assumes a distinctive character. This first sense of the Other plays a determinative role in whether I am initially sympathetically or antipathetically inclined toward the Other; these feelings are also subject to revision.

As the Other is generally disclosed from the first moment with a distinctive, though premature, sense, this cannot be understood as the appresentation or co-presentation of certain generic attributes—"sad," "bossy," "polite," etc.—onto a mere moving body. Although I will use such adjectives to describe the person after the fact, the actual presence of the Other involves a "saturation" and specificity of sense, which make the mere ascription of generic predicates insufficient. For this reason, it is always more revelatory of a person's character to recount the concrete and situated behavior of a person than to ascribe generic predicates. The anecdote is more revealing than generic predication, as an anecdote involves *imagining* the situation in a way that does more justice to the sensible-intelligible unity and specificity of the scene.[80]

It is out of a history of such encounters with an Other, as a *biography of the relationship* begins to unfold, that the Other comes to an ever-richer disclosure for me. There are, of course, innumerable elements involved in *getting to know* someone, such as trust, increasing intimacy, etc., which have not been considered. However, the general manner in which the sense of an Other unfolds and takes on an irreducible and

---

80 The significance of the *imagination* for a twofold disclosure is taken up in Chapter 4.

individual significance has been outlined. Out of understanding the Other in many situations a picture and sense of character or personality emerges. In his *Farbenlehre* (*Theory of Colours*), Goethe offers the following illuminating description:

> strictly speaking, it is useless to attempt to express the nature of a thing abstractedly. Effects we can perceive, and a complete history of those effects would, in fact, sufficiently define the nature of the thing itself. We should try in vain to describe a man's character, but let his acts be collected and an idea of the character will be presented to us.[81]

In this respect the character in a play presents a purification and simplification of the logic of life. A good dramatist (or novelist) does not *develop* his characters through having one personage linguistically describe another personage (although this might play a role). The playwright presents the actions of a character within complex scenes and situations. Out of the manner in which the personage acts in the situations portrayed in the many scenes of a play, the character of the personage emerges. The sense of the character contextually arises from the scenes. As a result, the character emerges with a meaning much richer and more specific than would otherwise be possible. Characters such as Hamlet or King Lear or Cordelia thereby resemble living, inexhaustible individuals. However, there are, of course, important differences between dramatic personages and real persons, only a few of which will be mentioned. The characters of a play are written by the playwright and once the play is written it is set in stone, although it forever remains open to fresh interpretations. A person, in contrast, writes herself into the drama of life. The past of a biography resembles a character in a play that the person has already co-authored along with Others, while the present and future are matters that each person continues to co-author and have their sense as *possibility* rather than as *actuality*. In encountering the Other I also differ from an audience member who can participate in the whole drama from a superior vantage point, sympathizing with the characters but viewing them from a distance. In encountering and relating to Others, in *Sein* as *Mitsein*, I am included as an actor on the stage of life, and cannot exit to gaze upon it as a spectator; I-am-in-the-world, and am implicated in the disclosure, self-expression, and actions of Others.

---

81 Johann Wolfgang von Goethe, *Sämtliche Werke nach Epochen seines Schaffens: Zur Farbenlehre*, vol. 10, ed. Karl Richter et al. (Munich: Carl Hanser Verlag, 1989), 9; *Theory of Colours*, transl. Charles Lock Eastlake (London: Frank Cass & Co., 1967), xvii.

Phenomenology and the Problem of Dualism   63

There is an absolutely central element that has, more or less, been left out of the above considerations. This is language; not as the physiognomy or tone of an Other's voice, but as the communication of an Other's *thoughts*. The two are obviously interrelated; the tone of voice can, for instance, indicate the difference between something ironically, humorously, sincerely, or sarcastically *meant*; a change in tone with identical diction can *mean* fundamentally different things. Nevertheless, it makes sense to distinguish (even if they cannot ultimately be divided) between the physiognomic aspect of the voice and the *thought* content. The reason for having concentrated on the former lies in the fact that the later chapters are primarily concerned with the twofold disclosure of non-linguistic beings (in the human sense of "linguistic") and the present task is to prepare the ground for what follows. However, language as the communication of the *thoughts* of an Other obviously plays the most central of roles in *getting to know* a human Other and requires some discussion.

In conversing with an Other and learning her thoughts on numerous matters, in a certain sense, the most complete communion of I and Other is possible. The person is no longer a *manifestation* or *presence* for me but rather another center of, and perspective on, the world. As Merleau-Ponty states,

> In the experience of dialogue, there is constituted between the other person and myself a common ground; my thought and his are inter-woven into a single fabric, my words and those of my interlocutor are called forth by the state of the discussion, and they are inserted into a shared operation of which neither of us is the creator. We have here a dual being, where the other is for me no longer a mere bit of behaviour in my transcendental field, nor I in his; we are collaborators for each other in consummate reciprocity. Our perspectives merge into each other, and we co-exist through a common world. In the present dialogue I am freed from myself, for the other person's thoughts are certainly his; they are not of my making, though I do grasp them at the moment they come into being, or even anticipate them ... It is only retrospectively, when I have withdrawn from the dialogue and am recalling it that I am able to reintegrate it into my life and make of it an episode in my private history, and that the other recedes into absence ...[82]

While conversing with an Other, I spontaneously think his words/thoughts. The more attentively I listen the more a distinct awareness

---

82 Merleau-Ponty, *Phenomenology of Perception*, 413.

of myself recedes into the background. I think thoughts that may be foreign to my worldview and interpret the world in light of them.[83] Only after the fact of *thinking what the Other says* can I formulate a personal response. Understanding (as cognitive capacity) oscillates between thinking with the Other and formulating my own response and perspective. Thus, *understanding* is not reducible to solipsism, as it oscillates between my and the Other's perspectives. There are naturally mis-*understandings*; however these are deficient moments of *understanding*.

The claims I am making for *understanding* might seem exaggerated. However, while these claims present an ideal situation they correspond to the essence of understanding and dialogue. Genuine dialogue presupposes that "we understand each other" and is the clearest example of the universality of language and understanding. Understanding is essentially self-transcending and language is essentially intersubjective; their co-operation enables a conversation to be *a* conversation, a *single* conversation. If one thinks a conversation starting from the notion that subjects are separated islands one will never adequately conceive what takes place in a conversation. Conversing is an oscillation in the *shared* world of language and thought. We rightly speak of *partners* in a conversation; there is *one* conversation in which a plurality of persons *take part*.[84] The more I listen to the Other, the more I forget myself and the articulate thought of the Other takes center stage. Language in this way opens up another center of the world. The world is always an *interpreted* world; it is disclosed in relation to a world-view. In thinking the Other's thoughts I see the world accordingly; I *literally* understand the world from the perspective of an Other. Along with the distinctive *presence* of an Other this is a further reason why an Other can *enrich* my world. My world is enriched through learning to see the world from the intellectual vantage point of an Other. Of course, in everyday encounters the Other as *presence* and the Other as *thinking self* are co-determining, just as in the more limited case, *what* a person says and her *tone* of voice implicate one another.

---

83 The gesture of genuine understanding is not egocentric but ec-static; it gives itself over to the theme. There is an irreducible "I-ness" but the I surrenders itself to make space for the Other or the theme.
84 One might object that such a conversation assumes agreement and does not allow for *argument, tension,* and *disagreement*. However, an argument is still a mode of conversation in that it presupposes *understanding* and a *shared* language; there can be no *absolute* dis-agreement or difference. Even if two people do not speak the same language they will still *understand* the Other "as another human being" and will be able to communicate to a minimal degree. Moreover, they can *potentially* understand the foreign language, and as children had the *capacity* to learn *any* language.

Conclusion of Chapter

With regard to the disclosure of the Other, the operation of an intentionality or understanding with a *receptive* character has been demonstrated. The explication of terms such as "impression," "charisma," and "presence" revealed what, following Merleau-Ponty, could be called a *chiasmic* disclosure of the Other.[85] This disclosure is *relational* in the strong sense of the word, in which the relating must be conceived as more fundamental than the *relata*. It also involves a richness that undermines the view that in perceiving the Other, I am limited to the givenness of the Other's body, while psychological aspects are appresented. Furthermore, this givenness of the Other eludes any sort of "a priorism," as the content does not have its genesis outside and prior to the lived encounter, but is born in the spatio-temporality of the lived encounter itself. Nor is it "a posteriori" in any Empiricist sense of the word. This is another way of saying that it concerns an *essence* that is *relationally disclosed*.

The primacy (in so far as such a term is valid) of a pre-dualistic givenness of the human Other was also illustrated in the discussion of the *expressive Leib* and the perception of individuated senses. These phenomena reveal an indissoluble unity of the sensible and the intelligible in a manner that resembles the working of a work of art.

After distinguishing a spectrum of disclosures of the Other, which might be arranged on a scale from poorer to richer (the richest being correlative to an intentionality of love), we were able to give a phenomenological account of the process of *getting to know* another individual and the emergence of an individuated sense and character. This knowing is not an imposition of meaning from a detached point of view, but an understanding *out of* lived events. The way in which a character emerges out of the scenes of a play, or the way in which the sense of a symphony emerges out of its many movements, provide good analogies for the nature of this kind of understanding (though the limitations of such analogies must be taken into account).[86] It is out

---

85 Although I am drawing a great deal from Merleau-Ponty's philosophy there are essential points where I diverge from his thought. Despite the brilliance of Merleau-Ponty's descriptions of the living body in contrast to "objectifying" conceptions of the body I still regard Merleau-Ponty's thought as one-sidedly *emphasizing* the bodily. In this sense my appropriation of terms such as "chiasm" bear slightly different nuances of meaning to the meaning of these terms in Merleau-Ponty's thought. Precise points of divergence from Merleau-Ponty's thought are articulated in the following chapters.

86 One limitation, which has not yet been explicitly mentioned, is the fact that, although we might speak of artworks as being "ensouled," there is a clear difference between a human being and a work of art. To put it in crude terms one could say that the human being is "self-moving" whereas an artwork

of such an *involved* or *participational* understanding that a sense of the individual Other unfolds, a sense that cannot be acquired otherwise.

Solipsistic philosophical arguments concerning the impossibility of knowing the existence of an Other are based on problematic and erroneous grounds. They assume that understanding is subjective, a view which we have rejected on various grounds. They then treat the problem within a reflective vacuum. The surest evidence that I am awake and not asleep is the character of the actual experience of being awake (in contrast to sleeping), in comparison to which philosophical doubt offers less compelling evidence. The task lies then in explicating this evidence rather than denying it or trying to reconstruct it with weaker or inferior logical evidence. Likewise, the surest evidence of the existence of other individuals is the living experience of Others, and not a "philosophical proof" that Others exist. In the life-world we never have any doubt in the existence of Others; the task then is to explicate this *fact*. The above explication showed that the sense of the other individual attains a haecceity that could never be generated by simply projecting universal concepts on a screen of the Other's body. Nor is it a sense that could be generated on the basis of an analogizing apperception based on an original givenness of my own interiority. The sense of the other individual as an individual is born from the understanding of living encounters.

There is naturally a great deal more that could be said concerning the manner in which the Other is disclosed in the life-world, and even the most extensive analysis would be insufficient. With the simplest of objects a complete disclosure is out of the question, let alone with another, individual, human being who is not only inexhaustible as an actuality but whose essence is always in the mode of a not yet realized *possibility* or *potentiality* of self-realization. To unconcealment belongs concealment and there is no complete unconcealment. However, understanding is the possibility of unconcealment and is self-transcending in its innermost essence. As aforementioned, this does not mean that non-dualistic disclosure is a total disclosure. Rather, "non-dualistic disclosure" implies a disclosure where the sensible and the intelligible, the physical and the spiritual, the particular and universal, the individual and meaning, are revealed as aspects of a holistic phenomenon. It was the task of the above considerations to articulate such a phenomenon on the basis of a phenomenology of the life-world in the mode of everydayness, and the very limited treatment has sufficed to achieve this task. Such a disclosure was shown to involve

---

requires an agent outside of itself; a piece of music does not perform itself, a book does not write itself, etc., whereas my *Leib* is something I move from within.

an understanding which on its noetic side (as "intentional act") cannot be regarded as the imposition of a meaning from a detached vantage point, but rather involves an activity which is equally a passivity or receptivity.

The above considerations have explicated the structure and features of a twofold disclosure of other human beings, which involves a close intertwining of the sensible and the intelligible and an active-passivity. The question might now be raised as to whether it is possible to demonstrate an equivalent disclosure of other beings. Can the phenomena of other-than-human Nature, for instance, be disclosed in an analogously twofold or non-dualistic manner? In my opinion, within the horizon of a phenomenology of the life-world in the mode of everydayness this would only be possible to a limited extent. Nevertheless, the boundary between the everyday or ordinary and the extraordinary is certainly a blurry one. Already within the horizon of the everyday a spectrum of richer and poorer disclosures was discernible. The disclosure of the individual Other correlative to love was distinguished as belonging to the richer end of the spectrum. Such a disclosure is far from ordinary or mundane but it is an experience shared by many. Moreover, most, if not all, of us have at least once been struck by the beauty of an aspect of the natural world, which we would find hard to put into words. Such experiences could also belong to a phenomenology of the life-world within the horizon of the "everyday" but at the "richer" end of the spectrum. If such seldom and privileged disclosures still belong to the horizon of the "everyday," why then is there a need to break with this horizon at all? Has space not already been made for the entire spectrum of human experiences? The answer to the first question is articulated on the basis of a negative answer to the second question: Space has *not* been made for the entire spectrum of human experiences. If we turn, for instance, to the writings of certain mystics we find claims to experiences or disclosures of the numinous which take place *beyond* the horizon of "common" (even if rare) human experiences. To do justice to the claims to such disclosures the horizon of the everyday must be left. While it could be stated that the *borderline* of the *everyday* (richer disclosures within the horizon of the "everyday") touches the *threshold* of the *extraordinary* or *exceptional* and in this way there is a continuum between them, this blurry boundary is nevertheless an important and valid distinction. The subsequent chapters will demonstrate the meaningfulness of this distinction through explicating Rilke's exceptional non-dualistic vision of things. This non-dualistic vision is similar in structure to the twofold disclosure delineated above. It involves an active-passivity, an intertwining of the sensible and intelligible, and a reversal of intentional-directionality. However, Rilke's vision was achieved through a *praxis* of seeing that is not part and parcel of daily life; in turn, it reveals the structure of a twofold vision to a more profound degree and extends beyond the sphere of the human to the wider natural world. The logic of this move from the human Other to a poetic vision of Nature might be supported by the following claim by Scheler:

> Man's point of entry into identification with the life of the cosmos lies where that life is nearest and in closest affinity to his own, namely *in another man*. He who has never known the Dionysian ecstasy of emotional union between man and man, it matters not how, will also find the living, dynamic side of Nature, *natura naturans* (as opposed to *natura naturata*, with which science and the symbolic approach to the study of Nature are solely concerned) for ever a closed book to him.[87]

---

[87] Scheler, *The Nature of Sympathy*, 108. Waldenfels also makes the related point that a dialogical view of self and other has implications for a more intertwined perspective (intertwining of inner and outer) on other areas, including art, perception, space, etc. Waldenfels, *Das Zwischenreich des Dialogs*, 62.

Two Learning to See: Rilke and the Visual Arts

The problem of dualism, as an existential, epistemological, ontological, and creative problem, was central to Rilke's entire development. While he did not address dualism through philosophical reasoning, the centrality of this problematic is reflected in his biography and writings as a whole. Rilke's response to dualism transformed in the course of his poetic and personal development. The focus of the present work is on the way in which Rilke formulated and responded to this problem in his middle period (approx. 1902–10). His approach to dualism will be considered from two primary directions.

The present chapter and the subsequent chapter (Chapter 3) explicate Rilke's formulation of the problem of dualism in the middle period and his experiential resolution of this problem through the *praxis* of a certain manner of *seeing*. Rilke's twofold seeing not only enabled an experiential overcoming of dualism but also offered a central source of inspiration for the composition of his most accomplished poetic work of this period, the *Neue Gedichte* (*New Poems*, 1907) and *Der neuen Gedichte anderer Teil* (*New Poems: The Other Part*, 1908).[1] Furthermore, these poems foster a twofold vision of things for the reader's imagination. The latter is the main theme and argument of Chapter 4. In short, Chapters 2 and 3 focus on Rilke's seeing, while Chapter 4 focuses on the significance of Rilke's poetry, more specifically the *Neue Gedichte*, for an overcoming of dualism.

There are two essential questions that must, at least in part, be addressed at this point, in order to legitimate the turn to Rilke. These questions could be formulated as follows:

---

1 While the *Neue Gedichte* first appeared in two separate volumes, published in 1907 and 1908 respectively, these volumes are two parts of a single body of work. Whenever I mention the *Neue Gedichte* without further specification, I am referring to both parts as a unified collection. See Luke Fischer, "Perception as Inspiration: Rilke and the *New Poems*."

1. Why turn to Rilke and his poetry in order to advance the prior *philosophical* discussion of the problem of dualism?
2. Why, more specifically, has the choice been made to focus on Rilke's middle period and the *Neue Gedichte*? If the problem of dualism was central to Rilke's whole development why not turn to the later Rilke and his maturest works, *Duineser Elegien* (*Duino Elegies*, 1922 [published in 1923]) and *Die Sonette an Orpheus* (*The Sonnets to Orpheus*, 1922 [published in 1923])?[2]

Thus far the problem of dualism has been addressed through an examination of the perception of the human Other in the life-world. The reason for this focus lay in the fact that it demonstrates in a readily accessible manner the existence of a non-dominative way of understanding and its correlative non-dualistic disclosure, in other words, a twofold seeing. This twofold seeing, in which the sensible and the intelligible are closely intertwined, was articulated through a phenomenological reflection on the kind of perception that is operative in our everyday, pre-theoretical being-in-the-world. As the human Other was our focus, this naturally gives rise to the question as to whether such a mode of unconcealment can extend to other regions of being. My contention is that Rilke can lead us into further regions in a way that would not be possible were we to remain within a phenomenology of the life-world in the mode of everydayness. The primary domain that will be explicated following Rilke is that of Nature and, more specifically, landscape, animals, and plants.[3] Thus, one reason for turning to Rilke is that he can lead us beyond the horizon of a phenomenology of the everyday, but in a way that is continuous with the previous considerations.

Rilke's solution to the problem of dualism was neither a metaphysical monism in the sense of a philosophical system nor

---

2 The reason why we are not focusing on the earlier Rilke will be made clear in the course of this chapter.
3 Rilke's way of seeing was not, however, limited to the natural world. Correlatively, while the *Neue Gedichte* contains a number of poems that thematize "natural things," there are also numerous poems that thematize works of art, architecture, human figures, as well as biblical and mythological subjects, etc. I have chosen to capitalize "Nature" in this chapter for a few reasons. First, it is in keeping with the capitalization of "Other" in the preceding chapter, and, as in the former case, serves to emphasize the importance of the subject matter. Second, Rilke's conception of Nature shares much in common with the Romantic conception of "Nature" as a holistic reality with a divine significance. While in environmental philosophy and ecocritical theory there are lively debates about, and critiques of, the concepts of "Nature" and "nature," these do not require discussion in the present context. See, for instance, Timothy Morton, *Ecology without Nature: Rethinking Environmental Aesthetics* (Cambridge, MA: Harvard University Press, 2007).

a matter of phenomenological *reflection*. It resulted from the cultivation of a radically self-less seeing of things that is not immanent to the everyday and differs from a purely philosophical methodology. This praxis of seeing was largely inspired by the example of visual artists—the Worpswede artists (Otto Modersohn, Paula Modersohn-Becker, Clara Westhoff [later Clara Rilke], and others), Auguste Rodin, and Paul Cézanne, in the respective chronological order. Among other things this praxis of seeing led to an exceptional, non-everyday disclosure of Nature that overcomes our ordinary estrangement from the natural world and is not attainable by purely philosophical means. Chapters 2 and 3 thus elaborate two answers to the first question listed above. First, Rilke's vision is continuous with the structure of seeing outlined in the previous chapter but enables a non-dualistic disclosure of Nature that transcends the horizon of a phenomenology of the life-world in the mode of everydayness. Second, Rilke's seeing demonstrates a non-dualistic disclosure that cannot be achieved by a purely philosophical methodology. Nevertheless, this seeing, as will be shown, is implicitly phenomenological and can be explicated as a phenomenology of the exceptional. Chapter 4 will further demonstrate Rilke's unique significance for an overcoming of dualism through the argument that his *poetic language* can foster a twofold vision (for the imagination) in a manner superior to philosophical language.

In response to the second question above, it can be stated that the Rilke of the middle period and the *Neue Gedichte* link up directly with the problematic as it has been elaborated thus far. Although there is no doubt that Rilke's response to the problem of dualism continued to evolve into the late period, his maturest works—the *Duineser Elegien* and *Die Sonette an Orpheus*—are not as immediately phenomenological in character as the *Neue Gedichte*. Furthermore, the praxis that facilitated the inspiration of the later works is less directly connected to our previous phenomenological considerations; the concern with the world of perception is far more evident in Rilke's middle period than in his later work. While a comprehensive answer to the question as to whether the *Duineser Elegien* and *Die Sonette an Orpheus* ultimately offer a more profound response to dualism is beyond the scope of the present work, further aspects of this question are discussed in the second section of Chapter 3. However, there are additional reasons for privileging Rilke's middle period.

Rilke's late work can be more adequately understood and is less susceptible to misunderstanding, on the basis of a previous engagement with his work from the middle period. Hence, a consideration of the middle period provides a kind of prolegomenon for an evaluation of Rilke's later response to dualism. Lines such as, "Was draußen *ist*, wir wissen aus des Tiers/ Antlitz allein ... [what *is* outside, we know from the animal's/ countenance alone]" (Die Achte Elegie, *Duineser Elegien*) take on a deeper sense if one has previously engaged with the dynamic, physiognomic portrayal of particular animals in the *Neue Gedichte*.[4] More importantly, the most decisive lines of the *Duineser Elegien* (from The Ninth Elegy), "Erde! unsichtbar!/ Was, wenn Verwandlung nicht, ist dein drängender Auftrag?/ Erde, du liebe, ich will ... [Earth! invisible!/ What if not transformation, is your urgent charge?/ Earth, dear one, I will]," can be more appropriately understood against the background of the middle period.[5] Although the specific dynamic between the poet and the invisible alters in the later period, the basic character of the Rilkean invisible, an invisible that is by no means in opposition to the visible, is more susceptible to misunderstanding if interpreted without reference to the middle period. In that the *Duineser Elegien* present a "worldview," an evaluation and formulation of the situation and vocation of humanity in the universe, they have a more abstract, philosophical character. This "abstractness" contrasts with the concrete, detailed portrayal of things in the *Dinggedichte* (thing-poems) of the *Neue Gedichte*.[6] In this portrayal it is more immediately ascertainable that the Rilkean invisible/interior/super-sensible is not the opposite of the visible/exterior/sensible.[7] Moreover, in the years following the composition of the *Duineser Elegien* and *Die Sonette an Orpheus* Rilke was primarily occupied with writing poems in French. Some of the French collections of poems, such as *Les Quatrains Valaisans*, are reminiscent of the *Neue Gedichte* in the concreteness of their depictions (although they have a more elusive and ethereal character than the *Neue Gedichte*—no doubt due to differences between the French and the German language as well as to the different stage of life and work in which they were written).[8] It would be legitimate to regard

---

4 KA 2, 224. For a discussion of Rilke's later vision of animals (and its connections to Franz Marc's animal paintings) see Luke Fischer, "Animalising Art: Rainer Maria Rilke and Franz Marc"; Luke Fischer, "Die Animalisierung der Kunst: Rainer Maria Rilke und Franz Marc," in *Mythos-Geist-Kultur: Festschrift zum 60. Geburtstag von Christoph Jamme* (Munich: Wilhelm Fink Verlag, 2013), 335–48.
5 KA 2, 229.
6 The consideration of poems in Chapter 4 is, for the most part, limited to *Dinggedichte*. While the *Dinggedicht* is a type of poem characteristic of the *Neue Gedichte* there are also numerous poems that do not fit into this genre.
7 For a good explication and defense of the view that the invisible of the later Rilke is in important senses continuous with the invisible of the middle period, see Hermann Meyer, "Die Verwandlung des Sichtbaren: Die Bedeutung der modernen bildenen Kunst für Rilkes späte Dichtung," in *Zarte Empirie: Studien zur Literaturgeschichte* (Stuttgart: J. B. Metzlersche Verlagsbuchhandlung, 1963).
8 See Bernhard Böschenstein, "R. M. R.s französische Gedichte," in *Rilke – ein europäischer Dichter aus Prag*, ed. Peter Demetz, Joachim W. Storck, and Hans Dieter Zimmermann (Würzburg: Königshausen & Neumann, 1998), 191–200.

these poems as aiming to perform something of the transformation (*Verwandlung*) that Rilke articulates as an ideal in the *Duineser Elegien*. The task of transformation as the later Rilke conceived it would thus be not so different from what he was already pursuing at the time of the *Neue Gedichte*. Such observations also speak in favor of the unity of Rilke's oeuvre.

The poem "Wendung" ("Turning") of 1914 is often regarded as a programmatic presentation of the ideal of the late period in contrast to the middle period; it formulates a change in Rilke's conception of the task of transforming the visible into its invisible equivalent. The well-known lines toward the end of the poem read as follows:

Denn des Anschauns, siehe, ist eine Grenze.
Und die geschautere Welt
will in der Liebe gedeihn.

Werk des Gesichts ist getan,
tue nun Herz-Werk
an den Bildern in dir ...[9]

The work of vision, of the face ("Gesicht"), is done; the task is now "heart-work" ("Herz-Werk") on the pictures ("Bildern") within. This certainly marks a transition from a more outward perception—the work of vision or *Schauen*—to an inner work—"Herz-Werk." However, this work of love is on the *pictures* or *images* within, and thus raises the question: What is the origin of these pictures, which the work of love needs to further transform? These pictures resulted from the work of seeing. Without this seeing, therefore, there would be no pictures for the *Herz-Werk* to transform. It is the "Werk des Gesichts" that stands at the center of Rilke's middle period. The later work then, also in this sense, is not a radical break with the middle period but marks a further transformation of the fruits of the middle period. In other words, the later work should be understood through the middle work, as the further development of a single motif.[10]

The focus of the present and subsequent chapter is not on an interpretation of the poems of the *Neue Gedichte*. Rather, the aim is to

---

9 "For beholding, see, has a boundary./ And the more deeply perceived world/ wants to flourish in love.// Work of vision is done,/ do heart-work now/ on the images within you." KA 2, 102.

10 For a good discussion of the development of Rilke's conception of *Verwandlung* or transformation, and its relation to his reception of the thought of Rudolf Kassner, see Gerhart Mayer, *Rilke und Kassner: eine geistige Begegnung* (Bonn: H. Bouvier u. Co. Verlag, 1960).

explicate Rilke's formulation of the problem of dualism, his praxis of seeing, and its correlative non-dualistic disclosure of Nature. Rilke's conception of the dualistic condition and his practice of seeing were intimately bound up with his challenges and identity as a poet; had Rilke not conceived the experience of duality in a certain way, and had he not sought to overcome this condition by way of a certain praxis, the *Neue Gedichte* would have never come into being. In this sense, the following considerations concern the background and inspiration of the *Neue Gedichte*. A non-dualistic disclosure of things granted the inspiration for numerous poems in the *Neue Gedichte*. *Dichten*—the composing of poems—was clearly part and parcel of this non-dualistic disclosure of things. The primary goal of Chapters 2 and 3, however, is to consider this inspiration, in so far as is possible, in abstraction from Rilke's composition (the act of writing) of the poems. When specific poems are discussed in these chapters, they serve the purpose of illuminating the background of the *Neue Gedichte*. With respect to the *Neue Gedichte* such an abstraction is to some degree possible. Rilke's *Dichten* is only conceivable on the basis of a certain praxis, a certain *way of knowing*, which involved a transformation of experience *prior* to the moment of writing and provided an essential germ for the compositional task.[11]

Rilke's work in the middle period was intimately connected to his engagement with a number of visual artists; this is not surprising considering the centrality of vision for Rilke, whom Rudolf Kassner characterizes with the epithet, "Augenmensch" ("visual-person").[12] Early in the middle period Rilke was intensively involved with the artist colony in Worpswede, and married one of the younger artists in the community, Clara Westhoff. In 1902, in a period of financial need, he received a commission to write a monograph on the more famous Worpswede artists at that time.[13] In this monograph, *Worpswede*, and other writings Rilke shows signs of the first formulations of the central ideal of his middle period. In the introductory chapter of *Worpswede* Rilke clearly articulates the problem of human/nature dualism as a problem of vision. For this reason, this text will provide the starting point for our explication of Rilke's response to dualism.

The most significant influences on Rilke's ideal of the middle period were Rodin and Cézanne. Rilke's two essays on Rodin (1903

---

11 I return to this theme toward the end of Chapter 3.
12 Rudolf Kassner, *Rilke: Gesammelte Erinnerungen 1926–1956*, ed. Klaus E. Bohnenkamp (Pfullingen: Neske Verlag, 1976), 13, 34.
13 The painters featured in *Worpswede* are Fritz Mackensen, Otto Modersohn, Fritz Overbeck, Hans am Ende, and Heinrich Vogeler. The monograph was written in 1902 and first published in 1903.

and 1907)—published together in *Auguste Rodin*—and his *Briefe über Cézanne* (1907) offer clear presentations of Rilke's assessment of these artists.[14] Rilke characterizes Rodin's and Cézanne's manner of seeing things, as well as their translation of vision into their respective art forms—sculpting (primarily) in the case of Rodin, painting in the case of Cézanne.[15] However, Rilke's writings on Rodin and Cézanne provide more than an interpretation of these artists. They mirror the ideals Rilke himself was forming at the time, and the practice of seeing he was cultivating in connection to his own art. (There are, moreover, significant points of connection between Rilke's understanding of Cézanne and the evaluation of Cézanne by eminent phenomenologists such as Heidegger and Merleau-Ponty.) The primary reason for turning to Rodin and Cézanne is in order to understand Rilke more deeply. The treatment of these three artists would become confusing were they to be considered simultaneously. Therefore, two sub-sections are devoted to Rodin and two sub-sections are devoted to Cézanne. They explore each artist's way of seeing and its translation into the work of art. These two moments provide a model for the two parallel moments in Rilke's creative process (perception and poetic composition) and establish the context for intermedial comparisons between Rilke and these visual artists. While in the present chapter Rilke's understanding of artistic vision is primarily explored in relation to his engagement with visual artists, Chapter 3 draws these considerations to their culmination through a more exclusive explication of Rilke's seeing.

Rilke's Formulation of the Problem of Dualism

The first edition of *Worpswede* (written in 1902) was an illustrated monograph on the Worpswede artists and in the introduction Rilke discusses general issues concerning landscape painting. In this context Rilke clearly formulates a problem of dualism with regard to Nature and sketches a path by which the human estrangement from Nature might be remedied.[16]

The introduction begins with the remark that anyone who wanted to write a history of portraiture would have a difficult task "but, at

---

14 The first essay on Rodin was published in 1903. In 1907 a second essay (derived from a lecture that was first given in 1905) was added to the first. The *Briefe über Cézanne* (*Letters on Cézanne*) were first published posthumously. The letters were written to Clara Rilke at the time of Rilke's intensive engagement with the works of Cézanne that were exhibited in the Cézanne retrospective at the Salon d'Automne in Paris from October 6–22, 1907.
15 Rilke also took a great interest in Rodin's drawings. For our purposes, however, we will limit ourselves primarily to a discussion of Rodin's sculptures.
16 It is typical that the problem of dualism and its potential resolution are closely intertwined with Rilke's reflections on art.

any rate, he would be dealing with human beings ..."[17] Rilke thereby relativizes the difficulty of writing a history of portraiture in contrast to the greater challenge of writing a history of landscape painting. The reason for this assessment is based on the connection he draws between our general understanding of things and their painterly depictions. He writes, "With human beings, we are in the habit of learning much from their hands and everything from their face, in which, as on a dial, the hours are visible which cradle and carry their soul."[18] The visible appearance of the human being is a physiognomic language that we all understand; we can see through the visible (face and hands, etc.) to the invisible meaning (soul). This twofold understanding of the Other in the life-world facilitates our interpretation of the visual language of portraiture. The language of portraiture is the language of the human appearance (i.e., "body language"), with which we are familiar through our ordinary perception of human Others. What is most pertinent in the present context is not Rilke's interpretation of the nature of portraiture, but his view that we are habituated to seeing the interrelation of the visible and the invisible in the case of the human Other. Rilke's claim precisely corresponds to the reason why we began our phenomenological treatment of the problem of dualism (Chapter 1) with the perception of the human Other.

Just as Rilke draws a parallel between the appearance of the Other in the life-world and portraiture, so too he draws a parallel between our understanding of Nature and landscape painting. However, whereas in connection to the human Other we are accustomed to seeing through the visible to its invisible meaning, Nature is a closed book for our ordinary perception. Nevertheless, already at the beginning of *Worpswede*, Rilke assumes that a twofold understanding of Nature is a prerequisite for an adequate grasp of landscape painting. The important point for us is Rilke's view that our ordinary perception of Nature is deficient. Rilke's pertinent assumptions can be summed up as follows:

1   The human form is a language and Nature is a language.
2   We generally understand the human form in a twofold manner—we perceive the invisible meaning of the visible.
3   The language of Nature is not generally understood by us.

---

17 A translation of the introduction of *Worpswede* can be found under the title "Worpswede" in the volume cited here. Rilke, "Worpswede," in *Where Silence Reigns*, trans. G. Craig Houston (New York: New Directions Books, 1978), 6. KA 4, 308.
18 "Worpswede," 7. KA 4, 308.

While Rilke's analogy between human appearance and the appearance of Nature or landscape intimates the possibility of a twofold vision of Nature, no concrete elaboration of this possibility is provided at this point in the text. The need for a twofold seeing of Nature (analogous to our perception of the human Other) is suggested, but the means of realizing such a vision are not elaborated. Rilke describes our general estrangement from Nature in the following words:

> whoever was to write the history of landscape would find himself immediately without aids, at the mercy of what was alien, unrelated, incomprehensible to him ... landscape is without hands and has no face – or rather it is all face and has a terrible and dispiriting effect on man by reason of the great and incalculable quality of its features ... For let it be confessed: landscape is foreign to us, and we are fearfully alone amongst trees which blossom and by streams which flow. Alone with a dead person one is not nearly so defenceless [*preisgegeben*] as when alone with Trees ... For, however, mysterious [*geheimnisvoll*] death may be, life that is not our life is far more mysterious, life that is not concerned with us [*das nicht an uns teilnimmt*], and without seeing us, celebrates its festivals, as it were, at which we look on with a certain embarrassment, like chance guests who speak another language.[19]

As with respect to dualism in general, the following question must be raised in relation to our estrangement from Nature: Is this dualistic situation ontologically fundamental or is it merely correlative to a certain epistemic mode? In other words: Is Nature in its very being opposed to the human mind, or is it a certain manner of being-in-the-world that makes Nature *appear* removed from us? The affirmation of the former would, as previously illustrated (Chapter 1), lead in the direction of a metaphysical dualism. The affirmation of the latter would raise the further question as to whether other modes of "knowing" Nature could overcome this human/nature dualism. Is it possible for Nature to disclose itself in a twofold manner that is analogous in structure to the disclosure of the human Other in the life-world?

In the above excerpt Rilke already clearly intimates an affirmative answer to this question. We are ordinarily unaware of the "life" of Nature; this "life" is "mysterious" to us. In ascribing a hidden life to Nature and comparing humans to guests who cannot read Nature's "language" or "face," Rilke suggests that a dimension of Nature is concealed from our everyday modes of being-in-the-world.

---

19 "Worpswede," 6–7. *KA* 4, 308.

In philosophical terms, we are ordinarily only aware of Nature as *naturata* ("object") and not as *naturans* ("activity" or "life"); we perceive the manifestations of Nature's life but cannot decipher them. While we are able to perceive the "souls" (the invisible) of human beings through the visible language of gesture, the "life" (invisible) of Nature is unknown to us. If we are to overcome this estrangement from Nature, we must learn to read the face of Nature and institute a mode of being-in-the-world that differs from our everyday modes of being. Rilke characterizes our ordinary relationship to Nature as follows:

> The ordinary man, who lives with men, and sees Nature only in so far as she has reference to himself, is seldom aware of the problematic and uncanny relationship. He sees the surface of the things, which he and his like have created through the centuries, and likes to believe that the whole earth is concerned with him because a field can be cultivated, a forest thinned, and a river made navigable. His eye, focused almost entirely on men, sees Nature also, but incidentally, as something self-evident and available [*Vorhandenes*] that must be exploited as much as possible.[20]

This utilitarian and instrumental comportment toward Nature limits our perception to Nature's "surface." Nature's "life" remains hidden and unknown. There is an implicit dualism in our ordinary relationship (or lack of genuine relationship) to Nature. Nature is a surface without depth or interiority. Interiority is merely subjective and human, while Nature appears as an exterior without any intrinsic depth. Were this polarization of interior and exterior unable to be overcome, then our estrangement from Nature would be irremediable and an adequate (experiential) overcoming of human/nature dualism would be, in principle, impossible. For Rilke, however, this experienced estrangement from Nature is correlative to a certain way of being-in-the-world and is not insurmountable. At this point Rilke introduces a developmental perspective on the problem of dualism. This developmental conception provides an important key toward the possible transcendence of dualism.

Rilke's Developmental Conception of the Dualistic Condition

Rather than regarding the human estrangement from Nature as a simple fact Rilke introduces a developmental conception which interprets the *dualistic condition* as emerging out of a *pre-dualistic condition*.

---

20 "Worpswede," 8–9; translation altered. *KA 4*, 310.

He then indicates the way toward a possible *post-dualistic condition*. The child is the figure of a pre-dualistic manner of being-in-the-world, while the ordinary adult is representative of the dualistic condition. The teenager is placed at the point of transition between these two forms of being-in-the-world. It soon becomes clear that the artist or poet is the figure who represents a post-dualistic condition. Rilke characterizes the child as follows:

> Children see Nature differently; solitary children in particular, who grow up amongst adults, foregather with her [Nature] by a kind of like-mindedness [*Gleichgesinntheit*] and live *within* her, like the smaller animals, entirely at one with the happenings of forest and sky and in innocent obvious harmony with them.[21]

In Rilke's writings the child repeatedly appears as a figure of *participation*. By "participation" I mean a pre-dualistic state, a state prior to a sense of detachment from the world. The child, for Rilke, is *one* with the happenings of Nature. This pre-dualistic state also involves a more profound *revelation* of Nature than that which is granted to the adult. These lines from the poem "Kindheit" in the *Neue Gedichte* exemplify this view:

Kindheit

Es wäre gut viel nachzudenken, um
von so Verlornem etwas auszusagen,
von jenen langen Kindheit-Nachmittagen,
die so nie wiederkamen – und warum?

Noch mahnt es uns – : vielleicht in einem Regnen,
aber wir wissen nicht mehr was das soll;
nie wieder war das Leben von Begegnen,
von Wiedersehn und Weitergehn so voll

---

21 "Worpswede," 9; my emphasis. KA 4, 310. Scheler expresses the following similar view to Rilke: "our primary knowledge of Nature is itself a knowledge of the *expressive aspect* of living organisms; mental phenomena therefore (which are invariably presented only within a structural context), are always given, in the first instance, in unities of expression ... does such knowledge precede, accompany or follow a knowledge of the (inanimate) physical world? Our answer will be that it precedes it. Thus the primitive, like the child, has no general acquaintance with 'deadness' in things: all his experience is presented as *one* vast field of expression ..." Scheler, *The Nature of Sympathy*, 218.

80   The Poet as Phenomenologist

> wie damals, da uns nichts geschah als nur
> was einem Ding geschieht und einem Tiere:
> da lebten wir, wie Menschliches, das Ihre
> und wurden bis zum Rande voll Figur ...[22]

The first line tells us that it would be good to give much thought to childhood (which has become so lost to us) in order to be able to say something concerning it. Childhood is then characterized by its "long afternoons" that never returned. The "long childhood-afternoons [langen Kindheit-Nachmittagen]" obviously suggests more than afternoons that are factually longer than at other times of year (i.e., summer afternoons in contrast to winter). The expression implies that the experience of temporality and time is different in childhood. The second verse begins with "Noch mahnt es uns" ("it still admonishes us"). What sense can we make of these lines? It is clear that something belonging to childhood has been lost but continues to admonish us. This is then qualified with the phrase "perhaps during rainfall [vielleicht in einem Regnen]," which draws in the natural world. The second line of the second verse elaborates that we no longer know what it—the rainfall—wants from us. Thus, a difference between adult experience and the childhood experience of natural events is suggested. It is the subsequent six lines that most concern a participative view of childhood. These lines could be translated as follows:

> never again was the life of encountering,
> of reuniting and continuing as full

> as at that time, when nothing happened to us other than
> what happens to a thing and to an animal:
> when we lived, like human-matters, what belongs to them
> and were filled with figure [*Figur*] up to the brim ...

I have translated the substantivized infinitive "Begegnen" with the English word "encountering." The word "Begegnen" is sometimes translated as "meeting"; however, "meeting" corresponds more

---

22 "Childhood// It would be good to reflect much, in order/ to convey something of what is so lost,/ of those long childhood-afternoons,/ which never as such returned – and why?// It still admonishes us – : perhaps during a rainfall,/ but we no longer know what it means;/ never again was life so full of encountering,/ of reuniting and continuing// as at that time, when nothing happened to us other than/ what happens to a thing and to an animal:/ when we lived, like human-matters, what belongs to them,/ and were filled with figure up to the brim ..." KA 1, 473–4.

closely to the noun "Treffen" in German. "Begegnen" suggests a chance meeting or serendipitous encounter. In recounting a chance encounter with someone on the street one uses the verb "begegnen" rather than "treffen." "Begegnen" also implies the coming together of two things; "gegnen" in "be-gegnen" clearly relates to "gegen," which implies "opposition" as in "gegenüber" ("opposite") and the German word for object, "Gegenstand"—that which stands opposite. These senses of "Begegnen" correspond most closely to "encounter," as to encounter something is at once *to engage with* something and *to be engaged by* something. This life of encountering, of reuniting, and continuing was "never again ... as full as at that time." Thus adulthood is impoverished relative to the childhood experience of things.

The idea of childhood participation comes to its most definitive expression in the first two lines of the third verse, which convey an identity between the life of the child and the life of things. The child is not locked in a prison of subjectivity; rather, it is radically ec-static—the child's life is the life and happenings of the things it encounters. The time of childhood, first characterized by the long afternoons that never returned, is the time when happenings are the happenings of things. Here there is not yet a diremption between the inner life and an exterior world. As similarly described in *Worpswede*, the child is "entirely at one with the happenings of forest and sky."[23] Childhood is a pre-dualistic state of being; it is not aptly characterized as a coupling or synthesis of what we later understand by the words "inner" and "outer." Such a characterization would remain dualistic as "inner" would be understood as the interiority of a subject rather than as the inner life of things. Childhood is prior to the division of inner and outer and thus could be called both pre-dualistic and pre-synthetic (synthesis presupposes difference).[24]

This interpretation of childhood can be gleaned from many of Rilke's writings. In terms of the middle period, there are pertinent passages in his novel, *Die Aufzeichnungen des Malte Laurids Brigge* and a number of poems from the *Neue Gedichte*. A consideration of "Mädchen-Klage" ("Girl's Lament")—the second poem in the *Neue Gedichte*—will suffice for the present purposes.

---

23 "Worpswede," 9; my emphasis. *KA 4*, 310.
24 A pedantic reader might object that childhood behavior presupposes some kind of distinction between self and world. However, my point is that a sharp division or separation between inner and outer, self and world, etc. does not yet exist for the child. Moreover, as we will see, the distinction between these realms gradually emerges and widens.

Mädchen-Klage

Diese Neigung, in den Jahren,
da wir alle Kinder waren,
viel allein zu sein, war mild;
andern ging die Zeit im Streite,
und man hatte seine Seite,
seine Nähe, seine Weite,
einen Weg, ein Tier, ein Bild.

Und ich dachte noch, das Leben
hörte niemals auf zu geben,
daß man sich in sich besinnt.
Bin ich in mir nicht im Größten?
Will mich Meines nicht mehr trösten
und verstehen wie als Kind?

Plötzlich bin ich wie verstoßen,
und zu einem Übergroßen
wird mir diese Einsamkeit,
wenn, auf meiner Brüste Hügeln
stehend, mein Gefühl nach Flügeln
oder einem Ende schreit.[25]

In the first verse of "Mädchen-Klage" childhood is described in the third person. In the second verse the "I" of the adolescent girl appears and reflects upon her childhood. A transition and change from childhood to adolescence is indicated by this shift in pronouns. In the third stanza the adolescent girl's sense of being shut out from a previous state of participation is articulated, which serves to explain the poem's title—"Mädchen-Klage" ("Girl's Lament"). She laments her new condition in its contrast to the experience of childhood.

As in the poem "Kindheit" the child is here presented as inhabiting a state of radical sympathy with things. This sympathy, however, cannot be understood in terms of the adult, who starts with the sense of an

---

25 "Girl's Lament// This inclination, in the years,/ when we were all children,/ to be often alone, was mild,/ for the others the time passed in strife,/ and one had one's side,/ one's vicinity, one's expanse,/ a way, an animal, a picture.// And I thought still, that life/ never ceased to give,/ that one considers oneself within./ Am I in myself not in the encompassing?/ Will what is mine no longer console/ and understand me as when I was a child?// Suddenly I am as though exiled,/ and my loneliness becomes/ something too vast for me,/ when, on the hills of my breasts,/ standing, my feeling cries for wings/ or for an end." KA 1, 449–50.

opposition between Self and Other, which is remedied, in part, by a cultivation of sympathy toward Others. Rather, this sympathy is a basic mode of being prior to the diremption of self and world. The first verse conveys a childhood mood of basic harmony in contrast to the others (the adults presumably) who spent their time in strife. The child has a "vicinity," an "expanse," a "way," an "animal," a "picture"—the child identifies with all of these things. This time of participation comes to its highest expression in the fourth line of the second verse. In this line the adolescent girl simultaneously reflects on her changed condition and on the sense of participation which characterized her childhood. Her uncertain condition is voiced in the question, "Bin ich in mir nicht im Größten?" The fact that she poses this question at this point shows that she is no longer "im Größten" as she was in childhood. This line could translated as, "Am I in myself not in the greatest?" However, a more accurate translation of the sense might be, "Am I in myself not in the encompassing?" The child is portrayed as being one with the "world-all"; the child is *within*, rather than excluded from, the "all-encompassing." The first two lines of the second stanza are especially revealing of the surplus meaning that is granted to the child; these can be translated as, "I thought still, that life/ never ceased to give." Childhood is thus presented as a time when life and things seem to give an infinity and inexhaustibility of meaning, when there is no want of meaning.

Rilke articulates childhood as a time of experiential monism—as pre-dualistic—and as a time when the world, Nature, and things, offer themselves with an excess of significance. To employ terminology from the French phenomenologist, Jean-Luc Marion, phenomena as revealed to the child are generally "saturated phenomena," phenomena given with a surplus or superabundance of meaning.[26] Moreover, it is clear that the ec-static character of the child, its "pre-ego-centric" manner of being, is intimately connected to this "excessive" disclosure of things. It can be concluded that "childhood," for Rilke, signifies *a distinctive manner of being-in-the-world, which must be understood in its intrinsic wholeness.*

It should now be clear that when Rilke refers to the normal dualistic relationship to the natural world, he is specifically referring to the adult experience. Adolescence is a kind of intermediate phase. In reference to "Mädchen-Klage" it was already indicated that adolescence marks the period of transition from childhood participation to a dualistic condition. The teenage girl mourns the loss of the childhood manner of being-in-the-world but, in a certain sense, this childhood way of being

---

26 For a good introduction to the idea of the "saturated phenomenon" see Jean-Luc Marion, *Being Given: Toward a Phenomenology of Givenness.*

is still close enough for her to recollect its specific character. The shift from the third person description in the first stanza to the first person description in the second stanza signifies the emergence of a separation between self and world, "I" and "not-I." This conception of adolescence as an intermediate phase between the pre-dualism of childhood and the dualism of adulthood is also expressed in *Worpswede*. After the lines that describe children as "one with the happenings of forest and sky and in innocent obvious harmony with them," Rilke writes:

> But just because of this, there comes later for boys and girls that lonely period filled with deep, trembling melancholy, when they feel unutterably forlorn, just at that time of their physical maturing; when they feel that the things and events in Nature have *no longer*, and their fellow-men have *not yet*, any concern for them [*an ihnen teilnehmen*] ...[27]

The adolescent inhabits a kind of nowhere land between childhood participation in Nature and adult estrangement. It *seems* inevitable, from Rilke's account thus far, that the only path available leads from the childhood state of monism through the nowhere land of adolescence to the dualistic state of adulthood. From the beginning of *Worpswede* Rilke has assumed that we (adults) are estranged from Nature and individual maturation now seems to be a one-way track from monism to dualism.

However, Rilke presents another possibility, which is implicitly and explicitly connected to his conception of the artist. The artist is an *exceptional* adult who cultivates a different relation to childhood. It is, in part, through the artist's cultivation of a different relation to the pre-dualistic condition that the attainment of a post-dualistic experience of Nature is made possible. Later in the text Rilke quotes the German Romantic painter Philipp Otto Runge, and identifies his words with the aspirations of the Worpswede artists. "Runge wrote: 'we must become children if we want to achieve the best.' They [the Worpswede artists] want to achieve the best, and they have become children. They see everything in one breath, people and things ..."[28]

In "becoming a child" again, the artist regains the participative vision of things characteristic of childhood. This might seem to imply the view that art involves regression. Yet this is not the case. The nature of the artist's distinctive relation to childhood can be gleaned from the poem "Die Erwachsene" ("The Grownup") in the *Neue Gedichte*.

---

27 "Worpswede," 9; translation altered. *KA 1*, 310.
28 "Worpswede," 21. *KA 4*, 324.

Die Erwachsene

Das alles stand auf ihr und war die Welt
und stand auf ihr mit allem, Angst und Gnade,
wie Bäume stehen, wachsend und gerade,
ganz Bild und bildlos wie die Bundeslade
und feierlich, wie auf ein Volk gestellt.

Und sie ertrug es; trug bis obenhin
das Fliegende, Entfliehende, Entfernte,
das Ungeheure, noch Unerlernte
gelassen wie die Wasserträgerin
den vollen Krug. Bis mitten unterm Spiel,
verwandelnd und auf andres vorbereitend,
der erste weiße Schleier, leise gleitend,
über das aufgetane Antlitz fiel

fast undurchsichtig und sich nie mehr hebend
und irgendwie auf alle Fragen ihr
nur eine Antwort vage wiedergebend:
In dir, du Kindgewesene, in dir.[29]

Here, as elsewhere, Rilke characterizes childhood as ec-static and "at-one" with the world. In the first verse childhood is described with the simile that it carries the world like the Ark of the Covenant ("Bundeslade"). This suggests a unity of the earthly and the divine, the phenomenal and the numinous, the visible and invisible—a unity that is at once a "Bild" (image) and "bildlos" (imageless). Along with the descriptions of childhood in the second strophe as bearing all manner of things like a full jug ("vollen Krug"), this portrayal is consistent with Rilke's general view of the wholeness of childhood experience. In the transition between the second and third verse it is said that a veil quietly glided over the open visage ("Antlitz"). This suggests an emerging duality and partition between self and world,

---

29 "The Grownup// That all stood on her and was the world/ and stood on her with everything, fear and grace,/ the way trees stand, growing and erect,/ wholly image and imageless like the Ark of the Covenant/ and solemnly, as if placed on a people.// And she bore it; bore high overhead/ the flying, the fleeing, the remote,/ the tremendous, the yet unlearned/ calmly as the water-bearer carries/ the full jug. Till in the midst of play,/ transforming and preparing for something else,/ the first white veil, quietly gliding,/ fell upon the opened visage// almost opaque and never to lift itself again/ and somehow to all her questions/ responding vaguely with only one answer:/ in you, you who-were-a-child, in you." KA 1, 477.

and the loss of a more participative vision of things in the transition from childhood to adulthood. The veil is almost opaque ("undurchsichtig") and will never again ("nie mehr"—"nevermore") lift itself. However, the last lines state that a vaguely communicated answer seemed to respond to all of her (the adult's) questions. Presumably, these questions relate to the veil, to the partition that has divided self and world. The answer quietly given to these questions is, "In dir, du Kindgewesene, in dir." The answer is, "within you ..." It is clear that this "within you" has something to do with the possibility of lifting the veil in order to achieve a reconciliation of self and world and the rediscovery of a childlike wholeness. After the first "In dir" comes a comma and then "du Kindgewesene." The expression "Kindgewesene" is untranslatable as a single word and suggests the developmental character of the present, as does the ordinary German word for adult, "Erwachsene." "Erwachsene" can easily be translated with the English word "grownup." However, the word "Kindgewesene," coined by Rilke, conveys an inverse perspective on this development. "Erwachsene" or "grownup" implies that becoming an adult involves growing beyond childhood. However, the answer that quietly utters itself to the adult is, "In dir, du Kindgewesene, in dir." In other words, "Within you, you who-were-a-child, within you." The answer to the problem of dualism then, the possibility of lifting the veil, lies in the rediscovery of childhood or the childlike within. In the adult, who is defined by *having been* a child, who once enjoyed a pre-dualistic condition, the childlike can be rediscovered. In the rediscovery of the childlike, Rilke discerns the possibility of a movement toward a post-dualistic disclosure of Nature. This understanding of the childlike is also reminiscent of the statement in the Gospel of Matthew (18.2–6) that only those who become like children can enter the kingdom of heaven.

In *Malte*[30] Rilke also thematizes the importance of maintaining a certain connection to childhood in adulthood. Malte states, "If I insisted that my childhood was past, in that same moment everything to come [*alles Kommende*] was gone ..."[31] For the protagonist the future seemed to lose all promise, unless he could maintain a connection to his childhood. This promise of the future is the possibility of a reunified vision, a transcendence of the condition of estrangement that, for the most part, constitutes adulthood.

Rilke frequently asserts the importance of recollecting one's childhood. This no doubt facilitates the relation to childhood that has already been discussed. However, there is an additional significance

---

30 *Malte* is an abbreviation for Rilke's novel *Die Aufzeichnungen des Malte Laurids Brigge*.
31 KA 3, 594.

in recollection. Although we have characterized childhood in terms of participation and excess meaning, there is also a certain *deficiency* in childhood. Articulating this deficiency serves to demonstrate that the artist's exceptional relation to childhood and the childlike is not a matter of regression. What then is the deficiency in childhood? It pertains to childhood's pre-reflexivity. This insufficiency lies in the fact that, as Ruth Hermann so aptly puts it, "'Kindheit' wird erst dann zu einem Thema, wenn sie vergangen ist [Childhood only becomes a theme once it is past]."[32] In other words, for the child, "childhood" is not thematized. The essence of childhood is not reflectively, and therefore, not completely grasped and experienced by the child. This pre-reflective state is, moreover, constitutive of childhood. The meaning of childhood can thus only be properly (reflectively or consciously) grasped by the adult. The task of recollecting childhood involves grasping for the first time *consciously* the child's manner of being-in-the-world. Through recollection, the nature of childhood can be raised to self-consciousness. However, while recollection raises childhood experience to self-consciousness, remembering a pre-dualistic state is not in itself sufficient to overcome dualism.

In light of the above, let us consider the following passage from *Worpswede*, in which Rilke articulates the difference between the ordinary adult and the artist:

> finally, some of them make up their minds and join these people in order to share their work and their fate, to be useful, to be helpful, to serve the enlargement of life somehow, whilst the others, unwilling to leave the Nature they have lost, go in pursuit of her and try now, *consciously* and by the use of their *concentrated will*, to come as near to her again as they were in their childhood *without knowing it* [*ohne es recht zu wissen*]. It will be understood that the latter are artists: poets or painters, composers or architects, fundamentally lonely spirits, who, in turning to Nature, put the eternal above the transitory, that which is most profoundly based upon law above that which is fundamentally ephemeral, and who, since they cannot persuade Nature to concern herself with them, see their task to be the understanding of Nature, so that they may take their place somewhere in her great nexus [*Zusammenhänge*].[33]

Some individuals, in the course of their development, accommodate themselves to the adult world, others, namely artists, "go in pursuit

---

32 Ruth Hermann, *Im Zwischenraum zwischen Welt und Spielzeug: Eine Poetik der Kindheit bei Rilke* (Königshausen & Neumann, 2001), 14.
33 "Worpswede," 9; translation altered; my emphasis. *KA 4*, 311.

of her [Nature] and try now, consciously and by the use of their *concentrated will*, to come as near to her again as they were in their childhood without knowing it." Therefore, the artist's connection to childhood is not a matter of regression (nor does recollection suffice); rather, it involves *consciously instituting* a childlike manner of being-in-the-world. The artist thereby achieves a *knowing* unity with Nature in contrast to the *unknowing* unity that is characteristic of childhood.

For the Rilke of the middle period the way toward an overcoming of dualism lies in the cultivation of a certain manner of *seeing*. In the introduction to this chapter attention was drawn to Rilke's retrospective characterization of his work of the middle period, in the poem "Wendung" of 1914, as "das Werk des Gesichts"—"the work of vision [of the face]." It is important to mention this once again, because the childlikeness consciously fostered by the poet (and artist) is the basic mood of artistic *seeing*. It is also worthwhile to recall the earlier quotation from *Worpswede* following Rilke's reference to Runge, in which Rilke describes the Worpswede artists as having learnt to *see* things like children again.[34]

In what way is artistic seeing childlike? The most essential aspect of this artistic and poetic disposition is its active-passivity or receptivity. In the previous chapter an active-passivity was distinguished in the twofold perception of the human Other in the life-world. The active-passivity of Rilke's "seeing" is continuous with this everyday perception, but more radical in a number of ways. First, it is *consciously instituted* by the poet and not already implicit to the perception of the Other in the life-world.[35] Second, it is both *more active and more passive* at the same time. This is, of course, a contradiction as far as the terms are concerned (the very expression "active-passivity" is already a contradiction in that "active" and "passive" are antonyms). Although contradictory at this level, however, the expression points to a concrete mode of mind that is best described by this paradoxical formulation. "Passivity" implies an attitude of *reception*; however, this reception is not a mere passivity in the sense of the philosophical tradition of Empiricism. "Activity" indicates an act of the mind, but this act does not have the sense of domination or imposition that is often ascribed to mental activity in transcendental idealism (Kant). This activity has the character of what we usually ascribe to passivity, namely a gesture of suffering (*passio*), and vice versa.[36] The

---

34 "Worpswede," 21. *KA 4*, 324.
35 This is not to say that a genuine "openness" or "receptivity" to human Others requires no cultivation.
36 If such a notion appears to some readers as nonsensical then I ask them to reflect on the implicit meaning of the concept of inspiration. We certainly do not regard inspiration as a merely passive state but rather as involving intense concentration, alertness, and activity. However, inherent to the meaning of inspiration, even as it is employed by many contemporary poets (although

second claim, then, is that this active-passivity is an intensified active-passivity in comparison to the active-passivity (or passive-activity) which was described in the previous chapter. It involves an active submission of the gaze to the phenomena of perception, in relation to which the phenomena *reveal themselves* more deeply. Third, this active-passivity is not solely directed toward the human realm but is also *directed toward Nature* or operative in a vision of other-than-human Nature.

The basic character of the child's way of being can be understood as a radical active-passivity. However, the child does not need to foster this disposition consciously as it is the child's basic, or given, manner of being. The child's essential gesture was characterized above as ec-static, as participating in things and events, and as one with its surroundings; the child's basic gesture is sympathetic but in a pre-dualistic sense. The child's manner of being is also depicted by Rilke as a fundamental *Gelassenheit*, as an impartial, unconditional letting-be; this is clearly thematized in the first half of "Die Erwachsene" where the child is described as carrying the world "gelassen wie die Wasserträgerin den vollen Krug." Other qualities that can be ascribed to the child's way of being, as understood by Rilke, are: "naiveté," "unknowing," "openness," "wonder," "selflessness," and "unpremeditatedness." It is also precisely these qualities that enable the child to experience things as disclosed with an "excess" and "superabundance" of meaning. The qualities of "naiveté" and "unknowing" are far from negative traits; they are conditions that enable a privileged disclosure of things. The overarching character of all these qualities can be distinguished as an active-passivity or a passive-activity. It is this radical active-passivity (natural and effortless for the child) that must be consciously instituted by the poet in order to enable a post-dualistic disclosure of Nature. Rilke already articulates this view early in his engagement with the Worpswede artists. In a journal entry of September 11, 1900, written while Rilke was residing in Worpswede, one can see how the artist's consciously cultivated way of seeing resembles the child's manner of being-in-the-world:

> Something like selflessness lies in this kind of participation in Nature. I am gradually beginning to understand this life, which enters through large eyes into eternally waiting souls. This daily attentiveness, wakefulness and readiness of the outwardly turned

---

they might not attribute the source of inspiration to a muse), is the notion of a gift or a reception. Inspiration is an activity but it cannot be arbitrarily or forcefully willed by the subject. The word implies a notion of active-passivity.

senses, this thousandfold seeing and always looking away from oneself ... this being only eye, free of all calculation.[37]

The poet or artist selflessly participates in Nature and consciously actualizes the ec-static gesture of mind that is the natural gesture of the child; attentively, wakefully, the artist looks away from him- or herself. It is not only in direct reference to the child that Rilke presents artistic seeing as a radical active-passivity. This gesture of active-passivity, as a *sine qua non* of the poet, is present in manifold variations in both his poetry and prose.[38] These ideas will be further elaborated in the later discussion of Rodin and Cézanne.

Rilke and Romanticism

Much of the above seems to place Rilke squarely within the tradition of Romanticism. Rilke's conception of the poet's relation to childhood and the artist's privileged vision of Nature reveals close affinities between Rilke and the Romantics. H. R. Klieneberger, in concluding his essay "Rilke and the 'Change of Sensibility': An Introduction," locates Rilke's place within modernism, with the epithet that Yeats ascribed to himself, namely, as belonging to the "last Romantics."[39] In this essay, and in the chapter "Romanticism and Modernism in Rilke," Klieneberger draws out a number of parallels between Rilke and Novalis, and Rilke and Wordsworth.[40] Although Rilke was unlikely to have been very familiar with Wordsworth, significant parallels between the two poets can easily be demonstrated.

Wordsworth's Ode, "Intimations of Immortality from Recollections of Early Childhood," presents a developmental conception of the passage from childhood to adulthood that bears many resemblances to Rilke's conception. One need only consider the most well-known verse:

> Our birth is but a sleep and a forgetting:
> The Soul that rises with us, our life's Star,
>   Hath had elsewhere its setting,
>   And cometh from afar:

---

37 Rilke, *Tagebücher aus der Frühzeit*, ed. Ruth Sieber-Rilke and Carl Sieber (Leipzig: Insel Verlag, 1942), 266.
38 The poem "Der Tod des Dichters" ("The Death of the Poet") in the *Neue Gedichte* is, for instance, exemplary of this view; Rilke portrays the poet as a figure of radical participation. KA 1, 461–2.
39 H. R. Klieneberger, "Rilke and the 'Change of Sensibility': An Introduction," in *Rilke und der Wandel der Sensibilität*, ed. Herbert Herzmann and Hugh Ridler (Essen: Die Blaue Eule Verlag, 1990), 18.
40 H. R. Klieneberger, *George, Rilke, Hofmannsthal and the Romantic Tradition* (Stuttgart: Hans-Dieter Heinz Akademischer Verlag, 1991).

> Not in entire forgetfulness,
> And not in utter nakedness,
> But trailing clouds of glory do we come
>   From God, who is our home:
> Heaven lies about us in our infancy!
> Shades of the prison-house begin to close
>   Upon the growing Boy,
> But he beholds the light, and whence it flows,
>   He sees it in his joy;
> The Youth, who daily farther from the east
>   Must travel, still is Nature's priest,
>   And by the vision splendid
>   Is on his way attended;
> At length the Man perceives it die away,
> And fade into the light of common day.[41]

I will leave to one side the belief in the pre-natal existence of the soul that is advocated in the opening eight lines of this verse, although this belief was also held by Rilke.[42] In the remaining eleven lines we find a conception of the passage from childhood to adulthood that is almost identical to Rilke's. Wordsworth, like Rilke after him, regarded childhood as a kind of prelapsarian state in which there is a unity of the finite and the infinite, the phenomenal and the numinal; "Heaven lies about us in our infancy." Manfred Engel also notes this kinship between the conception of childhood in Rilke and Romanticism, in his statement that, "Like the Romantics, the child is regarded by him [Rilke] as a being who is still closer to nature, less limited, and more immediately and unconsciously connected to the whole of creation."[43]

Like Rilke, Wordsworth also outlines the path of development as a gradual expulsion from the Eden of childhood. The youth for Wordsworth is somewhere between childhood existence and the impoverished condition of the adult. In adulthood the superabundant light of childhood finally "fades into the light of common day."

Furthermore, Wordsworth regarded the poet as a figure who preserves a special relation to childhood, and thereby does not allow a

---

41 William Wordsworth, *Poetical Works* (Paris: A. & W. Galignani and Co., 1828), 249.
42 See, for instance, Gísli Magnússon, *Dichtung als Erfahrungsmetaphysik: Esoterische und okkultistische Modernität bei R. M. Rilke* (Würzburg: Königshausen & Neumann, 2009), 120ff.
43 Manfred Engel, "Nachwort [Afterword]," in *Die Aufzeichnungen des Malte Laurids Brigge*, by Rainer Maria Rilke (Stuttgart: Philipp Reclam, 1997), 342.

complete break with childhood to occur, which is the common path of development. Moreover, he regarded the preservation and cultivation of a childlike openness as essential in maintaining a deeper perception of things. These views are simply and succinctly articulated in the short poem of 1802, "The Rainbow."

> My heart leaps up when I behold
>   A Rainbow in the sky:
> So was it when my life began;
> So be it when I shall grow old,
>   Or let me die!
> The Child is father of the Man;
> And I wish my days to be
> Bound each to each by natural piety.[44]

Wordsworth's "the Child is father of the Man" resembles the end of Rilke's poem "Die Erwachsene" which speaks of the "grownup" as the "one-who-was-a-child" ("Kindgewesene"). For Wordsworth, as for Rilke, it is essential for the poet to maintain a childlike disposition and this "natural piety" facilitates a privileged disclosure of the natural world.

These are just a few of the numerous common threads that unite Rilke with the project and ideals of Romanticism. I do not wish to deny these affinities between Rilke and Romanticism. In fact, it is largely the elements that place Rilke in continuity with Romanticism that are of the utmost interest. However, were Rilke simply a "late Romantic," in the sense of a Romantic born a century late, then my privileging of Rilke as opposed to the Romantic tradition would be quite arbitrary.

The reasons for turning to Rilke in order to address the problem of dualism are manifold. In terms of the views that Rilke shared with the Romantics, it can be argued that Rilke realized some of these ideals in ways that surpass the historical Romantics. In *Worpswede* Rilke states,

> There was a great love of Nature in the German Romantics. But they loved her as the hero of a story by Turgeniev loved his sweetheart, of whom he said: "I am particularly fond of Sophia when I sit with my back to her, that's to say, when I think of her, when I see her before my mind's eye, especially in the evening, on the terrace ..." Only one of them, perhaps, has looked Nature in the face: Philipp Otto Runge, the Hamburg artist, who painted the Nightingale Bush and the Morning. The great miracle of the sunrise has not been painted like that again. The increasing light,

---

44 Wordsworth, *Poetical Works*, 15.

rising silent and radiant to the stars, and on the earth beside the cabbage field, still completely saturated with the strong dewy depth of night, in which a little naked child – Morning – is lying. Everything here has been *seen* and *seen* again [*alles geschaut und wiedergeschaut*] ...⁴⁵

In the first part of the above passage Rilke shows a certain sympathy for Romanticism, more specifically Romantic painting, but he is also critical. Rilke's critique here can also be understood as a self-critique. This passage, written in 1902, has a janus-head quality; it looks forward to an ideal that Rilke had not yet realized (which achieved its ultimate poetic realization in the *Neue Gedichte*) and backwards as a critique of the inadequacy of his earlier *Stimmungslyrik* ("mood-poetry"). Rilke characterized his earlier *Stimmungslyrik* as a poetic expression of the moods that Nature inspired in him.⁴⁶ This is similar to his general characterization of Romantic artists. Rilke is sympathetic to the general direction of Romanticism in its acknowledgment, in short, of Nature as a "thou" as opposed to a mere inanimate mechanism—nature as "living" rather than "dead."⁴⁷ However, Rilke believes that the Romantics, for the most part, remained too subjective. In the above appraisal of Runge as an exception, Rilke gestures in the direction he was to travel himself. The picture "Morning," by Runge, shows that

---

45 "Worpswede," 15; my emphasis. *KA 4*, 317.
46 A good retrospective self-characterization by Rilke of his earlier *Stimmungslyrik* (of which *Das Stundenbuch* is representative), and the contrasting ideal which informed the *Neue Gedichte*, can be found in his *Briefe über Cézanne*. There he states, "If I were to come to visit you, I would surely also see the splendor of moor and heath, the hovering bright greens of meadows, the birches, with new and different eyes; and though this transformation is something I've completely experienced and shared before, in part of the Book of Hours [*Das Stundenbuch*], nature was then still a general occasion for me, an evocation, an instrument in whose strings my hands found themselves again; I was not yet sitting before her; I allowed myself to be swept away by the soul that was emanating from her; she came over me with her vastness, her huge exaggerated presence, the way the gift of prophecy came over Saul; exactly like that. I walked about and saw, not nature but the visions she gave me. How little I would have been able to learn from Cézanne, from van Gogh, then." Rilke, *Letters on Cézanne*, trans. Joel Agee, Foreword by Heinrich Wiegand Petzet (New York: Fromm International Publishing Corporation, 1985), 48–49. From now on I shall refer to the *Letters on Cézanne* as LC. *KA 4*, 615–616.
47 Chapter 4 includes a discussion of Rilke's connection to forms of biology in the Romantic tradition.

everything has been "seen and seen again." It is not a picture painted by someone whose back is toward Nature.[48]

While such a summary representation of Romanticism is inadequate, and if one thinks of Romanticism in the broadest sense (not in contradistinction to Classicism) then one can hardly say of Goethe (as a scientist and poet), to take a pre-eminent example, that he did not observe Nature closely enough.[49] Moreover, it sounds absurd to claim that Wordsworth, Novalis, Hölderlin, and other major poets of the Romantic era were not close observers of Nature. Nevertheless, I think there is a certain legitimacy to Rilke's characterization, if one compares Cézanne, for instance, to the Romantic painters, or Rilke, to the Romantic poets. Rilke's most accomplished work of the middle period, the *Neue Gedichte*, illustrates a deeper penetration, and a more exact and concentrated depiction of things than is, for the most part, to be found in the poetry of Romanticism. Rilke, in his novel, has Malte say, "Er war ein Dichter und haßte das Ungefähre … [He was a poet and hated the approximate]."[50] This statement clearly reflects Rilke's own striving and values. This striving is far from a rejection of Romanticism; it reveals the further development of a certain tendency in Romanticism. The Romantics, against the mechanistic view of Nature—which was spread by a growing scientism in connection with the achievements of modern physics and industrialization—fostered an alternative way of understanding Nature. The Nature of Romanticism was primarily organic Nature, and this organicism provided an alternative to the mechanistic view of Nature. The faculty that disclosed Nature as organic, and as animated rather than mechanical, was the imagination, rather than intellect or reason. Nature, for the Romantics, was something with which a communion was possible, in contrast to the Nature of modern physics, which has more and more established a picture of Nature that compels us to feel estranged from her.[51] In *Worpswede* Rilke shows himself to be implicitly and explicitly sympathetic to these features of Romanticism, but he regards the treatment of Nature in Romantic *works of art* as remaining too generic. If the Romantics discovered and revived such an understanding of Nature, a Nature that could be disclosed as a "thou" rather than as an

---

48 Although one might beg to differ with Rilke's criticisms of Romantic art, I hold the view that Rilke attained to a degree of detail and "objectivity" in his poetry, particularly in his *Dinggedichte*, that is unprecedented in the history of lyric poetry.
49 On Goethe's contemporary significance for thinking about Nature and the environment, see "Goethe and Environmentalism," Special Section of the *Goethe Yearbook* 22 (2015), ed. Luke Fischer and Dalia Nassar.
50 In *Malte* the statement refers to the French poet Félix Arvers. KA 3, 572.
51 See Carolyn Merchant, *The Death of Nature: Women, Ecology, and the Scientific Revolution* (San Francisco, CA: HarperCollins, 1983 [1980]).

"it," then the next step might be regarded as a deeper penetration of the particulars of Nature within an organicist context.[52] It is precisely this ideal that informed Rilke's practice of seeing in the middle period. Thus Rilke's aspirations in the middle period do not involve a rejection of Romanticism; rather he seeks to realize to a higher degree ideals that were to some extent formulated by the Romantics. If the Romantics could claim that, "All art should become science [*Wissenschaft*] and all science art. Poetry and philosophy should be made one,"[53] then Rilke, in some of the *Dinggedichte* of the *Neue Gedichte*, fulfilled a *component* of this demand to a degree unmatched by any of the Romantic poets themselves.[54] The detail, concentration, and "objectivity" in the portrayal of things grant these poems a scientific or cognitive dignity such that they fulfill the demand that poetry become science (*Wissenschaft*) or knowledge, while still remaining poetry, to an especially high degree.

There are many motifs that connect Rilke to Romanticism. A comparison of the thematization of death in Rilke and Novalis, for instance, would be highly interesting and sufficient for an independent monograph. Novalis's endeavor to "Romanticize the world" through a synthesizing of the sensuous and the spiritual, the lower and the higher, etc. also shares important affinities with Rilke's views of the deeper identity of the sensuous and the spiritual.[55] The centrality of concepts concerning transformation, becoming, and metamorphosis in the era of Romanticism and German Idealism (Novalis, Schelling, Hegel, Goethe, Coleridge) and their relationship to the central role

---

52 In the last few decades there has been a revival of interest in Romanticism due to its potential to address significant aspects of the present ecological crisis. See, for instance, Jonathan Bate, *Romantic Ecology: Wordsworth and the Environmental Tradition* (London: Routledge, 1991); Gernot Böhme, *Für eine ökologische Naturästhetik* (Frankfurt am Main: Suhrkamp, 1989), 96ff.; Kate Rigby, *Topographies of the Sacred: The Poetics of Place in European Romanticism* (Charlottesville, VA: University of Virginia Press, 2004).
53 Friedrich Schlegel, *Kritische Friedrich Schlegel Ausgabe*, vol. 2, ed. Ernst Behler (Paderborn: Schöningh, 1958), 161.
54 I emphasize that Rilke achieved a component of this ideal in that his poetry has an epistemic value. However, Rilke is not exemplary of the other component of this ideal, namely that *philosophy and science* become poetic. In contrast to Rilke, the German Romantics, Friedrich Schlegel and Novalis, *philosophized* in a poetic manner; they sought to bring philosophy closer to poetry (their philosophical employment of the fragment—a non-systematic form that encourages intuitive leaps of thought—is one example of this endeavor). See the discussion below.
55 Novalis [Friedrich von Hardenberg], *Novalis Schriften: Die Werke von Friedrich von Hardenberg*, ed. Richard Samuel, H.-J. Mähl, Paul Kluckhorn, and G. Schulz, vol. 2 (Stuttgart: W. Kohlhammer, 1960–88), 545, Nr. 105.

96   The Poet as Phenomenologist

of *Verwandlung* (transformation) in Rilke's poetics would also be a theme worthy of detailed exploration.[56] Thus, there are numerous inherent relationships between Rilke and the tradition of Romanticism. However, differences between Rilke and Romanticism should not be overlooked. One ostensible difference is the absence of any explicit or independent philosophy in Rilke. There is no question that although (as I have suggested) Rilke realized a "scientific objectivity" in his poetry that surpasses the Romantics and although his poetry contains an immanent philosophical significance, he is inferior to the Romantics (some of them) when it comes to philosophy in the explicit sense. Novalis and Coleridge were, in addition to being poets, penetrating philosophical thinkers, whereas in Rilke there is no *independent* and *explicit* philosophy.[57] Rather, as Käte Hamburger has elaborated, in the case of Rilke we find *a body of poetry in the place of a philosophy*.[58] In other words, Rilke's "philosophy" is inherent to the poetry and as poetry (Rilke's poetry is philosophically significant without being didactic). This situation relates to the task of the present work, namely, to make explicit the internal philosophical significance of Rilke's vision and poetry.

While a detailed exploration of Rilke and Romanticism is beyond the scope of this work, the subsequent considerations of Rilke's place within a broader art-historical context will build on the preceding observations. The central task of this and the following chapter is to articulate Rilke's way of seeing and its correlative non-dualistic disclosure of things.

Rilke's Engagement with Rodin and Cézanne: The Formulation of "das Werk des Gesichts"

Early in Rilke's novel, *Malte*, one finds the well-known lines, "Ich lerne sehen. Ich weiß nicht, woran es liegt, es geht alles tiefer in mich ein

---

56   For an elaboration of Goethe's view of art as a higher metamorphosis of Nature see Luke Fischer, "Goethe contra Hegel: The Question of the End of Art," *Goethe Yearbook* 18 (2011): 127–58.

57   It may be worthwhile to mention that there has been a recent renewal of interest in Early German Romanticism as a distinctive *philosophical* movement. Manfred Frank and Frederick Beiser have been two of the most influential scholars in this development. See, for instance, Manfred Frank, *Einführung in die frühromantische Ästhetik* (Frankfurt am Main: Suhrkamp, 1989); Frederick Beiser, *The Romantic Imperative: The Concept of Early German Romanticism* (Cambridge, MA: Harvard University Press, 2003); Dalia Nassar, *The Romantic Absolute: Being and Knowing in Early German Romantic Philosophy, 1795–1804* (Chicago: University of Chicago Press, 2013); Dalia Nassar, ed., *The Relevance of Romanticism: Essays on German Romantic Philosophy* (New York: Oxford University Press, 2014).

58   Käte Hamburger, *Philosophie der Dichter*, 268.

und bleibt nicht an der Stelle stehen, wo es sonst immer zu Ende war. Ich habe ein Inneres, von dem ich nicht wußte [I am learning to see. I do not know what it consists in; everything enters me more deeply and no longer remains at the place, where it, otherwise, always came to an end. I have an interior, of which I did not know]."[59] Malte, in many ways Rilke's fictive alter ego, speaks of learning to see and a correlative transformation in the experience of vision. Already from these lines it is, moreover, clear that this seeing involves an extra-ordinary relationship between "inner" and "outer." It will be demonstrated shortly that Rilke himself learnt to see in a new way in the middle period, and that this seeing, among other things, enabled a non-dualistic disclosure of Nature. It will be shown that the interior, of which Malte says he formerly knew nothing, is an interiority no longer in opposition to the world, but in a sense yet to be clarified, the interior of the world itself. However, before turning to an explicit elaboration of Rilke's vision it is important to consider the two most significant artists for Rilke in the middle period, namely Rodin and Cézanne. In his engagement with these French visual artists, Rilke formulated the ideal of a distinctive manner of being-in-the-world, a praxis of seeing, and the translation of vision into the composition of the work of art. Although Rilke did not establish the personal connection to Cézanne that he cultivated with Rodin (Cézanne died the year before Rilke's intensive engagement with his work), Cézanne assumed for him an even greater significance than Rodin.[60]

As we are primarily concerned with the background of the *Neue Gedichte*, the consideration of Cézanne may raise some questions. While as early as 1900, and again in 1905, Rilke mentions Cézanne in letters to Clara Rilke, it was not until the 1907 Cézanne retrospective at the Salon d'Automne (October 6–22, 1907) that Rilke developed a profound appreciation for Cézanne's work.[61] This means that Cézanne can only be regarded as exercising a significant and direct influence on the second part of the *Neue Gedichte* (*Der neuen Gedichte anderer Teil*) and not on the first part, and therefore, not on the *Neue Gedichte* considered

---

59 *KA 3*, 456.
60 In the letter of February 26, 1924 to Alfred Schaer, Rilke states that since 1906 Cézanne has been the most significant example for him. Rilke, *Briefe*, vol. 2, 1914–26 (Wiesbaden: Insel Verlag, 1950), 440.
61 Before 1907, Rilke was also familiar with writings by art historians that discussed Cézanne's work. His prior reading and his earlier viewings of some of Cézanne's paintings no doubt provided a background for Rilke's decisive encounter with Cézanne. See Ralph Köhnen, *Sehen als Textkultur: Intermediale Beziehungen zwischen Rilke und Cézanne* (Bielefeld: Aisthesis Verlag, 1995), 108–113.

as a whole.⁶² However, for a number of reasons this fact does not negate the legitimacy of relating Cézanne to the entire *Neue Gedichte*. Rilke's *Briefe über Cézanne* (*Letters on Cézanne*) were written shortly after the publication of the first part of the *Neue Gedichte* and, as will be seen, Rilke's assessment of Cézanne is directly connected to his evaluation of his own work, in particular the *Neue Gedichte*. Moreover, Rilke came to recognize in Cézanne an artist who had pursued a path deeply related to his own path as a poet; the discovery of Cézanne was, no doubt, an *Ereignis* (significant event), yet this *Ereignis* was simultaneously a clarification of Rilke's own artistic ideals. Even in the "new poems" written prior to his awakening to Cézanne, Rilke recognized a deep affinity between his own work and Cézanne's art.⁶³

Rilke identifies two crucial moments in the creative processes of Rodin and Cézanne. These two moments are: 1) the practice of a way of seeing, and 2) the translation of a vision of things into the composition of the work of art. The creative process of both the sculptor and painter involves the perception of things or models—human models, artifacts, landscapes, etc.⁶⁴ The sculptor and the painter then seek to translate what is disclosed to their vision into their respective mediums (through their craft). These two moments are intimately connected and scarcely divisible in the artistic process. However, for the sake of conceptual clarity these two moments will be considered, as far as is possible, separately.

There are widespread tendencies today to consider artworks in abstraction from the vision out of which they are born. While the artwork is the ultimate articulation of this vision, one of the central claims of this book is that artistic *seeing*, such as Cézanne's seeing of the landscape, is of central importance. For the artist (the artists under consideration) there is always a movement or dialogue between *seeing* and *composition*, which is at the same time a meaningful relation between the *world* and the *work*. Pervasive contemporary tendencies lose sight of this relation. The "aesthetic attitude" regards artworks as isolated aesthetic objects.⁶⁵ Post-modern criticism affirms the "death of the author" and dissolves the "referent" in an internal play of linguistic

---

62 Rilke's intensive engagement with Cézanne began shortly after he finished the first part of the *Neue Gedichte*. Rilke completed the first part of the *Neue Gedichte* in July of 1907.
63 See, for instance, *LC*, 63. *KA 4*, 622.
64 Of course, in abstract or non-figurative art the model to a great extent disappears. However, this is not the case with the still figurative work of Rodin and Cézanne, despite Cézanne's historically significant role in the development of abstract painting.
65 See Gadamer's critique of aesthetic consciousness. Hans-Georg Gadamer, *Wahrheit und Methode*, 94ff.; *Truth and Method*, 77ff.

signifiers. Post-modern theory and criticism thus disconnect the work from the personal *vision* of an author and lose sight of the referent or world beyond the text. The attention given here to a *perception of the world* that precedes the complete work of art is one way in which these tendencies are challenged. Moreover, I explicate this *seeing* as deeply significant even when it does not culminate in a successful work of art; it is nothing less than a twofold vision of things and an experiential overcoming of dualism.[66] This affirmation of a distinctive relation between the world and the work can also be regarded as a contribution to the ecocritical reaffirmation of the significance of the referent in contrast to post-modern theory. The current environmental crisis calls for a renewed consideration of our relation to the natural world, and the nature or environment that is suffering as a result of human actions is more than a linguistic construct. As Kate Rigby explains, "While acknowledging the role of language in shaping our view of the world, ecocritics seek to restore significance to the world beyond the page."[67] For the purposes of the present concerns this statement can be expanded to include works of art in a more general sense (one could, for instance, substitute "language" with "art," and "beyond the page" with "beyond the work").

For these reasons the character of this seeing and its translation into the work (and the work of art itself) will be considered as *distinctly* as possible. Two sub-sections focus on the two moments (seeing and its translation) as they appear in Rodin. Another two sub-sections do the same for Cézanne. For a number of reasons the treatment of Cézanne is especially significant. Cézanne came to assume a greater importance for Rilke than Rodin; toward the end of his life Rilke stated that Cézanne remained his supreme example.[68] Cézanne's importance for the whole development of modern art is difficult to over-estimate. Merleau-Ponty and Heidegger both came to value Cézanne as one of the most, if not *the* most, significant modern painters. Merleau-Ponty found in Cézanne a kind of "painter-phenomenologist," who was an important influence on both his earlier phenomenology and his later phenomenological *ontology*. The late Heidegger saw in Cézanne's late works a painterly analogue of his own efforts to overcome metaphysics,

---

66 In this respect my claims might also be regarded as an argument for the pedagogical significance of artistic practice, irrespective of the quality of the resulting works. When I am set with the task of drawing something, to offer an obvious example, I am called to perceive what I draw in a more exact, lively, and intimate manner than a casual everyday glance at things.
67 Kate Rigby, "Ecocriticism," in *Introducing Criticism at the 21st Century*, ed. Julian Wolfreys (Edinburgh: Edinburgh University Press, 2002), 154–5.
68 See n. 60.

a "post-metaphysical painting."[69] Thus for Rilke, Heidegger, and Merleau-Ponty, Cézanne was of crucial importance; moreover, their reflections on Cézanne intersect in significant ways. The proximity between Rilke and Cézanne is at the same time a proximity between Rilke and phenomenology. Thus, the treatment of Cézanne also paves the way for my phenomenological interpretation of Rilke.

Prior to turning to Rodin and Cézanne in particular, the basic disposition that Rilke envisages as necessary for the artist is elaborated in a way that builds on the earlier discussion of "childlikeness" and "active-passivity." While the treatment of Rodin and Cézanne bears an independent value, it should be kept in mind that the primary purpose is to provide a broader context within which to understand Rilke. The two moments considered in Rodin and Cézanne—a non-dualistic vision and its artistic embodiment—shed important light on the relation between Rilke's vision and poetry (the focus of Chapters 3 and 4 respectively).

The Disposition of the Artist

Rilke's various writings clearly indicate that being an artist calls for a certain manner of being-in-the-world. In the previous sections this manner of being was discussed with respect to features that Rilke shares with Romanticism. It was suggested that an artistic way of being and seeing involves the conscious institution of a radical "active-passivity." This idea comes into further relief in Rilke's texts on Rodin and Cézanne. After Heidegger's hermeneutic phenomenology, it should be evident to us that the way in which things show themselves is inseparable from a certain manner of being-in-the-world.

Already in *Sein und Zeit* Heidegger elaborated the view that "understanding" (*Verstehen*) and "dispositions" (*Befindlichkeiten*) are equally fundamental or originary (*gleichursprünglich*) in their role of disclosing the world and ourselves.[70] (He identifies both with the structural moment of "being-in," which belongs within the total structure of "being-in-the-world.") Heidegger thereby rejected and transformed the traditional view of "moods," or more generally "affects," as unessential to truth.[71] Although the disclosive significance of moods or disposi-

---

69 See Christoph Jamme, "Der Verlust der Dinge: Cézanne – Rilke – Heidegger," *Deutsche Zeitschrift für Philosophie* 40 (1992): 385–97; Günter Seubold, *Kunst als Enteignis: Heideggers Weg zu einer nicht mehr metaphysischen Kunst* (Bonn: Bouvier Verlag, 1996).
70 Heidegger, *Sein und Zeit*, 130ff.
71 For an extensive discussion of Heidegger's departure from the metaphysical interpretation of the human being as the "rational animal" and the traditional prioritization of the rational over the "affective," see Paola-Ludovika Coriando, *Affektenlehre und Phänomenologie der Stimmungen: Wege einer Ontologie und Ethik des Emotionalen* (Frankfurt am Main: Vittorio Klostermann, 2002), 120ff.

tions is not conceptually elaborated in Rilke, he similarly regarded the *cultivation of certain dispositions* as essential to the manner in which the world and things are disclosed.

In *Auguste Rodin* (a monograph in two parts) Rilke portrays the artist (in this case Rodin) as existing in a privileged harmony with the whole of Nature.[72] Both Rodin's general manner of being and his artistic productivity are characterized in this way. In *Auguste Rodin* (First Part, 1903) Rilke states,

> He [Rodin] felt where one [*man*] must begin; a calmness in him showed him the true way. At this point is revealed that deep agreement with Nature, which is characteristic of Rodin and which has been described so well by the poet Georges Rodenbach, who calls him simply "an elemental force" …[73]

In *Auguste Rodin* (Second Part, 1907) Rilke writes,

> Here, in the solitude of his country dwelling [in Meudon], he has learnt to embrace this Life with still greater faith and love. It reveals itself [*Es zeigt sich*] to him now as to one of the initiated, it no longer hides itself from him, it has no distrust towards him. He recognizes it in what is small and in what is great; in what is scarcely discernible [*im kaum mehr Sichtbaren*] and in what is immense [*Unermeßlichen*]. It is present in his rising up and in his going to rest and in the night watches; the simple old-fashioned repasts are filled with it, the bread and the wine; it is in the joy of a dog, it is in the swans and in the shining flight of doves. It is present in all its fullness in every tiny flower and is a hundredfold in every fruit. Any cabbage leaf from the kitchen garden makes proud display of it, and rightly so [*und mit wieviel Recht*]. How it delights to shimmer in the water and how happy it is in the trees! And how it takes possession of the existence of men where it can, when they do not resist [*Und wie nimmt es, wo es kann, das Dasein der Menschen in Besitz, wenn sie nicht sträuben*].[74]

---

72 Rilke was commissioned to write a monograph on Rodin in 1902. He arrived in Paris on August 28, 1902 and took up residence there in order to make a personal connection to the artist and see him at work. The monograph was published for the first time in 1903. On the basis of a lecture first given in 1905 a second part was added to the monograph and both parts appeared for the first time in a single volume in 1907.
73 Rilke, *Auguste Rodin*, trans. G. Craig Houston (Mineola, NY: Dover Publications, 2006), 5; translation altered. From now on I shall refer to *Auguste Rodin* as *AR*. KA 4, 409.
74 *AR*, 59–60; translation altered. KA 4, 473.

The artist, Rodin, enjoys a particular at-oneness with the whole *life of Nature*, and the above passages indicate clear points of connection between *Worpswede* (1902) and the two-part monograph on Rodin (1903 and 1907). Early in *Worpswede* we encountered Rilke's claim that Nature's life is hidden from us. This claim was soon qualified and relativized in relation to Rilke's view of developmental psychology; the life of Nature is hidden from the *ordinary* adult. In the above excerpt Rilke affirms that for the "extra-ordinary" adult, the artist Rodin, the *life* of Nature is no longer hidden.⁷⁵ Rodin is as though "initiated" into this ordinarily hidden dimension of Nature. In the discussion of *Worpswede* it was seen that the privileged disclosure of Nature granted to the artist depends on the maintenance of a childlike openness to things. "Childlikeness" is only one ascription among many, which denote a state of mind characterized by an active-passivity. The end of the above passage indicates that a calm and receptive disposition grants Rodin a privileged revelation of the life of Nature—"how it [Life] takes possession of the existence of men where it can, when they do not resist."⁷⁶ Rodin's calm disposition allows Nature to reveal itself.

The advocation of an active-passivity—a letting-be—is found in Heidegger under the name of *Gelassenheit*.⁷⁷ It is not surprising that Rilke, in the letter to Clara Rilke of October 19, 1907 (see below), employs this word. Although the *word* "Gelassenheit" does not have the central significance that it accrues in the later Heidegger, Rilke employs a number of words which circumscribe a range of meaning that is close to the Heideggerian sense of *Gelassenheit*. Rilke states (this time with regard to his own requirements as an artist),

> how of one piece is everything we encounter, how related one thing is to the next, how it gives birth to itself and grows up and is educated in its own nature, and we basically just have *to be* [dazusein], but simply, devoutly [*inständig*], the way the earth is [*da ist*], and gives her consent to the seasons, bright and dark and whole in space, not asking [*verlangend*] to rest upon anything other than the net and influences and forces in which the stars feel secure.⁷⁸

---

75 The significance of "life" in Rodin will be elaborated in the course of our discussion.
76 If it is not yet completely clear that an attitude of *Gelassenheit* is implied by this quotation, it will become clear in the light of the subsequent discussion.
77 See also Rilke's conception of inspiration as presented in the first poem of the *Neue Gedichte*, "Früher Apollo." KA 1, 449.
78 LC, 69–70; translation altered. KA 4, 625.

Learning to See: Rilke and the Visual Arts   103

At the beginning of the subsequent paragraph he mentions *Gelassenheit* explicitly: "Some day the time and *Gelassenheit* and patience must also be there in order to continue writing the Notebooks of Malte Laurids Brigge ..."[79]

In the block quotation above Rilke advocates a general attitude of letting-be. Such letting-be enables a kind of harmony with the whole of Nature and the cosmos and a sense for the interrelatedness of all beings ("how of one piece is everything we encounter, how related one thing is to the next"). It is certainly possible to see an affinity here to Heidegger's notion of being homely on the earth and beneath the sky.[80] In the second passage, with the mention of "Gelassenheit" and "patience," Rilke relates this world-attunement to the possibility of his own creative work, in this instance, the writing of his novel, *Malte*. A connection between *Gelassenheit*, Nature, and artistic creativity is also affirmed in Rilke's statement regarding Rodin that, "it lies in the essence [*im Wesen*] of this mighty genius to have as much time as Nature and to produce like her."[81]

Rodin's *Gelassenheit* is a kind of harmony with the time of Nature. This time is clearly much slower than the haste and distraction of modern technological existence. It is also more fruitful—Rilke again perceives an affinity between Rodin's artistic creativity and the creativity of Nature. To return for a moment to the earlier discussion, one notices here another relationship between Rilke and Romanticism (and German Classicism—Goethe, for instance) in the association of natural productivity and artistic productivity (Schelling and Coleridge are two notable representatives of this view).[82]

With respect to both Rilke and Heidegger, an understanding of *Gelassenheit* must take into account the word's "effective history," as their usage bears clear traces of its earlier meaning. The word dates back to German mysticism of the late Middle Ages, which both the thinker and the poet received.[83] However, the meaning of *Gelassenheit*,

---

79 LC, 70; translation altered. *KA* 4, 625.
80 See, for instance, Heidegger, "Bauen Wohnen Denken," in *GA* 7 (2000 [1951]), 150ff. Cf. Yen-Hui Lee, *Gelassenheit und Wu-Wei: Nähe und Ferne zwischen dem späten Heidegger und dem Taoismus* (PhD diss., Albert-Ludwigs-Universität, Freiburg, 2001), 60.
81 AR, 63; translation altered. *KA* 4, 477.
82 For an account of the relation between natural productivity and artistic productivity in Goethe, see Luke Fischer, "Goethe contra Hegel: The Question of the End of Art."
83 Both Rilke and Heidegger explicitly draw on the work of authors from the mystical tradition. For a detailed discussion of similarities and differences between Heidegger's later thought and Meister Eckhart, see John D. Caputo, *The Mystical Element in Heidegger's Thought* (New York: Fordham University Press, 1986). See also n. 87.

in the middle Rilke and the later Heidegger, is not identical to Christian mysticism. For Meister Eckhart *Gelassenheit* is the precondition for the possibility of the *unio mystica*—the marriage of the soul with *God*. Through letting go of the world the mystic is able to experience the God who transcends the world and is not of this world. While in Rilke and Heidegger there is also a connection between *Gelassenheit* and a possible appearance of the divine, their understanding of *Gelassenheit* is more closely connected to the possibility of the world and things being disclosed in a deeper light (though this is also a dimension of Eckhart's thought[84]). For Rilke *Gelassenheit*, among other things, enables a privileged disclosure of the natural world. In Heidegger *Gelassenheit* allows a more profound disclosure of Being and presents an alternative to the attitude of the "dominating subject" of metaphysics and the calculative thinking characteristic of the technological age.[85]

The overcoming of dualism must be thought and experienced in terms of an active-passivity. This necessity is already evident in Eckhart. Eckhart's best-known statement could be paraphrased in the words, "my seeing of God is at the same time God's seeing of me"; to see God is to be seen by God and vice versa.[86] This mystical vision is at one and

---

84 Caputo draws attention to a structural parallel between the relationship between creatures and God in Eckhart and beings and Being in Heidegger. Eckhart speaks of the necessity to "find God in things," which relates to "Heidegger's own insistence that we find Being itself in beings." Caputo, *The Mystical Element in Heidegger's Thought*, 185.

85 See Heidegger, "Die Frage nach der Technik," in *GA* 7, 7–36; "Zur Erörterung der Gelassenheit," in *GA* 13, 37–74; "Überwindung der Metaphysik," in *GA* 7, 67–98. In the present work a number of connections are drawn between Rilke and Heidegger. In light of this fact the reader may ask why more space has not been given to a specific treatment of Heidegger's own interpretation of Rilke. I have already mentioned some reasons for this omission in the Introduction. One important reason is that an adequate assessment of Heidegger's reading of Rilke would probably require a separate monograph. My interpretation of Rilke is not in perfect agreement with Heidegger. However, I always clearly bring into view what I regard as mutually illuminating connections between Heidegger's and Rilke's work. While I continue to elaborate points of connection and difference between Heidegger and Rilke, I largely leave it to the reader to assess the relationship between my reading of Rilke and Heidegger's interpretation of Rilke. I may offer a more explicit and elaborate interpretation of Heidegger's reading of Rilke at a later date. In my article on Rilke and Franz Marc I briefly mention some of my disagreements with Heidegger. Luke Fischer, "Animalising Art: Rainer Maria Rilke and Franz Marc," 54ff., n. 7.

86 Meister Eckhart states, "Daz ouge, dâ inne ich got sihe, daz ist daz selbe ouge, dâ inne mich got sihet, min ouge und gotes ouge daz ist éin ouge und éin gesiht und éin bekennen und éin minnen." Meister Eckhart, *Die deutschen Werke*, vol. 1, trans. Josef Quint (Stuttgart: 1958), 201.

the same time my activity of seeing and my suffering to be seen.[87] There is thus a radical coincidence of seer and seen, a radical non-dualism. In this instance, it is wrong to speak of a subject constituting an object. An "object" that is constituted by a subject is a "subjective object" or a mirror of the subject. In Eckhart's statement, to see is to be seen and to be seen is to see; in seeing I am seen by that which I see. That which I see is not a passive object that is informed by my active gaze. I and that which I see are simultaneously active and passive, doing and suffering, seeing and being seen. This passive-activity or active-passivity indicates the broader significance of *Gelassenheit* with regard to the problem of dualism.[88]

Another term that Rilke employs frequently in *Auguste Rodin* and the *Letters on Cézanne*, which belongs in the general spectrum of the "childlike" and *Gelassenheit*, is that of "poverty" (*Armut*). Rilke does not simply mean "financial poverty" but primarily a disposition or mood of non-possession, openness, and trust that may be connected to financial poverty. Rilke ascribes this disposition to van Gogh, Rodin, and Cézanne. Of Rodin he says the following:

> when love of work failed, poverty drove him to it. Poverty without which his life would be unthinkable. He never forgets that it made him one with the beasts and flowers, devoid of possessions amongst all those who possess nothing, who depend on God and on him alone.[89]

---

87 In Heidegger's essay "The Turning" ("Die Kehre") there is a passage that is structurally so similar to Eckhart's statement concerning the coincidence of my seeing with God's seeing that it is hard not to regard it as a paraphrase of Eckhart. Heidegger states, "Only when man, in the disclosing coming-to-pass of the insight by which he himself is beheld, renounces human self-will and projects himself toward that insight, away from himself, does he correspond in his essence to the claim of that insight. In thus corresponding man is gathered into his own [*ge-eignet*], that he, within the safeguarded element of world, may, as the mortal, look out toward the divine." Heidegger, *The Question Concerning Technology and Other Essays*, trans. William Lovitt (New York: Harper, 1977), 47; "Die Kehre," in *GA* 79 (2005 [1949]), 76.

88 Anthony Steinbock in his book, *Phenomenology and Mysticism*, speaks of the active-passivity involved in various forms of mystical experience. He explicates the character of mystical experience as follows: "It is God who is 'active' in relation to which our participation in the experience is 'passive.' We do not cause or provoke epiphanic givenness; it is experienced as grace. Our 'activity,' as it were, is receiving." Anthony J. Steinbock, *Phenomenology and Mysticism: The Verticality of Religious Experience* (Bloomington, IN: Indiana University Press, 2007), 139.

89 *AR*, 56; translation altered. *KA* 4, 469.

This poverty, this state of non-possession, enables the artist to identify with the things of Nature, making "him one with the beasts and flowers … who depend on God and on him alone." This passage is a clear allusion to Christ's teaching of poverty in the New Testament. In Luke 12 we find,

> I bid you put away anxious thoughts about food to keep you alive and clothes to cover your body. Life is more than food, the body more than clothes. Think of the ravens: they neither sow nor reap; they have no storehouse or barn; yet God feeds them. You are worth far more than the birds! … Think of the lilies: they neither spin nor weave; yet I tell you, even Solomon in all his splendour was not attired like one of these …[90]

While there is a strong affinity between Rilke's characterization of poverty and the passage from the New Testament, Rilke places a special emphasis on becoming one with the "beasts and flowers," thus suggesting that the artist's possessionless disposition enables a special revelation of the creatures of Nature.

In the *Letters on Cézanne*, Rilke speaks of van Gogh as one "in whom something of the spirit of Saint Francis was coming back to life" and as someone who "sees everything as a poor man."[91] It is clear that this seeing of things as a poor man means that the things, thereby, show themselves more richly. Rilke states that *things* in van Gogh's paintings remind "one of the 'saints' he promised himself and resolved to paint at some much later time."[92] "Ordinary" things appear in van Gogh's paintings with an aura of the holy. The reason why van Gogh can paint things in such a way, according to Rilke, is because he sees the "nameless" (in other words, the ineffable, the unfamiliar, the holy) in them.[93] Later in the *Letters on Cézanne* he writes that, "One has to be poor unto the tenth generation … One has to be able at every moment to place one's hand on the earth like the first human being."[94] Here it is clear that poverty is connected to a kind of open-mindedness or conscious naïveté, the ability to receive the world with a pure sense of wonder that is not glazed by the film of familiarity.

These considerations have explicated Rilke's view that a cultivated mood of childlikeness, of unpossessiveness or poverty, of renunciation, of *Gelassenheit*, is a precondition for a privileged disclosure of things.

---

90 Luke 12.22–4, 27. *The New English Bible* (Oxford: Oxford University Press, 1970), 91.
91 *LC*, 20. *KA 4*, 602.
92 *LC*, 18. *KA 4*, 601.
93 *LC*, 18, 20, 40. *KA 4*, 601–2, 611.
94 *LC*, 73–4. *KA 4*, 627.

Another quality Rilke repeatedly emphasizes in his middle period is "impartiality." Impartiality is regarded as a necessary condition for the possibility of a truthful vision of things; if impartiality is lacking then things, or phenomena, cannot show themselves as they are—disclose themselves. This attitude of impartiality could be formulated as the demand on the artist to transcend habitual and conventional sympathies and antipathies. Such an attitude is inseparable from what could be called Rilke's "truth aesthetics," and perhaps it would be better here to re-enlarge the meaning of the word "aesthetic" to incorporate its older meaning, still in use by Kant (the "transcendental aesthetic"), of the perceptible generally.[95] The artist's manner of seeing should transcend "likes" and "dislikes." It should let things show themselves from themselves without distorting them with emotional reactions and conventional responses.

This impartial vision should not, however, be understood as a "moodless" or "dispositionless" vision. As Heidegger rightly claims, there is no such thing as a moodless state.[96] Even indifference is a mood—a way of relating to the world which reveals the world and ourselves in a particular light. To understand "impartiality" as moodless would also contradict what has just been elaborated. Nevertheless, the mention of emotions that distort perception might seem like a regression to a pre-phenomenological, subjective view of affective life. However, this is not the case; the nature of affects is more nuanced and complex.

Aspects of Gernot Böhme's phenomenological view of atmospheres can help to paint a more complete picture of the range of affects.[97] Böhme has clearly illustrated the existence of a fundamental class of non-subjective affects which, following the "new phenomenology" (*neue Phänomenologie*) of Hermann Schmitz, he calls "atmospheres" (drawing on the usage of everyday speech but transforming the term into a philosophical concept). "Atmospheres" are "quasi-objective"

---

95 More recently Gernot Böhme has elaborated a general phenomenological aesthetics. See Gernot Böhme, *Aisthetik: Vorlesungen über Ästhetik als allgemeine Wahrnehmungslehre* (Munich: Wilhelm Fink Verlag, 2001). We will draw on Böhme's important work on a phenomenology of "moods" and "atmospheres" at various points in the further course of this book.
96 Heidegger, *Sein und Zeit*, 134.
97 Gernot Böhme's works are more well known in Germany than in the Anglophone world. For an introduction to his view of atmospheres and the ecocritical significance of this concept, see Kate Rigby, "Gernot Böhme's Ecological Aesthetics of Atmosphere," in *Ecocritical Theory: New European Approaches*, ed. Axel Goodbody and Kate Rigby (Charlottesville, VA: University of Virginia Press, 2011), 139–52.

feelings or moods.[98] Atmospheres can be sensed in the natural and the human world, and Böhme demonstrates that these atmospheres are pre-reflectively given and cannot be understood as subjective projections. To offer an example from the human world, suppose that you enter a room where a meeting is taking place and immediately sense a "tense" or "serious" atmosphere.[99] As examples from the natural world, one can think of the "radiant" atmosphere of late-afternoon sunlight shining through leaves or the crisp atmosphere of a cool morning.[100] However, it is possible to have an emotional reaction to a surrounding atmosphere. One becomes annoyed, for instance, at having to attend the "serious" meeting when it would be preferable to sit outside in the sun and eat an ice cream. Or, a person walks beside a river and while watching the sun shimmer on its surface rejoices over the fact of being alive. (This also opens up questions of whether one is in *harmony* with a particular atmosphere or not. One can attend a party and become attuned to the festive mood, or one can experience oneself as an outsider and dislike being there. One can feel at home in a particular city or suffer "culture shock." In the latter case in each example, one's personal mood is in a *dissonant* relation to the surrounding atmosphere.) In these instances an emotion emerges as a secondary response to a "quasi-objective" mood or atmosphere. In this limited sphere and particular moment the common view of affects as "subjective" is to a certain degree right (only to a certain degree because affects must ultimately be understood within the broader context in which they belong). This emotional response does not belong to the *atmospheric appearing of the phenomenon*; rather, it is a way of personally relating or reacting to the pre-given phenomenon.

With these considerations in mind, the relations and distinctions between dispositions, atmospheres, and secondary emotions can be explicated. Dispositions can be understood as what Paola-Ludovika Coriando calls *Grundstimmungen*; these are fundamental affective attunements of self and world.[101] Atmospheres are more local embodied experiences of a kind of objective or "quasi-objective" (to follow Böhme) feeling, which, however, presuppose certain dispositions. For instance, without a certain *calm* and *receptive* disposition one is not able to properly sense (*"spüren"*) atmospheres. A genuine awareness of atmospheres presupposes a tranquil receptivity. Perhaps one of the reasons for the widespread lack of awareness of atmospheres

---

98 Gernot Böhme, *Anmutungen: Über das Atmosphärische* (Ostfildern vor Stuttgart: Edition Tertium Arcaden, 1998), 8.
99 Cf. Böhme, *Aisthetik*, 46–7.
100 Cf. Böhme, *Anmutungen*, 35ff.
101 See n. 102.

Learning to See: Rilke and the Visual Arts   109

and for the subjective interpretation of affects is the fact that we generally fail to cultivate the necessary disposition and sensibility to make atmospheric phenomena genuinely conscious (they remain elusive and unobserved), and thus to an extent our affects are subjective.[102] However, the qualification should be made that affective life is one of great fluidity and metamorphosis, such that these phenomena cannot be ultimately divided or separated, and they often pass into one another. Moreover, it will shortly be elaborated how "affects" vary in status with regard to their world-disclosive significance.

After this slight but necessary detour we can return to the theme of impartiality. It is instructive to recall Rilke's retrospective clarification of the *Neue Gedichte* as poems about "*things* felt" rather than his feelings toward things.[103] Here Rilke had in view the distinction between the feeling of atmospheres and subjective or secondary affects (although he did not use this terminology). Rilke's demand on the artist to cultivate an impartial attitude is a demand to transcend an aesthetics of the "beautiful" in the narrow sense of the word—"beauty" as defined by its opposition to the "ugly." To be sympathetic to the "beautiful" and antipathetic toward the "ugly" is to be partial in one's vision. The artist's way of seeing must acknowledge impartially the character of what would normally be repulsive or attractive. This is also not disconnected from *Gelassenheit*; Rilke develops the idea of artistic impartiality

---

102 Coriando and Böhme are two of the most significant recent contributors to a phenomenological articulation of the affective but I am unaware of any dialogue between the two philosophers. This may have to do with the fact that Coriando's work is strongly aligned with Heidegger and hermeneutic phenomenology, whereas the main influences on Böhme's work are Hermann Schmitz and Goethe. Nevertheless, Coriando's interpretation of Hölderlin's latest poems can be understood in the way in which I have related ideas in Böhme and Coriando. Coriando regards a harmony or "*Ein-klang*" as the fundamental disposition or *Grundstimmung* of Hölderlin's latest poems which primarily thematize the seasons. This *Grundstimmung* of *Einklang* is what enables the particular *Stimmungen* of the different seasons to be experienced by the "soul" or the *Gemüth* of the poet (Paola-Ludovika Coriando, *Affektenlehre und Phänomenologie der Stimmungen: Wege einer Ontologie und Ethik des Emotionalen*, 187–207). In Böhme's terminology the seasons are atmospheric phenomena; the seasons are sensed to have different atmospheres. Thus, if one writes "atmospheres" in place of the *Stimmungen* of the seasons in Coriando's considerations of the late Hölderlin, then one is provided with another example of the relationship between "disposition" (what Coriando calls "Grundstimmung") and "atmosphere" that I have articulated.
  Böhme relates his conception of the "affective" to Heidegger's conception of *Befindlichkeit* but also distinguishes his views from Heidegger's. His main disagreement with Heidegger concerns Heidegger's lack of attention to the "living body" or *Leiblichkeit*. See Böhme, *Aisthetik*, 73–86.

103 Letter of February 3, 1923, "À une Amie." Rilke, *Briefe*, vol. 2, 1914–26, 389.

in the same letter of October 19 where he speaks of the necessity of *Gelassenheit*. There, as well as in *Malte*, he notes the exemplary significance of Baudelaire's poem "Une Charogne" ("A Carcass") in which a decomposing carcass is vividly portrayed.[104] Rilke sees in Baudelaire, particularly in "Une Charogne," an artist who does not shy away from the ugly but presents what ordinarily would be regarded as repulsive as truthfully as possible.

> First, artistic perception had to overcome itself to the point of realizing that even something horrible, something that seems no more than disgusting, *is*, and shares the truth of its being with everything else that exists. Just as the creative artist is not allowed to choose, neither is he permitted to turn his back on anything: a single refusal, and he is cast out of the state of grace and becomes sinful all the way through.[105]

This impartiality is essential in that it enables a truthful revelation of things that is uncolored by attractions and aversions. It facilitates an openness to all phenomena. This open-mindedness is not merely "theoretical" and might be described as a phenomenological or existential open-mindedness. One of Rilke's most significant articulations of this open-mindedness is in his *Briefe an einen jungen Dichter* (*Letters to a Young Poet*), written between 1903 and 1908. In the letter to Franz Kappus of August 12, 1904 he writes,

> We must accept [*annehmen*] our existence [*Dasein*] as *far* as is possible; everything, even the incredible, must be a possibility.

---

104 LC, 67. KA 4, 624. Rilke regarded Cézanne's way of seeing things as impartial in this way and was impressed to find out that the late Cézanne valued this poem highly and could recite it by heart. Rodin was also a deep admirer of Baudelaire and praises "Une Charogne" for the same reasons as Rilke, namely its impartiality and its transcendence of an aesthetics of the beautiful in the narrow sense (J. A. Schmoll gen. Eisenwerth, *Rodin-Studien: Persönlichkeit – Werke – Wirkung – Bibliographie* [Munich: Prestel-Verlag, 1983], 93). The place where Rilke himself most obviously demonstrated such an impartiality is in *Malte*, with its depictions of the poor, the decrepit, outcasts, beggars, the sick, death, the supernatural, and the general sense of nihilism that pervades the protagonist's experience of Paris. However, some of these themes are also addressed in the *Neue Gedichte*. Coriando also examines *Malte* in her discussion of fundamental moods or *Grundstimmungen* in *Affektenlehre und Phänomenologie der Stimmungen* (pp. 208–32). However, the main theme of Coriando's inquiry in this instance is the temporal finitude of human life and the significance of an authentic relationship to death (and life). An assessment of Coriando's interpretation of *Malte* in this light would lead us too far afield.

105 LC, 67. KA 4, 624. In *Malte* there is an almost identical passage. See KA 3, 505.

Learning to See: Rilke and the Visual Arts   111

Fundamentally speaking this is the single courage that is demanded of us: to be fearless toward the strangest, the most miraculous, and the most inexplicable phenomena that can encounter us. That human beings were cowardly in this sense has damaged life infinitely; the experiences that are called "apparitions," the entire so called "world of spirits" [*Geisterwelt*], death, all these things that are so related to us, as a result of daily resistance have been expelled from life to such a great extent that the senses with which we could grasp them have atrophied ...[106]

The above passage illustrates the extent of Rilke's understanding of "impartiality" and open-mindedness. Due to aversion and closed-mindedness our experience of the world has become superficial and we have lost the capacity to perceive the most significant phenomena. The artist is called to transcend these limitations.

Manfred Engel elucidates Rilke's understanding of "impartiality" as "an indiscriminate 'unselective seeing [*unwählerisches Schauen*]' ... that in 'hard matter-of-fact-ness [*harter Sachlichkeit*]' ... accepts all aspects of reality, no longer drawing a distinction between the beautiful and the ugly, the pleasant and the disgusting, the familiar and the strange."[107] Engel interestingly chooses the verb "to accept" (*akzeptieren*), in speaking of an impartial acceptance of all aspects of reality.[108] This links

---

106 *KA* 4, 541–2.
107 Manfred Engel, "Nachwort [Afterword]," in *Malte*, 331. "Unwählerisches Schauen" and "harte Sachlichkeit" are expressions used by Rilke in "Die Bücher zum wirklichen Leben" (*KA 4*, 652) and his letter to Jakob von Uexküll of August 19, 1909 (*Briefe aus den Jahren 1907–1914*, vol. 3 [Leipzig: Insel Verlag, 1930], 72) respectively. It should be qualified, however, that the expression "harte Sachlichkeit" is employed by Rilke in reference to Uexküll's lack of understanding for the *Neue Gedichte* in comparison to his admiration of Rilke's earlier poetry. Uexküll saw an impersonal character in the *Neue Gedichte* and complained that the poems show no awareness of the reader. Rilke justifies the poems but then confesses that there are perhaps certain deficiencies. It is in this context that Rilke speaks of "harte Sachlichkeit" as well as "lack of feeling" ("Ungefühlsmäßigkeit"). I do not think that "*harte* Sachlichkeit" ("hard matter-of-factness" or "hard objectivity") is a completely adequate characterization of the *Neue Gedichte* nor do the best poems involve a lack of feeling. I would rather speak of an "objectivity of feeling" than a lack of feeling or "hard matter-of-factness." (Later I elaborate the meaning of "Sachlichkeit" and "objectivity.") This said, the quotation from Engel draws out the significance of "impartiality," and "harte Sachlichkeit" in the above passage resonates with the "courage" advocated by Rilke in the preceding quotation and his ideal of a "sachliches Sagen."
108 As it is common practice today to interrogate the political implications of a philosophical concept I would like to say a few words about the objections that might be made to the notions of acceptance and *Gelassenheit* developed

to our previous consideration of "openness" and suggests a relation between impartiality and *Gelassenheit*, in that *Gelassenheit* involves a gesture of acceptance, an allowing or *letting*-be. Without impartiality *Gelassenheit* is not wholly attainable, as a lack of impartiality implies a turning away from certain realities and a resulting imprisonment in the subjective. Thus Rilke claims that the artist's "state of grace" is lost if there is a lack of impartiality.[109] This "state of grace" recalls the privileged disclosure of Nature granted to Rodin—the life of Nature that reveals itself to human beings "when they do not resist."[110]

Under the words "Gelassenheit," "poverty," and "impartiality" a richer picture has been presented of what was intimated in the earlier discussion of the poet's maintenance of a "childlike" openness to things.[111] The artist and poet's manner of being-in-the-world involves the cultivation of an extra-ordinary active-passivity. We always inhabit particular dispositions, and the way in which phenomena and the world reveal themselves is in light of these attunements.[112] However, not all dispositions are equally significant; the cultivation of certain dispositions enables things to reveal themselves more deeply. Both the later Heidegger's emphasis on *Gelassenheit* and Rilke's characterization of "childlikeness," "poverty," "impartiality," and "Gelassenheit" can be understood in this way. Rilke regarded such dispositions as essential to the work of the artist and as enabling a privileged disclosure of the world.[113]

---

in this chapter. One could raise the objection or simply present the view that such an attitude of acceptance and *Gelassenheit* would necessarily imply, in the practical sphere, a political quietism. However, this is an unnecessary conclusion. By "acceptance" and "Gelassenheit" a disposition of mind is meant; the significance of this disposition lies in allowing a phenomenon to show itself in its truth. In so far as this is the case, it does not represent a political quietism, though it would be contrary to rash, impulsive, decisions to political problems. Moreover, I regard this disposition of *Gelassenheit* as essential to a genuine ethic. It is only after first allowing a phenomenon to show itself, reveal its character to us, such that we know what we are dealing with, that a mature practical response is possible. Finally, the humility of *Gelassenheit* is a disposition that contrasts radically with the greed for power and domination that is the root of so much injustice in the world.

109 *LC*, 67. *KA 4*, 624.
110 *AR*, 60; translation altered. *KA 4*, 473.
111 Other prominent and related terms in Rilke that we have not investigated include "solitude" (*Einsamkeit*) and love. However, for our purposes what has been elaborated suffices.
112 See Heidegger, *Sein und Zeit*, 134ff.
113 I regard it as still true today, even after the phenomenological work of Scheler, Heidegger and many others, that our general cultural understanding of "affects," "feelings," "emotions," "moods," etc. is fairly superficial. It is still common, for instance, to think of knowledge and insight as pertaining

Learning to See: Rilke and the Visual Arts   113

How does this notion of active-passivity relate to Rilke's interpretation of Rodin's and Cézanne's artistic processes? Rilke was impressed by the fact that both Rodin and Cézanne drew inspiration from a practice of seeing. As a poet he had felt subject to an unpredictable inspiration that came and went like a breeze. In the example of Rodin and Cézanne he found artists who *worked* consistently, in two different applications of "work." First, work in the sense of a praxis of seeing—"das Werk des Gesichts"—and, second, in the sense of the work of composition or the craft—*Handwerk*.

---

to the intellect but as bearing little relationship to states of mind or dispositions (moreover, through the reach of popular media and the "culture industry" as well as the role of specific technologies in modern communication, superficial moods are more pervasive than ever). We recognize that the passions must be tamed for the intellect to pursue its tasks with clarity but this is about the extent of our common cultural knowledge. We have little understanding of moods as attunements to the world and of the fact that certain insights are not possible without the cultivation of particular states of mind. We see the negative role that certain passions and emotions can have on our cognitive life, but not the *disclosive* (or "positive") character of dispositions. This is most clearly visible in the fact that there is nothing equivalent for the life of "affects" to the sophistication of our intellectual education or *Bildung* (earlier cultural forms such as monastic life at least implicitly involved a *Bildung* of dispositions). Or, to offer another example, think of how unusual it would be for a teacher to say: "you don't understand what I am talking about because you have not attained the requisite state of mind." As I have indicated, the writings of Coriando and Böhme offer a more recent contribution to our understanding of affective life. Another earlier, though within philosophical circles less well-known thinker, who developed an expanded conception of moods and dispositions (at the same time as Max Scheler; they were familiar with each other's work) as necessary for attaining certain insights into the world is Rudolf Steiner (Steiner also attended Franz Brentano's lectures in Vienna). In Steiner's lectures, *Die Welt der Sinne und die Welt des Geistes* [*The World of the Senses and the World of the Spirit*], for instance, he outlines four moods that must be respectively cultivated, in order to arrive at a true knowledge of the world. These moods are: "Staunen, Verehrung, weisheitsvoller Einklang mit den Welterscheinungen, Ergebung in den Weltenlauf ... [wonder, reverence, wisdom-filled harmony with the phenomena of the world, surrender to the course of the world ...]" (Rudolf Steiner, *Die Welt der Sinne und die Welt des Geistes*, Gesamtausgabe, vol. 134, 1979 [1911/12], 27). While Steiner's perspective differs from Heidegger's in a number of respects, for one in that he maintains the traditional metaphysical terms "soul" and "spirit" (in contrast, for instance, to Heidegger's use of *Dasein*), he nevertheless regards moods as essential to truthful insight and as a kind of *world-attunement* in ways that are akin to Heidegger. More recently, Böhme has drawn on aspects of Steiner's and Goethe's theories of color in connection to his elaboration of atmospheres (Gernot Böhme, *Atmosphäre: Essays zur neuen Ästhetik* [Frankfurt am Main: Suhrkamp, 1995], 76–7).

With regard to the first sense, it might seem as though the opposite of a spirit of *Gelassenheit* were implied; namely, the attempt to induce inspiration by a forceful effort of will. However, this work of seeing or vision involves an active-passivity, an activity with a receptive gesture. To regard it as the attempt to "willfully produce" inspiration is a misunderstanding and constitutes a failure to grasp the reality of an activity that is receptive and void of domination. Hermann Meyer in his essay "Rilkes Cézanne-Erlebnis" characterizes Rilke's understanding of perception in relation to an oft-cited letter that he wrote shortly before his intensive engagement with Cézanne:

> Half a year before the "Cézanne-experience," in a letter from March 8 written on Capri, Rilke sought to describe the riddle of this willed "will-lessness" [*willentliche Willenlosigkeit*] and the coincidence [*Ineinssetzung*] of the exterior and the interior. "Seeing [*Das Anschauen*] is such a miraculous matter, concerning which we know so little; in seeing we are completely turned outward, but right when this is the case to the greatest extent, things seem to take place within us, which have longingly waited to be unobserved, and during which they, intact and with strange anonymity, fulfill themselves within us, without us, – their meaning grows in the object outside."[114]

Meyer characterizes this seeing as a willed or deliberate "will-lessness," a "willentliche Willenlosigkeit"; it is an activity with the gesture of passivity. Rilke describes this seeing as an almost anonymous process, as though for the ec-static gaze meaning burgeons in the very thing seen—"wächst in dem Gegenstand draußen ihre Bedeutung heran." The interior meaning of this perception is not granted through introspection but through a kind of looking away from oneself, what could be called an "extro-spection," through an ec-static identification of the gaze with the perceived "object." It is as though this seeing is in-spired by the thing seen, receives its meaning from the thing. Hence, this work of vision can by no means be understood as a mere "willing" or "forcing" of inspiration, which would clearly be a contradiction in terms; it must be conceived as an active submission of the gaze. Perhaps the act of listening to music provides a more readily accessible example of such an intentional gesture; when one is truly attentive to the unfolding of a piece of music, one lets it sound, lets it mean or speak; one is "given over" to the music. (As T. S. Eliot wrote in relation to privileged experiences of music, "you are the music/ while the music

---

114 Hermann Meyer, "Rilkes Cézanne-Erlebnis," in *Zarte Empirie*, 260.

lasts."[115]) This is the essential gesture of the seeing that Rilke regards as vital to Rodin's and Cézanne's (and his own) artistic productivity.

Rodin's Physiognomic Vision

Rodin's perception was a dynamic, physiognomic, and exact vision of things (particularly the animate body) that cannot be understood in dualistic terms. This sub-section is devoted to explicating these key characteristics of Rodin's vision. The French word *modelé* plays an important role in Rilke's understanding of Rodin. Rilke's interpretation of *modelé* has a threefold significance. *Modelé* pertains to Rodin's perception of things, it is the basic principle of sculptural form, and it refers to Rodin's process of sculpting. The present sub-section focuses primarily on the first of these meanings, while in the subsequent sub-section other aspects of *modelé* are considered.

In the early stages of Rilke's personal interaction with Rodin he recounts anecdotes in his letters to Clara Rilke that include discussions of *modelé*. While Rilke, at least in his early letters, is unable to find a suitable translation of the word, as a first indication it could be said that *modelé* designates the modeled surface of things or modeling (but modeling not in a sense that is restricted to plastic works of art). *Modelé* pertains to the expressive character of three-dimensional form, perceived as an interrelation of concave and convex "surfaces." Rilke discusses Rodin's perception of the *modelé* of natural things and the human body:

> Le Modelé ... I know what that means: it is the constitution of planes, as distinct from contours, that which fills out all contours. It is the law and relationship of these planes. You see, for him there is *only* the *modelé* ... on all things, on all bodies ... And what he meant was something like this: What concerns me, that is, what concerns the sculptor par excellence, is not the study or seeing of colors or contours, but that which constitutes sculpture, surfaces ... What must it have been for him when he felt that hitherto no one had looked for this basic principle of sculpture! It was his to find: thousands of things offered it to him: above all the naked body.[116]

---

115 T. S. Eliot, "Four Quartets," in *The Complete Poems and Plays* (London: Faber and Faber, 1969), 190.
116 Rilke, *Selected Letters 1902–1926*, trans. R. F. C. Hull (London: Quartet Books, 1988), 8–9; translation altered. Rainer Maria Rilke and Auguste Rodin, *Der Briefwechsel und andere Dokumente zu Rilkes Begegnung mit Rodin*, ed. Rätus Luck (Frankfurt am Main: Insel Verlag, 2001), 47–8. From now on *Der Briefwechsel und andere Dokumente zu Rilkes Begegnung mit Rodin* will be referenced as *AR dt*.

116 The Poet as Phenomenologist

Rodin's basic way of perceiving the world is closely tied to his art (but this does not imply that the two moments cannot be distinguished for the purpose of conceptual clarity). The language of *form* is of utmost importance to a sculptor. However, this does not yet describe the basic constituents of form and is a bit like saying that painting concerns figures and shapes. Just as the fundamental elements of painting are *colors and their relations*, so the basic constituents of sculpture are *surfaces and their relations* as constitutive of form. However, Rodin perceives these surfaces in a specific manner. While a surface can be regarded as two-dimensional, Rodin views surfaces as the outer limits of a depth or volume. This is intimated by Rilke's statement that the *modelé* is that which "fills out all contours" and is clearly expressed by Rodin's following characterization: "When you model [*modelez*], never think in surface, but in relief. Your spirit must conceive of every surface [*superficie*] as the extremity of a volume that pushes from behind. Picture the forms as if they were pointing toward you."[117]

In this description from *Le Testament*—a brief text by Rodin that was discovered shortly after his death (1917)—Rodin advises sculptors to regard surfaces as the limit of a volume and as directed toward the viewer, as opposed to seeing them in merely two-dimensional terms.[118] This view of *modelé* was intimately connected to Rodin's conception of the *life* of natural things. Thus he states that, "All life emerges from a center, then it germinates and blossoms from inside to outside."[119] In the *modelé* Rodin perceives a lawful manifestation of the life of Nature which is at the same time the language of sculpture. Rilke recounts how Rodin held up a snail's shell and proclaimed, "Voilà le modelé grec."[120] Rodin sees all things according to the *modelé*, which is at the same time the basic principle of his art. He learns the principle of his art from the world, and his art informs his perception of the world.

The description of *modelé* as constitutive of form might seem to imply a static conception of form. However, Rodin was primarily concerned with *life*, which he regarded as essentially in *motion* and *dynamic*. Speaking for Rodin, Rilke states,

> There was no such thing as calm, not even in death; for in decay, which is also movement, even what was dead was still

---

117 Auguste Rodin, *Das Testament* (*Le Testament*) (Überlingen: Werner Wulff Verlag, 1946). This edition has no page numbers.
118 Rodin also regarded this understanding of *modelé* as the secret of ancient Greek sculpture, which he mentions shortly after the next quotation from *Le Testament*.
119 Rodin, *Das Testament*.
120 AR dt, 48.

subordinate to life. In Nature there was only movement; and an art that wished to give a credible interpretation of life, might not take for its ideal a calm which was non-existent.[121]

In the previous sub-section we discussed Rodin's general attunement to the life of Nature. In the above excerpt this "life" assumes a more definite meaning. "Life" refers primarily to natural and human processes and the expressive meaning that is revealed in dynamic forms. While *modelé* may initially seem to imply the static arrangement of concave and convex surfaces, Rodin regarded the *modelé* of things in dynamic terms. *Modelé* concerns the expressive significance of momentary gestures and features. This is evident in Rilke's rhetorical questions, which could easily pass for a passage from a text by Merleau-Ponty:[122] "let us for a moment consider whether everything before us, everything we observe, explain, and interpret, does not consist simply of surfaces? And what we call mind and soul and love: are these things not only a slight transformation on the small surface of our neighbour's face?"[123]

The *surfaces* of the face are seen in their slight transformations and momentary movements. These convey an expressive significance in which we perceive "mind and soul and love." In short, *modelé* refers to the perception of three-dimensional form in terms of a dynamic and expressive interrelation of surfaces.

Rilke and others who personally knew Rodin admired his avid observation of all natural beings and his participation in the life of Nature.[124] However, what was most central to Rodin, as is evident from his sculptures, was the *modelé* of the human body. For Rodin, the word "Nature" is as comprehensive as the word "Being" and could be regarded as a synonym of Being (but with the specific connotations

---

121 *AR*, 12. *KA 4*, 417. In connection to the centrality of the concept of "life" in Rodin's views, J. A. Schmoll speaks of an intrinsic affinity between Rodin and Bergson. J. A. Schmoll, *Rodin-Studien*, 94.
122 Consider, for instance, the following statement from Merleau-Ponty's essay, "Cézanne's Doubt": "Other minds are given to us as incarnate, as belonging to faces and gestures. Countering with the distinctions of soul and body, thought and vision is of no use here, for Cézanne returns to just that primordial experience from which these notions are derived and in which they are inseparable." Merleau-Ponty, "Cézanne's Doubt," in *The Merleau-Ponty Aesthetics Reader: Philosophy and Painting*, ed. Galen A. Johnson and Michael B. Smith (Evanston, IL: Northwestern University Press, 1993 [1945]), 66.
123 *AR*, 46; translation altered. *KA 4*, 458.
124 This is evident in Rilke's accounts. See also Auguste Rodin, *Rodin on Art and Artists: Conversations with Paul Gsell*, trans. Romilly Fedden (New York: Dover Publications, 1983); Helene Nostitz, *Rodin in Gesprächen und Briefen* (Dresden: Wolfgang Jess Verlag, 1949 [1927]).

that are carried by "Nature" in contrast to the more indeterminate character of "Being".[125] For this reason, Rodin regards the human body as a pre-eminent manifestation of Nature and he perceives no significant rift between the natural and the human.[126] Nevertheless, the consideration of Rodin's physiognomic perception of the living human body will involve a certain restriction in light of our broader concerns. However, many characteristics pertaining to Rodin's perception of the human being will prove significant to our later consideration of other-than-human Nature.

A keen and disciplined observation of human models was central to Rodin's artistic process. Two pertinent features of Rodin's perception of models are its dynamic, physiognomic character and its exactitude. By "physiognomic" I mean that it involves an understanding of expressive meaning.[127] However, this physiognomic vision is significantly *dynamic*. Rodin does not pursue a science of physiognomy that seeks to isolate static features and correlate them with psychological qualities. Rather, his vision is concerned with the *living moment* of expression and is dynamic in a twofold sense. The "object" or noema of this vision is fundamentally *in movement* and *temporal*, and the act of seeing or noesis is concentrated on the *living present* of this noema. The formulation "dynamic physiognomic vision" taken as a whole

---

125 Rodin's all-encompassing conception of Nature is reminiscent of Goethe. See also n. 121.

126 Rodin also saw the human body in terms of correspondences and analogies with other natural beings and phenomena. This is expressed, for instance, in the *modelé* of his sculptures which often resemble and have been compared to the surfaces of natural phenomena. There is moreover a cosmological dimension to Rodin's artistic worldview, which is mentioned by various authors, including Rilke, Gsell, Nostitz, and Schmoll. We will not explore these aspects of Rodin's work in detail, though they are not insignificant with regard to Rilke, whose poetry often involves analogies between the natural and the human as well as cosmological aspects (these features of Rilke's work are discussed in Chapter 4). The following record of Rodin's words by Nostitz offers an example of the cosmological aspect: "The body of the human being is a temple and has heavenly forms" (*Rodin in Gesprächen und Briefen*, 41). With a similarly cosmological sense Rilke says of the *modelé* and central *planes* of Rodin's sculptures: "the given details are brought together in strongly marked surface-units, until finally they adjust themselves, as if under the influence of rotating forces, in a number of great planes, and we get the impression that these planes are part of the universe [*Himmel-Globus*] and could be continued into infinity" (*AR*, 51. *KA 4*, 463).

127 Rodin's physiognomic vision is continuous with our consideration of the *expressive Leib* in the previous chapter. However, Rodin's highly *schooled* and *cultivated* physiognomic vision can be regarded as a *refinement* and *deepening* of the kind of seeing that is operative in our common perception of Others in the life-world.

thus refers to an act of seeing that divines the significance of *expressive movement*. Furthermore, as will be illustrated, this seeing is *exact*.

Rilke offers many examples of Rodin's devoted and diligent perception of models. Speaking of Rodin's preparations for his sculptures of Victor Hugo, Rilke writes, "For the figure of the poet himself Rodin made many studies. Hidden in a window niche of the Hôtel Lusignan during Victor Hugo's receptions, he observed and noted down hundreds upon hundreds of the aged poet's movements and every expression of his animated countenance."[128]

Rodin, of course, did not usually need to be so surreptitious in his observations (at this time he was still an unknown sculptor). The study of models through observation and drawing played a crucial role in his creative process. Rodin often received inspiration for his sculptural works through the revelations of momentary gestures and poses of his models. Generally he did not arrange his models in preconceived poses; rather, he let the models move freely around the studio until he caught sight of a particularly expressive gesture.[129] In *Auguste Rodin* (First Part) Rilke describes this as follows: "Rodin had the theory that if unapparent movements made by the model, when the latter believes himself or herself to be unobserved, were caught rapidly, they would contain a vividness of expression which we do not surmise [*ahnen*] because we are not accustomed to follow them with keen alert attention ..."[130] In his attentiveness Rodin discovers the expressive significance of a momentary gesture which he immediately seeks to translate onto the page. A little later Rilke writes:

> He catches his model unawares, in habitual or accidental attitudes, under the stress of effort and whilst prey to lassitude, seizing every incipient expression. He knows every transitory expression of feature, knows whence comes the smile and whither it departs. He lives through a human face as through the scene of a drama in which he himself takes part; his place is in the midst of it, and nothing that occurs is indifferent to him or escapes him. He refuses to be told anything about the person, he wants to know only what he sees. But he sees everything.[131]

The dynamic physiognomic character of Rodin's study of models is clearly discernible in the above; Rodin "knows every transitory expression of feature." The ec-static, participative disposition of this

---

128 *AR*, 32. *KA 4*, 439.
129 *Rodin on Art and Artists*, 10ff.
130 *AR*, 26; translation altered. *KA 4*, 432.
131 *AR*, 30. *KA 4*, 436.

120   The Poet as Phenomenologist

vision is also clearly articulated in the analogy of the human face with a drama in which he "takes part" and "is in the midst of." This vision is given over to its "object"; one could say that it is *there*, with that which it sees. The comprehensive nature of this seeing is summed up in the final sentence with "he sees everything." The other prominent feature of this vision is its *exactitude*. With regard to Rilke's estimation of exactitude we might recall the statement from *Malte*, "Er war ein Dichter und haßte das Ungefähre [He was a poet and hated the approximate]."[132] The *detailed* character and *exactitude* of Rodin's vision are tersely formulated in the statement that "nothing that occurs is indifferent to him or escapes him." Rodin's seeing of his models differs greatly from Rilke's characterization of his own earlier perception of Nature as the reception of a vague inspiration. Rodin is alert to every movement and feature of the models. However, the exactitude of this gaze does not reduce what it perceives to the status of an inanimate object; it is not the objectifying and analytic gaze of the scientist that "murders to dissect." This vision is simultaneously *physiognomic, participational, and exact*.

The dynamic, physiognomic exactitude of Rodin's vision can be further explicated in relation to the *modelé* of the human body. Earlier we considered Rilke's characterization of *modelé* in terms of "surfaces" that are expressive of psychological and spiritual meanings ("mind and soul and love"). It should also be recalled that Rodin regarded these surfaces as the limit of a volume. Elsewhere Rodin connects this perception of the surface in depth to an awareness of the expression of muscles on the surfaces of the body. While Paul Gsell's record of Rodin's words in the following account concerns the *modelé* of sculptures, it also pertains to Rodin's perception of models:

> Instead of imagining the different parts of a body as surfaces more or less flat, I represented them as projectures of interior volumes. I forced myself to express in each swelling of the torso or of the limbs the efflorescence of a muscle or of a bone which lay deep beneath the skin.[133]

Gsell refers to Rodin's perception of "muscles in movement" as follows:

> In this way he has learned to read the feelings as expressed in every part of the body. The face is generally considered as the only mirror of the soul; the mobility of the features of the face seems to us the only exterior expression of the spiritual life. In reality there is not a muscle of the body which does not express

---

132   *KA 4*, 572.
133   *Rodin on Art and Artists*, 22.

the inner variations of feeling. All speak of joy or of sorrow, of enthusiasm or of despair, of serenity or of madness. Outstretched arms, an unconstrained body, smile with as much sweetness as the eyes or the lips.[134]

The truth of this statement can be ascertained through a simple observation. When I am in a tense "state of mind" this comes to expression at the same time in the tension of my muscles. When I am inwardly relaxed my muscles are at the same time more relaxed. Thus it is obvious that the appearance of the muscles of a person can be "read" physiognomically and, moreover, that this applies for every detail of the body. As Rodin states, "in a running man, not only the legs but the whole body takes part in the action, helping the legs; in sleep, it is the whole body which relaxes, rests, not only the head."[135] Rodin's schooled perception discerned the expressive significance in the smallest and most exact details.

In this discussion of *exactitude* it is important to take the opportunity to consider the related concept of "objectivity." The value of "objectivity" is often ascribed to the middle Rilke;[136] however, this word should be applied with caution and qualification. Rilke clearly appreciated an "objectivity" in Rodin's seeing. However, the artist's vision has nothing to do with the "objectifying" thought of science that was discussed in the previous chapter. One of the benefits of our common understanding of artistic vision lies in the fact that we would never naïvely assume, as we do with respect to scientific observation, that artistic perception concerns a pure in-itself which is detachable from *human participation*. Thus, artistic vision cannot be "objective" in the sense of "objectifying" science or metaphysics. The word "objectivity" is also suggestive of "physicality." However, in the case of Rilke and Rodin "objectivity" cannot be understood in this reductive and superficial sense. This *reductive* sense is constitutive of the modern natural-scientific view that only those properties that count as "physical" are "objective"—for instance, the size, mass, and shape of something (or if the primary/secondary quality distinction is rejected, the color and smell of things as well). This scientific gaze reduces what it sees to the status of an *inanimate* object. If Rodin's vision (or Rilke's vision) is to be called "objective," then this has to mean that it involves a revelation of the

---

134 *Rodin on Art and Artists*, 10.
135 Auguste Rodin, "Rodin's Reflections on Art," recorded by Henri Charles Étienne Dujardin-Beaumetz, trans. Ann McGarrell, in *Auguste Rodin: Readings on his Life and Work*, ed. Albert Elsen (Englewood Cliffs, NJ: Prentice Hall, 1965), 172.
136 This ascription of objectivity is connected to a number of statements by Rilke as well as to characteristics of his poems. See, for instance, the consideration of "sachliches Sagen" later in this chapter and the discussion of Rilke's "Dinggedichte" in Chapter 4.

"things themselves," a revelation in which, however, more is revealed than what reductionism and science would allow.[137] While the "physical properties" that most concern a sculptural perception of things are the "surfaces" rather than colors, sounds, or smells, these surfaces are perceived in their *expressive* significance. Moreover, Rodin's vision is *exact*, but not in the sense of an analysis of merely "physical" properties; rather, it discovers a *physiognomic* or *expressive* significance in every detail. It shares the characteristic of *exactitude* with scientific observation but it does not reduce what it perceives to a lifeless object. In addition to being dynamic, physiognomic and exact Rodin's gaze is also *participative* rather than detached; it immerses itself in the phenomena. Thus, the word "objectivity" is only appropriate to the middle Rilke's understanding of perception and art if these qualifications are kept in mind.

In addition, "objectivity" has the connotation of truth. The opposite of "objective" is "subjective" in the sense of "merely subjective." The "subjective" is what pertains to personal experience but not to the world. Rodin's vision is certainly not "subjective" in this sense. His dynamic physiognomic vision is directed toward a deeper, non-reductive truth— an *essence* or *character*. In *Le Testament* Rodin claims that "Everything is beautiful for the artist as in every being and in every thing his penetrating gaze discovers the character, that is, the interior truth which shines within the form."[138] In his conversations with Gsell, Rodin emphasizes that the artist perceives the invisible animating spirit of Nature through its exterior. Rodin, as recounted by Gsell, states the following:

> It is a general belief that we [artists] live only through our senses, and that the world of appearances suffices us. We are taken for children who, intoxicated with changing colors, amuse themselves with the shapes of things as with dolls. We are misunderstood. Lines and colors are only to us the symbols of hidden realities. Our eyes plunge beneath the surface to the meaning of things, and when afterwards we reproduce the form, we endow it with the spiritual meaning which it covers.
>
> An artist worthy of the name should express all the truth of nature, not only the exterior truth, but also, and above all, the inner truth.
>
> When a good sculptor models a torso, he not only represents the muscles, but the life which animates them—more than the

---

137 The German word *Sachlichkeit* which Rilke often employs is, in this sense, less misleading than "objectivity"; *Sachlichkeit* suggests a vision that is adequate to the "things themselves" or "matters themselves." See the later discussion of Cézanne.
138 Rodin, *Das Testament*.

life, the force that fashioned them and communicated to them, it may be, grace or strength, or amorous charm, or indomitable will.[139]

Rodin's perception ultimately discovers the invisible animating principles or the life of forms; through a devoted attention to the "surface" an invisible depth is revealed. Rodin's physiognomic vision is clearly non-dualistic. Through attending to the visible, the *invisible side of the visible*, the animating principle of the visible, is revealed.

As a way of summarizing and further articulating the key differences between a vaguely inspired seeing (such as Rilke's earlier experience of Nature), the gaze of the scientist that "murders to dissect," and Rodin's artistic vision, I would like to offer a musical analogy. Someone with a musically untrained ear might hear a symphony and be deeply moved by it; this person senses the expressive whole, but only discerns the main motifs and melodies; this listener is unable to follow the complex interrelation of all the parts but receives a vague and lively impression of the whole. Another person with a trained musical ear may be able to follow every detail of the music but in the act of analysis lose a sense for its expressive and meaningful character; the piece of music is reduced to an object of analysis and the listener objectifies, rather than participates in, the music. The third possibility suggests a higher synthesis of the first and the second case; this applies to the person who can follow the expressive character of the music right into the different parts, feel how each part contributes to and is a development of the whole, and how an aspect of the whole comes to expression in each part. This third level is characteristic of the great composer, virtuoso musician, conductor, and ideal listener. This third level includes analysis and exactitude, but without "murdering" the vibrant appearance in order to take cognizance of the details. This corresponds to Rodin's manner of seeing his models—in the smallest details he lights on an expressive meaning.

From Ding to Kunst-Ding: *The Translation of Vision into the Sculptural Work of Art*

In both Rodin's and Cézanne's artistic work Rilke observed an intimate connection between a twofold seeing and artistic composition. Now that Rodin's dynamic physiognomic vision of his models has been sketched, we will focus on how this vision is translated into his sculptural work. Within the broader context of this book, the most pertinent concern at this moment is Rilke's view of the relation between *Ding* (thing) and

---

139 *Rodin on Art and Artists*, 80.

124   The Poet as Phenomenologist

Kunst-Ding (art-thing).[140] For our purposes *Ding* can be regarded as a synonym for "model" and, in the case of Rodin, *Kunst-Ding* implies sculpture.[141] The relation between *Ding* and *Kunst-Ding* is thus the relation between the model and the work, and in the case of portraiture which will be given special attention, the relation between the person and the portrait. Considered from the "I-pole"—from the vantage point of the artist's creative process, in contrast to the "objective" connection between the artwork and the world—the relation between *Ding* and *Kunst-Ding* involves the translation of perception into artistic composition. Drawing on the *perception of a thing* (*Ding*) the artist proceeds to *create an "art-thing"* (*Kunst-Ding*). Under the rubric of *Ding* and *Kunst-Ding* the relation between the model and the work, perception and artistic creation, will be explicated. In addition, consideration will be given to the holistic character of the work of art, Rodin's reinterpretation of the fragment, and further senses of *modelé*.[142] The discussion below highlights those aspects of Rodin's oeuvre that are pertinent to my reading of Rilke (little consideration is given to Rodin's more allegorical and symbolic works).[143]

In a letter which was, in part, previously discussed, Rilke draws a connection between the *modelé* of things and the *modelé* of sculptural works: "You see, for him there is *only* the *modelé* ... on all things, on all

---

140 The relation between *Ding* and *Kunst-Ding* elaborated here will be significant for our later consideration of Rilke's poetry. Many of Rilke's *Neue Gedichte* have been considered under the category *Dinggedicht* or "thing-poem." The character of Rilke's *Dinggedichte* can be illumined through understanding what is entailed in his distinction between *Ding* and *Kunst-Ding* in the case of Rodin. The *Dinggedicht* can be regarded as a species of *Kunst-Ding* (although, among other significant differences, a work of sculpture clearly has a "thingly" character to a greater extent than the more elusive, temporal existence of a poem). The notion of the *Dinggedicht* is discussed in more detail in Chapter 4.

141 Rilke was not a systematic thinker and is not consistent in his terminology, but for our purposes it is important to explicate his views in a more consistent and systematic manner. Rilke sometimes uses the word *Ding* to mean *Kunst-Ding*, whereas we will use the word *Ding* as a synonym for "model" and things other than works of art. This said, Rilke's use of *Ding* to mean *Kunst-Ding* can also be philosophically justified as the *Kunst-Ding* for Rilke, as we will see, is the most exemplary *Ding*.

142 Rilke's own use of "models" and the concept of portraiture will also prove to be essential to our understanding of Rilke.

143 For a more encompassing and detailed consideration of Rodin's work, see J. A. Schmoll's *Rodin-Studien*. While Rodin often only named his sculptures after the fact and even his more symbolic works often arose due to some immediate inspiration from the model, rather than through a theme that was chosen in advance, the more allegorical works, by virtue of their titles, suggest a less immediate relation to their models than portraits do. See Rodin, "Rodin's Reflections on Art," 163ff.

bodies, he detaches it from them, and after he has learnt it from them he makes of it an independent entity, that is a work of sculpture, a work of plastic art."[144] Rodin sees all things according to their *modelé* but he also makes an "independent entity" of the *modelé*. While all three-dimensional things can be seen in terms of their *modelé*, they do not usually consist solely of *modelé*. One can focus entirely on a person's *modelé*, but this entails the exclusion of other modes of appearance, such as the person's tone of voice or scent. In contrast, sculpture involves the creation of a new being that is constituted solely by its *modelé*. However, if the character of a person already comes to expression in the *modelé*, why does Rodin not fashion sculptures in the manner of perceptual realism or naturalism? The answer to this question has a number of facets.

To begin with, it is instructive to note that were a sculpture a mere copy of the model then it would be superfluous and actually reveal less than the model due to the essential limitations of the artistic medium. For Rilke, as will be seen, the *modelé* of the *Kunst-Ding* is a *perfection* of the *modelé* of the thing. This is because there is still contingency in the *modelé* of things whereas the *modelé* of the *Kunst-Ding* must contain no contingency, and departs from the *modelé* of things through achieving greater *perfection* and *necessity*. There are two particularly relevant aspects in which the *Kunst-Ding* perfects the *modelé*. The first aspect, which pertains to a feature of the *modelé* not yet elaborated, concerns the occupation of space and modulations of light and shadow. Rilke states the following (in one of his most famous passages on the relation between *Ding* and *Kunst-Ding*) in this regard:

> No movement misleads him anymore, since he knows that in the rise and fall [*Auf und Ab*] of a calm surface there is also movement and since he only sees surfaces and systems of surfaces that clearly and exactly determine forms. Because there is nothing uncertain for him in an object [*Gegenstand*] that serves him as a model [*Vorbild*]: there, a thousand small surface-elements are fitted into space and when he creates an artwork his task is: to integrate the thing more deeply, more firmly, a thousand times better into vast space, so that, so to speak, it does not budge if one shakes it.[145]

By a "thing" or *Ding* Rilke means a three-dimensional thing that appears in space, and more specifically, Rodin's models. The unique way in which things appear in space is intimately connected to how they catch

---

144   Rilke, *Selected Letters 1902–1926*, 8–9. *AR dt*, 48.
145   *AR dt*, 78.

the light through the angles and textures of the surfaces (while Rilke does not mention light specifically in the above passage he discusses its significance in numerous other places[146]). However, the *modelé* of the sculpture must be more perfect than that of spatial things; in Rodin's sculptures every surface has been shaped to enable the sculpture to stand securely in space and to catch light and shadow in particular ways. Relative to the sculptures, other things are more contingent in the manner in which they occupy space. There is moreover a significant temporal difference between *Ding* and *Kunst-Ding*. Whereas the appearance of a thing is transient, the sculptural work of art assumes a more enduring spatial existence. The following passage can serve to introduce a further respect in which the *modelé* of the sculpture exceeds that of the thing:

> It [the *modelé*] was his to find: thousands of things offered it to him: above all the naked body. It was his to transpose, that is to turn it into *his* expression, to accustom himself to saying *everything* through the *modelé* and *not otherwise*. Here, you see, is the second essential point in this great artist's life. The first was that he had discovered a new fundamental element of his art, the second, that he desired nothing more of life than to express himself and everything he possessed [*alles Seine*] entirely through this element.[147]

The clue here is that Rodin had to learn to say *everything* through the *modelé* and nothing else. This statement has a very broad significance. It can be applied to Rodin's entire oeuvre and paraphrased by saying that whatever theme Rodin wished to express, he sought to communicate through the language, and more specifically the *modelé*, of the human body. Thus, Rilke's characterization is as equally applicable to Rodin's treatment of myth and allegory as it is to his portraiture. However, it is the latter that is most pertinent to our concerns.

We assume that the task of portraiture is to express and disclose, through the visibility of the artwork, the personality, character, nature, or genius of the person portrayed. In ordinary life we get to know a person from many different angles—through a person's appearance, gestures, tone of voice, thoughts, and behavior in various contexts, etc. (see Chapter 1). Through various elements and senses the character of a person, to a certain degree, becomes manifest for us. The sculpted portrait, in contrast to the living person, can only address two of our senses—primarily sight, but also touch. In the life-world a person is

---

146 See, for instance, *AR*, 7, 45, 50. *KA* 4, 411, 457–8, 462; *AR dt*, 48–49.
147 Rilke, *Selected Letters 1902–1926*, 9–10; translation altered. *AR dt*, 48.

manifest through various avenues, whereas sculpture is limited to gesture and form, and must ultimately express *everything* through *modelé*. As aforementioned, the language of a work of art is a reduced language and it is now evident that this language is burdened with the paradoxical task of saying more with less. To put things more succinctly: the *invisible* that is manifest through multiple avenues in the living person must be said solely through *modelé* in the sculpture. However, if the *modelé* of the person is one of the avenues through which the invisible is disclosed, it is not yet apparent why the *modelé* of the sculpture should be anything more than a copy of the *modelé* of the person or model. The reason the sculpture must be more than a copy is because of contingencies at the expressive level. Just as contingencies in the way a *thing* inhabits space must be exceeded by sculpture, contingencies of expression must be surpassed.

In a person's appearance more disclosive and less disclosive elements can be discerned. A certain gesture, for instance, might typify a person, whereas a certain bodily mark or creases in clothes will reveal little or nothing. If Rodin were simply to copy the *modelé* of the model, then contingency would remain in the artwork. The artist grasps the invisible (character, for instance) that comes to partial expression in the visible. However, the visibility of the artwork must be even more expressive of the invisible than the visibility of the original. The artwork is thus akin to a further development or evolution of the tendency already operative in the original to manifest the invisible in the visible. A certain gesture is distinctive of a person; the sculptor learns from this and models this feature into the sculpture. However, other features of the model are less expressive and more contingent. In the sculpture nothing can be contingent. Every feature must contribute toward making the invisible visible. Therefore, every surface in its relation to other surfaces must be essential to the entire expression. Rodin thus states that "all the features must be expressive—that is to say, of use in the revelation of a conscience."[148] This is the second respect in which the *modelé* of the sculpture surpasses that of the original. Moreover, these considerations reveal how Rilke's aesthetics in his middle period occupies a position that is neither a form of perceptual realism nor a form of abstraction (in the strong sense).[149]

---

148 *Rodin on Art and Artists*, 54.
149 While he followed the ground-breaking developments in the visual arts in the early decades of the twentieth century, Rilke, even in his late period, was never wholly sympathetic to abstract art. Cézanne remained his supreme example because Cézanne maintained a balance between an independent artistic language and a commitment to Nature and "objective" representation. This point of view is evident, for instance, in Rilke's response to the works of Paul Klee. See Rilke, *Rainer Maria Rilke: Über moderne Malerei*, ed.

In his conversations with Gsell and Dujardin-Beaumetz, Rodin often sounds like he has a realist conception of sculpture. Gsell questions Rodin on this matter and it becomes evident that Rodin regards Nature (in his encompassing sense of the word) as possessing a visible and invisible side. The task of the artist is not to copy the visible, but to make the invisible more visible than it is otherwise. According to Rodin the artist *sees* the invisible and seeks to make it manifest, and in this light he contrasts his sculptures to what a cast of a model (the most perfect copy) might offer: "the cast only reproduces the exterior; I reproduce, besides that, the spirit which is certainly also a part of nature."[150]

In so far as the relation between *Ding* and *Kunst-Ding* (in the case of portraiture, the person and the portrait) pertains to the relation between the invisible and the visible, essence and appearance, the following comparison is instructive. The animate body (*Leib*) is disclosive of the personality; in other words, the soul comes to expression in the body. However, as was demonstrated, it does not come to perfect expression—contingency remains. In this sense, the creation of the work of art (the portrait) can be conceived as the creation of a more perfect body. Of course, the personality or person cannot literally inhabit this body like a living body. However, in this "more perfect body" it attains a more complete *visible* manifestation of its essence. It is for this reason that the work of art, according to Rilke, neither falls under the category of realism nor abstraction. *The work of art is a further development of an inherent principle in the original or the model, namely, to manifest the invisible in the visible.* The movement from *Ding* to *Kunst-Ding* is thus akin to a movement of progressive incarnation. I say "akin," because the personality cannot literally inhabit the work of art in the way in which it is operative in the living body.

At this point it is illuminating to consider Rilke's most succinct formulation of the relation between *Ding* and *Kunst-Ding*.

The thing is defined, the art-thing [*Kunst-Ding*] must be more defined; freed of all chance and indistinctness, removed from time and given space, it becomes lasting, capable for eternity. The model [*Modell*] seems, the art-thing is. So is the one the nameless

---

Martina Krießbach-Thomasberger (Frankfurt am Main: Insel Verlag, 2000), 117–19; Hermann Meyer, "Die Verwandlung des Sichtbaren: Die Bedeutung der modernen bildenen Kunst für Rilkes späte Dichtung." Elsewhere, I have discussed Rilke's close connections to the work of Franz Marc, both in their balance of figuration and abstraction and in their shared interest in animals. Luke Fischer, "Animalising Art: Rainer Maria Rilke and Franz Marc," 45–60; "Die Animalisierung der Kunst: Rainer Maria Rilke und Franz Marc," 335–48.
150 *Rodin on Art and Artists*, 11.

progression beyond the other, the silent and increased realization of the wish to be, which emanates from everything in Nature.[151]

Both in its occupation of space and time and in its disclosure of an invisible essence in every aspect, the sculptural work of art surpasses the thing by bringing its *modelé* to a superior degree of realization. This view does not elevate art above Nature through opposing the two, but rather through regarding the work of art as the higher fulfillment of a principle immanent in Nature.[152]

Having sketched in broad outlines the relation between *Ding* and *Kunst-Ding*, the model and the work of art, we will now consider in more detail how this translation is realized in Rodin's work. In the previous sub-section the dynamic character of Rodin's twofold vision was indicated, namely its attentiveness to the living present and fleeting gestures. This raises the question: How can the static medium of sculpture present *movement*? Rodin's solutions to this problem illustrate basic ways in which he surpasses perceptual realism. Perhaps the most obvious solution to this problem is manifest in *The Walking Man* (*L'Homme qui marche*), whose left leg is significantly longer than his right and thus enables the sculpture to lean forward with both feet on the ground and thereby suggests the temporal motion of walking. Merleau-Ponty comments on these matters in his essay, "Eye and Mind" ("L'Œil et l'esprit") (his description is more or less a paraphrase of Rodin's words in Gsell's account):[153]

> Movement, is given, says Rodin, by an image in which the arms, the legs, the trunk, and the head are each taken at a different instant, an image which therefore portrays the body in an attitude which it never at any instant really held and which imposes fictive linkages between the parts, as if this mutual confrontation

---

151 *AR dt*, 78.
152 The poem "Gesang der Frauen an den Dichter" in the *Neue Gedichte* thematizes this idea in its own way. *KA 1*, 461. From an ecocritical perspective, Kate Rigby has discussed some of the concerns raised by this kind of view (Rigby focuses on related views in Romanticism and Heidegger) of the relation between nature and art (*Topographies of the Sacred*, 92ff.). The main concern is that if art is conceived as superior to Nature then it could be regarded as more valuable than, and as a substitute for, Nature. Here is not the place for a detailed response to this concern (and it should be said that, in significant respects, I share Rigby's concern). Nevertheless, I think this issue can be diminished through an emphasis on the deep *relationship* between (and co-dependence of) Nature and art that this kind of view implies. See also Chapter 4, n. 34 and Fischer, "Animalising Art: Rainer Maria Rilke and Franz Marc."
153 See *Rodin on Art and Artists*, 32ff.

130   The Poet as Phenomenologist

of incompossibles could—and alone could—cause transition and duration to arise in bronze and on canvas.[154]

This is precisely the case for Rodin's *Saint John the Baptist* (*Saint Jean-Baptiste*)—a "non-fragmentary" work related to *The Walking Man*—and in principle holds for the armless and headless "Walking Man."[155] Merleau-Ponty proceeds to argue that painting and sculpture can thus reveal the world more truthfully than the photograph (earlier he also argues for the superiority of painting and sculpture over cinema). In the development of this thought, he again draws on Rodin:

> When a horse is photographed at that instant when he is completely off the ground, with his legs almost folded under him—an instant, therefore, when he must be moving—why does he look as if he were leaping in space? And why, by contrast, do Gericault's horses really *run* on canvas, in a posture impossible for a real horse at a gallop? It is because the horses in *Epsom Derby* bring me to see the body's grip upon the ground and that, according to a logic of body and world I know well, these "grips" upon space are also ways of taking hold of duration. Rodin said profoundly, "It is the artist who is truthful, while the photograph lies; for, in reality, time never stops." The photograph keeps open the instants which the onrush of time closes up forthwith; it destroys the overtaking, the overlapping, the "metamorphosis" [Rodin] of time. This is what painting, in contrast, makes visible, because the horses have in them that "leaving here, going there," because they have a foot in each instant.[156]

The same can be said of Rodin's headless "Walking Man," namely that he has a "foot in each instant," and thus can express the *movement* of walking.[157] Rodin defines movement as "the transition from one attitude to another" and his sculptures are able to manifest *transition* by suggesting the movement between two poses, or from one pose to another.[158]

---

154 Merleau-Ponty, "Eye and Mind," in *The Merleau-Ponty Aesthetics Reader: Philosophy and Painting*, 145.
155 For a detailed elaboration of the relation between *The Walking Man* and *Saint John the Baptist* see Werner Schnell, *Der Torso als Problem der modernen Kunst* (Berlin: Gebr. Mann Verlag, 1980), 25ff.
156 Merleau-Ponty, "Eye and Mind," 145.
157 Rilke refers to this sculpture as "that walking figure, which stands like a new word for the action of walking in the vocabulary of your feeling." AR, 47. KA 4, 459.
158 *Rodin on Art and Artists*, 32.

Learning to See: Rilke and the Visual Arts 131

However, Rodin also brought expressive movement into his sculptures in more subtle ways. Later in a previously (partially) quoted passage from *Auguste Rodin* (First Part) Rilke relates the connection between what I have designated Rodin's "dynamic physiognomic vision" and his sculpting of portraits.

> Rodin had the theory that if unapparent movements made by the model, when the latter believes himself or herself to be unobserved, were caught rapidly, they would contain a vividness of expression which we do not surmise because we are not accustomed to follow them with keen alert attention ... So, too, with portraits ... For, mistaken as it is to see in his plastic art a form of Impressionism, it was none the less the mass of exact and boldly seized impressions which provided him with the wealth of material from which he finally selected what was important and necessary, in order to unite it in mature synthesis [*um es in reifer Synthese zusammenzufassen*].[159]

Rodin's self-less gaze, his detailed study of his models, enables him to take note of gestures that are essentially expressive of the person. He can then sculpt the equivalent gestures in order to bring the essence to visibility in the sculpture. A good example of this view in the case of portraiture can be found in Rilke's letter to Samuel Fischer of April 19, 1906. There, in recounting Rodin's process of sculpting a portrait of George Bernard Shaw, Rilke states that Shaw's "entire being [*Wesen*] leaps into the bust from that spot [a part of Shaw's body], feature by feature with astonishingly increased intensity ..."[160] Rodin transfers the *essential* features of the model into the sculpture, such that the essence (*Wesen*) of the original comes to manifestation in the sculpture itself.

These essential gestures and features were often taken from many different moments (as is indicated from the block quotation above) and united in the sculptural portrait. In the features of a face, for instance, Rodin would combine expressions that could not occur at the same time. In this way the *life* and biography of the person were made manifest in the static medium of sculpture. The portrait is not merely the record of a moment in time, but a synthesis of many moments. Rilke writes,

> This mode of work leads to tremendous creations composed of hundreds upon hundreds of vital moments [*Lebensmomente*]: and such is, indeed, the impression we receive from these busts. The

---

159 *AR*, 26; translation altered. *KA* 4, 432.
160 Rilke, *Selected Letters 1902–1926*, 86; translation altered. *AR dt*, 174–5.

many widely separated contrasts and the unexpected transitions, which go to make up a human being and his continuous development, meet here in a felicitous union and are knit together by an inner force of adhesion. These people have been created from material brought from the most distant reaches of their personality, all the climates of their temperament are revealed in the hemispheres of their head.[161]

This synthesis of many features, movements, and times, might seem like it would compose an aggregate rather than the organic unity of an artistic whole. A mass of impressions implies a multiplicity. The unification of a multiplicity into a whole, however, cannot be attained through a simple fusing of diverse elements. A mere fusion of multiple elements would produce an aggregate (a kind of collage), and not the integrity and organic unity of a work of art. In his vision Rodin must already divine a whole in the many impressions. This is necessarily presupposed by his very ability to distinguish the essential and necessary from the unessential. The essential is that which is revelatory of the essence or whole. In various features and gestures Rodin perceives a partial manifestation of the invisible in the visible. It is this invisible, divined in selfless attentiveness to the model, that provides the principle for the formation of the work of art. Rodin's task of uniting all the gathered impressions into an artistic whole involves balancing the many suggested movements in relation to one another such that a dynamic equilibrium results.[162] The work of art must not completely diverge from the model because the model's visibility already partially expresses the invisible, but the sculpture nevertheless realizes an intensified synthesis of the most expressive features.

Rilke's description of Rodin's portrait of Balzac draws together many of the elements that have been discussed. In addition, an Expressionistic moment in Rodin's work comes to the fore which also belongs to the way in which the *Kunst-Ding* surpasses the *Ding*. (While in the case of Balzac—as with many of Rodin's works—literature also played an important role in the development of the plastic work, due to our concern with perception this will not be discussed in any detail.) Rilke explains how Rodin drew from every possible source to deepen his understanding of Balzac. "He [Rodin] visited Balzac's home, the landscape of Touraine, which constantly re-appears in his books, he read his letters, studied the existing portraits of Balzac, and he lived

---

161 AR, 30. KA 4, 437. For a detailed characterization of one of Rodin's works in this regard see Rilke's description of *The Man with the Broken Nose* (*L'Homme au nez cassé*) (AR, 10–13. KA 4, 415–18).
162 AR, 13. KA 4, 417.

through his works again and again ..."¹⁶³ On this basis and after numerous sculptural studies, according to Rilke, Rodin finally had an inner vision of how to portray Balzac, which was realized in his final portrait. Rilke states that, "Rodin had seen his Balzac in a moment of tremendous concentration and tragic exaggeration, and thus he depicted him. The vision did not pass; it was transformed."¹⁶⁴

In the expression "tragic exaggeration" Rilke further illustrates the manner in which Rodin's sculptures exceed "reality." However, it is this "exaggerated" depiction that enables Balzac to come to such an essential manifestation. Retrospectively, we can also see in Rilke's evaluation of Rodin an intimation of his place on the cusp of Expressionism. Rodin's sculptures often present figures in "unusual" or "unnatural" postures, but this does not divorce them from the inherent sculptural language of the world. Rather the language of sculpture is an intensification and evolution of this language, in the service of greater expression and symbolism. The following statement by Rilke reveals how in the case of portraiture the artistic whole achieves a greater manifestation of the essence of a person: "Rodin has given him [Balzac] proportions which are probably much greater than those of the writer's figure. He has understood the very essence of his nature, but he has not stopped with the limits of that nature; he has drawn this mighty contour about its ultimate, its most distant possibilities ..."¹⁶⁵

Rilke often describes the work of art as a kind of saying. It is a saying of the essence in the respective artistic medium. However, this saying is distinguished from a more reflective speech, whether it be intellectual criticism or chatter. Rilke claims that, "all talk is misunderstanding" and "insight is only within the work."¹⁶⁶ These statements are pertinent to the translation of vision, or the saying of the essence, in the work. In the *Letters on Cézanne* Rilke writes,

> Ideally a painter (and, generally, an artist) should not become conscious of his insights: without taking the detour through his reflective processes, and incomprehensibly to himself, all his progress should enter so swiftly into the work that he is unable to recognize them in the moment of transition.¹⁶⁷

Rilke regards a movement into the stance of reflection as entailing a loss of the insight that could be *said* through a more immediate artistic

---

163 *AR*, 38. *KA 4*, 445.
164 *AR*, 39. *KA 4*, 446.
165 *AR*, 37. *KA 4*, 444–5.
166 *LC*, 78. *KA 4*, 629.
167 *LC*, 75. *KA 4*, 628.

articulation of vision—a view which he presented as early as 1898 in his essay "Über Kunst."[168] How can this process be understood in relation to Rodin?

In the earlier consideration of *modelé*, attention was drawn to Rilke's identification of the word with the perception of a thing according to a system of surfaces or planes, expressive of its essence. He also describes *modelé* as the basic principle of Rodin's sculptural work. In a letter to Clara Rilke, Rilke employs the word to mean the process of transposing a vision of the *Ding* into the composition of the *Kunst-Ding*. As an attempt to articulate the difference between *saying* in the work of art and "talk [*Gerede*]," he states: "And have I not just had the experience with him, for which you prepared me years ago: that of the immaterial, the unintentionally formed—'like the worm, that makes its way from point to point in darkness?' in a word: of the modelé?"[169] Here the forming of the work of art, understood as the pre-reflective movement from *Ding* to *Kunst-Ding*, is described as *modelé*.

Rilke speaks of the thing according to *modelé*, the work according to *modelé*, and also regards *modelé* as the process of artistic composition (understood as a pre-reflective saying). A threefold distinction is therefore contained in the word. However, these three aspects are parts of the same and correspond precisely to what has been articulated. The *modelé* of the thing concerns the manifestation of the essence through the interrelation of surfaces. The *modelé* of the work or *Kunst-Ding* concerns a more perfect visible manifestation of the invisible or the essence. The process of composition involves divining the invisible, which comes to partial expression in the thing, and composing a form (the work of art) which is a more perfect sensible manifestation of the *same* invisible. In other words, the invisible which informs the thing, informs the process of composition, and leads to a more perfect visible formation of the invisible, which is the work of art or *Kunst-Ding*. In terms of sculpture this means that the essence which comes to partial expression in the *modelé* of the thing is divined by the sculptor and, in turn, informs the modeling of the sculpture, which achieves a more perfect *modelé*.

Before turning to Rilke's characterizations of specific sculptures that will serve in the further elaboration of the wholeness of the work of art and the holistic nature of the fragment, here is an appropriate place to correct certain misrepresentations and misunderstandings of Rilke in the secondary literature. Rilke's conception of art often leads him to describe works as self-sufficient and self-contained. Furthermore, in the secondary literature this quality has often been attributed to Rilke's *Neue Gedichte*. A one-sided understanding of this self-sufficiency has fostered many

---

168 *KA 4*, 114–20.
169 *AR dt*, 199.

interpretations of Rilke's poems as exemplary of "aestheticism" and an attitude of "art for art's sake."[170] The poem (or work of art) is regarded as bearing no reference to anything outside itself. There is an implicit tension in these interpretations because they fail to resolve the apparent contradiction between Rilke's notion of the artwork's self-sufficiency on the one hand, and his emphasis on the artist's selfless attentiveness to the world on the other. The aestheticist interpretation of Rilke fails to make sense of how Rilke can affirm both of these views. However, this apparent contradiction can be resolved through understanding that the wholeness of the work of art or its self-containment lies precisely in the fact that an invisible of *things* and the *world* attains a more perfect visibility *in* the work of art. Hence, one can say that the work of art as a self-contained whole is revelatory of things in the world. I regard this as the only coherent interpretation of Rilke's many reflections on art and his own poetry.[171] That Rilke understood the work of art as a revelation of the *world* is evinced in the concluding sentence of *Auguste Rodin* (First Part). Rilke describes Rodin's complete devotion to his medium as involving a "certain renunciation of life." However, "just by the patience of such renunciation did he win life: for the world offered itself to his chisel."[172] This view should be kept in mind in any consideration of Rilke's poetry.

Various aspects of the wholeness of the work of art have already been explicated, particularly with respect to portraiture. A consideration of Rodin's most famous sculpture, *The Thinker* (*Le Penseur*) can further our understanding of the holistic character of the work of art and of the relation between *Ding* and *Kunst-Ding*.

The title of the sculpture, *The Thinker*, implies an archetypal figure or universal character. Thinking is an *invisible* activity. This invisible, of course, comes to visible expression in any person deeply immersed in thought. However, for aforementioned reasons, it will never be the case that every visible aspect of a person's appearance will be expressive of contemplation; there is always contingency. The sculpture in contrast increases and perfects the visibility of the invisible. In the

---

170 See, for instance, Ralph Köhnen, *Sehen als Textkultur: Intermediale Beziehungen zwischen Rilke und Cézanne*, 94. See also n. 228. Paul de Man offers a similar reading of Rilke's poetry as referring to nothing beyond the text. Paul de Man, *Allegories of Reading: Figural Language in Rousseau, Nietzsche, Rilke, and Proust* (New Haven, CT: Yale University Press, 1979), 20–56. On Paul de Man's interpretation of Rilke, see also Anthony Phelan, "Rilke and His Philosophical Critics," in *The Cambridge Companion to Rilke*, ed. Karen Leeder and Robert Vilain (Cambridge: Cambridge University Press, 2010), 185–7.
171 For a more detailed discussion of a similar view, see Michael Kahl, *Lebensphilosophie und Ästhetik: Zu Rilkes Werk 1902–1910* (Freiburg: Rombach Verlag, 1999). See also Fischer, "Animalising Art: Rainer Maria Rilke and Franz Marc."
172 *AR*, 41. *KA* 4, 449.

sculpture, every gesture, every curve of the body, must reveal the state of contemplation. The wholeness of the work of art lies in the fact that every aspect contributes toward the expression of this invisible. The work of art thereby achieves a more perfect sensible manifestation of the *invisible* state of thinking than any person in the world. Rilke says of *The Thinker*, that the "whole body [*Leib*] has become a skull and all the blood in his veins has become brain."[173] In other words, every aspect of the sculpted figure is expressive of contemplation. Just as a portrait must express the character of a person through every visible aspect, so does *The Thinker* bring a more general invisible to a higher and more integral manifestation. Every aspect of a work of art contributes to the manifestation of the essence and thus the work is "whole" to a superior degree than any "thing."

Other significant respects in which Rodin's work exemplifies the distinctive wholeness of the work of art pertain to his modern interpretation of the fragment and torsi. J. A. Schmoll and Werner Schnell have provided comprehensive explications of Rodin's fragments and his important place in the historical development of the fragment.[174] Here, only a few key points will be considered.

Rilke was very aware of the significance of the fragment in Rodin's work. Martina Krießbach-Thomasberger comments that in view of the development of twentieth-century sculpture Rilke's insights into Rodin's work are remarkable, particularly his recognition of the *modelé* and the value of the fragment.[175] There were many influences on Rodin's reinterpretation of the fragment and torsi, two of which were the use of sculptural fragments in architecture and Rodin's avid interest in, and collection of, antique sculptures (which, of course, are mostly bequeathed to us as fragments).[176] Nevertheless, while there are precedents to Rodin's work, Rodin was a forerunner and innovator in his conscious employment of the fragment and in his interpretation of the fragment as a complete work.

Rodin's work reveals that fragments and torsi can be artistic wholes. In the work of art, the part itself can be a whole, independently of what is commonly regarded as a whole. This provides another example of Rodin's modernity; Rodin's use of the fragment was an important step

---

173 *AR*, 22. *KA 4*, 428.
174 Schmoll, *Rodin-Studien*, 99–160; Schnell, *Der Torso als Problem der modernen Kunst*.
175 Martina Krießbach-Thomasberger, "Rilke und Rodin," in *Rilke – ein europäischer Dichter aus Prag*, ed. Peter Demetz, Joachim W. Storck, and Hans Dieter Zimmermann (Würzburg: Königshausen & Neumann, 1998), 150.
176 In his early days in Brussels (1872–6) Rodin himself worked on architectural sculptures that included the deliberate use of the fragment. See Schmoll, 148ff.; Schnell, 10ff.

in the liberation of artistic language, and in particular, the language of sculpture (thus both in his gestures toward Expressionism and in the role of the fragment, Rodin made important steps away from perceptual realism toward a greater independence of the work of art; while he is arguably not as significant as Cézanne in this respect, he indubitably played an important role). Rilke recognized this and articulates the wholeness of the fragment in various ways. He characterizes Rodin's sculpture, *The Inner Voice* (*La Voix intérieure*)—a symbolic figure of the muse that "lacks" arms and forms part of the Victor Hugo Monument—as being as "armless as life within."[177] In a similar vein Rodin himself tersely says of another version of the same figure: "Meditation—the enemy of action."[178] He further explains the symbolic meaning of the sculpture as follows: "My figure represents *Meditation*. That's why it has neither arms to act nor legs to walk. Haven't you noticed that reflection, when persisted in, suggests so many plausible arguments for opposite decisions that it ends in inertia?"[179] As symbolic of the inner life, *Inner Voice* and *Meditation* do not require complete limbs, which are suggestive of, and central to, *external action*.

Rilke also explicitly formulates the difference between the wholeness of an artistic composition and a common whole, and in this way draws out further differences between the *Ding* and the *Kunst-Ding*. After speaking of those who criticize Rodin's armless statues, he writes,

> Not long ago the same criticism was levelled against the trees of the Impressionists, cut off as they are by the edge of the picture; we very soon became accustomed to such an effect, learning to see and understand, in the case of the painter at any rate, that an artistic whole must not necessarily be identical with the usual thing-whole, that, independent of it, there arise within the picture itself new unities, new associations, relationships and adjustments. It is the same in sculpture. The artist has the right to make one thing out of many and a world out of the smallest part of a thing. Rodin has made hands, independent, small hands which, without forming part of a body, are yet alive. Hands rising upright, angry and irritated, hands whose five bristling fingers seem to bark like the five throats of a Cerberus. Hands in motion, sleeping hands ... Rodin knows that the body consists of

---

177 AR, 47. KA 4, 459.
178 Rodin, quoted in Schmoll, *Rodin-Studien*, 129. In earlier versions of the work, the figure had arms, but Rodin came to regard them as unnecessary. In independent versions of the work (presented on its own rather than as part of a larger composition) it was also given the name *Meditation* (*La Méditation*).
179 *Rodin on Art and Artists*, 68.

so many stages for the display of life, of such life as in any and every part can be individual and great, and he has the power to bestow on any part of the vast, vibrating surface of the body the independence and completeness of a whole.[180]

The fragment is a case in which the *Kunst-Ding* is distinguished from a regular thing in a decisive manner. We normally think of arms, legs, heads, etc., as parts of the complete *Gestalt* of the human figure; they are parts of a whole. However, the fragment illustrates that the formal and expressive wholeness of the work of art can depart from the "usual thing-whole"; the work of art is a new kind of independent unity. Rodin's hands do not need to be connected to bodies; they are independent works of art with an integrity of expression (from our present vantage point after the history of twentieth-century art it is easy for us to grasp this point, but at the time Rilke was writing, Rodin's fragments belonged to the forefront of the artistic avant-garde). The artistically formed "part" is a whole in itself. However, even in this case there is not an opposition between Nature and art. As Rilke states, "Rodin knows that the body consists of so many stages for the display of life ... and he has the power to bestow on any part ... the independence and completeness of a whole." In his torsi, and in his fragments (such as hands), Rodin brings the life manifest in these parts of the living body to an intensified and holistic expression. In the example of *The Thinker* we discussed how the whole comes to expression in each part; this already implies a sense in which *the whole is in each part*. The fragment realizes this general character of the work of art to a further degree. It not only illustrates that the whole is in each part, but shows that *the part can be a whole*.

While Rilke eloquently articulated the nature of the artistic whole and the fragment in prose, his most concentrated and striking depictions of this theme are contained in his poetry. *Der neuen Gedichte anderer Teil* includes the dedication "*A mon grand Ami Auguste Rodin*," and begins with the famous poem "Archaïscher Torso Apollos," the complementary poem to "Früher Apollo," which opens the first part of the *Neue Gedichte*. Later "Archaïscher Torso Apollos" will be considered from other perspectives, but in the present context it will serve to further illustrate the nature of artistic wholeness. It is worthwhile to recall that Rodin was an avid collector of antique sculptures, and his love of classical sculpture (in the mostly fragmentary forms, in which it is bequeathed to us) was a definitive influence on his sculptural reinterpretation of the torso and fragment. A comprehensive understanding of Rilke's poem requires an awareness of this background and the fact

---

180 *AR*, 16–17. *KA 4*, 421–2.

that "Archaïscher Torso Apollos" is an implicit tribute to the French sculptor.[181]

Archaïscher Torso Apollos

Wir kannten nicht sein unerhörtes Haupt,
darin die Augenäpfel reiften. Aber
sein Torso glüht noch wie ein Kandelaber,
in dem sein Schauen, nur zurückgeschraubt,

sich hält und glänzt. Sonst könnte nicht der Bug
der Brust dich blenden, und im leisen Drehen
der Lenden könnte nicht ein Lächeln gehen
zu jener Mitte, die die Zeugung trug.

Sonst stünde dieser Stein entstellt und kurz
unter der Schultern durchsichtigem Sturz
und flimmerte nicht so wie Raubtierfelle;

und bräche nicht aus allen seinen Rändern
aus wie ein Stern: denn da ist keine Stelle,
die dich nicht sieht. Du mußt dein Leben ändern.[182]

This sonnet portrays an archaic sculpture of Apollo, whose head is missing and only the torso remains.[183] It begins with the statement that we never knew the "tremendous head" ("unerhörtes Haupt"). The second line surprises us in that it proceeds to describe a feature of the former head. Only its eyes are mentioned (this is not insignificant as

---

181 See n. 180 and n. 184.
182 "Archaic Torso of Apollo// We did not know his tremendous head,/ in which the eyeballs [*Augenäpfel*] ripened. Yet/ his torso still glows like a lamp [the word "Kandelaber" means "candelabrum"; however, at the time the poem was written it also referred to a type of gas lamp],/ in which his gaze, only turned low,// persists and gleams. Otherwise the bow/ of the breast could not dazzle you, and in the quiet turning/ of the loins a smile could not travel/ to that center, which bore procreation.// Otherwise this stone would stand disfigured and short/ under the shoulders' transparent fall/ and not shimmer like a predator's coat;// and not break out from all its borders/ like a star: because there is no place/ that does not see you. You must change your life." *KA 1*, 513.
183 For a discussion of the relation between "Archaïscher Torso Apollos" and the antique torso (now recognized as belonging to the Early Classical style) that may have inspired the poem (as well as of the poem "Früher Apollo"), see Ulrich Hausmann, *Die Apollosonette Rilkes und ihre plastischen Urbilder* (Berlin: Verlag Gebr. Mann, 1947). Cf. Paul Böckmann, *Dichterische Wege der Subjektivierung* (Tübingen: Max Niemeyer Verlag, 1999), 338, n. 50.

Apollo is a god of light; in the later discussion more attention will be given to the images connected to light and vision in the poem) with the untranslatable word, "Augenäpfel." "Augenäpfel" means "eye-balls" but contains the metaphor "eye-apples," which is elaborated in the organic image of the eyes having "ripened" in his head; among other things this suggests Rilke's view of the intimate relation between Nature and art. The enjambment to the third line is preceded by the word "but [aber]." The reader is thus both surprised and prepared to find out that, although the head—the center of vision—is missing, the torso still glows like the light in Apollo's former eyes, only less brightly, like a gas lamp turned down low ("Kandelaber" can refer to a type of street lamp with multiple arms that was common in Paris during Rilke's time as well as to a candelabrum). The sonnet then proceeds to describe in subjunctive formulations (one of Rilke's preferred grammatical moods) the necessity in the fact that the torso gazes (this is reminiscent of Rilke's characterization of hands that "bark" in *Auguste Rodin*) and the integral relation of the remaining parts of the sculpture. Rilke articulates the same kind of relation between part and whole in his description of Rodin's *The Man of Early Times* (*L'Homme des premiers ages*).

> Here was a life-sized nude figure showing life which was not only equally great in every part but which was, as it seemed, everywhere endowed with the same sublimity of expression. What was expressed in the face, the pain and effort of awakening together with the desire for this awakening, was written on the least part of the body; each part was a mouth uttering it in its own manner. The most searching eye could not discover in this figure any place less alive, less definite, less expressive than another ...[184]

As in the archaic torso of Apollo, what is expressed in the face is expressed in every aspect of the body, with the important difference that in the archaic torso the head and the legs no longer literally remain. Nevertheless, what once came to expression in Apollo's bright gaze continues to reveal itself, only less brightly, in the remaining torso. Formerly the head gazed, and this gaze was also articulated in the rest of the torso, but even now the torso continues to gaze and dazzle the beholder, the "you [*du*]" of the poem. This reveals both the original wholeness of the work of art, in which the head and body of Apollo were aspects of a single expression, and the fact that *the wholeness of the part* is manifest in the remaining torso. This brief consideration suffices to demonstrate how Rilke's sonnet vividly and tersely conveys the idea

---

184 AR, 14. KA 4, 419.

of aesthetic wholeness that he also discovered in Rodin.[185] While there is an obvious difference between a historical torso that was originally "complete" and Rodin's deliberately created torsi, it should now be evident how a recognition of the intrinsic wholeness of a historical torso could naturally develop into the deliberate torso.[186]

In addition to aesthetic wholeness, "Archaïscher Torso Apollos" emphatically conveys the revelatory power of the work of art. The poem can end with "you must change your life [du mußt dein Leben ändern]" because the work of art has mediated a disclosure, opened up a new perspective for the viewer. This event of insight and transformed perception ripens into the judgment "you must change your life."

The main points established in this sub-section can now be summarized. Through his dynamic physiognomic vision Rodin perceives the essence of the thing which comes to a partial manifestation in its *modelé*. Informed by this essence he composes the sculptural work of art in which every aspect of the *modelé* serves to articulate this essence. The creation of the *Kunst-Ding* thus brings forth a new being that is a more perfect sensible manifestation of the essence of the *Ding* and reveals the thing in its essence. In the *Kunst-Ding* every aspect mutually serves in the manifestation of the invisible essence and in the articulation of the whole. The consideration of the fragment further explicated the independence of the artistic whole from the "thing-whole," and demonstrated how a part can itself be a whole. However, in this independence it is no less a manifestation of the essence that it embodies.

Cézanne's Participative Vision

Rilke characterizes Cézanne's seeing in similar ways to Rodin's. However, in certain respects his descriptions of Cézanne are even more emphatic. The discussion of Cézanne will draw us closer again to the broader problematic of Nature and dualism, in contrast to the focus on the human body in Rodin. While Rilke does make significant statements about Cézanne's vision of Nature, in the *Letters on Cézanne* (*Briefe über Cézanne*) he offers more detailed depictions of still-lifes and portraits and gives less attention to Cézanne's landscapes. The precise reasons for this are unclear (the Cézanne retrospective at the Salon d'Automne [October 6–22, 1907] included the display of twenty

---

185 Schmoll also suggests that the precise characterizations of the expressive surfaces of the sculpture bear directly on the significance of *modelé* in Rodin. Schmoll, *Rodin-Studien*, 105ff.
186 "Historical torso" is the terminology used by Schnell for torsi that due to historical and natural reasons are bequeathed to us as torsi, as opposed to being originally created as torsi. Schnell, *Der Torso als Problem der modernen Kunst*, 10.

landscape paintings[187]). However, from certain remarks, it is clear that Rilke highly esteemed Cézanne's landscapes. It is important to keep in mind that the *Letters on Cézanne* were not originally intended for publication; they were posthumously published letters that Rilke wrote to Clara Rilke at the time of his decisive awakening to Cézanne and consist of his early attempts to characterize and understand Cézanne's art (this is not to deny their great literary merit or Rilke's remarkable ability to convey linguistically the visual experience of Cézanne's pictures).[188] Rilke did contemplate writing a monograph on Cézanne as he had done for Rodin but he came to doubt, among other things, his capacity to be "objective" in his characterizations of art, as his personal artistic questions as a poet were always closely intertwined with his reflections. Despite Rilke's self-appraisal, his *Letters on Cézanne* have been positively received by art historians and contributed in significant ways to the reception of Cézanne.[189] Due to Rilke's interest in the genre of landscape painting (evinced, for instance, in *Worpswede*) and scattered statements that reveal his profound admiration of Cézanne's landscapes, I suppose that had Rilke written a monograph on Cézanne he would have articulated the breakthrough in landscape painting achieved by Cézanne and built on his earlier discussions of this genre. Because of these limitations in Rilke's reflections (as well as other reasons yet to be elaborated), the treatment of Cézanne will be supplemented by sources that extend beyond Rilke's interpretation of the French painter; nevertheless, the treatment is fundamentally in tune with Rilke's understanding. In keeping with the aforementioned structure, the present sub-section focuses on Cézanne's way of seeing, while the subsequent sub-section explicates how this way of seeing is translated into his paintings.

---

187 Pierre Sanchez, *Dictionnaire du Salon d'Automne. Répertoire des exposants et liste des œuvres présentées 1903–1945*, vol. 1 (Dijon: Échelle de Jacob, 2006), 301. See Justus Lange, "'Es geht alles tiefer in mich ein und bleibt nicht an der Stelle stehen, wo es sonst immer zu Ende war.' Rilke und Cézanne – ein Blick aus kunsthistorischer Perspektive," *Blätter der Rilke-Gesellschaft* 30 (2010): 212–30. The exhibition also included twelve portraits, eleven still-lifes, as well as other pictures.
188 Ralph Köhnen speaks of the essayistic character of Rilke's *Letters on Cézanne* and elaborates numerous analogies and parallels between Cézanne's paintings and Rilke's writings of the middle period. Köhnen, *Sehen als Textkultur: Intermediale Beziehungen zwischen Rilke und Cézanne*, 112ff.
189 Kurt Badt (1956) and Gottfried Boehm (1988) are, for instance, two notable art historians who draw on Rilke and positively assess his contribution to our understanding of Cézanne. Other connections between Rilke and the historical reception of Cézanne will be articulated in the course of our considerations. Kurt Badt, *Die Kunst Cézannes* (Munich: Prestel-Verlag, 1956); Gottfried Boehm, *Paul Cézanne: Montagne Sainte-Victoire* (Frankfurt am Main: Insel Verlag, 1988).

Rilke's description of Cézanne's vision contains many of the same features that we identified in his interpretation of Rodin. Rilke characterizes a self-portrait by Cézanne with the striking analogy of a dog seeing into a mirror and taking its appearance for another dog.[190] While this passage in the *Letters on Cézanne* reveals a great deal about Rilke's understanding of Cézanne's art and style, Rilke also sees in the portrait a revelation of Cézanne's "objective" and ec-static *perception of the world*, and the latter is presently our main concern.

> The strong structure of this skull which seems hammered and sculpted from within is reinforced by the ridges of the eyebrows; but from there, pushed forward toward the bottom, shoed out, as it were, by the closely bearded chin, hangs the face, hangs as if every feature had been suspended individually, unbelievably intensified and yet reduced to utter primitivity, yielding that expression of uncontrolled amazement in which children and country people can lose themselves, – except that the gazeless stupor of their absorption has been replaced by an animal alertness which entertains an untiring, *objective* [*sachliche*] wakefulness in the unblinking eyes. How *great* this watching of his was and how unimpeachably *accurate*, is almost touchingly confirmed by the fact that, without even remotely interpreting his expression or presuming himself superior to it, he reproduced himself with so much humble objectivity, with the unquestioning, matter-of-fact interest of a dog who sees himself in a mirror and thinks: there's another dog.[191]

In the above excerpt I have emphasized the words "great," "accurate," and "objective" (*sachlich*), which echo Rilke's accounts of Rodin's vision. The dog analogy is also reminiscent of Rilke's account of seeing in the previously cited letter from Capri of March 8, 1907, in which he describes the ec-static gesture and "strange anonymity" of "das Anschauen."[192]

Joachim Gasquet speaks of Cézanne's vision as a "poetry of the exact."[193] This concern with exactitude is reflected, for one, in the role that knowledge of geology played in Cézanne's "meditation

---

190 For a detailed consideration of Rilke's view of the dog–human relation see Kári Driscoll, *Toward a Poetics of Animality: Hofmannsthal, Rilke, Pirandello, Kafka* (PhD diss., Columbia University, New York, 2014), 76–127. Rilke's perception of dogs is also a focus of Chapter 3 of the present work.
191 *LC*, 84–85; my emphasis. *KA 4*, 632–3.
192 Rilke, *Briefe aus den Jahren 1906–1907*, vol. 2, 214. See also n. 114.
193 Joachim Gasquet, *Joachim Gasquet's Cézanne: A Memoir with Conversations*, trans. Christopher Pemberton (London: Thames and Hudson, 1991), 95.

with a brush in his hand" on the Provençal landscape and Mont Sainte-Victoire.[194] According to Gasquet, Cézanne says that "in order to paint a landscape well, I first need to discover its geological structure" and "I need to know some geology – how Sainte-Victoire's roots work, the colours of the geological soils – since such things move me, benefit me ..."[195] The purpose of this knowledge is clearly not a matter of "theory," at least not in the modern sense of the word. This knowledge assisted Cézanne to *see* the landscape with greater precision and understanding; its role was analogous to that of anatomy for Renaissance painters in their portrayals of the human form.

While awareness of geological and topographical structure was crucial in the first stages of Cézanne's study of the landscape it was the perception of color which then became the focus. He was particularly attuned to gradations of colors. Just as Rodin saw all things in terms of the primary element of his art, the *modelé*, Cézanne saw all things in coloristic terms and was ceaselessly preoccupied with refining this vision. Gottfried Boehm, in his monograph on Cézanne's late pictures of Mont Sainte-Victoire, identifies a kind of phenomenological reduction at work here. Cézanne would suspend all habits of thought—scientific and everyday—and attune his gaze entirely to the play and gradations of color, to sensations of color, what he called "*sensations colorantes.*"[196] Cézanne often speaks of seeing all things in planes of colors, something which is reflected in his painterly technique. Rilke was aware of this and recounts Cézanne's diligent study of Mont Sainte-Victoire: "There he would sit for hours, occupied with finding and incorporating the '*plans*' [planes] (curiously, he refers to them again with the same word Rodin used)."[197] Rilke here notes the similarity between Cézanne and Rodin in the use of the word "planes" (we used "surfaces" and "planes" interchangeably in our discussion of Rodin); nevertheless, there are significant differences between the three-dimensional existence of sculpture and the two-dimensionality of painting whose primary element is color rather than form, and these differences inform Rodin's and Cézanne's perception in distinctive ways.[198] For Cézanne, gradations of color-planes did not have the value

---

194 Émile Bernard, "Memories of Paul Cézanne," in *Conversations with Cézanne*, ed. Michael Doran, trans. Julie Lawrence Cochran, intro. Richard Shiff (Los Angeles: University of California Press, 2001), 59.
195 *Joachim Gasquet's Cézanne: A Memoir with Conversations*, 153, 165.
196 Gottfried Boehm, *Paul Cézanne: Montagne Sainte-Victoire*, 54ff.
197 LC, 39. KA 4, 611.
198 Interestingly, as we will see, Cézanne's *plans* have a sculptural value in his paintings; they are central to his unique technique of modeling through color contrasts. However, this is, of course, different from the modeling of

of a mere property, or effect of light; the play of light and the colored surfaces of things were an expression of Nature itself. Thus, Cézanne states: "Colour, if I may say so, is biological. Colour is alive, and colour alone makes things come alive."[199] Similarly, he elaborates: "Nature isn't at the surface; it's in depth. Colours are the expression on the surface of this depth. They rise up out of the earth's roots: they're its life ..."[200]

Cézanne was attuned to colors and the play of light in such a way that they offered distinctive revelations of the landscape or Nature. This bears obvious similarities to the significance of *modelé* for Rodin. These statements about color already suggest an exceptional disclosure of Nature. In connection with such a disclosure, Rilke states,

> I also noticed yesterday how unselfconsciously different they are [the paintings], how unconcerned with being original, confident of not getting lost with each approach toward one of nature's thousand faces; confident, rather, of discovering the inexhaustible within by seriously and conscientiously studying her manifold presence outside.[201]

An "inexhaustible within" is discovered by Cézanne through a diligent and selfless attentiveness to Nature's appearance. Rilke's mention of Nature's "faces" might also be characterized as a physiognomic vision and conception of Nature (the meaning of this will be clarified in the course of the inquiry). The devoted outwardly turned gaze leads to the discovery of an *inexhaustible interior*. An interior or invisible is revealed through a deep attentiveness to the exterior or visible. Rilke does not explicate the precise status of this invisible. Nevertheless, it is clear that he discerns an epiphanic significance in it. Heinrich Wiegand Petzet, in his introduction to the *Letters on Cézanne*, relates Rilke's view to Cézanne's account of "being in front of the landscape [*vor der Landschaft*] and drawing religion from it."[202] This "religion" is obviously not a doctrinal content that Cézanne has access to in advance; rather, it is an epiphanic sense which is only disclosed in the course and process of meditating on the landscape. Petzet elaborates that this was "a religion for which this churchgoing

---

three-dimensional form in Rodin. Modeling in the case of painting is indirect, particularly in Cézanne, who largely avoids the use of line and suggests three-dimensional form primarily through color modulation.
199 *Joachim Gasquet's Cézanne: A Memoir with Conversations*, 162.
200 Ibid., 166.
201 *LC*, 47. *KA 4*, 615.
202 Heinrich Wiegand Petzet, "Foreword," in *LC*, xxiii–xiv. Petzet, "Nachwort [Afterword]," in *Briefe über Cézanne*, by Rainer Maria Rilke, ed. Clara Rilke (Frankfurt am Main: Insel Verlag, 1962), 56.

heathen did not have a name."²⁰³ Rilke compares Cézanne to van Gogh, stating that Cézanne sees and paints things as if they were "Saints."²⁰⁴ In other words, commonly perceived things assume an aura of the sacred or the holy; the artist gleans the divine in them. Cézanne need not literally paint saints or religious figures in order to present the holy or numinous because he finds it in "everyday" things and his surroundings.²⁰⁵

Rilke's attribution of an epiphanic dimension to Cézanne's vision of Nature is in complete accord with other documents concerning Cézanne's way of seeing and his "theoretical" views. Cézanne adheres, for instance, to the idea of the "Book of Nature" and describes the appearance of the landscape as "the spectacle which *Pater omnipotens aeterne Deus* unfolds before your eyes."²⁰⁶ However, as aforementioned, such views should not be regarded as mere statements of belief or the expression of a mere doctrine. Rather, there is clearly an *epiphanic dimension* in Cézanne's actual *experience* of Nature and Cézanne employs these ideas as a way of making this experience intelligible. Cézanne's accounts of his perception of Nature, and ultimately his paintings, evidence an epiphanic vision. Upon viewing a painting of Mont Sainte-Victoire Rilke proclaims that "not since Moses has anyone seen a mountain so greatly [*groß*]."²⁰⁷

---

203 Petzet, "Foreword," in *LC*, xvii. Petzet, "Nachwort," in *Briefe über Cézanne*, 56.
204 *LC*, 40. *KA 4*, 611.
205 This also fits Kurt Badt's interpretation of the "religious" in Cézanne; Badt saw in the dissolution of things in Cézanne's technique of painting in patches of colors, and the recomposition of things out of the *totality* of color contrasts, a deformation of the ordinary, everyday appearance of things in order to reveal them in a deeper ontological sense. Badt, *Die Kunst Cézannes*, 19–20, 172–3. It is worthwhile to note that Heidegger was familiar with Badt's Cézanne interpretation and corresponded with Badt. See Christoph Jamme, "Der Verlust der Dinge: Cézanne – Rilke – Heidegger," 392.
206 *Joachim Gasquet's Cézanne: A Memoir with Conversations*, 163. Rodin held the same view of Nature, as was implied in our earlier considerations. With specific regard to the analogy of the "Book of Nature" Rilke quotes the following words of Rodin: "L'artiste doit revenir au texte primitif de Dieu (so nennt er die Natur) [The artist must return to the original text of God (this is what he calls Nature)] …" *AR dt*, 150.
207 Rilke, quoted in Petzet, "Foreword," in *LC*, viii; my emphasis. Rilke, quoted in Petzet, "Nachwort," in *Briefe über Cézanne*, 51. While the poem "Der Berg" ("The Mountain") from *Der neuen Gedichte anderer Teil* ostensibly concerns the Japanese painter Katsushika Hokusai (1760–1849) and was written before the 1907 Cézanne retrospective at the Salon d'Automne, the poem can also be regarded as an implicit tribute to Cézanne's vision and numerous paintings of Mont Sainte-Victoire (*KA 1*, 583). In his commentary on the *Neue Gedichte* Ulrich Fülleborn remarks that although the poem was written before Rilke's awakening to Cézanne, "Der Berg" is an anticipation of Cézanne and the relation between the works of art and the mountain as presented by the poem corresponds closely to Cézanne's understanding of *réalisation* (*KA 1*, 1002).

It was not only the landscape which held this significance for Cézanne, but also the basic element of his art, color. Cézanne not only regarded colors as an expression of Nature's depth and life; he also perceived them in epiphanic terms. In this respect he states that "colours ... are the dazzling flesh of ideas and of God."[208] Color was for Cézanne far from being reducible to a "physical" property, let alone a "secondary property."

Cézanne repeatedly exhorts the artist to *submit* his or her gaze to Nature in a way which is continuous with our previous elaboration of artistic vision. It is clear that Cézanne means an *active submission* or active receptivity. More specifically, Cézanne describes two stages in his meditation on the landscape with brush in hand. The first involves becoming aware of the geological structure of the landscape (this would provide him with the means of sketching the overall architectonic of the picture); the second is where an acute and immensely concentrated awareness of the colors would take over (where the true painting would begin). In the reconstruction of Cézanne's views offered by Gasquet it is evident that this involved a deepening sense of participation in the landscape, which might be explicated as a deepening perception of the invisible through its visible manifestations. After characterizing the first stage in his perception of the landscape, Cézanne describes his immersion in the world of color as follows:

> His [the artist's] whole aim must be silence. He must silence all the voices of prejudice within him, he must forget, forget, be silent, become a perfect echo. And then the entire landscape will engrave itself on the sensitive plate of his being ... I become sharply, overwhelmingly aware of colour gradations. I feel as if I'm saturated by all the shades of the infinite. At that moment I and my picture are one ... I come face to face with my motif; I lose myself in it. My thoughts wander lazily. The sun penetrates my skin dully, like a distant friend, warming, fertilizing my laziness, and together we germinate ... Only with nightfall can I withdraw my eyes from the earth, from this corner of the earth with which I've merged.[209]

The artist suspends all preconceptions and immerses himself completely in a receptive activity of seeing. Simultaneously the landscape as a whole, "the entire landscape," articulates itself within this ec-static vision. This leads to a deepening sense of participation in which a heightened awareness of colors plays a central role; Cézanne here

---

208 *Joachim Gasquet's Cézanne: A Memoir with Conversations*, 168.
209 Ibid., 150–3.

ascribes an epiphanic significance to the colors in his mention of the "infinite." At this point he discovers his motif (a point to which we will return). This sense of uniting with the landscape is further articulated by the statement "together we germinate."

Merleau-Ponty offers an account of this participation in the landscape, which echoes much of the quotation from Gasquet above, and emphasizes the non-dualistic character of Cézanne's vision. In "Cézanne's Doubt" ("Le Doute de Cézanne") Merleau-Ponty writes,

> Motivating all the movements from which a picture gradually emerges there can be only one thing: the landscape in its totality and in its absolute fullness, precisely what Cézanne called a "motif." He would start by discovering the geological foundations of the landscape; then, according to Mme Cézanne, he would halt and look at everything with widened eyes, "germinating" with the countryside ... His meditation would suddenly be consummated: "I have a hold on my motif," Cézanne would say ... The picture took on fullness and density; it grew in structure and balance; it came to maturity all at once. "The landscape thinks itself in me," he would say, "and I am its consciousness."[210]

The statement "the landscape thinks itself in me" matches perfectly with the characterization in Chapter 1 of the kind of language which might be used to express a non-dualistic experience. Cézanne makes this statement in order to articulate his *vision and experience of Nature*, a vision intimately related to his praxis as an artist.

Cézanne often characterizes this holistic and participative vision of the landscape as involving the sense that the usual boundaries between things dissolve (this, as we will see, also finds clear expression in Cézanne's style). This dissolution of boundaries is connected to an invisible dimension of things and holds both for Cézanne's experience of the landscape and for the "objects" of his still-lifes. In the considerations of Rodin's portraiture the invisible was described in terms of the "personality" and the "essence" of the person. Cézanne attributes an analogous invisibility to the "objects" of his still-lifes and to Nature more generally. Of course, this does not imply that the landscape has a "personality," but it does mean that the painter divines an invisible significance in things. While such a view of "objects" might seem unusual, the task of a phenomenological investigation is not to determine the nature of things in advance, in accordance with some preconceived standard, but to seek the nature of things on the basis of

---

210 Merleau-Ponty, "Cézanne's Doubt," 67.

how they reveal themselves, while always being open to unforeseen modes of givenness. Cézanne says,

> We were talking about portraits. People don't think of a sugar-bowl as having a face, a soul. But it changes every day too. You have to know how to catch them, how to win them over, those gentlemen ... These glasses and plates, there's talking going on between them. Endless confidences ... As for flowers, I've given them up. They wilt right away. Fruit are more faithful. They love having their portraits done. It's as if they're asking to be forgiven for fading. They exhale their message with their scent. They reach you with all their smells and tell you about the fields they've left, the rain that made them grow, the dawns they've watched. When I'm outlining the skin of a lovely peach with soft touches of paint, or a sad old apple, I catch a glimpse of the reflections they exchange of the same mild shadow of renunciation, the same love of the sun, the same recollection of the dew, a freshness ...[211]

Cézanne, in his comparison of still-lifes to portraiture, suggests an invisible or interior dimension of things which belongs to the things themselves, and a sense of fluid interrelationships *between* things. His characterization of apples and peaches also evokes the sense that these fruits communicate their integral relationship to other aspects of Nature. As the passage progresses it becomes clear that colors and the play of light and reflections are crucial to this revelation of things:

> Why do we divide up the world? Does this reflect our egoism? We want everything for our own use. There are days when I get the impression that the universe is nothing more than a stream, an ethereal river of reflection, of dancing reflections around the ideas of man ... The prism is our first step towards God, our seven beatitudes. The celestial atlas of the great eternal whiteness, the diamond-studded zones of God ...[212]

Cézanne again emphasizes an epiphanic revelation of colors. He proceeds to characterize this sense of interrelation between things and their dissolving boundaries, in terms of an atmosphere that surrounds them and is closely linked to the (invisible) light which illumines them, makes them visible, reveals their colors.

---

211 *Joachim Gasquet's Cézanne: A Memoir with Conversations*, 220.
212 Ibid., 220.

Objects enter into each other ... They never stop living, you understand ... Imperceptibly they extend beyond themselves through intimate reflections, as we do by looks and words ... Chardin was the first to have glimpsed that and rendered the atmosphere of objects ... He perceived that whole encounter in the atmosphere of the tiniest particles, the fine dust of emotion that surrounds objects ... it's the enveloping reflection, the light, from the general reflection, it's the envelope ... That's what I'm after ...[213]

In the above discussion some essential features of Cézanne's vision have been sketched: its participatory character and correlative disclosure of Nature as a dynamic or emerging organism; the experienced dissolution of boundaries between things; the living and epiphanic significance of colors. As Cézanne's vision is intimately intertwined with the process of painting, the attempt to articulate the two independently poses difficulties. In the subsequent consideration of Cézanne's translation of vision into the work of art, the structure and character of this vision will also be further elaborated.

The Task of Réalisation and Cézanne's Sachliches Sagen

While there are affinities between Cézanne's and Rodin's translation of vision into the work of art, there are also differences. In the case of portraiture, in which the model is the person portrayed, there is, for Rodin, an immediate relation between perception and composition; the subject of the sculpture is the model. However, in a sculpture like *The Thinker*, not to mention Rodin's more symbolic works such as *Inner Voice* or *The Hand of God* (*La Main de Dieu*), the relation between the perception of the model and the subject of the work is not as direct.[214] Even if Rodin often only came up with the title of a sculpture after completing a work which was inspired by his perception of the model, titles with literary, allegorical, or symbolic connotations invite

---

213 Ibid., 220. While in the above quotations Cézanne's language is sometimes more flowery than one might expect (from Cézanne) and thus calls into question the extent to which Cézanne is speaking and Gasquet is embellishing his views, given that other independent memoirs recount similar perspectives the gist of Gasquet's account can be trusted.

214 By "immediate" in this case I mean that perception of something in the world is integral to the very *process* of artistic composition. Thus, painting *en plein air* involves a more "immediate" translation of perception than a fantasy creation. I do not mean an immediacy in the language of painting; in significant respects Cézanne broke with the language of direct representation or "copying" more than any painter before him. In this sense the task of translating vision, or more specifically *réalisation*, was, as will be outlined, incredibly indirect and complex.

the viewer to interpret the work symbolically rather than as a direct translation of the model.²¹⁵ For Cézanne, in contrast, there is almost always a more immediate attempt to articulate the thing before him in the work.²¹⁶ This is not restricted to the case of portraiture, but is also the case for still-lifes and landscapes. This attempt to articulate an equivalent of vision in the (visual) language of the painting—an equivalent of the landscape, for instance—he termed *la réalisation*. Rilke characterizes the manner in which Cézanne's paintings reveal things as a *sachliches Sagen* (objective saying). The aim of this sub-section is to explicate the process of *réalisation* and the meaning of a *sachliches Sagen*.²¹⁷ The main focus will be on Cézanne's landscape paintings, in particular the later paintings of Mont Sainte-Victoire.

It was previously described how Rodin deliberately modeled each surface with a view to each sculpture's *appearance* in light and space. In his paintings Cézanne goes further in the thematization of the *appearance* of things. The paintings of Mont Sainte-Victoire thematize the very emergence of visibility, and the landscape itself as an emergent whole. The meaning of this will be clarified through drawing on various sources. Most significantly, I will illustrate important affinities and connections between Rilke, Heidegger, and Merleau-Ponty in their receptions of Cézanne. Prior to the more detailed articulation of Cézanne's painterly translation of vision, Rilke's idea of a *sachliches Sagen* will be explicated in broad terms that serve to establish the general horizon of this interpretation.

Shortly prior to the transformation he experienced through encountering Cézanne's work—which he characterized with expressions such as "suddenly one has the right eyes" and "I notice more and more what an event this is"—Rilke made a comment about paintings by van Gogh which ties in with his idea of a *sachliches Sagen*.²¹⁸ The appearance of a horse in one of van Gogh's pictures is described as "an old horse, a completely used up old horse: and it is not pitiful and not at all

---

215 See n. 143.
216 There are of course exceptions to the rule. Various paintings of bathers are a notable exception as Cézanne painted them in his studio. However, he no doubt drew upon a wealth of direct perceptions of Nature and human figures (including bathers) in the composition of these paintings, and the theme of these pictures is clearly the bathers themselves and their integration with the natural environment. The paintings are not symbols of something else (allegories); any symbolic dimensions of the pictures are rooted in their explicit subject matter and their composition.
217 *Sachliches Sagen* might be translated as an "objective saying" or a "saying of the things themselves" or a "matter-of-fact saying." Its features are elaborated in the course of our inquiry.
218 LC, 43, 46. KA 4, 612, 614.

reproachful: it simply *is* everything they have made of it and what it has allowed itself to become."²¹⁹ The emphasis on "*is*" is Rilke's.

In seeking to articulate Cézanne's work a short time later Rilke repeatedly emphasizes the paintings' ability to say and reveal the *being* of things or the things themselves. This is part of the breakthrough that he identified in Cézanne's work. Thus he says of the fruits in Cézanne's still-lifes that "they [the fruits] cease to be edible altogether, that's how thing-like [*dinghaft*] and real they become, how simply indestructible in their stubborn presence [*Vorhandenheit*]."²²⁰ Cézanne's paintings reveal the *existence* of things, the facticity of their *being-there*. With regard to the Cézanne room in the Salon d'Automne Rilke states, "here all of reality is on his side: in this dense quilted blue of his and the reddish black of his wine bottles …,"²²¹ and of Cézanne's portraits he says, "It is this limitless objectivity [*Sachlichkeit*], refusing any kind of meddling in an alien unity, that strikes people as so offensive and comical in Cézanne's portraits …"²²² One of Rilke's most illuminating characterizations of Cézanne's ability to say the things themselves is the following:

> You also notice, a little more clearly each time, how necessary it was to go beyond love; it's natural after all, to love each of these things as one makes it: but if one shows this, one makes it less well; one *judges* it instead of *saying* it. One ceases to be impartial; and the very best – love – stays outside the work, does not enter it, is left aside, untranslated: that's how the painting of sentiments came about (which is in no way better than the painting of material). They'd paint: I love this here; instead of painting: here it is.²²³

Cézanne's paintings bring the very being of things before our eyes; they show the things themselves, say "here it is." There is a sense in which "thatness" and "whatness," "existence" and "essence" are *revealed* in their ultimate unity in Cézanne's pictures. Rilke was moved to find out that Cézanne in his old age could recite Baudelaire's poem "Une Charogne" ("A Carcass") by heart.²²⁴ In this poem Baudelaire, leaving aside the final verse, offers a vivid and detailed depiction of a rotting carcass without any disgust, emotional reaction or reflection. In

---

219 *LC*, 18. *KA 4*, 601.
220 *LC*, 32–3; translation altered. *KA 4*, 608.
221 *LC*, 29. *KA 4*, 606.
222 *LC*, 65. *KA 4*, 623.
223 *LC*, 50; translation altered. *KA 4*, 616.
224 Also see n. 104 and the earlier discussion of this poem.

Cézanne, Rilke perceives a further progression of this artistic striving to say the things themselves. In fact, it is in the following comparison of Baudelaire and Cézanne that Rilke uses the precise expression *sachliches Sagen* (however, the many aforementioned quotations contribute to the articulation of his view that Cézanne's paintings say the very being of things, reveal the things themselves):

> I'm sure you remember ... in The Notebooks of Malte Laurids Brigge, the place that deals with Baudelaire and his poem: "A Carcass." I was thinking that without this poem, the whole trend towards the objective saying [*zum sachlichen Sagen*] which we now seem to recognize in Cézanne could not have started; first it had to be there in all its inexorability. First, artistic perception had to overcome itself to the point of realizing that even something horrible, something that seems no more than disgusting, *is*, and shares the truth of its being with everything else that exists ...[225]

As Rilke places such an emphasis on "being" in his *Letters on Cézanne*, it is not surprising that Heidegger's later reception of Cézanne was influenced by Rilke, and that Heidegger strongly encouraged Heinrich Wiegand Petzet and Clara Rilke to publish the *Letters on Cézanne* as an independent edition.[226] While Heidegger's specific statements concerning Cézanne (whom the later Heidegger regarded along with Paul Klee as the most significant modern painter) and Being cannot be identified completely with Rilke's, and whether Rilke properly recognized the "ontological difference" is questionable, there is a clear proximity between Rilke and Heidegger to which we shall return. At this moment, however, it should be mentioned that the primary concern of this work is *phenomenological* and I agree with Jean-Luc Marion and others that phenomenology is not limited to the horizon of Being.[227] Even if Rilke does not formulate the "ontological difference," it is the way that the *phenomena themselves* are revealed that is of the utmost importance, and the way in which phenomena show themselves to a poet like Rilke or an artist like Cézanne clearly exceeds their capacities

---

225 *LC*, 67; translation altered. *KA 4*, 624.
226 Heinrich Wiegand Petzet, *Encounters and Dialogues with Martin Heidegger 1929–1976*, trans. Parvis Emad and Kenneth Maly (Chicago: University of Chicago Press, 1993), 142; Christoph Jamme, "Der Verlust der Dinge: Cézanne – Rilke – Heidegger," 390; "'Zwiefalt' und 'Einfalt.' Heideggers Deutung der Kunst Cézannes," in *Wege und Irrwege des neueren Umganges mit Heideggers Werk: ein deutsch-ungarisches Symposium*, ed. István M. Fehér (Berlin: Duncker & Humblot, 1991), 99–108. The first edition of the *Briefe über Cézanne* was published in 1952 by Insel Verlag.
227 Marion, *Being Given: Toward a Phenomenology of Givenness*, 27–39.

of *conceptual* articulation. Moreover, there is an important affinity between Heidegger and Rilke when considered in a larger cultural and intellectual context in that they both see an ontological significance (broadly speaking) in Cézanne's art, which contrasts strongly with any sort of "aestheticism," "art for art's sake," or "formalist" aesthetics.[228]

In the present context it is especially significant that Rilke sees in his own work a striving for the *sachliches Sagen* that he identified in Baudelaire's "Une Charogne" and in Cézanne's paintings. In one of the letters on Cézanne Rilke responds to a suggestion, initially made by Clara Rilke, of a connection between his own work and Cézanne. The "blue pages" below refer to the manuscript of the *Neue Gedichte*, which Rilke wrote on blue paper.

> You must have known while writing how good it would make me feel, that insight which inadvertently sprang from the comparison of the blue pages with what I've experienced in front of Cézanne. What you are saying and affectionately confirming for me is something I had somehow suspected, although I would not have been able to say how far I had developed in the direction corresponding to the immense progress Cézanne achieved in his paintings. I was only convinced that there are personal inner

---

228 While Ralph Köhnen's monograph on Rilke and Cézanne, *Sehen als Textkultur: Intermediale Beziehungen zwischen Rilke und Cézanne*, is illuminating and rigorous in many respects, I cannot agree with his identification of Cézanne and Rilke with Mallarmé (p. 94). Köhnen does a good job of explicating the role of "construction" (as opposed to imitation or straightforward representation) in the work of Cézanne and Rilke, but he overemphasizes (my disagreement is one of *emphasis*) "construction" at the expense of the ideal of truth and "objectivity" which were central to Cézanne and Rilke. Not surprisingly, he is not entirely sympathetic to the ontological interpretations of Cézanne (pp. 93ff.). In contrast, I regard the ontological side of Cézanne's work to be evident in his paintings, his process of painting, the role of perception (if Cézanne had not been attempting to express his *vision of Nature* in painting there would have been no need to paint *en plein air*), the notion of *réalisation*, and his verbal utterances about his work. If Cézanne's paintings were simply a matter of free "construction," *réalisation* would not have posed such a great difficulty for him, because he would have only had to worry about the *formal* completeness of the picture. While much of Monet's work (though this is also not wholly true of Monet) might be regarded as a freer "musical" construction, a harmonious composition of colors for the sake of the composition itself (needless of the "objects" according to Kandinsky), this is definitely not true of Cézanne, who regarded a lack of "objectivity" as the shortcoming of Monet (see Max Imdahl, *Farbe: Kunsttheoretische Reflexionen in Frankreich* [Munich: Wilhelm Fink Verlag, 1987], 19ff.). I am more in agreement with the ontological interpreters of Cézanne such as Rilke, Kurt Badt, Max Imdahl, Merleau-Ponty, Heidegger, Gottfried Boehm, Christoph Jamme, Günter Seubold, and others.

reasons that make me see certain pictures which, a while ago, I might have passed by with momentary sympathy, but would not have revisited with increased excitement and expectation. It's not really painting I'm studying ... It was the turning point in these paintings which I recognized, because I had just reached it in my own work or had at least come close to it somehow, after having been ready, probably for a long time, for this one thing which so much depends on.[229]

In other words Rilke thinks that in the *Neue Gedichte*, even prior to his awakening to Cézanne, he was pursuing a similar or the same ideal that is so profoundly realized in Cézanne's paintings. Moreover, he esteems his poetry as having achieved this ideal to a great extent. He had "just reached it in" his "own work or had come close to it somehow." While not all of Rilke's poems in the *Neue Gedichte* can be interpreted in terms of a *sachliches Sagen*, Rilke's self-assessment is completely in line with my interpretation of poems in Chapter 4.[230]

With this background in mind the following question can be pursued: What, more precisely, is involved in Cézanne's painterly translation of vision, what he called *la réalisation*? In turn, what are the characteristic features of Cézanne's paintings? The following excerpt from the *Letters on Cézanne* thematizes Cézanne's *sachliches Sagen* and the idea of *la réalisation*, and thus offers a helpful entry into these questions:

> Actually without joy, it seems, in a constant rage, in conflict with every single one of his paintings, none of which seemed to him to achieve what he considered to be most indispensable. *La réalisation* he called it ... The compelling, the attainment of the thing [*Dingwerdung*], the intensified and even indestructible reality reached through his own experience of the object [*Gegenstand*], this seemed to him to be the innermost purpose of his work ...[231]

The task of realization is to achieve in the medium of painting a perfect equivalent of the deeper reality of the thing that is revealed in Cézanne's experience. As in the case of Rodin, the goal is also a transformation or metamorphosis of the thing ("Dingwerdung") into a

---

229 LC, 63. KA 4, 622.
230 The expression *sachliches Sagen* or "objective saying" obviously contains a double significance, which can be illustrated by writing "*objective* saying" or "objective *saying*." Up to now we have emphasized the former, namely that Cézanne's pictures say the *being of things*. We will soon elaborate the latter, the *how* of this pictorial *saying*.
231 LC, 34; translation altered. KA 4, 608.

156   The Poet as Phenomenologist

superior form of existence in the work of art.[232] In a passage to which we shall return (which concerns a portrait of Madame Cézanne) Rilke characterizes this transformation as follows:

> the color does not preponderate over the object, which seems so perfectly translated into its painterly equivalents that, while it is fully achieved and given as an object [*Gegenstand*], its bourgeois reality is at the same time relinquishing all its heaviness to a final and definitive picture existence.[233]

The "object" is perfectly translated into the language of painting and thus transformed or even transfigured into the more subtle body of colors. However, what in more detail is involved in the process of *réalisation* and how is it manifest in the example of landscape painting?

In the previous sub-section Cézanne's "motif" was mentioned. Richard Shiff is right to say of Cézanne that, "from the start, his motif is on the canvas as well as in the world."[234] Cézanne, along these lines, speaks of a "pictorial truth in things."[235] It is what Merleau-Ponty called "the landscape in its totality and in its absolute fullness" which he sought to translate into its painterly equivalent. A passage was also previously quoted, where Cézanne (in Gasquet's account) speaks of coming "face to face" with his "motif." The passage continues with Cézanne recounting the day that follows his first discovery of the "motif":

> A lovely morning follows; gradually the geological structures become clear to me, the strata, the main planes of my picture, establish themselves, and mentally I draw their rocky skeleton … I begin to distance myself from the landscape, to see it. With this first sketch, these geological lines, I detach myself from it. Geometry – the measurement of earth. A tender feeling comes over me and from the roots of this feeling rises the sap – colour. A sort of deliverance. Colour that expresses the radiance of the heart, that gives an outward form to the mystery of vision, that links earth and sun, the ideal and the real! An airy, coloured logic suddenly ousting sombre, stubborn geometry. Everything becomes organized: trees, fields, houses. I am seeing. In patches of colour. The geological foundation, the preparatory work, the

---

232 "Transformation" or "Verwandlung" is a central theme throughout Rilke's work. See n. 10.
233 *LC*, 81. *KA 4*, 630–1.
234 Richard Shiff, "Introduction," in *Conversations with Cézanne*, xxviii.
235 *Joachim Gasquet's Cézanne: A Memoir with Conversations*, 71.

world of the drawing, gives way; it has collapsed as if struck by a natural disaster. A cataclysm has carried it off and breathed new life into it. A new stage begins. The real one! The one where nothing escapes me, where everything is dense and at the same time fluid, natural. Only colours exist now, and in them brightness, the being whose thoughts they are, this aspiration of the earth towards the sun ... A minute in the life of the world passes. To paint that minute in its precise reality! Forgetting everything else for its sake. To become that minute. To be, in other words, the sensitised plate. To convey the image of what we see, forgetting everything that appeared before.[236]

After sketching the topographical structure of the landscape the process of painting and coloration takes over. Cézanne, as aforementioned, primarily regarded the landscape in terms of planes of colors. However, he also experienced the landscape as a seamless whole in all its elements. A clear reduction is involved in the attempt to translate the *landscape as a whole* onto the canvas. Cézanne has to and desires to say *everything* by means of the colors. This wholeness of Cézanne's experience is mirrored in the fact that he built up various parts of the canvas at the same time. He did not paint separate things, he let the things emerge out of the daubs of color which he added in various places at once. The picture itself emerged as a whole within which the "objects" in the picture also emerged. This mirrors his sense of the landscape itself as an organic totality. Rilke had some knowledge of this procedure and states,

> While painting a landscape and a still life, he would conscientiously persevere in front of the object, but approaching it only by very complicated detours. Beginning with the darkest tones, he would cover their depth with a layer of color that led a little beyond them, and keep going, expanding outward from color to color, until gradually he reached another, contrasting pictorial element, where, beginning at a new center, he would proceed in a similar way.[237]

This attempt to translate a vision of the landscape into color contains an evident difficulty pertaining to the fact that the landscape incorporates many qualities other than color. It is three-dimensional, relatively warm or cold, includes sounds and aromas, etc. Multifarious sensible qualities belong to the landscape in its fullness. Furthermore, invisible

---

236 *Joachim Gasquet's Cézanne: A Memoir with Conversations*, 153–4.
237 LC, 34. KA 4, 609.

dimensions of experience must also be translated into the modulation of colors on the canvas. Boehm offers a good explanation of the difficulties of translation and elucidates the reasons for Cézanne's persistent dissatisfaction with his attempts of "realization":

> His difficulties result, to begin with, from the far reaching abstraction inherent to this process … In Nature what appears, for instance, as the warm gleam of a crag illuminated by the sun, the reflection of light and the intermittent shadows of adjacent trees, what appears as the radiant blue of the sky, the dull breath of darkness, what appears as the glistening warmth of the vicinity and the coolness of the distance, what appears as thousands of grasses, flowers, leaves, animals, stones … in the painting only a patch of color can correspond to all this, a piece of matter that the brush flatly distributes. The difficulty of realization has to do with the overcoming of this rift, with surmounting this distance. Is there a more accelerated [*beschleunigtere*] abstraction, is a deeper rift conceivable, than that between Nature and painting? Painting can only succeed if with … the distribution of color on the canvas, a perfect equivalent of reality can be generated.[238]

The painting seeks to realize the fullness of the landscape or reality with the limited means of colors and their interrelations. Cézanne himself speaks, in this respect, of how colors must assume a synaesthetic significance in the painting. In Gasquet's reconstruction Cézanne says, "the pure blue smell of pine, which is sharp in the sun, ought to blend with the fresh green smell of meadows in the morning, and with the smell of stones and the distant marble smell of Sainte-Victoire. I have not achieved that effect. It must be achieved by the colors themselves …"[239] Elsewhere Cézanne speaks of his particular use of "blue tints to create the impression of air" and "depth."[240] In this sense a certain abstraction is necessitated, a kind of re-formation of Nature on the canvas; however, Cézanne's departure from representation does not result from an effort to detach the picture from an internal bond with the landscape or things, but stems from his attempt to say "everything"—everything revealed to Cézanne's exceptional vision—with the limited means of color. Whereas Nature can speak in color, form, sound, smell, warmth, etc., the painting must reveal all this in color. Cézanne wants the painting to be an equivalent of the landscape in its fullness. This is the task of *réalisation*.

---

238 Gottfried Boehm, *Paul Cézanne: Montagne Sainte-Victoire*, 57–8.
239 *Joachim Gasquet's Cézanne: A Memoir with Conversations*, 151.
240 Ibid., 163.

Cézanne's pictures are composed of patches or planes of color. Boehm importantly points out the fact that the individual colors (this is most apparent in his late paintings of Mont Sainte-Victoire) have no representative or meaningful value when viewed in isolation. It is only in the contrasts and gradations, in the relating of the colors, that they assume a value. This use of color to suggest other dimensions of the world is most clearly discernible in the fact that the patches of color in their interrelations—interrelations which can only be established through the work of the viewer's eye—at the same time serve to articulate the contours of the "objects." The relations of colors are simultaneously an appearance of colored things in the picture and the appearance of three-dimensional form. In Cézanne, coloration and modeling have become one and the same. Cézanne was completely conscious of this fact. According to Émile Bernard, Cézanne said,

> There is no line; there is no modeling; there are only contrasts … Modeling results from the perfect rapport of colors. When they are juxtaposed harmoniously, and when they are all present and complete, the painting models itself … Drawing and color are not distinct from one another; gradually as one paints, one draws. The more harmonious the colors are, the more precise the drawing will be. Form is at its fullest when color is at its richest. The secret of drawing and modeling lies in the contrasts and affinities of colors.[241]

In the discussion of Rodin's sculptures, attention was drawn both to the expressionistic and to the spatial and lustrous significance of the part/whole relation (these two moments can be distinguished conceptually but are obviously not divided; the *modelé* is both at the same time). In Cézanne's pictures not only is each part a visible expression of the invisible and determined in relation to light, each part is also related to every other part in the *dynamic emergence* of, for instance, the mountain's visibility. As the viewer traces the gradations of colors and sees them in relation, the "objects" in the picture *appear*; Mont Sainte-Victoire emerges ever more fully as the eye relates the colors to one another and perceives them in relation. Günter Seubold characterizes this process with regard to two late paintings, one of the gardener Vallier, the other of Mont Sainte-Victoire:

> The *Gestalt* of Vallier is in no way fixed; it forms itself for the tarrying observer, who through his/her own "production" must bring the planes into relation with each other – and who thereby

---

241 Émile Bernard, "Paul Cézanne," in *Conversations with Cézanne*, 38–9.

concedes that different "ways" [Bahnen] can be followed, that in the painting lies the potential for completely different connections. Similarly with *Montagne Sainte-Victoire*: The eye places at one moment these, in the next moment those, planes in connection with each other, at one moment follows one logic, in the next moment another, generates here a house, a tree, a path, which then also take shape in different ways and can thereby assume another "look" [*Aussehen*].[242]

Rilke was aware of the revolution in painting that had occurred in Cézanne's use of color. He states that, "no one before him [Cézanne] ever demonstrated so clearly the extent to which painting is something that takes place among the colors, and how one has to leave them alone completely, so that they can settle the matter among themselves."[243] He proceeds to give an elaborate characterization of the dynamic interrelation of colors and how they are reciprocally involved in the generation of the picture. He thus describes one of the portraits of Madame Cézanne:

> In the brightness of the face, the proximity of all these colors has been exploited for a simple modeling of form and features: even the brown of the hair roundly pinned up above the temples and the smooth brown of the eyes has to express itself against its surroundings. *It's as if every place were aware of all the other places*—it participates that much; that much adjustment and rejection is happening in it; that's how each daub plays its part in maintaining equilibrium and in producing it: just as the whole picture finally keeps reality in equilibrium ... To reach the peak of its [the red color of the armchair] expression, it is very strongly painted around the light human figure, so that a kind of waxy surface develops; and yet the color does not preponderate over the object, which seems so perfectly translated into its painterly equivalents that, while it is fully achieved and given as an object, its bourgeois reality is at the same time relinquishing all its heaviness to a final and definitive picture existence. Everything, as I already wrote, has become an affair that's settled among the colors themselves: a color will come into its own in response to another, or assert itself, or recollect itself. Just as in the mouth of a dog various secretions will gather in anticipation at the approach of various things—consenting ones for drawing out

---

242 Günter Seubold, *Kunst als Enteignis: Heideggers Weg zu einer nicht mehr metaphysischen Kunst*, 114.
243 LC, 75. KA 4, 627–8.

nutrients, and correcting ones to neutralize poisons: in the same way, various intensifications and dilutions take place in the core of every color, helping it survive contact with others. In addition to this glandular activity within the intensity of colors, reflections … play the greatest role: weaker local colors abandon themselves completely, contenting themselves with reflecting the dominant one. In this hither and back of mutual and manifold influence, the interior of the picture vibrates, rises and falls back into itself, and does not have a single unmoving part.[244]

Rilke ends his vivid depiction with the statement that there is not a single "unmoving part" in the picture—so dynamically interrelated are the colors in the appear*ing* of the picture (we previously saw the significance of movement in Rodin's sculptures; in Cézanne, movement plays an even greater role).[245] The picture also becomes freed of its representational character to a greater extent than in previous painting, as the elements of the picture only take on a significance with regard to the other elements of the picture; a patch of color, as already stated, signifies and contributes nothing if considered in isolation. However, this greater independence of pictorial language—which Émile Bernard identified as early as 1891 in his statement that Cézanne "opened to art this amazing door: painting for itself"—while paving the way toward later abstraction in painting, cannot be understood as a removal of the picture from any reference to the world.[246] Of course, abstract painting also need not be understood as a total loss of reference (this is only one interpretation); however, with complete abstraction there is no longer any obvious reference in the form of figurative representation, while in Cézanne representation still plays an inextricable role even though

---

244 *LC*, 80–2. *KA 4*, 630–1.
245 While the portrait of Madame Cézanne that Rilke describes was painted much earlier (1877) than the late pictures of Mont Sainte-Victoire, Cézanne's late work is in many respects simply the most radical execution of principles that can already be ascertained from the beginning of Cézanne's mature work (from around the time of his study with Camille Pissarro in 1872). Ralph Köhnen offers a good overview of the phases of Cézanne's work and their internal connection; he draws on Lionello Venturi's distinctions of four main phases but emphasizes the continuity in Cézanne's development from around 1871. Ralph Köhnen, *Sehen als Textkultur*, 70–98.
246 Émile Bernard, "Paul Cézanne," *Les Hommes d'aujourd'hui*, no. 387 (February–March 1891): n.p., quoted in Richard Shiff, "Introduction," in *Conversations with Cézanne*, xxix. For a discussion of a synthesis of abstraction and referential meaning in a related but slightly different context, see Luke Fischer, "Animalising Art: Rainer Maria Rilke and Franz Marc"; "Die Animalisierung der Kunst: Rainer Maria Rilke und Franz Marc".

the space of the painting achieves greater autonomy than earlier painting.[247]

The fact that the "objects" in Cézanne's pictures are not isolated but emerge in relation to other "objects," and finally arise out of the interrelations of shared colors, correlates directly with Cézanne's account of his vision, in which the ordinary boundaries between things dissolve. Rilke's statement that "it's as if every place were aware of all the other places" is reminiscent of Cézanne's remark that, "objects enter into each other ... Imperceptibly they extend beyond themselves through intimate reflections, as we do by looks and words." Furthermore, as the viewer reads the picture, sees the colors in relation, the "objects" take shape and dynamically emerge. This serves to thematize at once both *reality itself as emergent and dynamic, and the place of the seer in the emergence of the spectacle of vision.*

Like Rilke before him, Merleau-Ponty perceived in Cézanne's paintings a revelation of the things themselves. In "Eye and Mind," Merleau-Ponty mentions Cézanne's notion of *réalisation* and says the following with reference to paintings of Mont Sainte-Victoire:

> The painter, any painter, while he is painting, practices a magical theory of vision. He is obliged to admit that objects before him pass into him ... in short, that the same thing is both out there in the world and here at the heart of vision—the same or, if you like, a similar thing, but according to a coefficient similarity which is the parent, the genesis, the metamorphosis of being into its vision. It is the mountain itself which from out there makes itself seen by the painter; it is the mountain that he interrogates with his gaze.
>
> What exactly does he ask of it? To unveil the means, visible and not otherwise, by which it makes itself a mountain before our eyes ...[248]

In the paintings themselves the emergence of the mountain out of the totality of pictorial elements thematizes both the process of perception and the Being of the mountain, and ultimately reveals the intertwining of Being and vision. Merleau-Ponty thus speaks of "the metamorphosis

---

247 It is worthwhile to note that Rilke was never wholly sympathetic to abstraction in art. He regarded complete abstraction as a symptom of the "loss of things" in the technological age and while art involves a transformation of things it should seek to reveal things in their wholeness, rather than departing entirely from representation. For an insightful elaboration of these themes see Hermann Meyer, "Die Verwandlung des Sichtbaren; Die Bedeutung der modernen bildenen Kunst für Rilkes späte Dichtung," in *Zarte Empirie: Studien zur Literaturgeschichte*. See also n. 149.
248 Merleau-Ponty, "Eye and Mind," 127–8.

of being into its vision"; this concerns both what makes the mountain a mountain and what makes it a mountain for us. Cézanne found the means of disclosing this relationship in the characteristics of his paintings that we have considered; the *formation* of the mountain in the picture is at the same time its formation in our perception of the picture. Thereby, the mountain is neither revealed as a merely static reality nor is vision revealed as a mere passive registration of already complete "objects." How can the "still," "unmoving" mountain itself, however, be thought in such dynamic terms?

Temporality plays a key role in Cézanne's paintings as it also did for the Impressionists. For the Impressionists it was the *moment* that was defining—the apparition of a momentary vision and its felt character. For Cézanne the momentary, the ephemeral, also played a significant role. However, as Hermann Meyer and others have put it, Cézanne wanted to overcome Impressionism with the means of Impressionism.[249] Cézanne is not concerned with the mere *impression* of things, he is concerned with the things themselves, a point emphasized by Merleau-Ponty and others.[250] With the means of Impressionism he wants to get to the things themselves. The "instant" that Cézanne wants to capture is not that of a subjective impression, but a moment in the self-revelation of a Nature that is both ever-changing and ever-the-same, transient and lasting. Cézanne states,

> Nature is always the same, and yet its appearance is always changing. It is our business as artists to convey the thrill of nature's permanence along with the elements and the appearance of all its changes. Painting must give us the flavour of nature's eternity ... If, as I perceive them, these volumes and values correspond on my canvas to the planes and patches of colour that lie before me, that appear to my eyes, well then, my canvas 'joins hands'.[251]

This is a unification of Parmenides and Heraclitus and is not far from some of Heidegger's characterizations of the Greek understanding of *physis*.[252] The dynamic character of the picture thus tells not only of the involvement of the seer in the appearance of the seen, but also of

---

249 Hermann Meyer, "Rilkes Cézanne-Erlebnis," 248–9.
250 Merleau-Ponty, "Cézanne's Doubt," 62. See also Gosetti-Ferencei, *The Ecstatic Quotidian: Phenomenological Sightings in Modern Literature and Art*, 160. See also n. 223.
251 *Joachim Gasquet's Cézanne: A Memoir with Conversations*, 148.
252 See, for instance, Heidegger, "Vom Wesen und Begriff der Φύσις: Aristoteles, Physik B, 1," in *GA* 9 (1976 [1939]), 239–301.

Nature itself as dynamic and permanent at once. Boehm describes this dynamic significance of the paintings in terms of the relation between *natura naturans* ("nature naturing") and *natura naturata* ("nature natured"), nature as "process" and nature as "object," the latter being a moment of the former:

> The motif is a manifestation of this process, the result, and not the point of departure of painting ... Thus the *Montagne* shows us ... that Nature is not something that already *lies before us*, but something, that *forms* itself, that "becomes," when it claims existence. Max Raphael articulates this state of affairs with maternal imagery: "Cézanne sees as a farmer [*Bauer*] the earth in its process of giving birth ... It is a *hieros gamos* as rebirth in the consciousness of humanity. Cézanne identifies himself with the *terra creatrix* in the state of *creare*, with its pains and aches; he postulates and experiences himself as the principally, adequate representative of the *creator mundi omnipotens*." This state of affairs can be more precisely described as the synthesis of a becoming Nature (*natura naturans*) and a Nature that has become (*natura naturata*). What is certainly decisive is to see this relationship as a unity of the contradictory ... In the late-work it becomes completely clear that he sought the fusion of the seemingly irreconcilable, of above and below, of stillness and movement, of time and being.[253]

It is the landscape itself as both emergent and stable, changing and the same, temporal and lasting that is manifest and revealed in the paintings.[254] It is Nature not merely as "object" but Nature as "naturing" (*naturans*), a Nature which in the verbal sense maintains itself in being. In connection to our earlier considerations, it could be said that the *naturans* is the invisible of Nature, the *naturata* is the visible, and Cézanne's paintings seek to disclose this twofoldness in its dynamic unity. Along similar lines Boehm describes the paintings as interpreting the "Book of Nature" for us, and mentions Cézanne's emphasis on the "cone," the "sphere," and the "cylinder" as both key forms for painting

---

253 Gottfried Boehm, *Paul Cézanne: Montagne Sainte-Victoire*, 101–2.
254 In this respect, I should add that while I am sympathetic to many aspects of Badt's ontological interpretation of Cézanne, he does not properly recognize the *dynamism* in Cézanne's pictures and interprets Being in overly static terms. He sees that Cézanne, in contrast to the Impressionists, seeks a lasting reality but overemphasizes this (see, for instance, Badt, *Die Kunst Cézannes*, 120ff.). Boehm's interpretation is superior in that Boehm clearly brings out the "unity of the contradictory" in Cézanne rather than simply opposing the ephemeral and the lasting.

and letters of Nature's alphabet, but these details need not be elaborated in the present context.[255] Earlier than Boehm, Max Imdahl offered a similar interpretation of Cézanne's pictures of Mont Sainte-Victoire. Imdahl's characterization of *Montagne Sainte-Victoire* (1904–06, Basel, Öffentliche Kunstsammlung) unites various central aspects of our inquiry thus far.

Cézanne's picture is an image constituted by patches of color [*Farbflecken*], by mere "sensations colorantes," which as such signify nothing outside themselves and whose combination generates an autonomously ordered coloristic system. The coloristic system effectuates the appearance of the landscape, it brings forth the landscape out of itself. As this coloristic system Cézanne's picture is the phenomenon of a seeing sight [*sehendes Sehen*], namely a sight that abandons all objective foreknowledge and re-cognition. As the appearance of a landscape the picture is the phenomenon of a recognitive sight [*wiedererkennendes Sehen*], in so far as a landscape is an object of recognitive sight. One can speak of a pictoriality [*Bildlichkeit*] in which seeing sight masters and enables recognitive sight—but also of a visibility of the world [*Weltgesehenheit*] in which the effectuated is made visible within the horizon of the effectuating or the *natura naturata* within the horizon of the *natura naturans*.[256]

Imdahl's characterization brings together (without elaborating the idea) the two main aspects of our consideration, namely Nature and perception or vision. Due to Cézanne's "coloristic system" the mountain is not presented as a pregiven static object. Rather the mountain only properly emerges as the result of the spontaneous perception of the viewer. The mountain is a recognizable object and in this sense relates to a *re-cognitive sight*; however, *re-cognition* of the mountain in the picture is the result of a spontaneous or *seeing sight*, a cognitive rather than recognitive seeing. (It has also been significantly remarked that there is a degree to which Cézanne's pictures enable me to see my seeing, enable me to become aware of seeing as a constructive process.[257]) At the same time this appear*ing* of the

---

255 Gottfried Boehm, *Paul Cézanne: Montagne Sainte-Victoire*, 60.
256 Max Imdahl, *Bildautonomie und Wirklichkeit: Zur theoretischen Begründung moderner Malerei* (Mittenwald: Mäander-Kunstverlag, 1981) (the passage quoted does not have a page number and appears beneath a reproduction of the painting that precedes the essay, "Cézanne – Braque – Picasso: Zum Verhältnis zwischen Bildautonomie und Gegenstandssehen").
257 Ralph Köhnen, *Sehen als Textkultur*, 90.

landscape thematizes the landscape itself as *naturans* and not only *naturata*. Thus there is a kind of convergence of the relation between *seeing* and *seen* and the relation of *naturing* (*naturans*) and *nature* (*naturata*) (this is also suggested by Merleau-Ponty's expression, "the metamorphosis of being into its vision"). In light of this observation, might one not venture the claim that Cézanne's pictures suggest a hidden unity between *noetic activity* and *nature as verbal* (or at least an identity of seeing and the seen [the be*ing* of what is seen] in the process of seeing), and "realize" for the viewer an equivalent of his non-dualistic experience, formulated in the statement: "The landscape thinks itself in me ... and I am its consciousness"?[258]

Boehm connects the dynamic open totality of the picture with Rilke's understanding of Cézanne's *sachliches Sagen* and thus illustrates the manner in which this *sachliches Sagen* can be interpreted, in my chosen terminology, as a non-dualistic or twofold disclosure. Boehm writes,

> Cézanne's "*Sachlichkeit*," which so greatly impressed Rilke, is the result of an activity of "Temperament," in other words the embodiment of emotional, imaginative, and cognitive capacities. The Montagne Sainte-Victoire demonstrates itself, therefore, as an outer view and an interior-image at the same time; the alternatives, either "exterior" or "interior," fall short, already due to the fact that the most primary features of an exterior-view—stable space and illuminated things—have disappeared. The eye of the painter (subsequently that of the viewer) enters with what is seen into a completely indissoluble dynamic unity. The process of Nature wills to be consummated. This process compels vision to co-operate and finally to participate, and distinguishes it fundamentally from a determinative and dissociated observation of a static state of affairs.[259]

In Cézanne's "sachliches Sagen," inner and outer, mind and landscape, vision and natural process are disclosed as an indissoluble or twofold unity.

---

258 The German Idealist, Friedrich Schelling, is probably the philosopher who has offered the most systematic account of the work of art as revealing a synthesis of the unconscious process of nature and the conscious activity of the human mind. However, Cézanne's art demonstrates this synthesis to a greater degree than the art of Schelling's time. While all art is inseparable from the activity of the appreciator, the role of the viewer in constructing the painting is greater with respect to Cézanne's works than with respect to Romantic paintings. F. W. J. Schelling, *System of Transcendental Idealism*, trans. Peter Heath (Charlottesville, VA: University of Virginia Press, 2001 [1800]), 219ff.
259 Gottfried Boehm, *Paul Cézanne: Montagne Sainte-Victoire*, 116–17.

While I do not wish to blur the differences between Rilke's, Merleau-Ponty's, and Heidegger's interpretations of Cézanne, there is an obvious proximity between them, which has been indicated and requires some further elaboration. Since significant attention has been given to Merleau-Ponty's understanding of Cézanne, I will now say a bit more about Heidegger's Cézanne-reception.

Though Heidegger did not write a treatise or monograph on Cézanne, Cézanne's significance for Heidegger has been elaborated by Christoph Jamme, Günter Seubold, and others, on the basis of a number of fragmentary statements. I will not reconstruct Heidegger's view here but describe a few of the essentials. Heidegger saw, particularly in Cézanne's late works, a painterly equivalent of the overcoming of metaphysics. He says in a "thought-poem"—what he calls a *Gedachtes*— addressed to René Char in 1971, that, "Im Spätwerk des Malers ist die Zwiefalt/ von Anwesendem und Anwesenheit einfältig/ geworden, 'realisiert' und verwunden zugleich,/ verwandelt in eine geheimnisvolle Identität [In the late-work of the painter the twofold/ of what is present and presence has become simple or one-fold/ 'realized' and resolved at once,/ transformed into a mysterious identity]."[260] Seubold articulates "Anwesenheit" ("presence" or "presentness") as the horizon within which a being appears and "Anwesendes" ("what is present") as the being that appears within a given horizon.[261] These, according to Heidegger, become, in a mysterious way, simple or "one-fold" ("einfältig") in Cézanne's pictures. Seubold and Jamme seek to elaborate this claim concretely with regard to Cézanne's late paintings. They explicate this in terms of the fact that Cézanne's pictures do not take beings for granted, nor do they take the horizon within which beings are given for granted. Rather, as a result of the dynamic interrelation of the colored planes and the participation of our seeing in the articulation of the picture (where "objects" take shape and retreat simultaneously with our "reading" of the picture), the paintings thematize beings as emergent, as appearing out of a pre-objective horizon; things are thematized in their emergence into presence (and retreating into absence), rather than as already present. Jamme states the following, in this respect:

> With this background in mind it is possible to decipher what is implied [by Heidegger] by the "twofold of what is present and presence." Cézanne dissolves in his pictures the fixed objectivity [*fixierte Gegenständlichkeit*] of his motif. The objects

---

260 Günter Seubold, *Kunst als Enteignis: Heideggers Weg zu einer nicht mehr metaphysischen Kunst*, 106.
261 Ibid., 108.

("what is present") are no longer determined in their meaning through the horizon of a metaphysical worldview or through a pragmatic frame of reference. Objectivity is led back to its possibilizing ground, to its "endowment, generation, appropriation [*Ereignung*]." Cézanne, according to Heidegger's thesis, thematizes in his "late-work" ... the "letting-presence" itself, and "no longer the presentation of what is present in its presence."[262]

This is obviously very close to Merleau-Ponty's evaluation of the significance of Cézanne. As we saw, Merleau-Ponty regards Cézanne's paintings as revelatory of what makes the mountain a mountain before our eyes, which concerns both the being of the mountain and its disclosure. While there are significant differences in the thought (and poetry) of Heidegger, Merleau-Ponty, and Rilke, within the horizon of the present work it can be said that they all share the view that Cézanne's paintings enable a revelation of *die Sache selbst*.

While Cézanne freed up painting to evolve an independent language no longer as immediately tied to representation, it has long been recognized as a mistake to regard the "self-sufficiency" of Cézanne's pictures as the existence of an art which has no reference to the world or no *Weltbezug*. The term "realization," the attempt to translate a vision of *the world* into the picture, loses all meaning if this *Weltbezug* is ignored. Rilke, Merleau-Ponty, and Heidegger rightly saw how Cézanne's paintings enable a deeper disclosure of things. In his biographical accounts of Heidegger, Petzet discusses the thinker's connection to Cézanne. The following passage can serve as a fitting conclusion to this sub-section, in its emphasis on the concrete relation between Cézanne's paintings and the Provençal landscape in which they were born:

> More than once, Heidegger returned from a trip to the land of Cézanne and encouraged me—not without urgency—to bring together in a book all the paintings of the master that show the Montagne and to write a text for it. Of course, a prerequisite would be that I myself go to Provence and look on the Montagne St. Victoire with my own eyes. For even the best reproductions of the paintings and watercolors are not capable of showing what the "holy mountain" has to say and what the painter then transformed into the language of his paintings. In order to convey something of this dialogue, one must himself have seen both—the mountains and the paintings.[263]

---

262 Christoph Jamme, "Der Verlust der Dinge: Cézanne – Rilke – Heidegger," 392.
263 Heinrich Wiegand Petzet, *Encounters and Dialogues with Martin Heidegger 1929–1976*, 142; translation altered.

Learning to See: Rilke and the Visual Arts 169

Conclusion of Chapter

The previous section sketched Rilke's relationship to the Romantics and indicated the direction in which Rilke sought to move beyond the Romantic relationship to Nature. In *Worpswede* Rilke refers to Runge as an exception, as someone who was not inspired by Nature in a general way, but rather had *seen* the things he painted "again and again." It is evident from the explication in the present section that Rilke appraised Rodin and Cézanne as generally surpassing the artists of the Romantic era in their diligence and devotion to *seeing*. It is particularly clear that Rilke esteemed Cézanne's vision as involving a discipline and devotion to the detailed study of Nature and an "objectivity" (an "*inspired* objectivity") that are unmatched by the Romantic artists. Similarly, and this is most emphatic in Cézanne, he regarded their works of art as disclosive of the things themselves. The following chapters will reveal the deep affinity between these aspects of Rodin's and Cézanne's work, and Rilke's vision and poetry. Chapter 3 is primarily devoted to Rilke's way of seeing, while Chapter 4 explicates the twofold significance of his poetry.

Three Rilke as Seer: A Twofold Vision of Nature

The main task of the present chapter is to elaborate Rilke's parallel practices to those of Rodin and Cézanne, and to show how Rilke's seeing accomplished a non-dualistic vision of Nature. Although Rilke's practices have already been implied to a certain extent in the discussion of his engagement with visual artists, the present task is to articulate Rilke's vision more explicitly. This will bring the previous considerations of artistic vision to their culmination.

It is evident from *Worpswede* and his writings on Rodin and Cézanne that Rilke does not envisage the overcoming of dualism in philosophical terms, not even in terms of a phenomenological explication of what is implicit in the everyday life-world. Chapter 1 demonstrated that a phenomenology of the life-world in the mode of everydayness accomplishes a more adequate (experiential) overcoming of dualism than a metaphysical monism. Building on Chapter 2, the present chapter will show how Rilke's vision transcends the everyday (and its phenomenological explication[1]) and opens up a distinctive horizon for a phenomenology of the "exceptional" or "extra-mundane."

Attention was previously drawn to Rilke's contradistinction of the artist from the ordinary adult in *Worpswede*. The artist for Rilke (as for the Romantics before him) shares a special affiliation with, and maintains a childlike openness to, Nature. In his writings on Rodin and Cézanne, Rilke more emphatically describes a fundamental active-passivity, *Gelassenheit*, and poverty, conjoined to a selfless vision, as constitutive of the artist's manner of being-in-the-world. In the discussion of Cézanne, attention was drawn to *epiphanic* aspects of artistic vision. Thus, Rilke

---

1   As I discussed in Chapter 1 (and further discuss below), the phenomenological approach is itself exceptional (hence, for instance, Husserl's distinction between the "natural attitude" and the "phenomenological attitude") even if it is focused on everyday phenomena. Nevertheless, Rilke's poetic vision is exceptional in a different way from philosophical reflection.

presents the artist as an exceptional figure and, more importantly for our purposes, the artist's extra-ordinary manner of being facilitates a non-dualistic or twofold vision of Nature and the world. This highlighting of the exceptional or extra-mundane character of artistic vision, which includes a disclosure of the *divine* or *spiritual*, prompts the much-debated question concerning the relationship between Rilke and mysticism, namely whether, and if so, in what sense, Rilke should be regarded as a mystic. Due to the nature of the subsequent interpretation of Rilke, this question requires some discussion.[2]

In the contemporary context the words "mystic," "mysticism," "mystical" are often employed with critical or even polemical intentions. The "mystical" carries connotations of the "subjective," the "vague," the "unscientific," or even the "muddle-headed." That these predicates are inappropriate to Rilke's ideal in the middle period should already be apparent. Rilke valued "exactitude," "impartiality," and "objectivity." To recall *Malte*, "Er war ein Dichter und haßte das Ungefähre." Thus, if the middle Rilke is mystical, it is not in the sense of being "vague" and "subjective." That Rilke read and was influenced by authors in the mystical tradition is well known.[3] The contemporary Rilke-reception, however, tends to distance itself from mystical interpretations of Rilke, whereas in the early part of the twentieth century it was common to regard Rilke as a "mystical poet."[4] In the "non-mystical" reading of Rilke there is the tendency to oppose the terms "poet" and "mystic"; according to this view, Rilke's prime concern was poetry and this poetic concern can be detached from any consideration of mysticism. I regard this dichotomous treatment of the categories "poet" and "mystic" as a superficial consideration of the matter. First, many great poets have shared mystical strivings of one kind or another—Rumi, Blake, Novalis, Yeats, and countless others—and their vocations as poets *and* mystics cannot be easily, or

---

2 For a good discussion of some of the connections between Rilke and mysticism, see Martina Wagner-Egelhaaf, *Mystik der Moderne: Die visionäre Ästhetik der deutschen Literatur im 20. Jahrhundert* (Stuttgart: J. B. Metzler, 1989). See also Paul Bishop, "Rilke: Thought and Mysticism," in *The Cambridge Companion to Rilke*, ed. Karen Leeder and Robert Vilain (Cambridge: Cambridge University Press, 2010). For a comprehensive discussion of Rilke's connections to esotericism and occultism, see Gísli Magnússon, *Dichtung als Erfahrungsmetaphysik: Esoterische und okkultistische Modernität bei R. M. Rilke*. See also Gísli Magnússon, "Rilke und der Okkultismus," in *Metaphysik und Moderne: Von Wilhelm Raabe bis Thomas Mann*, ed. Andreas Blödorn and Søren R. Fauth (Wuppertal: Arco, 2006).
3 See n. 2. A comprehensive assessment of Rilke's interest in "esotericism," "occultism," "hermeticism," "mysticism," and "spiritualism" is beyond the scope of the present work.
4 Martina Wagner-Egelhaaf, *Mystik der Moderne*, 62.

at all, separated. Already for this reason, the opposition of "poet" and "mystic" is problematic. Second, poetry itself, as a form of language, bears many affinities to mystical writings; both seek to say the "unsayable" or "ineffable"; both negate and reveal the inadequacy of common language, whether it is through mystical "negative theology" or the poet's introduction of unfamiliar metaphors.[5] Both the poet and the mystic share a sense of dissatisfaction with more common forms of linguistic expression. Third, it should already be evident from our explication of Rilke's assessment of the artist as a privileged figure (particularly in the cases of Rodin and Cézanne) that characteristics are ascribed to the artist which derive from the mystical tradition—*Gelassenheit*, poverty, a vision of the holy. Hence, even if one agrees that Rilke was foremost an artist or poet (rather than a mystic), his conception of the artist and poet includes mystical aspects. Thus, *the opposition of poet and mystic is a false dichotomy and mystical elements are clearly attributable to Rilke.*

The title of this chapter, "Rilke as Seer ..." intentionally implies mystical connotations. "Seer" shares obvious affiliations with designations such as "mystic," "prophet," "clairvoyant," and "visionary." All these words suggest individuals who are "privileged with a first-hand experience of the divine" and this first-hand experience is a necessary condition that a person needs to fulfill in order to warrant any of these titles. However, specific reasons motivate the choice of the word "seer" in contrast to other synonyms. The verb "seer" bears a clear etymological relation to the present participle *"see*ing," and the infinitive *"to see."* It is in light of the central significance of seeing—*Schauen* and *Sehen*—that the word "seer" is an appropriate designation for the middle Rilke.

The verb "to see" is used with reference to a number of different contexts. Two of these contexts can be referred to as "sense perception" and "intellectual seeing." We say for instance "I *see* a tree," meaning "I have a sense perception of a tree." However, when someone tries to explain something to us and we finally understand what the person is trying to communicate, we say "now I *see* what you mean." The latter case concerns an "intellectual object" whereas the former case concerns a "sense object." With this in mind "the seer" could refer to "the one who sees" or "the one who is capable of seeing," but it should be clear by now that the seeing intended refers neither one-sidedly to "sense perception" nor to "intellectual seeing." *It is precisely the*

---

5 See Luke Fischer, "Metaphor and the Poetic Origin of Meaning," in *On Meaning: The Making of Civic Sense*, ed. Jose Ciprut (under review); Luke Fischer, "Owen Barfield and Rudolf Steiner: The Poetic and Esoteric Imagination," *Literature and Aesthetics* 21, no. 1 (2011): 136–58.

overcoming of this implicit dualism between a seeing of the intelligible in abstraction from the sensible and vice versa that is sought. Hence, "Rilke as Seer" implies Rilke's twofold vision. However, the "mystical" connotation of "seer" is also intended, but precisely with reference to a seeing that is twofold. This mystical characterization of Rilke does not imply an "other-worldly" attitude or a withdrawal from the sphere of perception. However, Rilke's perception in the middle period involves more than ordinary perception and includes an *epiphanic* or *numinous* dimension. It is these intertwined connotations that are intended by the words "seer," "twofold seeing," and the "mystical." *Moreover, it is only in such an "exceptional" vision of Nature that the possibility of an adequate overcoming of dualism (human/nature dualism) is glimpsed.*

While Rilke moves beyond a phenomenology of the life-world in the mode of everydayness, phenomenology as such is not limited to the everyday and Rilke's vision is in many respects implicitly phenomenological. Rilke shares the aspiration to overcome subject/object dualism and sensible/spiritual dualism which is common to many phenomenologists. Numerous parallels can be drawn between Merleau-Ponty's understanding of "living perception," the "chiasm," and "flesh," and Rilke's understanding of seeing. They both share the conception of an active-passivity in perception, and of a meaning which arises at the point of overlap between perceiver and perceived. The recent phenomenology of Jean-Luc Marion also shares many similarities with Rilke, particularly Marion's notion of the "saturated phenomenon."[6] Attention has already been drawn to examples of Rilke's interest in phenomena that bear the traits of "inexhaustibility," "surplus," and "excess." Indeed, many of Rilke's poems could be fruitfully interpreted as presentations of phenomena in the mode of "saturation." Heidegger also advocates a radical active-passivity, as aforementioned, under the name of *Gelassenheit*. Moreover, Heidegger sought to think behind the fateful dualism introduced by Plato into the history of philosophy, and to discover a thinking which is before the division between the "sensible" and the "intelligible." Käte Hamburger has pointed out many parallels between Husserl and Rilke and the centrality of "seeing" in both (Hamburger's interpretation of Rilke will be discussed in more detail in Chapter 4).[7] Hence, although Rilke was not influenced directly by phenomenology, and lived before

---

6 For a good introduction to the idea of the "saturated phenomenon" see Jean-Luc Marion, *Being Given: Toward a Phenomenology of Givenness*.
7 Käte Hamburger, "Die phänomenologische Struktur der Dichtung Rilkes," in *Philosophie der Dichter*.

Rilke as Seer: A Twofold Vision of Nature 175

the majority of phenomenologists of the twentieth century, there are obvious connections between Rilke and phenomenology.[8]

Moreover, important connections between Rilke and phenomenology can also be discerned with respect to mysticism. Both the later Heidegger and Marion share a serious interest in the mystical tradition. More recently Anthony Steinbock has explicitly drawn on mystics from the Abrahamic tradition in order to elaborate a phenomenology of religious experience.[9] This connection between the mystical tradition and the work of phenomenological philosophers is, I believe, far from arbitrary (see below). My central claim then, is that *although Rilke transcends the horizon of a phenomenology of the everyday, his whole tendency is implicitly phenomenological. Furthermore, there is an inherent relationship between mysticism and phenomenology.*

The phenomenological critique of previous philosophies results from the phenomenological privileging of a certain kind of givenness. Phenomenology privileges a "givenness-in-person." It is a lack of "givenness-in-person," a deficiency in "phenomenality," which is a major reason for the phenomenological critique of metaphysics. When I propose, "there is a picture hanging on the wall," the proposition can be verified by a "givenness-in-person." I either *see* that there *is* a picture on the wall or *see* that there is no picture on the wall. This is the moment of disclosure that Heidegger formulates in *Sein und Zeit*.[10] As was demonstrated in Chapter 1, the problem with metaphysical thinking is a lack of givenness, the deficiency of givenness regarding the matter (*Sache*) under consideration. This holds true for all metaphysics, or conversely it could be said that whatever bears this character is metaphysical. Whenever a thinker "objectifies" a reality as an "in-itself," which has no possible way of *showing itself from itself*, metaphysical thinking is taking place. Whether one postulates a purely physical reality as the ground of the world—a materialistic thing in itself—or a wholly transcendent God in this respect makes no difference. In both cases the object is "postulated" because it "cannot" be "given."[11]

In the 1927 lecture "Phänomenologie und Theologie" Heidegger makes the statement that contrary to the structure of other sciences the

---

8 Rilke did have some contact with the phenomenologist, Max Scheler but there is nothing to say that Rilke was deeply influenced by Scheler's writings. Many phenomenologists, in contrast, were influenced by Rilke—Heidegger and Gadamer are only two obvious examples.
9 Anthony J. Steinbock, *Phenomenology and Mysticism: The Verticality of Religious Experience.*
10 Heidegger, *Sein und Zeit*, 217ff.
11 See Chapter 1.

object of theology is not God.¹² The object of zoo-logy, for instance, is animals, whereas the object of theo-logy is not, in an analogous sense, God. While Heidegger makes this distinction on the basis of his view of the fundamental and distinctive role of faith in (Christian) theology, in contrast to other positive sciences (such as the natural sciences), this statement is also instructive for the present argument. If theology is metaphysical in the aforementioned sense, then (for different reasons than those given by Heidegger¹³) the object of theology is not God. The difference lies in the fact that God does not attain to a genuine givenness, whereas plants and animals do. Such a givenness is presupposed by a science such as zoology or sociology. The "objects" of the science of zoology are directly encountered and given in a way that is not true of metaphysical theology.¹⁴

This consideration brings to light the essential difference between mysticism and "metaphysical theology," and validates the former suggestion that there is an inherent kinship between phenomenology and mysticism. The difference between mysticism and "metaphysical theology" is a difference between a "givenness-in-person" and a deficiency of givenness. The latter directly experiences the divine, whereas the former deals with a postulated God. What fails to *appear* for the latter becomes *phenomenal* for the former. Thus, if one is a convinced phenomenologist and also bears an interest in the divine or the religious, then one is likely to be sympathetic to mysticism; "metaphysical theology" shows a deficiency in phenomenality whereas "mysticism" makes claims to a privileged givenness of the divine in person, as "first-hand experience." Hence, *a phenomenological and non-metaphysical approach to the divine implies mysticism, or mysticism could be regarded as a phenomenology of the divine.*¹⁵

Rilke's phenomenological and mystical disposition in the above sense is revealed by the following description by his friend and peer, the philosopher, Rudolf Kassner:

> Rilke's inner world is not founded on faith; rather Rilke, the man of sight [*der Augenmensch*], desires contact, wants to touch. Only in a world of contact is the beautiful, as it is described in

---

12 Heidegger, "Phänomenologie und Theologie," in *GA* 9 (1976 [1927]), 59ff.
13 My aim here is not to follow the details of Heidegger's thought in this lecture, but only to take his statement as an opportunity to point out one exemplary difference between metaphysical theology and zoology (as a representative science).
14 This conception of "metaphysical theology" is, of course, meant as a conceptual distinction and not as a description of everything that goes under the name of "theology," some of which might be properly "mystical" (see below).
15 Steinbock bears out this claim in detail in *Phenomenology and Mysticism*.

the first elegy, "nichts als des Schrecklichen Anfang [nothing but the beginning of terror]." His apostle is, therefore, not Paul, but Thomas, who places his fingers into the wound of the resurrected one.[16]

In other words, Rilke is not content merely to believe in the divine; rather, he seeks to experience the divine in person. He, "der Augenmensch," does not want to *believe* but rather wants to *see* and to establish direct contact with the numinous.

Perhaps more has been said than was strictly necessary in order to introduce the pertinent relationship between Rilke, mysticism, and phenomenology. However, these considerations serve to indicate that while Rilke's vision transcends the *everyday* and the horizon of many phenomenological studies, it can be regarded, at the very least implicitly, as a *phenomenology* of the exceptional.

Rilke's Seeing

The essential role of a cultivated *Gelassenheit* in Rilke's creative process was indicated in the previous chapter and can be gleaned from many of his writings. With this in mind, we will turn directly to Rilke's *praxis* of seeing, which is continuous with an active-passive disposition. That Rilke became a student of Nature, who stood before things and submitted his gaze to them in an analogous manner to Cézanne, is evident from numerous passages in his correspondences. In the previously cited letter of October 13, 1907 to Clara Rilke, he writes,

> If I were to come and visit you, I would surely also see the splendor of moor and heath, the hovering bright greens of meadows, the birches, with new and different eyes; and though this transformation is something I've completely experienced and shared before, in part of the Book of Hours, nature was then still a general occasion for me, an evocation, an instrument in whose strings my hands found themselves again; *I was not yet sitting before her* ... How little I would have been able to learn from Cézanne, from van Gogh, then.[17]

I have emphasized the statement, "I was not yet sitting before her." The idea of sitting "before [*vor*]" or "in front of" Nature is reiterated by Rilke in various contexts. By this he means that like a landscape painter who works *en plein air* he studied in detail the features of a landscape or

---

16 Rudolf Kassner, "Rainer Maria Rilke: Zum zwanzigsten Todestag 1946," in Rudolf Kassner, *Rilke: Gesammelte Erinnerungen 1926–1956*, 34.

17 LC, 48–9; my emphasis. KA 4, 615–16.

an aspect of Nature. Rilke relates that previously he was "not *yet* sitting before her," which means conversely that he has *now* learnt to sit before her (Nature) and, analogous to a painter, thus draws inspiration for his poetic works. Likewise, the statement that he could not have learnt from Cézanne or van Gogh at that time—when his attitude to Nature was less selfless—implies that he *has* learnt from them and *has* carried out analogous practices.

In a letter to a young female friend—"an eine junge Freundin"—of March 17, 1926 Rilke retrospectively characterizes the most significant events in his development as a poet. In this letter he again speaks of being "before" Nature but this time refers to Rodin. He writes,

> Russia ... became, in a certain sense, the foundation of my experiencing and receiving, just as, from the year 1902 on, Paris— the incomparable—became the basis of my desire for artistic form. Under the great influence of Rodin, who helped me ... to overcome a lyrical superficiality ... through the obligation ... to work like a painter or sculptor from Nature [*wie ein Maler oder Bildhauer, vor der Natur zu arbeiten*], relentlessly apprehending and copying. The first result of this strict, good schooling was the poem "The Panther"—in the Jardin des Plantes in Paris—to which one might ascribe this provenance.[18]

Influenced by Rodin's advice and example, Rilke became a diligent and selfless observer and learnt to work from Nature ("vor der Natur zu arbeiten") like a painter or sculptor. The first creative result of this apprenticeship to Nature was "Der Panther" (probably the most well-known poem in the *Neue Gedichte*). In other words, the inspiration for his poem "Der Panther" arose through this devoted perception of the animal.[19] That Rilke chooses to sum up the period of the *Neue Gedichte* and their background in this way justifies the view that this praxis of seeing and its translation into poetry (equivalent to the two moments in Rodin's and Cézanne's work) typifies his endeavors at the time.

Rilke's devotion to seeing led to a fundamental transformation in his sense and experience of Nature. Things assumed a deeper and more

---

18 Rilke, *Briefe*, vol. 2, 517.
19 A plaster-cast of an antique tiger in Rodin's studio was also a stimulus for the poem. However, this does not speak against Rilke's account, as some scholars might want to imply, because it would only speak against this account if Rilke conceived art as opposed to truth, if he conceived the status of art as fictional. An artistic presentation of an animal can clearly, and is ideally, revelatory of the essence of the animal. Art and perception mutually inform one another.

mysterious meaning. This is evident from a passage in the letter of August 8, 1903 to Lou Andreas-Salomé. Rilke's description also serves to build on our earlier discussion of the active-passivity of artistic vision. He explains,

> when I seek people they give me no counsel and do not know what I mean. And with regard to books I am just the same (just as helpless), and they also do not help me, as though they were still too human [*als ob sie noch zu sehr Menschen wären*] ... Only things [*Dinge*] speak to me. Rodin's things, the things on the Gothic cathedrals, the things of antiquity, all things that are perfect things. They point me to their prototypes: to the moving living world, seen simply and without interpretation as the occasion for things. I am beginning to see newly [*Ich fange an, Neues zu sehen*]: already flowers are often so infinitely much to me, and from animals have come stirrings [*Anregungen*] of a strange kind.[20]

The active-passivity of this vision is revealed by Rilke's dative characterization of things speaking or talking to him ("die Dinge reden zu mir"). Rilke's discussion of "things" or "Dinge" in this passage primarily refers to "art-things" or "Kunst-Dinge." This is indicated by his qualification that all "perfect things" speak to him and his listing of artworks. However, it is evident that his vision of Nature was transformed and his appreciation of art played a role in this transformation. The end of the passage reveals the aptness of stating that "natural things" also speak to him. For this reason, and for the purposes of clarity, our earlier conceptual distinction between *Dinge* and *Kunst-Dinge* can be maintained. It is not only *Kunst-Dinge* ("perfect things") that speak to him but also *Dinge* ("natural things" in this case)—flowers have taken on an inexhaustible meaning and from animals he has received strange incitements and stirrings ("Anregungen"). Thus *Dinge* and *Kunst-Dinge* came to "speak" to Rilke in a deeper and previously unknown way. The dative structure of Rilke's formulations reveals a reversal of ordinary intentional-directionality. It has already been stressed that Rilke's seeing does not dominate the phenomenon; rather, it is a kind of ec-static reception. Just as correlative to Rodin's *Gelassenheit* Nature assumes the character of an agent or activity, and as Meister Eckhart's vision is God's vision of him, in the above excerpt a reversal of the common understanding of intentionality is evident: "things speak to me."

The reversal of the common understanding of "intentional-directionality" in Rilke's letter is reminiscent of Marion's idea of

---

20 Rilke, *Briefe aus den Jahren 1902–1906*, vol. 1 (Leipzig: Insel Verlag, 1930), 116.

"counter-intentionality," of an intentionality that seems to proceed from the phenomenon and addresses the subject, rather than being confined by the subject's intention.[21] Rilke's seeing does not conform to a "subjective idealism," in which the appearance of the world is simply a reflection of the subjective categories and structures of the mind. Things actively reveal, and speak for, themselves. It is telling to contrast this gesture of active-passivity with Kant's formulation of the ideal attitude of the scientist toward Nature—a formulation that typifies much of the modern relationship to Nature and belongs to the Baconian tradition.[22] The reason for considering Kant's characterization is not in order to engage in a detailed critique of Kantian philosophy, which is well beyond the scope of the present work, but because it provides an instructive contrast to Rilke's attitude to Nature. In the "Preface" to the second edition of the *Critique of Pure Reason*, Kant states that the scientist (the knower of Nature) has learnt that he should approach Nature in the character of "an appointed judge who *compels* the witnesses to answer questions which he himself has formulated."[23] Physics owes its success in having learnt that "it must adopt as its guide ... that which it has itself *put* into nature."[24] It is clearly not an attitude of active-passivity that Kant is advocating as the proper attitude of the scientist. Moreover, correlative to this inquisitional attitude, there is no possibility that Nature would unconceal itself in a way that one would be called to characterize with the words, "die Dinge reden zu mir." The Kantian representation of the scientist implies an attitude of *imposition* rather than the contrary *receptive* disposition that is central to Rilke's understanding of the artist.

Kant's scientist "forces" or "compels" Nature to answer the scientist's questions in an analogous manner to a prosecutor compelling a witness to answer specifically directed questions. What Nature "says" in response to such an interrogation will be restricted by the terms *prescribed in advance* by the scientist. Rilke's attitude in contrast is thoroughly *non-a priori* and non-dominating; it is an active submission and the opening up of a space for Nature to disclose herself. If Kant's attitude is one of interrogation, Rilke's disposition is one of listening, letting-be, openness to the unforeseeable.[25] The former finds only

---

21 See, for instance, Jean-Luc Marion, *In Excess: Studies of Saturated Phenomena*, trans. Robyn Horner (New York: Fordham University Press, 2004), 113.
22 On the history of the modern relationship to Nature and its Baconian heritage see Carolyn Merchant, *The Death of Nature: Women, Ecology, and the Scientific Revolution* (San Francisco, CA: HarperCollins, 1983 [1980]).
23 Kant, *Critique of Pure Reason*, B. xiii; my emphasis.
24 Ibid., B. xiv; my emphasis.
25 One of Rilke's most beautiful articulations of the unforeseeability of certain revelations of things is the following tercet from sonnet X in the second part of

what it has put into Nature, whereas the latter can be *surprised* by an excess that it could have never anticipated—animals can make strange, unfamiliar impressions on the perceiver, flowers can reveal an *infinite* (clearly not *put* there by the "finite" subject) significance. In the present day, when so much of science has been reduced to the service of technology, the antithesis between Rilke's receptive gesture and science is only more apparent.[26] In that science has largely become subservient to political, economic, and pragmatic interests, much scientific inquiry—rather than expressing a pure desire for knowledge—is directed toward the goal of finding new ways of controlling nature that will aid technological progress and generate profits for corporations. Such scientific behavior involves an implicit reduction of knowing to the ability to control Nature. Genetic research for the purposes of genetic engineering is an exemplary case of this instrumentalization of science.[27] Rilke's active-passivity contrasts with this pervasive attitude of domination and manipulation. Moreover, an attitude of domination cannot possibly facilitate a non-dualistic disclosure of things. Such a disclosure presupposes a reciprocity between seer and seen that is only possible through an active-passivity or passive-activity. The observer who dominates the observed discovers little more than reflections of himself.

After mentioning in the passage quoted above that works of art refer him to the originals or prototypes, Rilke makes the statement, "Ich fange an, Neues zu sehen"—indicating a transformation in his vision; he is beginning to see "newly" or "new things" ("Neues"). This statement is reminiscent of the well-known words in *Malte*, "Ich lerne sehen ... [I am learning to see ...]."[28] It is clear from Rilke's characterization of the new significance of flowers and animals that this discovery involves something different from merely noticing previously unnoticed objects or properties. Rather, *the change is more fundamental; it involves a transformation in the entire meaning of his perceptions and the revelation of a new dimension.* The statement is also reminiscent of Malte's description of "eine veränderte Welt. Ein neues Leben voll neuer Bedeutungen [a changed world. A new life full

---

Die Sonette an Orpheus: "Aber noch ist uns das Dasein verzaubert; an hundert/ Stellen ist es noch Ursprung. Ein Spielen von reinen/ Kräften, die keiner berührt, der nicht kniet und bewundert." *KA 2*, 261–2.

26 See Heidegger's interesting discussion of the dominating attitude intrinsic to modern science and technology in "Die Frage nach der Technik," *GA 7*, 7–36. Also see Rilke's contrast of machine technology and art in sonnet X in the second part of *Die Sonette an Orpheus*. *KA 2*, 261–2.
27 See Craig Holdrege and Steve Talbott, *Beyond Biotechnology: The Barren Promise of Genetic Engineering* (Lexington, KY: The University Press of Kentucky, 2008).
28 *KA 3*, 456.

of new meanings]."²⁹ Rilke's "learning to see" or "Sehen-Lernen" involved a correlative transformation in the way he was addressed by things. This transformation of vision (as will be elaborated) suggests a transcendence of the horizon of the everyday and an exceptional way of seeing.

There are important parallels between Rilke's seeing of things and Rodin's perception of his models. In a letter to Clara Rilke of June 24, 1906 Rilke speaks of his own "models" as follows: "My relationship to my 'models' is certainly still false, especially since I really still cannot use any human models at all (Proof: I still do not make them) and after years am still occupied with flowers, animals, and landscapes ..."³⁰ Rilke refers to flowers, animals, and landscapes as his models, meaning that he sought to translate them into his poetry in an analogous manner to Rodin's sculptural process. Hermann Meyer comments on the apparent strangeness of Rilke's statement concerning his inability to "use any human models" in that he does "not make them."³¹ Rilke seems to mean that he has not been able to use human models for his poetry, yet at this point in time he had almost finished writing the second part of the *Neue Gedichte*, which contains numerous human figures. Rilke thus seems to be contradicting himself. However, he proceeds to distinguish his relationship to human models from his relationship to models drawn from the natural world—"flowers, animals, and landscapes." Meyer finds a resolution to this apparent contradiction in the interpretation that Rilke has not yet perceived human models as deeply and articulated them in poetry as successfully as non-human, natural beings. (This convincing interpretation lends support to my view that Nature occupied a privileged place for Rilke.)

How, precisely, does Rilke's perception of natural models relate to Rodin's perception of human models? We have already seen that Rilke's poem "Der Panther" arose through following Rodin's advice to observe and copy Nature like a painter or sculptor. There are a number of other animal poems in Rilke's *Neue Gedichte*, his prose pieces and letters describe encounters with animals, and The Eighth Elegy (Die Achte Elegie) in the *Duineser Elegien* focuses on the animal's place in the cosmos in contradistinction to humanity's estrangement from the universe.³² Although Rilke used animals, plants, and landscapes as his models (in Chapter 4 poems on these

---

29   *KA 3*, 505.
30   Rilke, *Briefe aus den Jahren 1907–1914*, vol. 3 (Leipzig: Insel Verlag, 1930), 282.
31   Hermann Meyer, "Rilkes Cézanne-Erlebnis," 264.
32   Luke Fischer, "Animalising Art: Rainer Maria Rilke and Franz Marc," 54ff.; "Die Animalisierung der Kunst: Rainer Maria Rilke und Franz Marc," 343ff.

various subjects will be analyzed), due to the special place of animals in Rilke's oeuvre, the following account of Rilke's perception of "models" will focus primarily on his vision of animals. (A discussion of the animal is also a logical progression from the consideration of the human Other in Chapter 1 and the consideration of Rodin's models in Chapter 2.)

In his book *Proust and Rilke: The Literature of Expanded Consciousness*, E. F. N. Jephcott speaks of Rilke's "systematic attempt to enter" the world of the animal "through empathy, or *Einfühlung*, an attempt which led to numerous poems on animals."[33] I am sympathetic to this characterization; however, the word "empathy" could be misleading. Empathy, as was illustrated in Chapter 1, is often understood in terms which ultimately imply solipsism. Rilke's seeing of animals cannot be understood in these terms. The submission of his gaze to the appearance of animals led to a deeper disclosure, in each case, of the animal's being. Scheler's characterization of "sympathy" is much more in line with the basic structure of Rilke's perception. "Sympathy," for Scheler, is not limited to a process of inferring the states of the Other on the basis of my own mental states (and private experiences). In Chapter 1 it was demonstrated that such a detour in our understanding of the Other is not necessary and, moreover, that this view cannot account for the phenomenological facts; the Other is revealed with a haecceity which, in principle, could not be constituted in this roundabout way. Furthermore, it was pointed out that if the theory of inference, or an analogous theory, were true then I could only see in Others a reflection of what I know of myself.

If the common understanding of "empathy" is applied to animals, it becomes only more problematic, for the main reason that animals are not the same kind of being as ourselves. An introjection of our own mental states into the appearance of animals is nothing more than an inappropriate "anthropomorphism"; such anthropomorphic projection clearly exists, and is perhaps our primary manner of relating to pets (that are also humanized to a certain degree through domestication). However, this does not mean that our perception of animals is limited to this possibility. There is also a widespread view that the animal and its environment or *Umwelt* are closed off from us; in other words, we have no way of really grasping the essence of an animal and its manner of being. This view is based on the same kind of thinking which regards the perception of depth or interiority in the human Other as inferred or derived from my own; the view that I am confined to my solipsistic private consciousness without any access to the specific character of the

---

33 E. F. N. Jephcott, *Proust and Rilke: The Literature of Expanded Consciousness* (London: Chatto & Windus, 1972), 129.

184   The Poet as Phenomenologist

Other. My earlier criticisms of this position need not be repeated, but it is important to point out the more serious consequences of this view when applied to the case of animals. In contrast to this view, I will articulate the possibility of a dynamic, physiognomic perception of animals that transcends anthropomorphic projection. Rilke's systematic attempt to enter the animal world facilitated a transcendence of solipsism and anthropomorphism and a disclosure, in each case, of the animal's being.

A statement by Scheler can serve to support the general horizon of the following interpretation of Rilke. Scheler's conception of "sympathy" with the "natural world" contrasts strongly with Husserl's view that to "empathize" with animals involves seeing the animal as an abnormal variation of myself.[34] Scheler states,

> We must dissociate ourselves, firmly and unreservedly, from the gross error of regarding the sense of unity with the universe as merely an 'empathic' projection of specifically human emotions into animals, plants, or inanimate objects—as sheer anthropomorphism, therefore, and a fundamental misapprehension of the real. On the contrary, it is man the microcosm, an actual embodiment of the reality of existence in *all* its forms, who is himself *cosmomorphic*, and as such the possessor of sources of *insight* into all that is comprised in the nature of the cosmos.[35]

As will be seen, Rilke's manner of seeing "natural things," including animals, could in many cases be aptly described as a kind of *cosmological* vision. His vision involves a *transformation* of the self rather than a *projection* of the self. This seeing accords with Keats' characterization of "negative capability" as the poet's ability to transform him- or herself, in a certain sense, into all things.[36]

In his letter to Clara Rilke of June 13, 1907 Rilke describes his perception of gazelles on the previous day in the Jardin des Plantes in Paris. Rilke's perception of the gazelles is akin to the "third level" of the musical analogy that was offered as an illustration of Rodin's detailed physiognomic vision of his models, a vision in which the parts express, and contribute to the revelation of, the whole. Approximately a month after writing this letter (July 17, 1907) Rilke wrote the poem

---

34   See Rudolf Makkreel, "How is Empathy Related to Understanding?," in *Issues in Husserl's Ideas II*, ed. Thomas Nenon and Lester Embree (Dordrecht: Kluwer Academic Publishers, 1996), 208–9.
35   Scheler, *The Nature of Sympathy*, 105.
36   John Keats, *Letters of John Keats*, ed. Stanley Gardner (London: University of London Press, 1965), 68, 98.

Rilke as Seer: A Twofold Vision of Nature   185

"Die Gazelle," which is included in the first part of the *Neue Gedichte*. The consideration of the letter here and the poem in the subsequent chapter will exemplify the connection between Rilke's perception and his poetry. There are a number of similarities between Rilke's letter and the poem; some metaphors, for instance, that Rilke uses to portray the gazelles in the letter were later employed in the poem. Thus, beyond the illustration of Rilke's connection to Rodin and Cézanne, this case is exceptionally helpful in drawing links between Rilke's seeing, inspiration, and poetic composition.[37] It offers a paradigmatic example of Rilke's "animal poems" and their background.[38] Rilke writes the following to Clara Rilke:

> Yesterday, by the way, I was in the Jardin des Plantes for the whole morning, before the Gazelles. Gazella Dorcas, Linné. There are two there and another by itself. They lay a few steps away from one another, ruminating, restful, looking. As women gaze out of pictures, so they gaze out from something [*aus etwas heraus*] with a soundless, definitive turn [*endgültige Wendung*]. And as a horse neighed, the one by itself listened, and I saw the radiating of ears and horns around her slim head [*das Strahlen aus Ohren und Hörnern um ihr schlankes Haupt*]. Were the ears of those in Al Hayat also so grey (contrasting like tin and gold with the hue of the other hair), with a soft, dark, branched marking inside? I saw only the one stand up for a moment, she lay down again straight away; but I saw, while they stretched and examined themselves, the marvelous work of their legs [*Läufe*]: (they are like rifles, out of which leaps are shot). I couldn't depart, so beautiful were they, and I felt exactly as I did before your delicate photography: as if they had only just been transformed into this *Gestalt*.[39]

In the first sentence of this passage Rilke speaks of having spent a whole morning "before [*vor*]" the gazelles. He did not just take a quick glance at them like a regular visitor to a zoo, but spent a long period of time observing them. Rilke again uses the expression "before [*vor*]," but in this case is more specific; he was not standing before Nature, but before the gazelles. He mentions their species, "Gazella Dorcas," which demonstrates his concern with exactitude. He proceeds to describe their appearance and behavior—they were lying, looking about, while

---

37 See also Luke Fischer, "Perception as Inspiration: Rilke and the *New Poems*."
38 Later in this chapter, as another example, I point out clear connections between a letter by Rilke and "Der Panther."
39 Rainer Maria Rilke, *Briefe aus den Jahren 1906–1907*, vol. 2 (Leipzig: Insel Verlag, 1930), 265–9.

peacefully ruminating. Rilke proceeds with more detailed descriptions; however, these are not coldly objective; rather they discern features in their expressive character and are steeped in wonder at the appearance of the animals. He describes the gazelles as looking out from something ("aus etwas heraus") in the way in which women gaze out from pictures with a silent, conclusive ("endgültige") turn. This analogy reveals much about Rilke's way of seeing.

What do portraits of women gaze out *from*? They gaze out of the space of the painting, the world of the painting, its interior space that is contained within the frame. Similarly the gazelles gaze out from something. They gaze out from the space of their being—from their world or *Umwelt*—which differs from the world of human beings, just as the space inside a painting is not space in the usual sense; we cannot enter the space of the painting in the way in which we can enter the space of the gallery. In the subsequent chapter, it will be shown how Rilke's presentation of animals relates to the work of his friend, the influential zoologist, Jakob von Uexküll, whose research centers on the connection between the animal and its *Umwelt*. For the moment, it suffices to say that the gazelles gaze out from the space of their own way of being. In Rilke's formulation we see his awareness of the animals' otherness, and his attempt to divine, through a participatory perception, the gazelles' way of being. Rilke's characterization intimates an intrinsic depth of the animal. The mention of women's faces in pictures also suggests something of the mildness and stillness, which comes to expression in the gazelles' look. A certain finality or necessity is implied by "definitive turn" ("endgültige Wendung"). What is Rilke getting at here?

A painting has the finality of an artistic composition which is connected to the coincidence of expression and appearance. Rilke discovers an analogous finality in the look of the gazelles. The analogy also implies an acknowledgment of the existence of the animals in their own right. We are all familiar with the manner in which a portrait can evoke the feeling that we are being looked at by the face in the painting (while at the same time of course looking at this face), as though its eyes were directed at us.[40] Similarly Rilke's seeing acknowledges the gaze that looks out from the animals, the animals' own look. The subsequent sentence further illustrates the way in which the gazelles relate to their environment (in this case not their natural environment but the Jardin des Plantes); one of the gazelles responds to the neighing of a horse

---

40 This sense of reversal that can occur in contemplating an artwork is a recurring theme in Rilke's poetry; the best-known poem, in which such a reversal takes place, is "Archaïscher Torso Apollos." This theme is further discussed in the present and subsequent chapter.

(presumably somewhere else in the Jardin des Plantes). Rilke proceeds to describe the way in which a gazelle responded, its listening, which draws his attention to the radiating of ears and horns around the slim head ("das Strahlen aus Ohren und Hörnern um ihr schlankes Haupt"). The word *Haupt* in German, in contrast to *Kopf* (the more common word for "head"), suggests the *expressive manner* in which a head is held rather than the head as merely an "objective" part of the human form. The substantive *Strahlen* ("radiating" or "beaming") likewise suggests more than the "physical location" and form of the ears and horns. The verb *strahlen* is often used in German in the sense in which we say in English, a person "beams" (*strahlt*) with joy. The grammatical structure of Rilke's statement implies that rather than the ears and horns "radiating," the "radiating" is embodied in ears and horns. To the sensitive reader an intimation of the epiphanic can be discovered in this description.

By this point Rilke has already conveyed many details of the gazelles' appearance and behavior—their ruminating, their manner of looking and listening, their heads, ears and horns—and always with the sense of an expressive unity or whole. He proceeds to describe the precise color, texture, and markings on the ears—the gazelles' grey ears "(contrasting like tin and gold with the hue of the other hair), with a soft, dark, branched marking inside." He describes having seen one of them stand to stretch and sit down again, and then states that while the gazelles stretched, he noticed the splendid work of their "legs" or "barrels" (*Lauf* can mean barrel [barrel of a gun] or leg; Rilke makes use of this double meaning). He then offers a magnificent simile in order to describe the manner in which gazelles run, which he has obviously also observed with great participation (it is not surprising that Rilke, a month later, employed the same simile in the poem, "Die Gazelle"). He likens the legs of the gazelles to barrels of a gun out of which leaps are shot. He thereby gives a marvelous portrayal of the specific character of the gazelle's run—the spring in its step—and its relation to the structure of the legs. Following on from this he claims that he was unable to tear himself away from the gazelles (although he has given his attention to them for a whole morning); this is not a detached gaze but a gaze with the mood of amazement or enchantment—a participative gaze. This gaze has the structure of an active-passivity; in taking hold of the thing seen, the gaze itself is taken hold of by the thing, to employ a formulation reminiscent of Merleau-Ponty.[41]

Rilke concludes the description of his time with the gazelles with another analogy to a work of art, this time comparing them to his

---

41 "… the idea of *chiasm*, that is: every relation with being is *simultaneously* a taking and being taken, the hold is held, it is *inscribed* and inscribed in the same being that it takes hold of." Merleau-Ponty, *The Visible and the Invisible*, 266.

feeling for Clara's "delicate photography." This again suggests a certain necessity in the appearance of the gazelles, a necessity similar to the expressive finality of a work of art. It is thus with the eyes of an artist that Rilke sees the gazelles. As Rodin sees his models Rilke sees the gazelles; Rilke's gaze is participative, exact, and sees everything in its expressive character—physiognomically. The gazelles, in their form, movement, behavior, and way of relating to their environment are revealed as expressive wholes. Rilke attempts to get at the essence of the animal in a way that transcends an opposition between essence and appearance, understanding and perceiving; just as the way to the essence of a piece of music is through an active submission to the sounding tones rather than through an abstract consideration, so Rilke seeks to discover the character of the animal through a participative gaze which is struck with wonder and divines an essence in conjunction with the appearance.

Earlier we turned to Rilke's statement that his models had been primarily flowers, animals, and landscapes. In this passage from the letter of June 13, 1907 a clear parallel is evident between Rilke's perception of his models and Rodin's physiognomic perception of human models. Rilke's physiognomic perception of the animal reveals its expressive sense. This "expressive sense" is disclosed in conjunction with the sensible appearing and not despite it; this expressive sense implies the concomitance of a twofold meaning of sense (sense perception and sense [i.e., meaning]—the visible and the invisible). Previously (in Chapter 2) attention was drawn to the oft-cited passage from Rilke's letter to Clara Rilke of March 8, 1907, in which he describes how in the ec-stasy of perception a meaning burgeons ("wächst"— "grows"), as it were, from the "object [*Gegenstand*]" while the gaze is surrendered to it.[42] Earlier in this letter Rilke also speaks of the coincidence of the appearance of things with a certain insight (*Einsicht*) into them.[43] Later in the same letter, this idea is elaborated in his characterization of transient impressions in the landscape of Capri that *non-arbitrarily* ("unwillkürlich") assume a symbolic character.[44] What does Rilke mean by this?

Though he does not specifically define what he means by "symbolic," it is clear from the context that Rilke is reiterating in different words

---

42 "Das Anschauen ist eine so wunderbare Sache, von der wir so wenig wissen; wir sind mit ihm ganz nach außen gekehrt, aber gerade wenn wirs am meisten sind, scheinen in uns Dinge vor sich zu gehen, die auf das Unbeobachtetsein sehnsüchtig gewartet haben, und während sie sich, intakt und seltsam anonym, in uns vollziehen, ohne uns, – wächst in dem Gegenstand draußen ihre Bedeutung heran ..." Rilke, *Briefe aus den Jahren 1906–1907*, 214.
43 Ibid., 213–14.
44 Ibid., 214.

what he has already stated; he does not impose a symbolic significance onto things, rather this significance seems to be granted by the things themselves while they are being perceived. This means that the invisible sense of the thing is not possessed in advance and then subjectively projected onto the appearance; on the contrary, the invisible sense arises without precedence *from the between* of seer and seen—in the "chiasm." Moreover, in the same letter it also becomes evident that *this invisible not only arises in the spatio-temporality of the ec-static encounter—in the out-turned gaze—but is also the very essence of the thing* (this point will be further elaborated in the course of this chapter).

Immediately after the previously quoted passage from this letter, Rilke describes how the "object" perceived in this ec-static gaze becomes the "only possible name" ("einzig möglicher Name") for the insight that coincides with this vision.[45] In other words, this insight is only recognizable (is only "named") in the moment of vision and the "object" perceived becomes the only proper symbol for this insight.[46] This characterization indicates the depth of the relationship between the invisible meaning and its visible manifestation. When, in the same letter, Rilke speaks of the non-arbitrary intensification of this kind of perception into the symbolic, he explicitly refers to this symbolic meaning as the "essence" ("Wesen") of the perceived.[47] Thus, it can be affirmed that the un*fore*seen invisible, which is revealed in the thing's attainment of a symbolic significance, *is* the invisible essence of the visible. Likewise, Rilke's perception of the animal is a twofold seeing in the strong sense: the revealed invisible is the essence of the visible. In other words, Rilke's seeing is a kind of phenomenological *Wesensschau*.[48] This interpretation is confirmed by a later letter.

In the letter to Magda von Hattingberg of February 17, 1914 Rilke describes an encounter with a dog in order to exemplify his way of

---

45 Ibid., 214.
46 These statements by Rilke also shed a great deal of light on the poetics of the *Neue Gedichte*; in particular, on Rilke's distinctive form of "Imagism" (see Wolfgang Müller, "Rilkes *Neue Gedichte* und der Imagismus," *Blätter der Rilke Gesellschaft* 30 [2010]: 231–45). As certain insights can only be recognized through the distinctive images of perception, a poetics that seeks to communicate these insights must concentrate on the portrayal of concrete images.
47 Rilke also emphasizes the significance of the epiphanic *instant* of this kind of vision (something that we will soon consider in more detail). His actual example is the momentary perception of a face. This description bears strong connections to the poem "Begegnung in der Kastanien-Allee" ("Encounter in the Avenue of Chestnuts") in *Der neuen Gedichte anderer Teil*. KA 1, 566.
48 Käte Hamburger interprets Rilke's poetry in terms of a Husserlian *Wesensschau*. I do not agree with her strictly Husserlian interpretation. See Chapter 4.

seeing.[49] He speaks here of *Sehen* but, more specifically, he uses the word *Einsehen* ("in-seeing"). Rilke's characterization both reinforces and elaborates on what has thus far been explicated. He writes,

> I love in-seeing [*Einsehn*]. Can you think with me how marvelous it is, for instance, to see into a dog while walking by, in-seeing (I don't mean seeing-through [*durchschauen*], which is, in contrast, only a kind of human gymnastics and where one immediately comes out again on the other side of the dog, only, as it were, regarding it as a window into the human lying behind it, not this) …[50]

It was previously mentioned that Rilke's way of seeing animals is not reducible to anthropomorphism and that it involves a spontaneous emergence of sense in the ec-stasy of vision. Here Rilke makes a clear distinction between what he calls "Einsehen" and a superficial, anthropomorphic perception of animals. In contrast to "in-seeing," "Durchschauen" looks through or past the animal, does not perceive its invisible nature. It does not see the animal as animal, perceive its specific animality, but regards it as if it were only a window onto humanity. In contrast, *Einsehen* involves,

> letting oneself [*sich einlassen*] into the dog, exactly into its center, to the place where it starts being a dog [*von wo aus er Hund ist*], there, where God, as it were, would have positioned himself for a moment, when the dog was complete, in order to oversee its first embarrassments and incidents and to affirm that it was good, that nothing was lacking, that one could not make it better.[51]

This passage is incredibly rich for the present purposes. To begin with, the active-passivity of this vision is once again evident; "Einsehen" involves "letting oneself [*sich einlassen*]" into the dog, whereas "Durchschauen" has an active but at the same time forceful character. To in-see in this case, is to let oneself into the very center that makes the dog a dog. Thus the inner aspect of this "*in*-seeing" is the interiority of the thing itself, the center from which the dog is a dog ("von wo aus

---

49 Although this is a later letter I agree with Jephcott that this characterization by Rilke clearly refers back to, or is at least continuous with, the middle period. Jephcott, *Proust and Rilke: The Literature of Expanded Consciousness*, 129.
50 Rainer Maria Rilke, *Briefwechsel mit Magda von Hattingberg "Benvenuta,"* ed. Ingeborg Schnack and Renate Scharffenberg (Frankfurt am Main: Insel Verlag, 2000), 114–15. From now on I shall refer to *Briefwechsel mit Magda von Hattingberg "Benvenuta"* as *Ben*.
51 *Ben*, 115.

er Hund ist"). This is an essence in the real and not merely nominal sense. Rilke's language here is reminiscent of his characterization of the gazelles staring "out from something" ("aus etwas heraus") yet more emphatic; Rilke, the seer, is now at the very center of the animal. Drawing on this earlier analogy, it could be stated that Rilke is no longer looking at the picture in a frame but has entered into the picture itself. This letter describes a deeper level of participation. Rilke's *Einsehen* is a *Wesensschau*, a seeing of the essence, an essence, however, that is not seen in abstraction from the phenomenon.

There is an obvious ontological dimension to Rilke's claims. Although it is clearly his seeing that enables such a disclosure of the animal, although this seeing is an epistemic process, it is apparent that what is disclosed has an ontological status. Rilke describes this center as the place where the dog starts being a dog and where God, as it were, would have located himself for a moment in order to acknowledge the perfection of his creation. This center is what ontologically makes the dog a dog, makes it *be* a dog. It is, of course, only in a type of knowing that has an ontological character that an overcoming of dualism is possible. If knowing and being are mutually exclusive then there is an inevitable dualism and division between them. A transcendence of dualism requires a form of knowing in which knowing participates in being and vice versa. Rilke's characterization of "Einsehen" clearly suggests such a two-way participation. For these reasons, Rilke's seeing demonstrates nothing less than an overcoming of dualism. This twofold seeing involves a coincidence of the sensible and intelligible, thatness and whatness, the visible and invisible, existence and essence, being and knowing. This mutual participation of being and knowing does *not* mean that knowing becomes identical to a *particular* being; Rilke does not literally become the dog; this is clear in his reference to the center of the animal as the *place* where *God* would have positioned himself. *Knowing* here involves *mentally* participating in the ontological essence (universal) of something—in this case, what makes the dog a dog. It is the "dogness" of the dog in a real sense and not in the sense of an abstract universal that has a merely nominal significance (i.e., the significance of a mere label or arbitrary classification).

Before further considering this letter, it is instructive to turn to the center of the earliest written, and probably most famous (along with "Archaïscher Torso Apollos"), of Rilke's *Neue Gedichte*, "Der Panther." The center of this poem is a center in two senses. First, as the middle verse of three verses, it is the structural or formal center of the poem. Second, it presents the center of the animal, in this case a caged panther, in a way that reveals the kind of *Einsehen* that Rilke describes in the letter to Magda von Hattingberg.

> Der weiche Gang geschmeidig starker Schritte,
> der sich im allerkleinsten Kreise dreht,
> ist wie ein Tanz von Kraft um eine Mitte,
> in der betäubt ein großer Wille steht.[52]

The panther's circular pacing is like a dance "around a *center* [Mitte]" where, numbed, "a great will stands." The center here, as in the case of the dog, is the center of the animal itself. Due to its confinement, the center of the panther cannot realize itself as it would in the animal's natural *Umwelt*. The "great will" at the panther's center would not be numbed if the panther were able to fulfill its nature in its proper *Umwelt*, if it were not restricted to an artificial caged environment. In connection to this poem one can speak of the center from which the panther is a panther in an identical sense to the letter's example of the dog. In these considerations, the earlier commentary on Rilke's physiognomic perception of gazelles is deepened. In the letter describing the gazelles there is an *intimation* of the "center" of the animals (the space out of which they gaze), while in "Der Panther" and the letter to Magda von Hattingberg, the depth of the animal is *explicitly* thematized. The latter examples more emphatically demonstrate that Rilke's perception of animals disclosed an interior which is not the opposite of the exterior, but rather an ontological depth of the thing itself.

In the sentence which follows the previously quoted excerpt from the letter to Magda von Hattingberg, Rilke indicates, in rather dramatic terms, the radically *participative* character of his seeing or "in-seeing."

> For a while one can endure being in the center of the dog, one must only watch out and be sure to leap out in due time, before its environment [*Umwelt*] wholly encloses one, because otherwise one would simply remain the dog in the dog and be lost for anything else [*für alles übrige verloren*].[53]

One must be careful, according to Rilke, not to remain in this ec-static center for too long otherwise the *Umwelt*, the environment from the dog's perspective, might close in around one and one would then remain forever trapped inside the dog. In anticipation of our later discussion, here it is apt draw on an image from the zoologist Jakob von Uexküll. Uexküll often likened the animal's world or environment (*Umwelt*) to a soap bubble. In *Theoretical Biology* (*Theoretische Biologie*),

---

52 "The supple gait of pliant strong steps/ which in the smallest of all circles turns,/ is like a dance of strength around a center,/ within which numbed a great will stands." *KA* 1, 469.
53 *Ben*, 115.

for instance, he states that "the space peculiar to each animal, wherever that animal may be, can be compared to a soap bubble which completely surrounds the creature ... The extended soap bubble constitutes ... the limit of its world."[54] In his letter to Hattingberg, Rilke is suggesting that *Einsehen* enables one, for instance, to enter the "soap bubble" of the dog with the related danger that one might not be able to exit this bubble and return to the human world. Although there is a slight sense of playful exaggeration in Rilke's claim, he later makes a point of emphasizing his earnestness (see below). His claim implies an active-passivity, and participation in the Other (the animal Other in this case) in the strongest sense.

An active-passivity, in the case of seeing, ultimately implies that the *act of seeing* assumes a gesture of *passivity* or *suffering*, as though *to see* simultaneously involved *being seen* by that which is seen. This is a reversal in the gaze, or more accurately, a reversal in "intentional-directionality" as it is ordinarily conceived and experienced. Such a reversal, as aforementioned, is necessary for an overcoming of dualism. It must no longer be the case that I as subject constitute the character of the object (a subjectified object), but rather, that the thing articulates its own character within my gaze, such that my gaze is akin to the suffering of the gaze of another. This "reversal in the gaze" is thematized by Rilke in numerous places. The following section from the poem "Wendung" presents an example of this reversal in intentional-directionality:

> Tiere traten getrost
> in den offenen Blick, weidende,
> und die gefangenen Löwen
> starrten hinein wie in unbegreifliche Freiheit;
> Vögel durchflogen ihn grad,
> den gemütigen; Blumen
> wiederschauten in ihn
> groß wie in Kinder ...[55]

Animals and lions stared into his open gaze. Flowers looked into him as into children. The gaze of the seer is the opening that suffers, or makes space for, the gaze of things.

---

54 Jakob von Uexküll, *Theoretical Biology*, trans. D. L. Mackinnon (New York: Harcourt, Brace & Company, 1926), 42.

55 "Animals stepped confidently/ into the open gaze, grazing,/ and the captive lions/ peered into it as into incomprehensible freedom./ Birds flew directly through it,/ the soulful gaze; flowers/ looked into it again,/ large, as into children ..." *KA* 2, 101–2.

One of the most striking poems in which Rilke conveys a reversal in the intentional-directionality of the gaze is "Schwarze Katze" in the *Neue Gedichte*. While the next chapter considers this poem in detail, at this point the analysis will focus on this reversal. Nevertheless, the entire poem is reproduced below, in order to provide the context for the final pertinent lines.

Schwarze Katze

Ein Gespenst ist noch wie eine Stelle,
dran dein Blick mit einem Klange stößt;
aber da, an diesem schwarzen Felle
wird dein stärkstes Schauen aufgelöst:

wie ein Tobender, wenn er in vollster
Raserei ins Schwarze stampft,
jählings am benehmenden Gepolster
einer Zelle aufhört und verdampft.

Alle Blicke, die sie jemals trafen,
scheint sie also an sich zu verhehlen,
um darüber drohend und verdrossen
zuzuschauern und damit zu schlafen.
Doch auf einmal kehrt sie, wie geweckt,
ihr Gesicht und mitten in das deine:
und da triffst du deinen Blick im geelen
Amber ihrer runden Augensteine
unerwartet wieder: eingeschlossen
wie ein ausgestorbenes Insekt.[56]

The reversal comes to its most extreme expression in the last lines of the poem. The first two-thirds of the poem describe a perceiver whose gaze is absorbed by the black cat. Toward the end of the poem, however, a turn or *volta* occurs, announced by "doch [but]." The cat no longer absorbs the gaze completely, nor is it like a place that resists the gaze

---

56 "Black Cat// A ghost is still like a place/ your glance bumps into with a sound;/ but there, in this black fur,/ your intensest gaze is dissolved:// as a madman, when he pounds/ into the darkness in complete rage,/ abruptly ceases and evaporates/ in the absorptive padding of a cell.// Thus all the glances that have ever met her/ she seems to conceal in herself/ so that, menacingly and disgruntledly,/ she can watch over them, and therewith sleep. But all at once, as if roused,/ she turns her face directly to your own:/ and there, unexpectedly, you meet your gaze again/ in the yellow amber of her round eye-stones:/ trapped like an extinct insect." KA 1, 545.

("dran dein Blick mit einem Klange stößt"). The cat is roused from its sleep and turns its gaze to the seer, and rather than the cat being the object of the seer's attention, at this moment the cat's gaze seems to constitute the seer. This is expressed in extreme terms, reminiscent of the previously cited quotation concerning the *Umwelt* of the dog. The eyes of the cat are compared to amber and the gaze of the seer to an insect which is trapped in the amber. The image of the trapped insect suggests that the gaze of the seer is helpless and has lost any sense of its own identity. This poem offers an extreme expression of an active-passive seeing, in which *to see a thing is, at the same time, to be seen by the thing*. This formulation intentionally recalls Meister Eckhart. Of course, the perception of an animal cannot be compared with the perception of God, or even with that of another human being; the latter, for instance, can involve an equal or symmetrical recognition of one another as *self-conscious* beings. A cat clearly cannot observe me with the same kind of self-consciousness as another human being; however, this is irrelevant to the main point. What is pertinent is the sense in which *things articulate their essence within Rilke's gaze*.[57] It is due to the fact that Rilke no longer experiences intentionality as a constitution of the meaning of objects on the part of a subject that he can also speak of flowers looking into him (as into children).[58] Natural things no longer stand over against him but assume a positively noetic character within his own noetic processes. His gaze is actively engaged in the emergence of meaning but at the same time suffers the meaning of things such that the things themselves take on the character of a mental or noetic activity. "Schwarze Katze" offers another point of connection between Rilke's characterization of "Einsehen" and the *Neue Gedichte*. By this stage it should be more evident how Rilke's learning to see involved a *real transformation* of the common experience and understanding of perception.

Later in the same letter to Magda von Hattingberg, Rilke indicates that this ontological, non dualistic, and participative *Einsehen* of the dog is typical of his *Einsehen* generally. He also further describes the epiphanic character of this seeing.

> Oh [*Ach*], will you laugh, dear confidante, should I tell you, *where* my supreme feeling, my world-feeling, my earthly blessedness has

---

57 In "Eye and Mind," Merleau-Ponty elaborates his idea of "chiasm" through drawing on André Marchand's statement, in reference to Paul Klee, that when he walks through a forest he has often had the feeling of being looked at by the surroundings. Merleau-Ponty, "Eye and Mind," 129. In Rilke one finds the same logic presented in a yet more radical way.
58 KA 2, 102.

been, thus must I confess it to you: this blessedness has been time and again, here and there, in such in-seeing, in the indescribable, swift, deep, timeless moments of this divine in-seeing [*göttliches Einsehn*].⁵⁹

The *exceptional* character of Rilke's seeing has already been articulated in a variety of respects. The incredible importance of this seeing for Rilke is also evident from the above. Rilke's feeling for the world, his earthly blessedness, is intimately connected to the "indescribable, swift, deep, timeless moments of this divine in-seeing." While the epiphanic dimension of this seeing was implied by Rilke's earlier mention of the center of the animal in relation to God, it is more directly conveyed in his description of this vision as a divine or godly in-seeing ("göttliches Einsehn"). There are a few reasons why I have chosen to characterize Rilke's vision as "epiphanic." First, there is a *numinous* or *spiritual* dimension to this vision that is aptly implied by "epiphany." Second, Rilke (in his letters, prose, and poetry) often emphasizes the *instantaneous* quality of this seeing; he often (though not always) emphasizes a momentary flash of insight. In this respect, the epiphanic in Rilke is exemplary of the broader literary meaning of "epiphany" that need not be overtly spiritual. In the above quotation, this sense is suggested by the adjective "swift" (*rasch*) and the emphasis on the "moments" or "instants" (*Augenblicken*) of insight. Third, its etymological connection to "phenomena" ("epi*phan*ic") and thereby to "phenomenology" is also apt.

In *Malte* and the *Neue Gedichte* there are many places that describe the appearance of things in an epiphanic or numinal light.⁶⁰ For the sake of continuity with the previous examples, I will consider another letter (written a couple of years after the middle period) in which Rilke speaks of an encounter with an animal, more specifically, of another encounter with a dog. In the letter of December 17, 1912 to the Princess Marie von Thurn und Taxis-Hohenlohe, Rilke writes:

> Alas [*Ach*], I have still not got over expecting the "new process" ["*nouvelle opération*"] as a result of human intervention, and yet

---

59 *Ben*, 115.
60 Consider, for instance, the following description in *Malte* of a man feeding sparrows: "Es dauert keine Minute, so sind zwei, drei Vögel da, Spatzen, die neugierig heranhüpfen. Und wenn es dem Manne gelingt, ihrer sehr genauen Auffassung von Unbeweglichkeit zu entsprechen, so ist kein Grund, warum sie nicht näher kommen sollen … je mehr Menschen sich um ihn sammeln, in entsprechendem Abstand natürlich, desto weniger hat er mit ihnen gemein … Wenn die Zuschauer nicht wären und man ließe ihn lang genug dastehn, ich bin sicher, daß auf einmal ein Engel käme und überwände sich und äße den alten, süßlichen Bissen aus der verkümmerten Hand." *KA 3*, 509–10.

what's the good, since it is my lot to pass by human kind, as it were, and reach some uttermost extreme, the very border of the earth; for instance recently in Cordoba a little ugly dog in the last stages of pregnancy came up to me; it was no laudable creature, and certainly full of accidental puppies, over whom no great fuss would be made; but since we were entirely alone she came over to me, as hard as it was for her, and lifted her eyes, enlarged from worry and inwardness, and desired my gaze, – and in her look there was truly everything that transcends the particular, to I know not where, into the future or the incomprehensible; it happened that she received a piece of sugar from my coffee, but over and above that, unspeakably so, we read in a sense the mass together; in itself the action was nothing but giving and receiving, yet the meaning and earnestness of our entire communication was boundless. This can, though, only take place on earth; it is on all accounts good, to have willingly passed through life, even if not at all heroically, – in the end one will be wonderfully prepared for divine relationships.[61]

Here Rilke recounts an encounter with a pregnant female dog in Cordoba. In the eyes of the animal he had seen "truly everything that transcends the particular" ("wahrhaftig alles, was über den Einzelnen hinausgeht"). The encounter with the animal takes on an inexhaustible meaning, opens into the "in-finite." The experience suggests the futural and the incomprehensible. These descriptions already indicate a religious or even mystical dimension. This numinous dimension is further emphasized in the metaphor that they said mass together and in Rilke's affirmation that on earth one is prepared for "divine relationships," which presumably become more evident in the afterlife. A simple encounter with an animal thus assumes divine proportions.

We have already articulated many features of Rilke's *Sehen* which demonstrate its non-dualistic character. In 1913 Rilke wrote two related prose pieces called "Erlebnis (I)" and "Erlebnis (II)." Although they were *written* after the period of the *Neue Gedichte*, in "Erlebnis (II)" Rilke refers back to an earlier experience (during his middle period) on the island of Capri, Italy.[62] In "Erlebnis (I)" and "Erlebnis (II)" Rilke seeks to communicate privileged experiences that revealed a deeper unity of mind and Nature—experiences in which mind and Nature,

---

61 Rilke, *Selected Letters 1902–1906*, 224–5; translation greatly altered. Rilke, *Briefe aus den Jahren 1907–1914*, 258–9.
62 Rilke resided on the island of Capri on two occasions. He was a guest at the villa of Alice Faehndrich from December 1906–May 1907 and from February–April 1908. See n. 66.

the earthly and the heavenly, were reconciled and revealed as aspects of a single whole. The experience portrayed in "Erlebnis (II)" concerns his perception (hearing) of a bird-call. As this description evokes in a striking and exemplary way Rilke's participational experience of Nature, it serves as a fitting conclusion to many of our considerations. The opening sentence of the excerpt below refers back to "Erlebnis (I)" which occurred at a later date in Spain.

> Later he thought he could recall certain moments, in which the potency [*Kraft*] of this one [a later experience—"Erlebnis (I)"] was contained, as in the seed. He recalled the time in that other southern garden (Capri), when a bird-call in the open and his inner consciousness were one, when it did not, as it were, break on the barrier of his body, but gathered both together into an unbroken space [*ununterbrochenen Raum*], in which there was only one region of the purest, deepest consciousness, mysteriously protected. On that occasion he had closed his eyes, so that he might not be confused by the contour of his body in such a generously granted experience, and infinity passed into him from all sides in so familiar a manner that he could believe he felt within himself the gentle presence of the stars which had now appeared.[63]

From the Middle Rilke to the Later Rilke

A number of characteristic features of Rilke's seeing of Nature have been illustrated. Attention has been drawn to its physiognomic character (a perception of the sensible and the intelligible as an expressive unity) and to the intimate connection between the visible and the disclosure of the invisible. This invisible was shown to be the invisible side of the visible or the interior of the exterior, and shown to include spiritual or epiphanic aspects. Furthermore, a kind of reversal of intentional-directionality was identified in Rilke's seeing. These points taken together suffice to illustrate the sense in which Rilke realized a non-dualistic or twofold disclosure of Nature. If one traces Rilke's development beyond the middle period (which has already been done in part) and investigates the meaning of key terms such as "Weltinnenraum" ("worldinnerspace"), "der Engel" ("the angel"), and "das Offene" ("the open") in his later writings, some of these features reveal themselves even more emphatically. It becomes even more apparent that the inner, for Rilke, *is* the other side of Nature and has a divine, mystical, or numinal aspect. The continuity between Rilke's seeing in the middle period and his seeing in the later period is also clearly discernible. In

---

63 Rilke, "An Experience (II)," in *Where Silence Reigns*, 36; translation altered. KA 4, 668–9.

"Erlebnis (II)," mentioned above, Rilke implies this continuity between his earlier and later vision, in that he regards an earlier experience of non-dualism—of the oneness of mind and Nature—as an anticipation of the later experience of non-dualism that he articulates in "Erlebnis (I)." For two reasons I have chosen to proceed with a few considerations of Rilke's development beyond the middle period. The first is that an illustration of certain continuities between the middle Rilke and the later Rilke serves to reinforce my interpretation of Rilke's seeing, while at the same time providing further support for the claim in the introduction to Chapter 2 that the later Rilke is in important respects continuous with the middle Rilke. Second, in the secondary literature notions such as *Weltinnenraum* are often treated with too little regard for the *experiences* which motivated their coinage and use. The term "Weltinnenraum" is often characterized as a *metaphysical* concept or understood *subjectively*. The word itself already points away from a subjectivistic interpretation in that "innen" (inner)—often regarded as solely belonging to the "subjective pole"—is placed between "Welt" (world) and "Raum" (space) which are commonly thought to belong more to the "objective pole"; the word thus suggests an interior *of the world* and not merely of an estranged subject. The fact that Rilke coined the word "Weltinnenraum" as an attempt to articulate "privileged experiences" suggests that it does *not* have a metaphysical character (in the critical sense in which the "metaphysical" has been defined in this work). *Weltinnenraum* does not have the status of a mere postulate but rather bears the status of a phenomenological category—an attempt to articulate the way something has shown itself in person. Hence, the second reason for venturing into a very limited consideration of the later Rilke is in order to provide a more adequate framework for understanding such words in Rilke and to support this generally non-metaphysical, phenomenological, and mystical reading of Rilke.

In the previously mentioned letter "an eine junge Freundin" of March 17, 1926 Rilke lists the three most important places in his life and development: Russia, Paris, and Spain.[64] For the middle Rilke Paris bore the greatest significance—his engagement with Rodin, his discovery of Cézanne, the city itself as an inspiration for his novel *Malte*, etc. Rilke's travels in Russia precede the middle period, while his stay in Spain played a decisive role in his later development—the most decisive experience being that of the town and landscape of Toledo, which has aptly been described as an experience of mystical participation.[65] Rilke's letters and other writings that

---

64 Rilke, *Briefe*, vol. 2, 517–18.
65 Hermann Meyer, "Die Verwandlung des Sichtbaren: Die Bedeutung der modernen bildenen Kunst für Rilkes späte Dichtung," 303–4.

pertain to his time in Spain are particularly illuminating with regard to central themes and terms in his later works, most importantly, "Weltinnenraum" and the "Engel." In the present context a consideration of the motif of the angel would lead us too far afield. However, the term "Weltinnenraum" is especially relevant and will be explicated in connection to "Erlebnis (I)" and "Erlebnis (II)," and to letters Rilke wrote in Spain.

It was during his stay in Spain in 1913 that Rilke wrote "Erlebnis (I)" and "Erlebnis (II)." As we have seen, "Erlebnis (II)" describes his experience of the bird-call on Capri as containing in a germinal form the later experience recounted in "Erlebnis (I)."[66] In what sense was the later experience a further unfolding of what Rilke had previously experienced? In Rilke's account of his experience of a bird-call he describes a non-dualistic experience. It is the monistic character of this *experience* that is important. If "Erlebnis (I)" is a further development of what was already intimated in this experience on Capri then it must involve a yet more radical sense of the unity of mind and Nature. This is precisely the development that takes place. In "Erlebnis (I)" many of the previously discussed features of Rilke's seeing are further emphasized. The text begins as follows:

> It might be a little more than a year ago, that something strange happened to him in the castle garden which sloped down fairly steeply to the sea. Walking up and down with a book, as was his wont, it occurred to him to lean against the forking of two branches, at about the level of his shoulder in a shrub-like tree, and immediately he felt himself so pleasantly supported in this attitude and given such ample rest, that he remained like this, without reading, completely absorbed into Nature [*völlig eingelassen in die Natur*],

---

66 As aforementioned, Rilke had two sojourns on Capri: from December 4, 1906–May 20, 1907 and from February 29–April 18, 1908. While I am not sure of the exact date of his non-dualistic experience of the bird-call, it seems quite likely that this experience occurred during December of 1906. My reason for this conjecture is due to a description toward the end of the poem that begins "Täglich stehst du mir steil vor dem Herzen." The latter is the first poem in the *Improvisationen aus dem Capreser Winter*, which Rilke arranged for possible publication in 1925 but which was first published posthumously in 1950. However, the mentioned poem was completed at the end of December 1906 on Capri and contains the following description of a bird-call, which bears striking resemblances to the experience recounted in "Erlebnis (II)": "Denn was soll mir die Zahl/ der Worte, die kommen und fliehn,/ wenn ein Vogellaut, vieltausendmal,/ geschrien und wieder geschrien,/ ein winziges Herz so weit macht und eins/ mit dem Herzen der Luft, mit dem Herzen des Hains/ und so hell und so hörbar für ihn …" *KA 1*, 373. See also Kári Driscoll, *Toward a Poetics of Animality: Hofmannsthal, Rilke, Pirandello, Kafka*, 109ff.

in a state of almost unconscious beholding [*Anschaun*]. Gradually his attention was awakened by a hitherto unknown sensation: it was as if almost imperceptible vibrations [*Schwingungen*] were passing from the interior of the tree into him … he was more and more surprised, indeed impressed, by the effect produced in himself by what was passing over into him without ceasing: he felt he had never been filled with more delicate vibrations [*leisere Bewegungen*—"quieter movements"], his body was being treated in some sort like a soul, and made capable of registering a degree of influence which could not really have been felt at all in the usual well-defined clarity of physical conditions. In addition to that, he could not, in the first moments, properly distinguish which sense it was by which he was receiving so delicate and pervading a communication; furthermore, the condition it was producing within him was so perfect and so persistent, different from all others … All the same, endeavouring always to account for the least perceptible experiences, he insistently asked himself what was happening to him and almost immediately found an expression which satisfied him, as he said aloud to himself that he had reached *the other side of Nature* [*er sei auf die andere Seite der Natur geraten*] … the expression gave him pleasure and he believed it to be almost completely apt.[67]

Here Rilke himself employs the expression the "other side of Nature" in order to describe an invisible dimension in his experience of a tree. The above description suggests an experience of reversal in intentional-directionality of a more radical kind than the earlier examples; the other side of Nature has in a quite literal sense become the agent, while the self has assumed the position of a pure witness.

A related change from the middle Rilke to the later Rilke pertains to his descriptions of experiences of non-dualism becoming less fleeting. Rilke's seeing in the middle period often involved *moments* of epiphany and such moments are a frequent theme in the *Neue Gedichte*, instants in which something is suddenly revealed in an unfamiliar and exceptional light. In "Erlebnis (II)" Rilke proceeds to describe his experience as expanding into a more sustained, or permanent, epiphany. Toward the end of "Erlebnis (II)" he writes:

> he could not fail to recognize that since the last experiences of these influences he was, as it were, finally delivered over to such relationships. A gentle something separated him from his

---

67 Rilke, "An Experience (I)," in *Where Silence Reigns*, 35; translation altered and my emphasis. KA 4, 666–7.

fellows by a pure, almost apparent, *between-space* [*Zwischenraum*], through which it was possible to pass over single items but which absorbed any relationship into itself ... they [other human beings] could not know that this kind of conquest had been won ... in a region beyond, a region having so little reference to human conditions, so that they would have called it "emptiness." The only thing by which he could address himself to them was, perhaps, his simplicity; it was reserved for him to speak to them of joy, when he found them too much involved in the opposites of happiness, and also to communicate to them something of his converse with Nature, things which they had ignored or only noticed in passing.[68]

Rilke speaks of finally being delivered over to such relationships. What were earlier experienced as momentary epiphanies of Nature's invisible side—an invisible that is not the opposite of the visible—became a more sustained way of seeing. In this context Rilke describes the disclosedness of an "intermediate space" or "between-space" ("Zwischenraum"). This formulation recalls his characterization earlier in "Erlebnis (II)" of the bird-call occurring in an "unbroken space" or "uninterrupted space" ("ununterbrochener Raum") where inner and outer were wholly united. Both of these expressions, which seek to convey an experience, call to mind the notion of *Weltinnenraum*. It is plainly clear that such experiences have a "mystical" character in the sense in which this word has been defined. This mystical dimension of Rilke's vision transcends the ordinary horizon of perception; it transcends the everyday or what is commonly accessible.

In the above, attention has been drawn to expressions—"between space," "unbroken space"—that bear a clear relation to Rilke's neologism, *Weltinnenraum*. These terms were employed by Rilke in order to describe privileged disclosures of Nature. In a poem written in 1914, not long after his stay in Spain, Rilke offers what for the present purposes could be called a "poetic definition" of *Weltinnenraum*.

> Es winkt zu Fühlung fast aus allen Dingen,
> aus jeder Wendung weht es her: Gedenk!
> Ein Tag, an dem wir fremd vorübergingen,
> entschließt im künftigen sich zum Geschenk.

---

68 Rilke, "An Experience (II)," 37–8; translation altered and my emphasis. KA 4, 669–70.

Wer rechnet unseren Ertrag? Wer trennt
uns von den alten, den vergangnen Jahren?
Was haben wir seit Anbeginn erfahren,
als daß sich eins im anderen erkennt?

Als daß an uns Gleichgültiges erwarmt?
O Haus, o Wiesenhang, o Abendlicht,
auf einmal bringst du's beinah zum Gesicht
und stehst an uns, umarmend und umarmt.

Durch alle Wesen reicht der *eine* Raum:
Weltinnenraum. Die Vögel fliegen still
durch uns hindurch. O, der ich wachsen will,
ich seh hinaus, und *in* mir wächst der Baum.

Ich sorge mich, und in mir steht das Haus.
Ich hüte mich, und in mir ist die Hut.
Geliebter, der ich wurde: an mir ruht
der schönen Schöpfung Bild und weint sich aus.[69]

The term "Weltinnenraum" clearly concerns a kind of non-dualism. The second verse ends with the phrase that "one is recognized in the other [eins im anderen erkennt]." The final line of the third verse defines "Weltinnenraum" as the "embracing and embraced [umarmend und umarmt]." However, this non-dualism does not solely pertain to Nature. Rilke is setting forth a view of non-dualism in more general terms. Were "Weltinnenraum" to refer solely to Nature, Rilke would have used the word "*Natur*innenraum" instead. Nevertheless, Nature clearly occupies a privileged place in the poem, as is shown by the mention of "evening light," "hillside-meadow" ("Wiesenhang"), the flight of birds, and a growing tree. It can, therefore, already be affirmed that the notion of "Weltinnenraum" is not without relation to the present problematic. Moreover, Rilke introduces the term in

---

69 "It beckons to feeling almost from all things,/ from every turning it blows here: Recall!/ A day, which we strangely passed by,/ decides in the future to become a gift.// Who reckons our yield? Who divides/ us from the old, the past years?/ What have we learned since the beginning,/ but that one is recognized in the other?// But that in us an indifferent thing turns warm?/ O house, o hillside-meadow, o evening light,/ all at once you bring it almost to our face/ and stand by us, embracing and embraced.// Through all beings extends the *one* space./ Worldinnerspace. The birds fly silently/ through us, right through. O, I who want to grow,/ I look without, and *in* me grows the tree.// I take care, and in me stands the house./ I guard, and in me is the guard./ Beloved, who I became: on me rests/ the image of the beautiful creation and weeps." KA 2, 113.

the stanza which says that "the birds fly silently through us" and the tree grows within him while it is seen ("in mir wächst der Baum"). It will be shown that in so far as "Weltinnenraum" includes Nature, the "Innenraum" of Nature should be conceived along the lines which have previously been established—as an invisible or interior which is the other side, rather than the opposite, of the visible or exterior, and bears an epiphanic character.[70]

As aforementioned, shortly before writing the "Weltinnenraum-Gedicht [Worldinnerspace Poem]" Rilke was in Spain (Ronda) and wrote "Erlebnis (I)" and "Erlebnis (II)." In a letter of January 14, 1919 to Adelheid von der Marwitz, Rilke recounts an earlier experience in Spain (1913) in reference to the recent publication of "Erlebnis (I & II)" and the poem "Der Tod."[71] In this letter Rilke describes an outer event of Nature simultaneously becoming an inner event and he employs the term "Innenraum" in the sense that I have suggested. In addition, he refers to his earlier experience of the call of a bird on Capri, recounted in "Erlebnis (II)." *Rilke is here clearly drawing a connection between his earlier and later experience of Nature in a way which matches precisely with the view I have set forth.* He states the following:

> In the poem "Death" ["Der Tod"] though, the moment is finally summoned, when for me (I stood on the wonderful bridge of Toledo at night) a tense slow arc of a star falling through *worldspace*

---

70 The later Rilke, in certain respects, conceived the task of *Verwandlung* (transmutation) of the visible into the invisible in more active and more abstract (or imaginal) terms. For the middle Rilke, the task of seeing could be formulated as a kind of "condescension" (in the old non-pejorative sense) to the things. This is reflected in the *Neue Gedichte* in so far as the subject, or I, is seldom present outside of its ec-static identification with a being. For the later Rilke the subject takes on a more active role in the *Verwandlung*. Both the subject and the things achieve a higher stage of existence through the *Verwandlung* of the visible into the invisible. In the *Duineser Elegien* this is reflected in the poetic self's declaration that it will embrace the task of *Verwandlung*, which is conceived as a reciprocal transformation of things (rather than a condescension to things) and the self. The space of the *Duineser Elegien* (and *Die Sonette an Orpheus*) is also mythopoeic or imaginal to a greater extent than the *Neue Gedichte's* world of concrete things. However, these differences between the middle Rilke and the later Rilke are more a matter of emphasis than kind, and as has been previously suggested in various ways, the different periods of Rilke's work ultimately complement and supplement (and overlap with) one another rather than contradict one another. For our purposes, the key point is that the primary character of the Rilkean invisible—an invisible which is not the opposite of the visible—remains consistent throughout his development. For a good treatment of the development of Rilke's concept of *Verwandlung* see Gerhart Mayer, *Rilke und Kassner: eine geistige Begegnung*.
71 They were first published in the *Insel-Almanach* (1919).

[*Weltraum*] at the same time (how should I say it?) fell through *inner-space* [*Innen-Raum*]: the dividing contour of the body was no longer there. And as this time through the eye, so at an earlier time this unity was announced through the ear: one time on Capri, as I stood in the garden at night, under the olive trees, and the call of a bird, in response to which I had to close my eyes, was simultaneously within me and outside, as in a single *undivided space* [*ununterschiedenen Raum*] of complete extension and clarity![72]

Rilke relates his experience of perceiving a shooting star, which, as it fell through "world-space [*Weltraum*]," simultaneously fell through "inner-space [*Innen-Raum*]." Without quite linking all these terms, Rilke basically describes this experience of a natural event—a shooting star—as "Weltinnenraum" or "worldinnerspace." He conveys a radical identification of the mind and Nature, stating that the contour of his body was no longer there. This coincidence of an outer event with an inner event as two aspects of a unity resembles a description of Nature in the "Weltinnenraum-Gedicht." In the poem Rilke writes, "I look *without* and *within* me grows the tree [ich sehe hinaus und *in* mir wächst der Baum]."[73] In the letter, the experience, which is mediated through *sight*— of the shooting star—is compared with the earlier *auditory* experience of a bird-call on Capri. With regard to the latter he employs a very similar expression to that used in "Erlebnis (II)"; in the letter he speaks of an "ununterschiedenen Raum [undivided space]"; in "Erlebnis (II)" he employs the expression "ununterbrochenen Raum [unbroken or uninterrupted space]." Rilke is clearly seeking to articulate the same idea and experience in these two almost-identical expressions.[74] In other words, *Rilke is identifying these two expressions. The fact that this experience of a bird-call on Capri occurred in 1907 or 1908 illustrates that the "Innenraum" of Nature disclosed to Rilke's seeing in the middle period is part of a continuum with his later conception of "Weltinnenraum."*[75] *Furthermore, in light of these considerations it can be concluded that "Weltinnenraum" is not a metaphysical concept devoid of any experiential basis; rather, it is grounded in Rilke's privileged experiences of a non-dualistic disclosure of Nature and the world. "Weltinnenraum" conceptualizes an experienced unity of mind and Nature.*

"Weltinnenraum" performs a similar function to the postulate of a single ground in metaphysical, monistic philosophies. For this

---

72 Rilke, *Briefe*, vol. 2, 119; my emphasis.
73 *KA 2*, 113; my emphasis.
74 We also saw in "Erlebnis (I)" Rilke's use of the word "Zwischenraum"— "between-space." I regard these four terms as synonymous: "Zwischenraum," "Ununterbrochener Raum," "Ununterschiedener Raum," "Weltinnenraum."
75 See n. 66.

reason it is understandable that within the secondary literature Rilke's notion of *Weltinnenraum* is often explicated as Rilke's metaphysics. However, in light of the development of twentieth-century philosophy and the reiterations of the "end of metaphysics"—most rigorously discussed by Heidegger who sought to develop a new kind of thinking beyond metaphysics—the relation between "Weltinnenraum" and the "metaphysical" requires further consideration in the present context. In that we have focused on the experiential background of an aspect of Rilke's poetic "worldview," and precisely formulated a valid and critical definition of metaphysics (its deficiency in "phenomenality"), it has been possible to make a case for a non-metaphysical, and rather, mystical (in the sense specified) reading of Rilke's notion of *Weltinnenraum*. My claim then is that Rilke's "Weltinnenraum" is not a metaphysical *postulate* but grounded in his transformed *experience* of the world, which included the disclosure of an invisible, an interior, that is the interior of things or of *the world* itself. If "Weltinnenraum" were simply regarded as a metaphysical concept it would, for the reasons articulated in Chapter 1, not fare any better as a solution to dualism than the other monisms discussed. At the very least then, I am arguing that the source which primarily motivated Rilke's coining of the term was non-metaphysical, and that this non-metaphysical reading finds much textual support. *The only adequate overcoming of dualism lies in an experiential disclosure of the invisible and the visible in their wholeness in each case. I regard "Weltinnenraum" as an attempt to give a name to such a disclosure.*

In having demonstrated that Rilke's later term—"Weltinnenraum"—can be of assistance in illuminating the middle Rilke and vice versa, the question might be posed as to why I have not chosen to focus on the later Rilke and his most encompassing work, *Duineser Elegien*? Why am I primarily concerned with the middle Rilke or, more specifically, with the *Neue Gedichte* and their background?

The *Duineser Elegien* formulate the task of humanity (in connection to the figure of the "angel" who stands for the one who has already completed the task) as a transformation of the visible world into an invisible one ("Verwandlung ins Unsichtbare").[76] This task is not formulated in the *Neue Gedichte*. However, in light of our problematic there are reasons for privileging the *Neue Gedichte* over the *Elegien*. The *Elegien* formulate the *task* of *Verwandlung*, the transformation of the visible into the invisible, and within the poems there are many moments where specific cases of *Verwandlung* are presented—in the perception of animals, the experience of a season, the lover's vision of the beloved. However, no collection gives as much weight to the visible

---

76 See Die Neunte Elegie (The Ninth Elegy) of the *Duineser Elegien*. KA 2, 227–9.

and the invisible in their belonging together as the *Neue Gedichte*. If there is any place where Rilke proves himself to be a poet who "haßte das Ungefähre [hated the approximate]," then it is the *Neue Gedichte*; the sensible features of things are often portrayed with a degree of detail and clarity that are arguably unmatched in the preceding history of poetry. However, the vividness of this portrayal of the sensible never has the character of a merely physical, or objectifying, description; there is always a concomitant expressive or invisible sense. The poems thereby do justice to the richness of sensible appearance while at the same time disclosing this appearance as the surface of an intrinsic depth (an invisible). Hence, in addition to the primary reason for turning to the *Neue Gedichte*, namely their phenomenological character, another reason is the wholeness of their presentation of things. Although the *Neue Gedichte* do not present an overall conception and evaluation of the human condition, they occupy an eminent position in Rilke's oeuvre due to their balanced twofoldness. Furthermore, the *Duineser Elegien* formulate the poetic task of transformation as a saying and praising of things ("Sag ihm [dem Engel] die Dinge ..."[77]). While they offer a grand legitimation of this saying, the *Neue Gedichte* accomplish this task in a more concentrated manner. Thus, the *Elegien* can be seen as an affirmation of, and later complement to, Rilke's earlier achievement, the *Neue Gedichte*.[78]

Rilke's *Sachliches Sagen*

Inspiration—when it *is* inspiration—, whatever its precise source, has the character of an active-passivity. Inspiration cannot simply be willed, nor is it passively given.[79] It involves a heightened mental activity with a receptive gesture. The word itself indicates this receptivity; to be "in-spired" is to "in-breathe" something, to take it in or receive it. The primary aim of this and the preceding chapter was to set forth the view that the inspiration of many poems in the *Neue Gedichte* had its source in a way of seeing that was nothing less than a privileged or extraordinary disclosure of the things themselves.[80] In this privileged disclosure things reveal themselves in a twofold manner; the invisible is

---

77 KA 2, 228.
78 In the Introduction I already mentioned the similarities between some of Rilke's latest poems—the French poems—and the *Neue Gedichte*. That these were written after the formulation of the task of *Verwandlung* in the *Duineser Elegien* also thereby vouches for a significant place of the *Neue Gedichte* within Rilke's overall achievement. The French poems, though significant, are not as masterful and complex as the *Neue Gedichte*.
79 See Owen Barfield, *Speaker's Meaning* (Middletown, CT: Wesleyan University Press, 1967), 68ff.
80 See also Luke Fischer, "Perception as Inspiration: Rilke and the *New Poems*."

no longer in opposition to the visible and interiority is the interior of the things themselves. In saying that this privileged disclosure of particular things inspired the *Neue Gedichte*, I am claiming that the poems were inspired by the *things themselves*. Many of Rilke's "new poems" are, or at the very least strive toward, an artistic *saying of the things themselves*. Rilke sought to articulate his vision of things in the poems. In turn, the poems themselves lead the reader to a privileged non-dualistic insight into phenomena. In the earlier discussion of Rilke's notion of *sachliches Sagen* in connection to Cézanne, this artistic ideal of saying the things themselves was elaborated. It will be helpful to consider again one of Rilke's most significant statements concerning this ideal. He writes,

> it's natural after all, to love each of these things as one makes it: but if one shows this, one makes it less well; one *judges* it instead of *saying* it. One ceases to be impartial; and the very best – love – stays outside the work, does not enter it, is left aside, untranslated: that's how the painting of sentiments came about ... They'd paint: I love this here; instead of painting: here it is.[81]

The task of the painter, following Rilke's interpretation of Cézanne, is not to portray a subjective interpretation of the thing; rather the painting should say or show "here it is." The painting should enable a disclosure of the thing itself, should enable the thing to show itself. The painting should not portray one's feeling toward the things, but say the things themselves.

Later in the same letter Rilke writes: "Can you imagine what that is like, and what it's like to experience this through him? ... In the poems, there are instinctive beginnings toward a similar objectivity [*Sachlichkeit*]. I'm leaving the "gazelle" as it is: it's good."[82] Rilke was unsure whether to include "Die Gazelle" in the *Neue Gedichte*. Here he expresses his decision to include it in the collection. It is clear from the passage that Rilke appraises himself as progressing toward a Cézanne-like objectivity in his poetry. This leaves open the question whether, and to what extent, Rilke attained the "objectivity" ("Sachlichkeit") that he esteemed in Cézanne (this question will be explored in Chapter 4). Although "Die Gazelle" is not Rilke's most accomplished poem in this respect, he clearly regarded it as approximating his poetic ideal in that he expresses his decision to include the poem in the *Neue Gedichte* after mentioning this ideal.

A rich background for appreciating the poem "Die Gazelle" has been provided by the explication of Rilke's way of seeing and his specific

---

81 LC, 50. KA 4, 616.
82 LC, 51. KA 4, 617.

description of contemplating the gazelles in the Jardin des Plantes. Attention was drawn to the way in which Rilke's seeing enabled a physiognomic disclosure of the animal. In Chapter 4 I will consider "Die Gazelle" as well as other "animal poems," and illustrate the continuity between Rilke's perception of animals and the imaginative vision facilitated by the poems. It will be revealed how the poems themselves, when appropriately actualized in the reader's imagination, accomplish a physiognomic, twofold disclosure of phenomena. In other words, the poems in their saying of things are *organs* of vision or insight into the things themselves. Poems are obviously not simply perceptions but complex linguistic works of art. The specific continuity between perception and these linguistic works will be explicated in Chapter 4, as well as further intermedial relations between Rilke's poetry and the works of Rodin and Cézanne. However, before doing so, I would like to draw out an important connection between Rilke and phenomenological philosophy that has not yet been explicitly thematized.

From the exegesis of Rilke's *sachliches Sagen* obvious connections to phenomenology have been indicated. However, in the earlier discussions of phenomenology the specific place of *language* was not considered. Language plays a central role in all philosophy, and in this respect it is not incorrect to regard philosophy as a form of literature; moreover, for the present purposes, this acknowledgment immediately brings poetry and philosophy into close proximity to one another. As far as *phenomenological* philosophy is concerned, Heidegger was the thinker who gave the most attention to the central role of language.

One of the most suggestive and well-known definitions of phenomenology is provided by Heidegger in *Being and Time*. Heidegger defines the meaning of the word "phenomenology" by way of an individual consideration of the words "phenomenon" and "logos." The "phenomenon" is defined as a specific way in which something can appear. More specifically it is described "as that which shows itself in itself."[83] He proceeds to define "logos" as the mode of discourse which lets something be seen concerning that which is under discussion.[84] Heidegger then offers his preliminary definition of phenomenology: "Thus 'phenomenology' means ... to let that which shows itself be seen from itself in the very way in which it shows itself from itself ... But here we are expressing nothing else than the maxim formulated above: 'To the things themselves! [*zu den Sachen selbst*]'."[85]

The similarity between Heidegger's definition and Rilke's conception of *sachliches Sagen* is clearly discernible. Phenomenology is

---

83 Heidegger, *Being and Time*, H. 28.
84 Ibid., H. 32–4.
85 Ibid., H. 34.

a saying that allows the things or matters (*Sachen*) to show themselves from themselves. It is not difficult to see that Rilke's *sachliches Sagen* can be properly regarded as a phenomenological demand for artistic saying. Significantly, there is also a more intimate connection between phenomenology and poetry, than between phenomenology and painting, in that both phenomenology and poetry say through the medium of language. It is apt to state that in these parallels between the middle Rilke and the early Heidegger a neighborhood of "Dichten und Denken" can already be seen, or more precisely—to fit in with the terminology of these respective periods—a proximity between Rilke's *Dinggedichte* and Heidegger's hermeneutic phenomenology. Broadly speaking both Heidegger and Rilke are concerned with a saying of the things or matters themselves.

If both phenomenological philosophy and the *Neue Gedichte* involve a saying which enables a self-showing of the things themselves, their manner of saying is, nevertheless, *not* the same. Philosophical phenomenology is not an art, nor does it create works of art in the manner of poetry (or painting). Yet the arts and philosophy both share what can be broadly described as a "logos-character." The essence of art and philosophy concerns the logos in that they seek to communicate insights and address human understanding. However, the *sine qua non* of the work of art is the radical indissolubility of the means of saying from what is said. A piece of music cannot be translated into "other words" or "other music" to the extent that philosophical prose can be translated or paraphrased. A philosophical idea can be paraphrased in different words and syntax, but a musical score cannot be paraphrased with different notes and intervals between them. The sonorous composition of a poem, what Ezra Pound calls *melopoeia*, is essential to its meaning to a far greater extent than the sound of philosophical prose.[86] In the work of art every aspect of the signifier assumes a communicatory significance; the sensible form attains the summit of non-arbitrariness.[87] As the French symbolist Paul Valéry explains with the analogy of human movement, most forms of language are a means of conveying a message; Valéry compares this to a walk whose significance lies in getting from location A (signifier) to destination

---

86 Ezra Pound, "How to Read," in *Literary Essays*, ed. T. S. Eliot (New York: New Directions, 1968 [1929]), 15–40. For a discussion of difficulties in translating Rilke's poetry see Luke Fischer, "Understanding through Translation: Rilke's *New Poems*," in *Perspectives on Literature and Translation: Creation, Circulation, Reception*, ed. Brigid Maher and Brian Nelson (New York: Routledge, 2013), 56–72.

87 We developed some of these points already with regard to the wholeness of the work of art in the section on Rodin and Cézanne.

B (signified).[88] In contrast, poetic language is akin to a dance, whose significance is in the movement itself. Poetic language is the opposite of referential language. While philosophical prose is a highly specialized form of language, its meaning is not as closely tied to its sensible form as poetic language. Although style, for instance, to a certain extent determines the meaning of philosophical prose, it does not assume the same level of significance as poetic form (or musical style). Hence, in a "poetic phenomenology" or a poetic saying of the things themselves, assonance, rhyme, alliteration, and rhythm must all serve in the disclosure of the matter (*Sache*) itself. These considerations serve to make a preliminary distinction between a poetic phenomenology and a philosophical phenomenology. (Further similarities and differences between Rilke's poetic phenomenology and phenomenological philosophy are explicated in the next chapter.)

Conclusion of Chapter

Since antiquity, in various guises, the artist has been regarded as an exceptional figure, as one whose works are mysteriously inspired and cannot be produced through mere talent or skill. In antiquity the poets thought of their works as dictations from a Muse, dictations whose law and meaning were beyond their comprehension (as Plato tells us), and in Romanticism, for instance, the artist was privileged with the status of a genius and a similar mystery surrounded his or her productive capacity. This "mystery" of art can be distinguished into two aspects. On the one hand, there exists the mystery of *artistic creation*, and on the other hand, there exists the mystery of *the work of art*. How do these two aspects show themselves in the case of Rilke's *Neue Gedichte*?

This chapter built on Chapter 2 and sought to present two interrelated matters: 1) Rilke's manner of being-in-the-world, his practice of seeing, and the correlative twofold disclosure of Nature; 2) the background and source of inspiration of the *Neue Gedichte*. These two aspects have been explicated as belonging to one and the same phenomenon. There is no doubt that Rilke was naturally gifted as a writer. Nevertheless, it has been demonstrated that the inspiration of the *Neue Gedichte* need not be consigned to the status of a complete mystery. The tendency to regard artistic inspiration as unfathomable is in many respects a failure to confront and seek to understand the genesis and nature of art. This tendency celebrates or criticizes the dark mystery without shedding any light on the matter. While I regard the *Neue Gedichte* as inspired poetry, there was a clearly and consciously instituted praxis of seeing that led to a transformation in

---

88 Paul Valéry, "Poetry and Abstract Thought," in *The Art of Poetry*, trans. Denise Folliot (Princeton, NJ: Princeton University Press, 1958), 52–81.

Rilke's vision and in turn enabled the composition of the poems. The source of inspiration need not be relegated to utter darkness. However, my stronger claim is that the inspiration of the *Neue Gedichte* was *a happening of truth*, a disclosure of the matters themselves which are in turn portrayed in the poems. In other words, the inspiration of the poems was a kind of *knowing*. A well-known passage in *Malte* describes the conditions necessary for the genesis of a poem. It begins as follows: "For the sake of a line of poetry, one must *see* many towns [*Städte sehen*], humans and things, one must be *familiar with* animals [*Tiere kennen*], one must *feel how* [*fühlen, wie*] the birds fly, and *know* [*wissen*] the gestures with which the small flowers open themselves in the morning."[89]

In the above passage Rilke outlines some of the necessary preconditions for the possibility of writing a line of poetry. For a significant reason I have emphasized particular words. To write poetry one "must *see* many towns, humans and things, ... be *familiar with* [or *know – kennen*] animals, *feel how* the birds fly, and *know* the gestures with which the small flowers open themselves." The italicized words all have a cognitive or epistemic character. Even the mention of feeling is not of a feeling *toward* something, which would imply a subjective attitude, but a feeling *how*. This feeling has the cognitive gesture of sympathy or participation; it involves, in the example given, feeling *how the birds fly*; it participates in the manner of *their* flight.[90] In other words, the starting point for the creative process of writing poetry is founded in a form of *knowing*, more specifically, a *twofold seeing* or *participative knowing*. Hence, artistic inspiration, in this case, is not a peculiar and mysterious category to be distinguished both from the epistemological and the ethical. On the contrary, the *Neue Gedichte* were inspired by a kind of knowing, moreover, a privileged kind of knowing, which transcends conceptual thinking and the "natural attitude," as well as the latter's phenomenological explication.

I will now address the mystery surrounding the work of art. It has been shown that Rilke saw his primary task in this period as that of translating a privileged vision into the composition of the work of art. Since at least the time of Kant, the mystery of artistic form and its excess of meaning has been a central problem of philosophical aesthetics. The richness and ambiguity of the work of art makes it irreducible to concepts, and the law of its form or composition, although it has a certain non-arbitrariness or necessity, also eludes conceptualization. However, just as the creation of Rilke's poems was

---

89 *KA 3*, 466; my emphasis.
90 This feeling might also be related to the earlier discussion (see the sub-section, "The Disposition of the Artist," in Chapter 2) of Gernot Böhme's conception of "atmospheres."

inspired by a certain kind of knowing, the wholeness of each poem is in-formed by this privileged participative knowing. Rilke makes a particular claim about Rodin that can be adapted and applied to Rilke himself. He speaks of Rodin's great knowledge of Balzac, which was necessary for the creation of the sculpture, *Balzac*. Rilke explains that, "Filled completely with the spirit of Balzac, Rodin now proceeded ... to build up the outward appearance [*äußere Erscheinung*]."[91] Analogously, it can be stated that Rilke (as result of his twofold perception), filled with the "spirit" of a caged panther or gazelles, proceeded to compose a poem which embodied and articulated his vision. Thus, the rule of the work of art is given to the poet, at least in part, by the inspired form of seeing that has been articulated. (It should perhaps be added that this is not to say that the poem is simply a pure expression of the "in-itself" or a pure mouthpiece of the "voice" of things. The voice of a poem [and the style of any work of art] manifests a distinctive subjectivity and human attunement to the world, and is, of course, a formation within a specific linguistic and poetic culture. Nevertheless, Rilke's poems manifest a deep attentiveness to their subject matters, and the poem can be understood as revealing a chiasm between self and world, language and being.)

As readers we encounter a poem whose wholeness strikes us with an excess of meaning. The (genuine) poem cannot be reduced to concepts or compositional rules. The intellect thus confronts an entity whose law exceeds its grasp. Works of art, and more specifically the poems in the *Neue Gedichte*, are irreducible to concepts, and always present a specific kind of excess, precisely because they bear the form of a superior kind of knowing. The light of the intellect confronts the appearance of a greater light in the form of the work of art. For this reason the ambiguity or richness of the poem is not a result of an epistemic inferiority to the concept, a vagueness instead of univocity, but a result of its superiority. The intellect is to the poem as the mole's eyes are to sunlight. This view that works of art, in the present case the *Neue Gedichte*, are inspired and informed by a higher kind of knowing than that of conceptual thinking, obviously has particular implications for literary theory and criticism; most significantly, the implication that a theoretical appropriation or explanation of a poem is ultimately inadequate. However, when a poem is really understood or actualized it is grasped with the *imagination* and not with conceptual reasoning. Hence, as I hope to illustrate, in an adequate imaginative engagement with a poem the intellectual standpoint is transcended. The genuine task of poetry criticism then, is not to substitute the poem with a theory but to keep in mental view the site that is opened by the

---

91 *AR*, 38; translation altered. *KA 4*, 445.

poem itself and to shed reflective light onto the poem without losing its reality in an attempt to translate it into concepts. It is with this, perhaps impossible, ideal in mind that I turn to the poems in the *Neue Gedichte*.

Four The *Neue Gedichte* as a Twofold Imagining of Things

Introduction

The *Neue Gedichte* (1907) and *Der neuen Gedichte anderer Teil* (1908) form one of Rilke's most distinguished poetry collections and represent his supreme poetic achievement during his middle period (1902–10). While as a collection they are perhaps less well known than his later masterpieces, *Duineser Elegien* (1922; published in 1923) and *Die Sonette an Orpheus* (1922; published in 1923), the two parts of *Neue Gedichte* contain many of his most famous poems ("Der Panther," and "Archaïscher Torso Apollos," for instance) and have been regarded by certain critics as his greatest accomplishment.[1] The most distinctive genre of poetry in the *Neue Gedichte* is known as the *Dinggedicht*— the "thing-poem" or "object-poem." The *Neue Gedichte* also includes poems that do not belong to this genre (love poetry and poems that reinterpret mythological and biblical themes); however, it is the *Dinggedichte* that are characteristic of the collection. Moreover, Rilke's *Dinggedichte* clearly demonstrate a phenomenological and non-dualistic vision of things that is continuous with his perception as explicated in the preceding chapter. Many of the *Dinggedichte* were directly inspired by Rilke's diligent praxis of perceiving the world in the manner of a visual artist and they provide the definitive poetic articulation of his twofold vision. These poems also reveal illuminating intermedial connections between Rilke's poetry and the visual artworks of Rodin and Cézanne. The main aim of this chapter is to demonstrate how Rilke's *Dinggedichte* articulate a twofold vision of things and thereby contribute to a phenomenological overcoming of dualism.

---

1 See Lawrence Ryan, "Rilke's *Dinggedichte*: The 'Thing' as 'Poem in Itself,'" in *Rilke-Rezeptionen*, ed. Susan L. Cocalis, Karin Obermeier, and Sigrid Bauschinger (Tübingen: Francke Verlag, 1995), 27–35.

The chapter is divided into two main sections. The first section focuses on the manner in which Nature is presented in a number of poems, beginning with a discussion of Rilke's animal poems. The second section extends to considerations of poems that thematize human figures and artifacts. Prior to these close analyses of specific poems, three central points are introduced that concern the general horizon of my interpretation: the *phenomenological* character of the *Neue Gedichte*; poetry as the language of *imagination*; and the characteristic features of Rilke's *Dinggedichte*.

The Phenomenological Character of the Neue Gedichte

Many poems in the *Neue Gedichte* are continuous with the previous articulation of Rilke's phenomenological seeing, and at the end of Chapter 3 close parallels were demonstrated between Heidegger's formal definition of phenomenology and Rilke's *sachliches Sagen*. Käte Hamburger is the literary critic who has made the most concerted effort to interpret Rilke in a phenomenological light. In her essay "Die phänomenologische Struktur der Dichtung Rilkes" Hamburger argues for a phenomenological interpretation of Rilke's work generally, and offers a phenomenological reading of a number of poems from the *Neue Gedichte*.[2] Hamburger points out the striking similarity between Rilke's "sachliches Sagen" and Husserl's "zu den Sachen selbst." She sees in Rilke's poetry a theory of knowledge or phenomenology of perception that is aware of the noetic-noematic correlation and the problem of constitution. She points to the centrality of *Schauen* or *Sehen* in Rilke and Husserl, regards Rilke's poems as executing the phenomenological reduction, and even identifies instances of a Husserlian *Wesensschau* in Rilke's poetry. Although I am in agreement with some of these points I do not agree with Hamburger's strictly Husserlian reading of Rilke, particularly with respect to the last two points—the phenomenological reduction and Husserlian *Wesensschau*.

Wolfgang Müller in his essay "Rilke, Husserl, und die Dinglyrik der Moderne" has rightly objected to aspects of Hamburger's interpretation.[3] He illustrates, for instance, that in her Husserlian reading of the poem "Blaue Hortensie" Hamburger overlooks essential elements (such as affective aspects) of the poem.[4] Müller concludes that although there are correlations between Husserl and Rilke (Müller regards Rilke's poems as thematizing the thing as a phenomenon constituted within perception), it cannot be said that Rilke performs the

---

2 Käte Hamburger, "Die phänomenologische Struktur der Dichtung Rilkes," 179ff.
3 Wolfgang Müller, "Rilke und die Dinglyrik der Moderne," in *Rilke und die Weltliteratur*.
4 Later in this chapter (in the sub-section, "Flower Poems") I discuss Hamburger's and Müller's interpretations of "Blaue Hortensie" in detail.

The *Neue Gedichte* as a Twofold Imagining of Things   217

phenomenological reduction as there are elements in his poems that would be excluded by the phenomenological reduction. I will not enter into the details of the disagreement between Hamburger and Müller here, as I would like to address the problem at a more general and encompassing level.

The main limitation in the discussion between Hamburger and Müller lies in the fact that the only phenomenologist who is considered in relation to Rilke is Husserl. In the earlier chapters I pointed out certain problems with Husserl's phenomenology and situated Rilke in closer proximity to Merleau-Ponty and Heidegger. While the preceding chapters articulated the phenomenological character of Rilke's seeing in terms that are not reducible to Husserl's philosophy, the present chapter will perform a similar task in relation to a number of Rilke's "new poems."

Although phenomenologists generally agree on the central significance of the phenomenological reduction, many phenomenologists have rightly pointed out that Husserl himself did not execute the reduction adequately.[5] The aim of the phenomenological reduction is to bring into view the how and what of the givenness of phenomena, while suspending the operation of all metaphysical conceptions, accepted scientific theories, and the naïve realism of the "natural attitude." As previously mentioned, I share Marion's view that Husserl's reduction is primarily (though not solely) a reduction to "objectness."[6] Moreover, this suggests that there are specific scientific prejudices that inform Husserl's considerations (we already illustrated some of these in the case of the givenness of the Other in Chapter 1). To say that Rilke does not perform the phenomenological reduction in a *Husserlian* manner (which is the content of Müller's claim) does not mean that Rilke's procedure is not *phenomenological*. Were one to regard the reduction as defining of phenomenological practice and to insist that only Husserl's execution of the reduction is adequate, then this would entail the absurd conclusion that thinkers such as Merleau-Ponty and Heidegger were *not* phenomenologists because their "phenomenological" analyses in particular cases conflict with Husserl's.

Moreover, if one grants that Rilke's ideal of a *sachliches Sagen* was the same as Cézanne's *réalisation* in the sphere of painting (as elaborated in the previous chapters) then one can draw on Merleau-Ponty in order to support the idea that Rilke, in his own way, performed a phenomenological reduction. In "Cézanne's Doubt" Merleau-Ponty clearly identifies Cézanne's practice of seeing and painting with the

---

5 See, for instance, Jean-Luc Marion, *Reduction and Givenness*.
6 Jean-Luc Marion, *Being Given: Toward a Phenomenology of Givenness*, 27ff.

phenomenological reduction or epoché and phenomenological description.[7] Rilke's vision is similarly phenomenological in a pre-eminent way, in that it involves a radical suspension of all preconceptions concerning things, in order to allow phenomena to reveal their own meaning.[8]

In this regard there are also crucial differences between Husserl and Rilke. If Rilke's perception has a "pre-scientific" character it is not in exactly the same sense as Husserl's phenomenology. This difference lies in the fact that Husserl's phenomenology of perception directs special attention to the life-world or *Lebenswelt* as it is given in the "natural attitude." When we are not engaged in scientific reflection we are involved in the everyday *Lebenswelt*. However, the specific character of the *Lebenswelt* has been distorted by scientific theories; the task of phenomenological reflection is to disengage these theories and bring into reflection the specific structure and character of the "pre-scientific" *Lebenswelt*. The *Lebenswelt* is in a sense the *everyday* world brought to phenomenological self-clarification. Although Rilke's perception involves a suspension of scientific and metaphysical theories, the purpose of this suspension is not to facilitate a description of the phenomenological structures implicit to the *Lebenswelt*. Rather, it is in order to enable an *exceptional* perception of things which transcends ordinary scientific conceptions as well as the givenness of things in the "natural attitude" and the latter's phenomenological explication. The reader may object to this particular distinction between the *everyday* and the *exceptional* and point out that Husserl's "phenomenological attitude," in contrast to the "natural attitude," is an *exceptional* state of mind.[9] However, the central point is that there is a difference of orientation between Rilke and Husserl. Rilke did not seek to uncover the structures of experience through a kind of philosophical *reflection*, nor is his perception limited to the horizon of everyday experience; rather he immersed himself more deeply in the process of *perception* and this led to an *exceptional* disclosure of things. In other words, this Rilkean disclosure is not attained through philosophical reflection, yet it is phenomenological in an analogous manner to Cézanne's vision as explicated by Merleau-Ponty.

A further difference between Rilke and Husserl lies in the fact that Rilke's seeing must be understood in terms of a *chiasmic* phenomenology

---

7 Merleau-Ponty, "Cézanne's Doubt," 59–75. Galen A. Johnson rightly says that "Merleau-Ponty found in Cézanne a paradigm of the phenomenological *epoché* and achievement of a prescientific perception of the visible" ("Phenomenology and Painting: 'Cézanne's Doubt,'" in *The Merleau-Ponty Aesthetics Reader*, 9).

8 Christoph Jamme in his essay "Der Verlust der Dinge: Cézanne – Rilke – Heidegger" points out significant connections between Rilke, Heidegger, Merleau-Ponty, and Cézanne.

9 See Chapter 1.

in contrast to Husserl's form of transcendental idealism. If Husserl went beyond Kant to discover the problem of constitution and the domain of phenomenology in its *concreteness* there is still a certain "Kantianism" and *a priorism* in his thought due to the manner in which all meaning is ultimately traced back to the acts of a transcendental subject. In this respect Rilke is far closer to Merleau-Ponty's chiasmic phenomenology in that the genesis of meaning in his artistic vision occurs at the juncture of seer and seen.

This brings us to Müller's objection to Hamburger's view that Rilke's poetry enables a Husserlian *Wesensschau* (an intellectual perception of the essential, universal structures of phenomena).[10] With regard to the example of "Blaue Hortensie" Müller claims that the articulation of the final blue of the petals in the poem should not be understood as a kind of *Wesensschau* (as a phenomenological articulation of their "blueness") but in light of the literary notion of epiphany—a moment of sudden and exceptionally vivid perception—which is also evident in the poems of William Carlos Williams.[11] At this point Müller entirely departs from any consideration of phenomenology, as though "epiphany" bears no relationship to a phenomenological *Wesensschau*. The reason Müller regards epiphany as different from a Husserlian *Wesensschau* lies in the fact that an epiphany does not have the a priori and rationalistic character of the *Wesen* of the Husserlian *Wesensschau*; an epiphany is more bound to the perceived phenomenon and is characterized by an excess. However, precisely at this point, where Müller departs from any further consideration of phenomenology, it is possible to see in Rilke's poetry a chiasmic phenomenology (Merleau-Ponty) of givenness in the mode of excess (Marion).[12]

In short, I agree, for the most part, with Müller's critique of Hamburger. However, in contrast to Müller, I consider Rilke's differences from Husserl as constitutive of his proximity to other phenomenologists. "Epiphanic perception" is nothing less than a chiasmic perception which involves a givenness of meaning in excess. This transcendence of the horizon of "objectness," or the givenness of "rich phenomena" as opposed to "poor phenomena," is not less

---

10 Müller, "Rilke und die Dinglyrik der Moderne," 26–7.
11 This is a weaker sense of "epiphany" than my use of the word in the previous chapter, in that my characterization of Rilke's epiphanic vision includes an emphasis on the religious and mystical connotations of the word. Nevertheless, Müller is right to emphasize the importance of epiphany in Rilke and his comparisons of Rilke's *Neue Gedichte* to the Anglophone movement of Imagism are also illuminating. With regard to the latter, see Wolfgang Müller, "Rilkes *Neue Gedichte* und der Imagismus," *Blätter der Rilke Gesellschaft* 30 (2010): 231–45.
12 See the discussions of Rilke's vision in Chapters 2 and 3.

phenomenological, but more phenomenological than the constitution of objects; it is a more profound and complete disclosure of the "things themselves." This is, moreover, connected to one of the significant tasks of phenomenology in the age of scientism. Phenomenology can partly be regarded as a response to scientific reductionism.[13] Scientism presents an objectivistic worldview, in which the subject is excluded and phenomena are reduced to physical and quantitative terms. In thematizing the "pre-scientific" life-world, phenomenology uncovers richer modes of givenness which have been overlooked and inappropriately reduced (in the sense of reductionism) by scientific thought. A phenomenology of *exceptional* givenness, such as the epiphanic phenomenology evident in Rilke's work, offers further contributions toward recovering and uncovering richer modes of givenness. The widespread tendency in the present age is to reduce richer forms of givenness to subjectivistic categories. Whatever cannot be accounted for in the terms of scientific reductionism is regarded as subjective. This point of view is in fact an inversion of the truth. Relative to exceptional forms of givenness, it is scientism that is subjective as it only allows for a limited and partial disclosure of things; a richer givenness is, so to speak, more "objective" in that it reveals more of the phenomenon.[14]

The numerous connections I have drawn between Rilke and Merleau-Ponty call for a brief mention of a slight but significant difference in their approaches and views. The previous chapter argued that Rilke's conception of the invisible does not have a metaphysical or merely postulated status, but is rather phenomenological. That Merleau-Ponty's view of the invisible is phenomenological rather than metaphysical should go without saying. However, the invisible revealed to Rilke's perception was shown to be epiphanic in the strong sense of the word—a disclosure of the numinal—whereas Merleau-Ponty's invisible bears a more agnostic status. In light of the present considerations, the Rilkean invisible can thus be regarded as part of a more profound disclosure. For this reason, the moments in Rilke's letters, poetry, and prose which articulate a phenomenological givenness of the divine or numinal must be interpreted as transcending the horizon of Merleau-Ponty's thought. What the poet and philosopher share in common though, is a chiasmic understanding of perception and a non-dualistic view of the relation between the visible and the invisible. In other words, Rilke shares Merleau-Ponty's view of

---

13 Cf. Shaun Gallagher, "Phenomenology and Non-reductionist Cognitive Science," in *Handbook of Phenomenology and Cognitive Science* (Dordrecht: Springer, 2010), 21–34.
14 Cf. Jean-Luc Marion, *Being Given: Toward a Phenomenology of Givenness*.

the intimate relation between the visible and the invisible; however, the Rilkean invisible is more clearly spiritual. I think that a fairly accurate idea of Rilke is given if one imagines him as Merleau-Ponty (in the form of a poet rather than a philosopher) with a good deal of Novalis or William Blake.

These considerations lead to a further significant point. Although Rilke's vision is essentially phenomenological, I am not subordinating Rilke to the thought of any phenomenological philosopher. My view is that Rilke's vision and poetry can *extend* phenomenology, and for that matter, philosophy itself. Due to the recognition of the problematic character of metaphysics within phenomenological philosophy, a different solution needs to be found to traditional metaphysical problems. Heidegger's view of the "end of philosophy" and his search for a new kind of thinking intimately related to poetry are closely connected to the present work.[15] It is a different response to this crisis of metaphysics and philosophy that I am pursuing in turning to Rilke. In so far as this response involves the articulation of a vision of the divine,[16] it also ventures beyond the boundaries of reason and metaphysics set up by Kant. It does this *not* through reclaiming the rights for reason which were excluded by Kant (whether problematically or not) but through articulating a different kind of perceiving and a different kind of thinking which transcend these boundaries in a distinctive way.

Now that the phenomenological horizon of the present approach to Rilke's poetry has been outlined, it is important to draw attention to a remaining crucial difference between Rilke and *philosophical* phenomenology, namely the difference between philosophical and poetic language.

Poetry as the Language of Imagination
The previous chapter explicated Rilke's twofold seeing of Nature as a phenomenological overcoming of dualism, an overcoming of the usual sense of human estrangement from the natural world. It also indicated how Rilke's twofold seeing generated the inspiration for many of the poems in the *Neue Gedichte*, particularly those poems which most obviously fall under the category of *Dinggedichte*. The present chapter aims to demonstrate how *the poems themselves facilitate a non-dualistic vision of things for the reader*. At this point this claim is likely to appear strange. How can a poem, which is a linguistic work of art and

---

15 See the Introduction.
16 In this respect I share Heidegger's view of the poet's task in the modern age, which he articulates with reference to Rilke, as a saying of the Holy. Heideggger, "Wozu Dichter?"

relatively abstract, bear any relation to things as they are revealed to sense perception?

In Chapter 3 two senses of the word "see" were explicated: perception (sense perception) and intellectual seeing ("I *see* what you mean"). Twofold seeing was described as involving an intimate connection of these two senses. However, the previous chapter gave special attention to the perceptual side or aspect of this twofold seeing. In this chapter the focus is on the intellectual aspect. It might be said that the previous focus was on a twofold perception while the present focus is on a twofold thinking (both belong to the broader category of twofold seeing). Many of Rilke's *Dinggedichte* foster a twofold thinking, a twofold disclosure of things *in thinking*.

"Two-foldness" implies a belonging together of two connotations of "sense"—meaning and the sensible. Yet how can there be a twofold seeing at the level of thinking, when thinking seems to be the very opposite of sense perception? The possibility of a twofold seeing in thinking can be intimated through turning to the following statement by Novalis:

> The imagination is the miraculous sense, which can substitute all our senses—and which already stands so much at our disposal [*in unserer Willkühr steht*]. If the outer senses seem to stand completely under mechanical laws—the imagination is clearly not bound to the presence and sensation of external stimuli.[17]

Imagination can stand in for the sensible but is clearly an intellectual operation and not a kind of sense *perception* (although it might be intimately related to perception). Imagination or imaginative thinking can *represent* the sensible at the level of thinking; it should be said, however, that by *represent* I do not mean re-presentation with its sense of repetition nor do I mean the German *Vorstellung*. I mean "represent" in the sense in which Gadamer uses the word in *Wahrheit und Methode*, in the sense, for instance, that one person can "represent" another in court.[18] The person who stands in for, or represents, another speaks on the other's behalf but does not necessarily say what has already been said by the other. New things can be revealed by the "representative" about the "represented." It is in this sense that imagination can stand in for, or "represent," the sensible.

It is in the imagination then, that the possibility of a twofold thinking—a twofold seeing with the mind's eye—can be discovered. Just as visible phenomena can mediate the disclosure of the invisible in

---

17 Novalis, *Novalis Schriften: Die Werke von Friedrich von Hardenberg*, vol. 2, 423.
18 Hans-Georg Gadamer, *Wahrheit und Methode*, 146ff.

The *Neue Gedichte* as a Twofold Imagining of Things   223

twofold perception, so can the invisible imagination reveal the nature of the visible. Twofold perception approaches the invisible through the visible, while twofold thinking approaches the visible through the invisible. Furthermore, these two processes complement and deepen one another. I will be able to more accurately imagine the manner in which a certain species of bird flies if I have closely observed this species in flight. In turn, the words of a poem can lead me to imagine an expressive manner of behavior that I have not yet perceived. In addition, it thereby calls me to expand my perception and notice what had up until now escaped my attention. Perception and imagination can extend and reinforce one another.[19]

The question whether language and thought are ultimately separable or inseparable, and their precise relation, is beyond the scope of this work. However, that there is an intimate connection between language and thought cannot be doubted following any serious reflection on the matter.

Philosophy and poetry share in common the fact that they exist through the medium of language, a point that was previously brought up in the comparison of Heidegger's definition of phenomenology and Rilke's idea of a *sachliches Sagen*. However, there is an important difference between philosophical language and poetic language which indicates a certain priority of poetic language with respect to a non-dualistic vision. *Poetic language fosters an imaginative thinking and can thereby more adequately show the sensible and the intelligible in their wholeness, in a twofold manner.* (This difference between philosophical and poetic language, however, should be understood more as one of degree than kind; philosophers, for instance, often resort to poetic

---

19 This account of the reciprocal deepening of perception and imagination is also indebted to the role of "exact sensorial imagination [*exakte sinnliche Phantasie*]" in Goethe's scientific studies and in the research of Goethean scientists. Goethe uses this specific expression in his reflection on Ernst Stiedenroth's *Psychologie zur Erklärung der Seelenerscheinungen* in *Zur Naturwissenschaft überhaupt, besonders zur Morphologie* but exact imagination plays a central role in all of Goethe's scientific studies, and scientists in the Goethean tradition have expanded the methodological conception of "exakte sinnliche Phantasie." Johann Wolfgang von Goethe, *Sämtliche Werke nach Epochen seines Schaffens: Zur Naturwissenschaft überhaupt, besonders zur Morphologie*, vol. 12, ed. Karl Richter et al. (Munich: Carl Hanser Verlag, 1989), 355; Johann Wolfgang von Goethe, *Scientific Studies*, trans. Douglas Miller (Princeton, NJ: Princeton University Press, 1994), 46. For a diverse introduction to contemporary Goethean science, see the essays in *Goethe's Way of Science: A Phenomenology of Nature*, ed. David Seamon and Arthur Zajonc (Albany, NY: SUNY Press, 1998). For a lucid account of the methodological conception of "exact sensorial imagination," see Craig Holdrege, *Thinking Like a Plant: A Living Science for Life* (Great Barrington, MA: Lindisfarne Books, 2013), 56–8.

formulations such as Hegel's famous statement involving the "owl of Minerva," and concepts can be found within poetry.)

It is interesting that Hegel can be drawn upon in order to support this view, as he understood poetry as the art of the imagination.[20] The difference between poetic language and other forms of language is defined by Hegel in connection to the role that the imagination plays in the former. He states,

> Using our ordinary intellectual mode of apprehension I understand the meaning of a word as soon as I hear or read it, without, that is to say, having an image of the meaning before my mind. If, for instance, we say 'the sun' or 'in the morning', the meaning is clear to us, although there is no illustration of the sun or dawn. But when the poet says: 'When in the dawn Aurora rises with rosy-fingers', the same *thing* is expressed, but the poetic expression gives us *more*, because it adds to the understanding of the object a vision of it, or rather it repudiates bare abstract understanding and substitutes the real specific character of the thing.[21]

In other words, poetic language calls for a concrete imagining of the phenomena themselves, an imaging of the appearances, which differs from the apprehension of a merely abstract universality.

Along these lines Hegel defines poetry as the "presentation of the truth ... which does not ... separate the universal from its living existence in the individual."[22] Poetic language calls for a concrete imagining of phenomena, and this imagining brings an incarnate universal to disclosure, a universal which is the very life of the particular. Hegel conceives poetic language in this sense as showing an original unity of essence and existence.[23] In other words, poetic language fosters a non-dualistic or twofold disclosure of things.[24] With

---

20 Hegel, *Aesthetics: Lectures on Fine Art*, vol. II, trans. T. M. Knox (Oxford: Clarendon Press, 1975), 959ff.
21 Ibid., 1002.
22 Ibid., 973.
23 Ibid., 1002.
24 Although I am drawing on Hegel to support my own view, there are numerous points in which I disagree with Hegel. Most importantly, I do not hold to his logic of *Aufhebung* or "sublation." Religion and, finally philosophy, are not the sublation of poetry. Hegel assumes that philosophical thought has access to the same universality as poetry but ultimately sublates it. My view, in contrast, is that "poetic thinking" and "poetic language" disclose a universality and get at the haecceity of things in a way which is not granted to conceptual language or philosophical thinking. Moreover, Hegel places philosophy above art and poetry in his logic of increasing spiritualization. However, it is precisely such a philosophical spirituality or abstractness which cannot bring into view the

regard to a number of Rilke's *Dinggedichte* this point will be demonstrated in a rigorous manner.

Of course, the role and relative significance of the poetic image and imagination differ greatly from poet to poet and tradition to tradition. In twentieth-century Anglophone poetry it is the movement of "Imagism" (and successive related movements) that is most strongly associated with the importance of the image. While Rilke's *Neue Gedichte* were written a few years prior to the advent of Imagism, concrete imagery plays a similarly central role in the *Neue Gedichte*.[25]

One of the main claims of this chapter is that Rilke's "new poems" express an *excess* which cannot be substituted by or paraphrased in an abstract conceptual language. This claim suggests that there is an implicit tension between literary criticism (especially poetry criticism) and its "object," a tension which is, to my mind, too seldom taken into consideration by literary critics. In poetry criticism *two forms of language*, and *two forms of thinking*, confront one another: the poetic and the conceptual or scientific (*wissenschaftlich*). Moreover, the specific goals of literary criticism often remain unarticulated. With the dominance of theories in literary theory and criticism today, *in practice*, texts are often treated as though they simply contain what can be better expressed in the conceptual or scientific language (*wissenschaftliche Sprache*) of some contemporary theory. This stands in strong contrast to the Romantic conception of the work of art as always *exceeding* and expressing *more* than what could ever be said in conceptual language. I hold to the view, as is clear, that a poem contains *more* than what can be paraphrased in conceptual terms.[26] In other words, any sort of criticism will always fall short of the poem. It will always be poor in comparison to the poetic work that it interprets. This then must also hold true for what is articulated in this chapter, as I am clearly undertaking a kind of philosophical literary *criticism*. What then do I aim to achieve?

My aim is not to replace the poems with a theory. I acknowledge an implicit tension between the conceptual language of this philosophical poetics and the linguistic works of art. This treatment cannot do justice to the rich ambiguity of the poems. However, in conjunction

---

point in which the spiritual and the sensuous interpenetrate one another. Poetry, in contrast, can perform such a twofold vision. The present work develops a conception of poetry that counters Hegel's view; it argues that poetry surpasses philosophy in important respects. See also Luke Fischer, "Goethe contra Hegel: The Question of the End of Art."

25 See Müller, "Rilkes *Neue Gedichte* und der Imagismus."
26 Of course, here I support the Romantics and depart strongly from Hegel's ultimate position. See n. 24.

with the phenomenological contextualization of the *Neue Gedichte* my commentary seeks to *point* to the non-dualistic disclosure that the *poems* are capable of accomplishing. Moreover, due to the fact that *contrasting* two things draws attention to the specific character of each thing, this thematization of the tension between poetic language and conceptual language will allow the special character of each (primarily the former) to come into relief. In addition, my approach differs both from the formalistic interpretations and the historical focus of much literary criticism; I regard the poems as a saying of being.[27] A poem is not an object; its essence cannot be determined reflectively. When a poem works, *is* itself, it does not oppose us as an object; rather, it is a happening, a temporal saying, a performance. The poem facilitates a disclosure and it is more an organ of vision than an object of consciousness. The formalistic tendencies within literary criticism tend to forget the true being of the poem and unwittingly reduce it to an "object" of criticism. Such an approach also naturally loses sight of the poem as a happening of truth, a saying which discloses. Truth (unconcealment) itself is not an object but an activity; it is a creative revelation, an event of illumination. Although my interpretation of poems below is also a conceptual, reflective treatment, it attempts to speak *with* and keep in sight this essential character of the poem, while recognizing the limitations of any critical commentary.

There are other significant differences between poetic language and conceptual language. These differences converge in what could be called the greater ambiguity of poetic language. However, this ambiguity should not be understood as a lack of clarity or vagueness, but on the contrary as a *surplus* or *excess* of meaning in comparison to conceptual language. If the aim of such language is to say and disclose a givenness of things in *excess*, then poetic language is not an inappropriate and imprecise language but the language that is adequate and proper to an *exceptional* givenness of things. The suggestive musicality of poetic language, the multivalent use of words, the formulation of new and foreign metaphors and similes, all serve to draw the reader into seeing what is portrayed in a richer and unfamiliar light. Although these features also play a role in philosophical language, they do so to a lesser degree. Philosophy has often described itself, for instance, as striving for univocity in expression as opposed to equivocity; the musicality and style of a philosophical expression do not bear the same degree of significance as these ultimately untranslatable features of a poem; metaphors play a significant role in philosophy and all forms of language but philosophy is not as productive in the creation

---

27 Cf. Heidegger, "Hölderlin und das Wesen der Dichtung," in *Erläuterungen zu Hölderlins Dichtung, GA* 4 (1951 [1936]), 42.

of new metaphors as poetry.[28] While there is not the space for a detailed consideration of these matters, in my reading of Rilke's "new poems" the significance of these aspects of his poetic language will be concretely demonstrated.

Rilke's Dinggedichte

The term *Dinggedicht* was first introduced by Kurt Oppert in 1926 in order to classify a type of poem that reached a certain climax in its historical development in Rilke's *Neue Gedichte*.[29] While Müller is right to criticize Oppert's characterization of the *Dinggedicht* as an "impersonal, epic-objective description of a being" for the reason that Rilke's *Dinggedichte* incorporate *subjective* experience, many details of Oppert's elucidation of the *Dinggedichte* are perceptive.[30] Oppert discerns intermedial connections between visual art and Rilke's *Dinggedichte*; he contrasts Rilke's concentrated depiction of things from occasional lyrical reflections; and he explicates the way in which the meaning of the poems is intertwined with the portrayal of things. The term *Dinggedicht* is also a fitting one in that it resembles Rilke's distinction between *Ding* and *Kunst-Ding* with respect to the work of Rodin. Due to the many connections between Rilke's *Dinggedichte* and Rodin's sculptures, it is illuminating to interpret Rilke's *Dinggedichte* as a species of *Kunst-Ding*.[31]

Although it is inadequate to regard all of the *Dinggedichte* within a single horizon, some pertinent common features can be isolated. The *Dinggedichte* are generally incredibly focused on the depiction of a perceptible thing. The way in which each thing is depicted could be said to foster an imagining where the sensible aspect of a thing and its meaning are given as a single phenomenon. Many of the poems facilitate a kind of physiognomic imagination, analogous to the physiognomic perception characterized in the previous chapters. Gestural, expressive portrayals of things are central to the poems, and in these respects the poems embody a chiasmic phenomenology and a phenomenology of expression. Things are often conveyed as expressive wholes, in such a way that the gestural dimension and the meaning cannot be divided.

Having mentioned the word "whole," it should be added that the "things" or *Dinge* as depicted in Rilke's *Dinggedichte* are also situated

---

28 See Luke Fischer, "Metaphor and the Poetic Origin of Meaning."
29 Kurt Oppert, "Das Dinggedicht: Eine Kunstform bei Mörike, Meyer und Rilke," in *Deutsche Vierteljahrsschrift* 4 (1926): 747–83.
30 Wolfgang Müller, "*Neue Gedichte/Der Neuen Gedichte anderer Teil*," in *Rilke-Handbuch*, ed. Manfred Engel (Stuttgart: J. B. Metzler, 2004), 298.
31 See the discussion of Rodin and Rilke in Chapter 2.

within larger contextual wholes. The thing does not come before the mind's eye as a mere isolated object, but as a phenomenon whose meaning is revealed through the manner in which it takes part in a larger context. It is often a specific scene which is brought before the mind's eye—the way a blind man ("Der Blinde") makes his way through the busy city of Paris, the way in which a panther ("Der Panther") relates to and is conditioned by its caged surrounding, a swan's relationship to land and water ("Der Schwan"), the movement of a ball between players ("Der Ball"). In this sense, one can also speak of Rilke's poems as offering a *hermeneutic*-phenomenological vision of things—hermeneutic in that the meaning of something is discovered through its relation to and place within a larger meaningful context, and phenomenological, as this meaning is incarnated in the *appearances* or the *phenomena*. However, in this respect a specific privilege of hermeneutic-phenomenological poetry can be seen in contrast to a hermeneutic-phenomenological philosophy. The latter has the advantage of articulating universal structures, but the former is better able to disclose the very meaning of *specific* things in their wholeness. The poems do not formulate the general structure of the part/whole relationship, but rather bring the very wholeness and meaning of a scene before the mind's eye. There are also clear cases where the poems illustrate things within a context which is beyond the horizon of a hermeneutic phenomenology in most of its forms (the later Heidegger is perhaps an exception). Things are sometimes presented within a context of what could be called *cosmological interrelationship*. At the end of "Die Rosenschale," for instance, the roses are said to contain "the vague influence of distant stars" ("den vagen Einfluß ferner Sterne"). With respect to these spiritual relationships between things, Rilke is closer to the mystical tradition, and more specifically, to the esoteric tradition with its view of correspondences between the earthly and the heavenly, than to hermeneutic phenomenology in its more well-known forms.[32] In short, the "thing" of Rilke's *Dinggedichte* is not an isolated "thing" (as some interpretations would have it), but a "thing" whose meaning and existence are bound to a larger contextual whole.[33]

---

32 See Antoine Faivre, *Access to Western Esotericism* (Albany, NY: SUNY Press, 1994), 10ff. See also Gísli Magnússon, *Dichtung als Erfahrungsmetaphysik: Esoterische und okkultistische Modernität bei R. M. Rilke*. This aspect of Rilke's work can also be fruitfully approached through Gaston Bachelard's phenomenological poetics. See Gaston Bachelard, *The Poetics of Reverie: Childhood, Language, and the Cosmos*, trans. Daniel Russell (Boston: Beacon Press, 1971). For further connections between poetic imagination and esoteric imagination, see Luke Fischer, "Owen Barfield and Rudolf Steiner: The Poetic and Esoteric Imagination."

33 I think that Anthony Phelan and William Waters (both of whom draw on Stefan Zweig's views of Rilke) are right to emphasize the significant role of

The *Neue Gedichte* as a Twofold Imagining of Things   229

In Chapter 2 Rilke's admiration for the dynamic character of Rodin's sculptures was discussed. Rodin's *Kunst-Dinge* or sculptures are not static but always evoke a sense of movement and thus imply temporality. However, with respect to time and movement, poetry has an advantage over sculpture.[34] A poem is essentially a temporal being. For Rilke's *Dinggedichte* this means that the time of the poem often coincides with the presentation of the temporal unfolding of an event or thing. Furthermore, this temporal unfolding is intimately connected to the twofold disclosure of things. The essence of a thing is not a-temporal, time-less, or purely abstracted from time, nor is it merely temporal in the sense of linear time. The twofold essence of things is better described as trans-temporal, and is grasped in the manner in which the meaning of a piece of music is grasped. It is neither an abstract entity outside of time nor discontinuous empirical time, but rather *a meaning that expresses itself in time, and makes of time a meaningful whole*. The temporal portrayal of things in Rilke's *Dinggedichte* corresponds at the imaginal level to the spatio-temporally situated character of the twofold perception outlined in the previous chapter, and also recalls the characterization of the *situatedness* of encounters with Others in Chapter 1. However, this point brings up an important difference between *Ding* and *Kunst-Ding*, or, in this instance, *Dinggedicht*.

Chapter 2 explicated Rilke's view of works of art—Rodin's sculptures and Cézanne's paintings—as *superior* presentations of the essence of a thing than the original thing itself. The essence of something comes to a higher expression in the work of art. This explains how Rilke can regard art as a revelation of Nature—moreover, as a higher revelation of Nature—while at the same time maintaining a non-realist (in the sense of perceptual realism) aesthetics. The failure to recognize this intimate relation between *Ding* and *Kunst-Ding* is a cause of great misunderstanding in much Rilke scholarship. Those who emphasize the self-contained character of the poems often end up interpreting Rilke in terms of an "art for art's sake."[35] However, this higher degree of self-containment is due to the necessity inherent to the work of art,

---

interconnections in the *Neue Gedichte*, in contrast to interpretations that treat the poems as isolated objects, though my interpretation is more thoroughly phenomenological than Phelan's. Waters offers an excellent synopsis of some of these interconnections in an overview of the *Neue Gedichte*. Anthony Phelan, *Rilke: Neue Gedichte* (London: Grant & Cutler Ltd, 1992); William Waters, "The New Poems," in *The Cambridge Companion to Rilke*, ed. Karen Leeder and Robert Vilain (Cambridge: Cambridge University Press, 2010), 59–73.

34 Cf. Judith Ryan, *Umschlag und Verwandlung: Poetische Struktur und Dichtungstheorie in R. M. Rilkes Lyrik der mittleren Periode* (Munich: Winkler Verlag, 1972), 24–5.
35 See Chapter 2.

in contrast to the contingency that remains in Nature, and this necessity is nothing less than a superior articulation of the *essence* of *things*.[36] I previously explicated this view by discussing the contingency in the appearances of things or *Dinge* relative to the essentiality of the work of art or *Kunst-Ding*. A particular crease in a person's pants, for instance, tells me less about the person than the look in her eyes. In the work of art, however, every aspect must be made expressive. In Rilke's poetry one finds the same kind of "essentialization" that is present in Rodin's works, but temporality plays a more central role. Rilke's poems do not simply re-present things as they are perceived. His poems are artistic compositions, not reports. They conjure for the mind's eye *unfolding events* in which *every aspect and moment* is revealing of the essence or meaning.

The above considerations serve as a general introduction to the horizon of my interpretation of Rilke's *Neue Gedichte*. Of course, many other significant features could be discussed here: the predominance of the sonnet form (and variations on this form) in the *Neue Gedichte*, whose structure is masterfully employed in the service of concentrated depictions and surprising turns; the complex relation between sound and meaning in the poems; the distinctive characteristics of Rilke's

---

36 As aforementioned, this kind of view of the significance of the work of art (including the poem), which shares strong similarities to Romantic and Heideggerian conceptions, has been of concern to ecocritics (see Kate Rigby, *Topographies of the Sacred*, 92ff.), in that it seems to make artworks more valuable than Nature and thereby tacitly legitimate anthropogenic environmental destruction. To convey this concern in overly crude terms, consider the following hypothetical claim: Since a particular poem about an endangered animal conveys the essence of the animal in a superior manner to the appearance of the animal itself, we need not worry about the possible extinction of the animal. While I share this ecocritical concern about views that in certain respects value art above Nature, I would like to intimate a couple of possible responses to this concern. First, I have argued that a work of art that thematizes a natural being is deeply related to the real essence of the natural being. Thus the artwork is not isolated from or independent of that which it depicts. Second, there is a certain ontological deficiency in the work of art if one compares it to Nature, which is self-engendering or autopoietic. The emergence of a work of art is dependent on the mediation of human labor; a poem or a painting does not bring itself into being in the way in which an animal brings itself forth and moves itself from within. In this respect, one can speak of an ontological deficiency in the work of art in comparison to the essence of natural beings. Hence, while the work of art might be the least arbitrary *presentation* of the essence, the ways in which it differs from natural beings mean that it cannot be a substitute for them. (Obviously a great deal more needs to be said about this topic and the primary concern of this book is, of course, not the elaboration of an ecopoetics but Rilke's response to the problem of dualism.)

metaphors and similes; the iconic aspects in Rilke's *Dinggedichte* and how they evoke the portrayed phenomena.[37] However, this introduction suffices to outline the most important features for the present context, and the significance of these various poetic devices for Rilke's *sachliches Sagen* will be illustrated in the course of the specific analyses.

In keeping with the trajectory of this inquiry, I will first explicate the twofold manner in which Nature is disclosed in the *Neue Gedichte*, devoting the most space to Rilke's "animal poems." Subsequently, I will turn to poems that focus on human figures, artworks, and artifacts and thereby demonstrate the broader significance of Rilke's *sachliches Sagen* for a poetic overcoming of dualism.

Nature as Poetically Disclosed
Animal Poems

The animals we find in Rilke's poetry are neither animals as we perceive them in everyday life nor animals as they are conceived and understood by mainstream, mechanistic science. These factors play a role in determining the generally subjectivistic and humanistic interpretations of Rilke's animal poems in the secondary literature. Such interpretations assume a metaphysics which has nothing to do with the phenomenological and ontological monism that comes to expression in all of Rilke's writings—his letters, poetry, and prose. Thus, they do not attain to the genuine site of Rilke's vision and poetry, namely an exceptional disclosure of things which involves a revelation of an invisible that is not reducible to the subjective or psychological but rather has an ontological status. Karl-Heinz Fingerhut, who has provided the most comprehensive monograph on the symbology of animals in Rilke's poetry, typifies the general direction of the majority of interpretations of Rilke's animal poems in the following statement:

> Thus, the figuration [*Gestaltung*] of animal-being in the *Neue Gedichte* is ultimately not the grasping and seeing of the "essence" of a particular animal beyond what is scientifically describable; it is above all a mirroring [*Bespiegelung*] and transfiguration of the human interior in the medium of the perceived natural object. Rilke's animal figures [*Tiergestalten*] are ... projections of the poetic interior onto a fitting object of the external world.[38]

---

37 For a good introduction to the typical characteristics of Rilke's *Neue Gedichte*, see Wolfgang Müller, "*Neue Gedichte/Der Neuen Gedichte anderer Teil*," in *Rilke-Handbuch*, 296–318. On Rilke's handling and adaptations of the sonnet form, see Judith Ryan, *Umschlag und Verwandlung*, 55ff.
38 Karl-Heinz Fingerhut, *Das Kreatürliche im Werke Rainer Maria Rilkes: Untersuchung zur Figur des Tieres* (Bonn: H. Bouvier u. Co. Verlag, 1970), 169.

Fingerhut takes this interpretation to its extreme in a footnote, referring to Rilke's animals as an "Objectification of Rilkean solipsism."[39] In the previous chapter it was demonstrated that Rilke's vision of animals was the very opposite of solipsism, that it entailed the transcendence of solipsism and dualism. The reason for these solipsistic or subjectivistic readings of Rilke's animal poems lies in the fact that many literary critics assume a dualistic metaphysics that is inadequate for Rilke's worldview and poetry, which challenge and overcome the oppositions between inner and outer, subjective and objective, the earthly and the spiritual. Although a dualistic way of thinking is pervasive in the age of scientism (what Schelling and Hegel would call a culture of *Verstand*, rather than *Vernunft*), it is strange that it should be so widespread in the human sciences or *Geisteswissenschaften*. It is even more striking in the case of Rilke as a radical monism with overtly mystical characteristics appears everywhere in his writings.

Fortunately, however, not all Rilke-interpreters adhere to the subjectivistic, humanistic reading of Rilke's animal poems. Käte Hamburger, Rudolf Eppelsheimer, and Monicka Fick, all in their own way present an interpretative horizon in which the poems can be regarded as thematizing a disclosure of the animals themselves.[40] Hamburger does this from a Husserlian phenomenological point of view, Eppelsheimer from an anthroposophical Goethean point of view, and Fick through drawing attention to Rilke's reception of the spiritualism of Carl du Prel, as well as the biology of Jakob von Uexküll (among other biologists).[41] Eppelsheimer and Fick are closer to my interpretation in so far as they recognize a genuinely esoteric or mystical dimension in Rilke's work and recognize Rilke's monism.[42] Although Fick does not

---

39 Ibid., 169, n. 155.
40 Hamburger, "Die phänomenologische Struktur der Dichtung Rilkes," 206ff.; Rudolf Eppelsheimer, *Rilkes larische Landschaft: Eine Deutung des Gesamtwerkes mit besonderem Bezug auf die mittlere Periode* (Stuttgart: Verlag Freies Geistes Leben, 1975), 101–20; Monicka Fick, "Organologisches Sehen oder die Verdichtung zur 'Umwelt': Rainer Maria Rilke," in Monicka Fick, *Sinnenwelt und Weltseele: Der psychophysische Monismus in der Literatur der Jahrhundertwende* (Tübingen: Max Niemeyer Verlag, 1993), 184–223.
41 On the significant connections between Rilke and Uexküll, see also Malte Herwig, "The Unwitting Muse: Jakob von Uexküll's Theory of Umwelt and Twentieth-Century Literature," *Semiotica* 134 (2001): 553–92.
42 I agree with some of the main points made by Eppelsheimer in his monograph *Rilkes larische Landschaft*. He characterizes Rilke, for instance, as a "spiritual phenomenologist," drawing on the twofold sense of the German word *Erscheinung* as "appearance" and "apparition" (p. 27). He also draws illuminating parallels between Rilke, Goethe, and Rudolf Steiner. However, at various points he over-interprets Rilke from an anthroposophical point of view without enough textual support, and does not address Rilke's own

The *Neue Gedichte* as a Twofold Imagining of Things   233

enter into detailed analyses of Rilke's animal poems, she points out some of the important connections between Rilke and contemporaneous developments in biology that in significant respects built on a Romantic heritage. The connection between Rilke and Uexküll is particularly relevant to our present concerns. It is not incidental that Heidegger and Merleau-Ponty drew on Uexküll's zoology in the context of their phenomenological and ontological considerations of Nature.[43] Heidegger appropriated many aspects of Uexküll's zoology and *Umweltforschung* in order to elaborate a conception of the organism and his thesis that the animal is "poor in world" or "*weltarm*" (in contrast to the world of *Dasein*).[44] Merleau-Ponty discovered in Uexküll many observations and ideas to support his project of a non-dualistic ontology of the "flesh."[45]

In important respects Uexküll's zoology could be characterized as a kind of hermeneutic phenomenology of the animal. It is hermeneutic in that Uexküll regards Nature as a meaningful whole rather than as *partes extra partes*.[46] Each part of nature must be contextualized within the whole and understood holistically rather than atomistically or in terms of a mechanical causality.[47] More specifically, the animal and its environment or *Umwelt*, according to Uexküll, constitute an irreducible and meaningful whole. Uexküll's approach is phenomenological to the

---

    disagreements with anthroposophy, which, in light of the horizon of his interpretation, is wanting of treatment. For a discussion of these matters and Rilke's relationship to esotericism, see Gísli Magnússon, "Rilke und der Okkultismus," in *Metaphysik und Moderne: Von Wilhelm Raabe bis Thomas Mann*; Gísli Magnússon, *Dichtung als Erfahrungsmetaphysik: Esoterische und okkultistische Modernität bei R. M. Rilke*.

43 See Brett Buchanan, *Onto-Ethologies: The Animal Environments of Uexküll, Heidegger, Merleau-Ponty, and Deleuze* (Albany, NY: SUNY Press, 2008).

44 Heidegger, *Die Grundbegriffe der Metaphysik*, GA 29/30 (1983 [1929/30]), 295ff. See also Brett Buchanan, *Onto-Ethologies*, 39ff.; Giorgio Agamben, *The Open: Man and Animal*, trans. Kevin Attell (Stanford, CA: Stanford University Press, 2004), 39ff.

45 See Merleau-Ponty, *Nature: Course Notes from the Collège de France*, 167ff. Merleau-Ponty drew on Uexküll's zoology to develop his "new ontology" of the "flesh" which sought a middle ground between mechanism and vitalism. See also Mauro Carbone, *The Thinking of the Sensible: Merleau-Ponty's A-Philosophy* (Evanston, IL: Northwestern University Press, 2004), 28ff.; Brett Buchanan, *Onto-Ethologies*, 115ff.

46 The importance of meaning, and more specifically, semiosis (signification and interpretation) in Uexküll's view of the animal's relationship to its *Umwelt* has been significant in the development of the interdisciplinary field of biosemiotics. Uexküll is widely regarded as a pioneer of biosemiotics.

47 This organic (rather than mechanistic) and holistic (rather than analytic) thinking also relates Uexküll's zoology to the Romantic tradition.

extent in which it focuses on the appearances and behavior of the living organism in its environment rather than seeking explanatory causes behind the phenomena. A wholeness of the animal, which Uexküll conceptualized with the notion of a *Bauplan* (body plan), is evident from the level of embryological development to animal-behavior—a wholeness not reducible to any single moment. The animal, through its anatomy, physiology, and behavior, is integrated into a corresponding *Umwelt*.[48] The specific character of the sense organs, for instance, is already an opening onto an *Umwelt*. The formation of the dog's nose, to offer an example, opens up an environment of smell not given to organisms with a less specialized sense of smell. The environment as distinctively accessible to the animal's sense organs is what Uexküll calls the *Merkwelt* (sense world). The world as it is significant to the animal's behavior is what he calls the *Wirkwelt* (effective world). The *Wirkwelt* is more truly the world as it is for the animal, because the animal does not merely receive neutral sense impressions (correlated to its organization) but responds to, and acts within, its environment. The wholeness which manifests itself in the harmonious integration of the animal and its *Umwelt* is what he calls an overarching *Planmäßigkeit* (conformity to a plan).[49] It is the notion of *Umwelt* and its connection to Nature as a whole which will prove most illuminating in my reading of Rilke's animal poems. Thure von Uexküll (Jakob's son) introduces the following general definition of the idea of the *Umwelt*, which is helpful for the present purposes:

> The *Umwelt*, which can be reconstructed from the observation of this ... score [musical score] of living features, is indeed generated by the subject [animal subject], because as the relational system of the subject the *Umwelt* comes into being and passes away with it. The *Umwelt* is, however, at the same time a composition of Nature, which encompasses the subject as well as its objects, which extracts the subject from the neutral things of the surrounding [*welche das Subjekt aus neutralen Dingen der Umgebung herausschneidet*] ... Jakob von Uexküll characterizes it thus: "The *Umwelten* are

---

48 Uexküll also distinguishes between lower and higher animals; the lower animals are integrated into an *Umwelt* but do not *have* an *Umwelt*. This *having* of an *Umwelt* (a representation of the *Umwelt*, so to speak) is what Uexküll calls the *Gegenwelt* (counter-world). As such distinctions are unimportant to my interpretation of Rilke, which focuses on higher animals, I am simply employing *Umwelt* in a way that includes *Gegenwelt*. Jakob von Uexküll, *Umwelt und Innenwelt der Tiere* (Berlin: Springer, 1909), 191ff.

49 Jakob von Uexküll and Georg Kriszat, *Streifzüge durch die Umwelten von Tieren und Menschen* [1934]; *Bedeutungslehre* [1940] (Frankfurt am Main: S. Fischer Verlag, 1970). See also Jakob von Uexküll, *Umwelt und Innenwelt der Tiere*.

autonomous unities, which interact with one another. And in this interaction a supra-subjective organization [*Planmäßigkeit*] of life reveals itself at every turn. Everywhere we recognize the presence of a great score, which reveals itself in thousands and thousands of duets—we need only think of the relationships between males and females, between predator and prey. But lifeless Nature is also included in this score, which immediately imposes itself on us in the relationship of the wings of birds to air and wind and the relationship of the fins of fish to water and current."[50]

The *Umwelt* is the world as it is for the living, embodied, animal subject. However, it is not reducible to this in so far as a supra-individual wholeness comes to expression in the animal's integration into its *Umwelt*. This integration is not only expressed in the animal's behavior, but also in its physiology and anatomy, which are essential aspects of the animal-whole. The physiology and anatomy of the animal are already adapted in a specific manner to its environment; thus there is a wholeness or *Planmäßigkeit* of life that circumscribes both animate and inanimate aspects of Nature as integral parts of itself. The wings of a bird and the air, for instance, exist in amazing reciprocity to one another. For this reason, a comparison of swallows and falcons in flight can mediate two different disclosures of air currents. A floating feather, moreover, illustrates the incredible adaptation of the feather to the element of air. A wholeness becomes evident in such relations which is not perceptible to the gaze which reduces everything to *partes extra partes*. As Brett Buchanan explains, Uexküll's emphasis on relationships entails an ontology of the animal, in which the being of any animal is itself shaped by its connections to significant others, both organic and inorganic.[51] Drawing on Goethe's poem (which itself draws on Plotinus) that speaks of the eye as being sun-like, Uexküll characterizes, for instance, the bee as flower-like and the flower as bee-like.[52] A century earlier Goethe himself had emphasized the significance of relationality in numerous ways.[53] With respect to animals

---

50 Thure von Uexküll, "Die Umweltforschung als subjekt- und objektumgreifende Naturforschung," in Jakob von Uexküll and Georg Kriszat, *Streifzüge durch die Umwelten von Tieren und Menschen; Bedeutungslehre*, xxvi.
51 Brett Buchanan, *Onto-Ethologies*, 33ff.
52 Jakob von Uexküll, *Streifzüge durch die Umwelten von Tieren und Menschen; Bedeutungslehre*, 158.
53 Uexküll greatly admired both Goethe's literary works and scientific works. See Gudrun von Uexküll, *Jakob von Uexküll*, 19, 93, 189. On connections between Goethe's and Uexküll's scientific views, see Frederick Amrine, "The Music of the Organism: Uexküll, Merleau-Ponty, Zuckerkandl, and Deleuze as Goethean Ecologists in Search of a New Paradigm," *Goethe Yearbook* 21 (2015).

and their environments, Goethe states that "the existence of a creature we call 'fish,' is only possible under the condition of the element we call 'water' ..."[54] Jakob von Uexküll often uses a musical analogy (as in the above quotation)—Nature's score or *Partitur*—to suggest the meaningful organization of Nature.[55] An integrity akin to a work of art or a musical composition comes to expression in the diversity of natural forms and their dynamic interrelationships. The natural world is, so to speak, a harmonious polyphony or a symphony, rather than an aggregation of discrete particulars. This musical analogy also implies that in order to grasp this wholeness, harmony, or conformity to a plan (*Planmäßigkeit*), it is necessary to attend to natural phenomena in a manner that is similar to the appreciation of a musical work; this wholeness is not understood through a process of abstraction.[56] As will shortly become clear, the virtue of poetry is that it can *perform* this wholeness imaginally.

The first animal poem I will consider is "Der Panther" as it is one Rilke's most accomplished and successful *Dinggedichte* and was the first of the *Neue Gedichte* to be written (1902 or 1903).

Der Panther
Im Jardin des Plantes, Paris

Sein Blick ist vom Vorübergehn der Stäbe
so müd geworden, daß er nichts mehr hält.
Ihm ist, als ob es tausend Stäbe gäbe
und hinter tausend Stäben keine Welt.

Der weiche Gang geschmeidig starker Schritte,
der sich im allerkleinsten Kreise dreht,
ist wie ein Tanz von Kraft um eine Mitte,
in der betäubt ein großer Wille steht.

Nur manchmal schiebt der Vorhang der Pupille
sich lautlos auf –. Dann geht ein Bild hinein,
geht durch der Glieder angespannte Stille –
und hört im Herzen auf zu sein.[57]

---

54 Goethe, *Scientific Studies*, 307.
55 For a more precise breakdown of the different ways in which Uexküll applies the musical analogy, see Brett Buchanan, *Onto-Ethologies*, 26–7.
56 See Chapter 2.
57 "The Panther/ *In the Jardin des Plantes, Paris*// His gaze has grown so tired from the passing/ of the bars, that it holds nothing anymore./ To him it seems as though there were a thousand bars/ and behind a thousand bars no world.// The supple gait of pliant strong steps/ which in the smallest of

In the secondary literature one mostly encounters interpretations of "Der Panther" which treat the panther as merely a symbol for a human state of affairs. According to these interpretations the poem has nothing, or very little, to do with a real caged panther; rather, the panther symbolizes Rilke's own existential predicament and sense of imprisonment in the city of Paris or represents some aspect of the human condition.[58]

After a little close consideration, the fact that so many critics execute humanistic interpretations (I have already suggested the primary reasons which motivate such interpretations) reveals itself as a kind of hermeneutic violence. First, the title of the poem is not "Selbst-Bildnis [self-portrait]" but "Der Panther." Second, the location of the caged panther is specified: the Jardin des Plantes. This specification is completely superfluous on a humanist-symbolic reading of the poem (the *existence* of a panther in a specific place is hermeneutically irrelevant to such a reading). Third, we know that the poem was inspired by Rilke's perception of a caged panther in the Jardin des Plantes, as well as an antique sculpture of a tiger in one of Rodin's studios.[59] Fourth, to mention another more general reason, Rilke's notion of a *sachliches Sagen*, articulated in the context of his reflections on Baudelaire (the poem "Une Charogne") and Cézanne, involved the formulation of a poetic ideal of saying the things themselves; in the present case there are numerous reasons to assume that the thing itself or the *Sache selbst* is the panther.

The question then arises as to what motivates the subjectivistic or anthropomorphic interpretation in this case. There are the biographical facts and their thematization in *Malte* (Rilke's own sense of being suffocated by Paris); however, this factor counts very little in comparison to the grounds just enumerated. A primary motivation for this interpretation is, most likely, the portrayal of the panther in the middle verse, which seems to present an interior depth of the panther that bears no similarity to our everyday perception of animals. Critics therefore speculate that it must be a projection or thematization of the human interior. In contrast, I regard this "interiority" as the presentation of a genuinely daemonic dimension perceived in the animal itself. The

---

all circles turns,/ is like a dance of strength around a center,/ within which numbed a great will stands.// Only sometimes the curtain of the pupils/ without a sound lifts up –. Then an image enters,/ passes through the limbs' taut stillness –/ and ceases in the heart to be." KA 1, 469.
58 For one example of this kind of approach to "Der Panther" see Brigitte Bradley, *R. M. Rilkes Neue Gedichte: Ihr zyklisches Gefüge* (Bern: Francke Verlag, 1967), 75.
59 See Chapter 3.

poem seeks to enact for the reader's imagination an *exceptional* or *privileged* givenness of the animal.

Fortunately, in the present case there are not only a few aforementioned literary critics who consider the poem as a revelation of the animal itself, but also two zoologists, namely, Jakob von Uexküll, and another zoologist in the same tradition, Hans Mislin.

Rilke first met Uexküll in 1905 and the poet and the biologist agreed in fundamental respects concerning the manner in which Nature should be observed.[60] Rilke took an interest in Uexküll's zoology (no doubt another sign that Rilke's interest in animals was more than merely aesthetic) and Uexküll was, already at that time, an admirer of Rilke's poetry.[61] In 1917, after reading Adolf Koelsch's article "Der Einzelne und das Erlebnis" in the *Neue Rundschau*, Rilke wanted to deepen his understanding of contemporary developments in biology that accorded with Uexküll's approach and he wrote to Uexküll asking him for advice. In Uexküll's reply to Rilke we see that the zoologist regarded "Der Panther" (which was written prior to the first meeting of the poet and the biologist) as demonstrative of an exceptional zoological vision. Uexküll states,

> that you possess an outstanding talent for biology and especially for comparative psychology is demonstrated by your poem "The Panther." The observation that you develop there is masterful. Perhaps you could try to hear a philosopher from the psychological school—but I think you are already too much of a master to still be a student.[62]

Uexküll regards "Der Panther" as a document of Rilke's exceptional zoological vision and considers his poetic observation of the animal as masterly ("meisterhaft"). Hans Mislin, who was a professor of zoology and a student of Uexküll's thought, elaborates on Uexküll's claim in his essay "Rilkes Partnerschaft mit der Natur [Rilke's Partnership with Nature]."[63] Before turning to Mislin's commentary on "Der Panther," it will be helpful to introduce some of the key ideas (with which I agree) that frame Mislin's interpretation of the poem.

Mislin begins his essay by commenting on the difference between ancient and mythic understandings of animals and the modern

---

60 Gudrun von Uexküll, *Jakob von Uexküll: seine Welt und Umwelt* (Hamburg: Christian Wegner Verlag, 1964), 56.
61 Rilke and Uexküll also read and discussed Kant's first *Critique* together. Kant had a significant influence on various aspects of Uexküll's biology.
62 Gudrun von Uexküll cites Jakob's letter in her book *Jakob von Uexküll: seine Welt und Umwelt*, 132.
63 Hans Mislin, "Rilkes Partnerschaft mit der Natur," in *Blätter der Rilke-Gesellschaft* 3 (1974).

The *Neue Gedichte* as a Twofold Imagining of Things 239

scientific conception. The latter according to Mislin no longer regards Nature as a "system of forces, movements, and energies."[64] Modern science generally considers Nature in mechanistic, inanimate terms and this view leads to a sense of human estrangement from Nature. In other words, our relation to Nature is no longer participative as it was when Nature was regarded as the expression of natural powers that were concomitantly divine powers. In Rilke, the poet of *Weltinnenraum*, Mislin sees a monistic, participational worldview, which could facilitate a new understanding of and reconciliation with Nature. According to Mislin, the poet rediscovers a symbolic or mythic significance (not in the subjectivist sense) to the animal which has disappeared with the development of modern science. However, Mislin does not see in Rilke a return to a pre-modern relationship to Nature, but rather a higher reconciliation of the ancient and the modern. For Mislin this reconciliation is most evident in "Der Panther." He writes,

> To begin with, in the scene of the panther's imprisonment [*Gefängnisszene*], everything is captured that suggests the original integrity of Nature and its injury through usurpation. The panther's being is grasped in both a concrete, sensory-motoric, as well as in an archaic-symbolic, manner. The movement of the panther is physiologically and physiognomically registered right into the particularities of muscle-tone. The mimesis of the eyes and pupils [*Augen- und Pupillenmimetik*] is seen in a sensory-physiological context, pursued in accordance with genuine holistic research [*Ganzheitsforschung*]. In reality, everything in the panther, which captivates and moves the natural scientist, is recorded. The symbolism of the poet has here incorporated the analysis of the scientist. Rilke thereby opens up the prospect of a new kind of natural *Wesensforschung* [study of beings] where the inner-world and outer-world are reintegrated into a new unity [*wieder zu neuer Einheit zusammenwachsen*].[65]

Throughout this passage Mislin is alluding to Uexküll's *Umweltforschung* and its attempt to understand the holistic relationship between the animal subject and its environment. The poem suggests the integral relation between the animal and its natural *Umwelt* and the way this relation is injured through the panther's confinement. Mislin notes the contextualized manner and the exactitude with which the details of the panther's movements and behavior are presented. Moreover, he implies that the poem is able to reveal the wholeness of the animal

---

64 Ibid., 39.
65 Ibid., 48.

in a way which incorporates and surpasses the observations of the natural scientist. The natural scientist may be moved by a "symbolic" givenness of the animal in his/her investigations but the scientist does not have the linguistic capacities to articulate the phenomenon in its concrete wholeness. As noted in the introduction to this chapter (in connection to Hegel), poetic language can bring the wholeness of a phenomenon before the imagination, and this is exactly what is accomplished by "Der Panther."

In the first stanza the numbed gaze of the animal is presented. Its natural environment has been replaced by the small enclosure surrounded by iron bars, and its gaze has grown tired, lost its natural vitality. The second stanza masterfully portrays the suppleness of the panther's muscles as it paces within its enclosure ("geschmeidig starker …"). This description is at the same time scientifically accurate and dynamically physiognomic. In the third line of the second verse the being of the panther is presented with a daemonic depth and mythic significance, which make its wearied circling nevertheless appear as a dance of strength or power ("ein Tanz von Kraft …"). However, this center of the panther no longer comes to its proper natural expression in its artificial environment. This privation is at the same time revelatory of the panther's relation to its natural *Umwelt*. The poem reveals the interdependence of animal and *Umwelt*. One can still see animals in a similarly deprived condition in the Jardin des Plantes today.[66] While observing them one has the feeling that one is not really seeing the animals themselves as they have been *denaturalized* by their confinement. The panther in this condition can no longer properly realize its being. The holistic relation between animal and *Umwelt* has been severed. The tension between the panther and its unnatural surroundings comes to the fore most strongly in the second verse in the inherent conflict between the dynamic, powerful being of the panther and its having been numbed ("betäubt") by its enclosure.

The third verse again characterizes the tired gaze of the panther, the eyes that only sometimes open to register anything ("Nur manchmal schiebt der Vorhang der Pupille/ sich lautlos auf …"). In the third verse, the meaning of Mislin's statement, that the mimesis of the eyes and pupils is demonstrated in accordance with genuine holistic science,

---

66 While the following example is anecdotal, I will mention it due to its pertinence. I visited the Jardin des Plantes a number of years ago (at the end of 2005) and among other animals, which were clearly suffering as a result of confinement, I saw a lonely wallaby (or perhaps it was a young kangaroo) and my immediate impression was "that's not really a wallaby." There was an immediate sense that through being deprived of its natural *Umwelt* the familiar animal (I grew up in Australia) was no longer itself and thus the visitors to the zoo were not in fact seeing a wallaby.

is most apparent. Uexküll discusses the dynamic interrelation of the animal's sense impressions and its behavior. In the wild, for instance, a panther has a certain way of relating to its prey. This relationship is not merely mechanistic, but the animal nevertheless has specified (in contrast to [the possibility of] human freedom) ways of responding to signs in its environment. The animal takes in its *Umwelt* in a certain way, but it is not only receptive but also effective; it responds or acts. The caging of the panther has led to the loss of this effective side. The image ceases to be; the panther cannot effectively respond to its perceptions ("ein Bild ... hört im Herzen auf zu sein"). As Geoffrey Winthrop-Young succinctly puts it, "'The Panther' is an *ex negativo* depiction of Uexküll's Umwelt."[67] The dynamic, holistic interplay between the animal and its environment has been eroded.

Rilke's interest in biology predated his first meeting with Jakob von Uexküll but deepened through and after their meeting. It is also significant to keep in mind that "Der Panther," in spite of its intrinsic connections to Uexküll's ideas, was written a few years before this meeting. In an informative article on Uexküll's influence on twentieth-century literature, Malte Herwig discusses Rilke's long-term interest in biology and perceptively remarks that "it is interesting to note how the keen observation that Rilke developed during his time with Rodin ... informed his perception of animals to a degree that won him laurels from these biologists."[68]

"Der Panther" is clearly not a report of a simple perception of the animal. It is selective in the features that it chooses to portray and one finds the same kind of "essentialization" that Rilke identified in Rodin's sculptures. Every feature serves in the articulation of the essence of the panther and its confined condition. The poem portrays the panther in a dynamic, gestural manner and vividly evokes the tension between the powerful being of the panther and the deteriorating effects of confinement. Rilke perceived a dynamism in Rodin's sculptures and his poetry carries this dynamism further. A sculpture can suggest temporality and movement but it does not itself unfold in time. In contrast, the poem is essentially temporal and the time of the poem incarnates the dynamic wholeness of the phenomenon. It makes the reader "see" the panther pacing in its cage and the weariness that comes to expression in its behavior. The poem, when properly understood, enacts for the reader a physiognomic disclosure of the animal at the imaginal level.

---

67 Geoffrey Winthrop-Young, "Afterword," in *A Foray into the Worlds of Animals and Humans* with *A Theory of Meaning*, by Jakob von Uexküll, trans. Joseph D. O'Neil (Minneapolis, MN: University of Minnesota Press, 2010), 232.
68 Malte Herwig, "The Unwitting Muse: Jakob von Uexküll's Theory of Umwelt and Twentieth-Century Literature," 562–3.

While my reading of "The Panther" has focused on the content and images in the poem, it should be added that all its formal characteristics serve in the evocation of the panther. Here I will only mention a few key characteristics. The steady iambic pentameter suggests the pacing of the animal. In the first stanza the assonance of the strong vowel, "e," which is reinforced by the end rhymes ("Vorübergehn," "mehr," "Stäbe," "hält," "gäbe," "Welt"), engenders a tone of hardness and pain. The line endings skillfully and aptly alternate between feminine and masculine rhymes. The shortness of the poem (twelve lines) serves the concentrated depiction and functions almost like a cage. The missing foot in the final line (it is tetrameter rather than pentameter) matches the sense that the image ceases in the panther's heart. These formal characteristics work in tandem with the semantics and images to evoke the scene.[69] To borrow Cézanne's term, the poem thus "realizes" the caged panther and reveals it to the mind's eye and the sensitive ear.

Although each of Rilke's *Dinggedichte* enjoys a relative self-sufficiency, the place of "Der Panther" in the first part of the *Neue Gedichte* is not without hermeneutic significance. In his book on the *Neue Gedichte*, Müller insightfully points out that "Der Panther" comes after "Der Gefangene," a poem which thematizes human imprisonment.[70] After "Der Panther" comes "Die Gazelle" which also articulates the animal in relation to its *Umwelt*. However, in this case the animal is presented in its natural *Umwelt*, without the tension of "Der Panther." The gazelle is in *harmony* with its *Umwelt*. The poem after "Die Gazelle" is "Das Einhorn" ("The Unicorn"), which does not present the "animal" in harmony with its *Umwelt* but as, in a certain sense, engendering its own *imaginary Umwelt*. While a close reading of all of these poems would lead too far afield, I will consider "Die Gazelle" as it is an animal poem, and the encounter which inspired it was previously discussed at length.

Die Gazelle
Gazella Dorcas

Verzauberte: wie kann der Einklang zweier
erwählter Worte je den Reim erreichen,
der in dir kommt und geht, wie auf ein Zeichen.
Aus deiner Stirne steigen Laub und Leier,

---

69 In the article "Understanding through Translation: Rilke's *New Poems*" I discuss the formal qualities of "Der Panther" in more detail and the difficulties these pose for the translator. Luke Fischer, "Understanding through Translation: Rilke's *New Poems*," 63ff.
70 Wolfgang Müller, *Rainer Maria Rilkes "Neue Gedichte": Vielfältigkeit eines Gedichttypus* (Meisenheim am Glan: Verlag Anton Hain, 1971), 195.

The *Neue Gedichte* as a Twofold Imagining of Things 243

und alles Deine geht schon im Vergleich
durch Liebeslieder, deren Worte, weich
wie Rosenblätter, dem, der nicht mehr liest,
sich auf die Augen legen, die er schließt:

um dich zu sehen: hingetragen, als
wäre mit Sprüngen jeder Lauf geladen
und schösse nur nicht ab, solang der Hals

das Haupt ins Horchen hält: wie wenn beim Baden
im Wald die Badende sich unterbricht:
den Waldsee im gewendeten Gesicht.[71]

If "Der Panther" is an exemplary *Dinggedicht* in its vivid and focused portrayal of its theme, then "Die Gazelle" is not as accomplished. Nevertheless, it is a beautifully composed sonnet and pertinent to the present discussion. The title and subtitle clearly express the subject matter of the poem. The thematized animal is the gazelle but more specifically the *Gazella Dorcas*, the same species that Rilke observed in the Jardin des Plantes.[72] The poem begins by naming the gazelle the "enchanted one" ("Verzauberte") and asks whether it is possible to *say* or *express* this enchanted being in a poem. In the first quatrain the gazelle is presented as the embodiment of an "unsayable" harmony which the poetic saying would like to adequate ("wie kann der Einklang zweier/ erwählter Worte je den Reim erreichen,/ der in dir kommt und geht …"). The "unsayable" is, of course, connected to an exceptional disclosure, the givenness of a phenomenon that seems impossible to convey in words.

A more concrete portrayal of features of the gazelle is first offered in the fourth line. The ears and horns are named and evoked as "Laub und Leier" ("leaf [foliage] and lyre"). This characterization serves in the first place to suggest the morphology of the ears and horns through their resemblance to opposite leaves (the ears) and the two arms of a

---

71 "The Gazelle/ *Gazella Dorcas*// Enchanted one: how can the consonance of two/ chosen words ever attain the rhyme,/ that in you comes and goes, as if to a sign./ Out of your brow rise leaf and lyre,// and all that is yours passes already in simile/ through love-songs, whose words, soft/ as rose petals, to the one who no longer reads,/ settle upon the eyes, which he closes:// in order to see you: carried, as though/ each leg were a barrel loaded with leaps/ and only held from firing, so long as the neck// inclines the head in listening: as when bathing/ in the woods a woman halts:/ the forest pool in her turned gaze [face]." Translated by Luke Fischer and Lutz Näfelt. KA 1, 469–70.
72 See Chapter 3 and Luke Fischer, "Perception as Inspiration: Rilke and the *New Poems.*"

lyre (the horns). This image, moreover, suggests the gazelle's harmonious integration into the natural world. However, this evocation also clearly involves mythological allusions which can be regarded as a further thematization of a phenomenality of the animal in excess—as unsayable. "Laub und Leier" bring to mind Apollo, the god of music and poetry, who wears the laurel wreath ("Laub" or "leaves") and bears the lyre—attributes which signify the domains under his auspices.[73] These oblique mythological allusions could be interpreted as the opposite of a *sachliches Sagen*, a saying of the things themselves. Such an objection is fostered by a dualistic opposition between myth and science, according to which myth is synonymous with fiction and reductive science possesses knowledge of the facts—what truly is. However, instead of habitually adopting this scientistic mentality, the following question can be asked: If the ideal of these poems is a saying of things as they show themselves from themselves why might they draw on mythological figures and allusions?

Mythology continues to inhabit poetry and art long after it has ceased to be the dominant mode of thinking. A development from mythological to rational thinking (philosophy and science) in European culture is illustrated by the documents which record the transition from Greek mythology to the mythopoeic philosophy of the Pre-Socratics and subsequently to the philosophy of Plato and Aristotle. Yet despite the fundamentally rational culture of modernity, mythological motifs continue to live and evolve in the arts and poetry. With respect to the theme of Nature, one need only consider the irreducible significance of mythology in the Romantic period in the works of poets such as Keats and Hölderlin. What is it then that motivates this persistent "mythologization" of Nature in the works of modern poets? One important reason concerns *the need to articulate a richer givenness of Nature which has been lost in, and eludes the terms of, modern scientific thought*. With respect to the poem presently under consideration the mythological allusions can be viewed as continuous with the thematization of the "unsayable" harmony that is manifest in the gazelle.

Apollo, the god and inspirer of poetry, surpasses in principle what any single poem can say (see "Früher Apollo," the first poem in the *Neue Gedichte*). The "saturated" givenness in the phenomenality of the gazelle's head, ears, and horns evokes a harmony or consonance

---

73 "Laub und Leier" might also be regarded as an allusion to Orpheus. In any case, both Apollo and Orpheus share in common the fact that they represent a supreme embodiment of poetry. Connections between "The Gazelle" and the later *Die Sonette an Orpheus* have been made by a number of scholars. See, for instance, Kih-Seong Kuh, *Die Tiersymbolik bei Rainer Maria Rilke* (Berlin: Ernst-Reuter-Gesellschaft, 1967), 68–77.

(*Einklang*) for the perceiver, which seems to surpass even the expressive capacities of poetry.

Nevertheless, the poem continues in its attempt to say what seems unsayable. Furthermore, to call something "unsayable" is at the same time to become involved in a paradox, in that this is already an attempt to say the unsayable. This is a linguistic procedure which shares much in common with negative theology. Through thematizing the inadequacies of language the speaker indirectly points his interlocutor in the direction of the "unsayable" phenomenon itself. "Die Gazelle" proceeds with this indirect method. The second quatrain tells us that all the qualities that properly belong to the gazelle already have their *likeness* or *simile* in love-songs (*Liebeslieder*). This reference to "love-songs" is an allusion to Solomon's *Song of Songs* where the gazelle is used a number of times as a simile for the "Beloved," but also relates to a larger literary tradition in which the gazelle has been symbolic of qualities such as love, beauty, and gentleness. That the gazelle lives already in similes also suggests that its elusive presence can only be captured indirectly or obliquely. The comparison of the words of love-songs to rose petals placed onto the eyes of a reader who no longer reads continues to invoke the gazelle as a manifestation of grace and gentleness. However, these adjectives ("grace" and "gentleness") are inadequate approximations, akin to verbal descriptions of music which offer little insight if they do not acquire their proper, individual determination through the experience of the *music itself*. Moreover, the poem and this gloss should not be understood as a mere projection of human inwardness onto the gazelle. As aforementioned, the gazelle has often been employed within the poetic tradition as a symbol of these qualities, which does not speak against, but rather for, my claim. The gazelle *can* be employed in such a way precisely because its *phenomenality* manifests these qualities.

It is in the third and fourth verse—the two tercets of the sonnet—that the poem attains to the kind of concreteness that "Der Panther" sustains throughout. The language, when actualized in the reader's listening and imagination (or *listening imagination*), facilitates a physiognomic disclosure of the animal's behavior which is as impossible to paraphrase as it is to substitute the sense of a piece of music with prosaic language. In stating this, it should be repeated that the primary intention of this commentary is *to indicate* or bring to explicit awareness what the poem itself reveals when adequately appreciated.

In the first tercet the legs of the gazelle are compared to the barrels of a gun which are loaded with leaps or jumps ("als/ wäre mit Sprüngen jeder Lauf geladen ..."). These do not fire for as long as the gazelle tilts its head and is absorbed in a state of listening. The behavior of the gazelle is here portrayed in a dynamic, physiognomic manner.

Although it is still, there is a dynamic tension in that the gazelle is in an *active* state of listening and could at any moment dash away on its powerful legs. The gazelle is suspended in a delicate space of listening; inner and outer are here conveyed in a pre-dualistic unity of manifestation.

The final analogy of the poem in the second tercet has been regarded as an allusion to the myth of Artemis or Diana, in which Actaeon eyes the goddess swimming naked.[74] I will not comment on this here; what has already been stated concerning mythology will suffice. The description of the "Waldsee im gewendeten Gesicht [forest pool in the turned gaze]" can be interpreted, following Müller, as a presentation of the unity of, and reciprocity between, the gazelle and its environment or *Umwelt*.[75] The gazelle and its *Umwelt* mirror one another and reveal an overarching harmony or *Einklang*, which strongly contrasts with the dissonance and tension between the panther and its caged environment. However, it is also the gazelle itself, in contrast to the fierce being of the panther, which embodies and discloses an epiphanic harmony. The sense of surprise in the final tercet and in the rhyming couplet (the final *volta* in this sonnet) evokes a moment of sudden insight into this harmony. Perhaps the rhyme or consonance of these two chosen words does capture the presence of the gazelle. On this note, it would be possible to argue that while "Die Gazelle" does not demonstrate the same degree of *Sachlichkeit* as "Der Panther," the obliqueness of the poem equally matches its theme.

"Der Schwan" is particularly interesting in the way it discloses the relationship between this aquatic bird and its *Umwelt*.

Der Schwan

Diese Mühsal, durch noch Ungetanes
schwer und wie gebunden hinzugehn,
gleicht dem ungeschaffnen Gang des Schwanes.

Und das Sterben, dieses Nichtmehrfassen
jenes Grunds, auf dem wir täglich stehn,
seinem ängstlichen Sich-Niederlasssen – :

---

74 See, for instance, Richard Francis Cox, *Figures of Transformation: Rilke and the Example of Valéry* (London: University of London, 1979), 42. Brigitte Bradley also regards "Laub" (foliage) in the last line of the first quatrain as an allusion to Artemis. Brigitte Bradley, *R. M. Rilkes Neue Gedichte*, 76.
75 Wolfgang Müller, *Rainer Maria Rilkes "Neue Gedichte,"* 195.

in die Wasser, die ihn sanft empfangen
und die sich, wie glücklich und vergangen,
unter ihm zurückziehn, Flut um Flut;
während er unendlich still und sicher
immer mündiger und königlicher
und gelassener zu ziehn geruht.[76]

The ostensible content of this poem clearly includes human-existential references. In mentioning this, I should take the opportunity to state that I am not entirely opposed to discovering a human meaning (i.e., the animal as symbolic of human matters) in Rilke's animal poetry. Already Kant, in the third *Critique*, with his notion of aesthetic ideas indicated the inexhaustible meaning of the work of art. It would be a mistake to limit the hermeneutic possibilities of a work of art to a fixed horizon. It is also the nature of metaphorical and figurative language to reveal *relationships* between things, including relationships between the human and the natural world.[77] However, a careful analysis of this poem reveals that the primary or foreground sense is the animal itself, in this instance the swan. To disregard this foreground sense in the majority of Rilke's animal poems is, for reasons already articulated, to perform a hermeneutic violence. The present interpretations of the animals in Rilke's *Neue Gedichte* aim to act as a corrective to the one-sidedly humanist readings that pervade the secondary literature.

The toil of life and the passage of dying are intrinsic to the content of "Der Schwan." However, the fact that the swan is the central image of the poem and the way in which the text enacts a physiognomic disclosure of the animal in relation to its *Umwelt* should not be overlooked. The first two stanzas involve similes that can be read bi-directionally: the swan's walk and the way it lowers itself into the water is compared to a human being who attends with difficulty to life's chores and is in the process of dying. However, the title names the theme as "Der Schwan" and the final verse focuses more

---

76 "The Swan// This toil, to proceed heavily and as if bound/ through what remains undone,/ resembles the unmade gait of the swan.// And dying, this no longer holding/ to the ground on which we daily stand,/ his anxious letting himself down – :// into the waters, which gently receive him/ and which as though happy and gone by/ recede beneath him, tide upon tide;/ while he infinitely still and sure/ ever more maturely and regally/ and serenely deigns to glide." Translated by Luke Fischer and Lutz Näfelt. *KA 1*, 473.
77 See Luke Fischer, "Metaphor and the Poetic Origin of Meaning." On the possibility of reading "Der Schwan" both as a human-existential poem and as an animal poem, see William Waters, "The *New Poems*," in *The Cambridge Companion to Rilke*, 62–4.

exclusively on the swan, while the analogue of dying recedes into the background. Hamburger, moreover, convincingly argues that the swan is the central theme of the first two verses. She regards the "Mühsal" ("toil") and the "Sterben" ("dying") as metaphors which serve to articulate the character of the swan's walk and the way it lowers itself into the water; were this not the primary meaning, then the nominative case of "Mühsal" and "Sterben" and the dative case of "Gang" and "Niederlassen" would be reversed.[78] In other words, the images of human toil and dying serve to characterize the swan's behavior rather than vice versa. While I concur with Hamburger's emphasis, the very fact that these two subjects can mutually illuminate one another means that the poem is open to being read both ways. Nevertheless, I am largely in agreement with Hamburger when she writes that "the swan is not a symbol, but a 'phenomenon'—the thing to be depicted, which the title declares."[79]

The way in which the poem transitions from the first two verses to the final verse is revelatory of the relation of the swan's anatomy and behavior to elements of its *Umwelt*—land and water. The poem begins with the description of the toil of someone who must proceed through unfinished tasks while feeling as if tied up or bound ("Diese Mühsal, durch noch Ungetanes/ schwer und wie gebunden hinzugehen"). This toil is said to resemble the gait or walk of the swan. Already on the basis of the first two lines, one knows that the writer of this poem has closely observed the way swans walk. These lines also testify to the manner in which perception and imagination can reinforce one another. If one closely observes the walk of swans and then re-reads the poem, one experiences how perception and imagination can be mutually illuminating. There is something almost pained in the walk of the swan which makes the opening comparison so fitting. A swan looks heavy and as if bound when it walks. The appearance of its anatomy on land—its large body carried on thin legs and webbed feet—makes it hardly seem suited to the activity of walking. It is as though the swan were not really made to walk, which is the idea communicated by the third line of the poem ("ungeschaffnen Gang des Schwanes"). Of course, webbed feet are intimately related to the element of water and are clearly more adapted to swimming than walking. These observations recall Uexküll's statement that even lifeless Nature is written into the score of Nature as is shown by the interrelationships between birds' wings and the air. In "Der Schwan" the same kind of interrelationships are evident in the way in which the swan's anatomy and behavior relate to the elements of land and water.

---

78 Käte Hamburger, "Die phänomenologische Struktur der Dichtung Rilkes," 206.
79 Ibid., 207.

The *Neue Gedichte* as a Twofold Imagining of Things   249

In the second verse the process of dying, or letting go of life, is given as an analogy for the swan's anxious entrance into the water. The passage from this life into the afterlife is like the swan's transition from one element into another one, from land into water.

The movement from the first two stanzas to the longer final stanza resembles a modulation from a minor key to a major key in a piece of music. There is an intensification or *Steigerung* in the manifestation as the swan enters the fluid medium; the swan seems to come into its own. In contrast to its awkward walking it now glides almost effortlessly on the surface of the water; it is "still and sure [still und sicher]" rather than seeming "heavy and as if bound [schwer und wie gebunden]." While there was something pained in its walk, in the water it is at ease as it glides on the current and appears ever more regal. (There is also a suggestion of the epiphanic in the characterization of the swan's graceful movement and the poem's allusion to the afterlife or the heavenly realm.) The alteration in tone from the first two stanzas to the final stanza is evoked both by the changing imagery and the modulation in phonemes. In the first stanza, the harder, heavier, and darker vowels such as "e," "u," and "a" ("Ungetanes," "gebunden," "hinzugehn," "Schwanes," etc.) together with the density of consonants (the consonance on "d," "g," "n," and "ch") that almost make certain words into tongue twisters ("ungeschaffnen") enact a feeling of awkwardness. To speak these words in the trochaic pentameter resembles the experience of toil. The assonance on "e" and the hissing repetition of "s" ("Sterben," "dieses," "Nichtmehrfassen," "täglich," "stehn," "Niederlassen," etc.) in the second verse similarly evoke a sense of anxiousness. The single sentence that bridges the gap between the second stanza and the third stanza kinaesthetically and typographically depicts the swan's downward entrance into the water, and the third stanza appropriately begins with the enjambment "into the waters" ("in die Wasser"). In contrast to the earlier stanzas, the brighter phoneme, "i," and the fluid consonant, "l," become more predominant in the final verse ("in," "die," "sich," "glücklich," "Flut," "still," "königlicher," etc.) and thus complement and enrich the image of the swan's graceful movement.

The images, content, and music (*phanopoeia*, *logopoeia*, and *melopoeia* in Ezra Pound's terminology[80]) of "Der Schwan" work in concert to disclose the interrelationship between the swan and its *Umwelt*. The swimming swan and the walking swan are virtually contradictions in their phenomenality. The former is often an "object" of beauty, the latter never. In the different responses that these appearances spark, the relationship between behavior, anatomy, and the elements of land

---

80   Ezra Pound, "How to Read," in *Literary Essays*, 25.

and water is revealed. Thus, while "Der Schwan" includes human-existential references, these references serve in the physiognomic disclosure of the swan and its *Umwelt*.

Before turning to appearances of other aspects of Nature in the *Neue Gedichte*, we will consider one more animal poem, "Schwarze Katze."

Schwarze Katze

Ein Gespenst ist noch wie eine Stelle,
dran dein Blick mit einem Klange stößt;
aber da, an diesem schwarzen Felle
wird dein stärkstes Schauen aufgelöst:

wie ein Tobender, wenn er in vollster
Raserei ins Schwarze stampft,
jählings am benehmenden Gepolster
einer Zelle aufhört und verdampft.

Alle Blicke, die sie jemals trafen,
scheint sie also an sich zu verhehlen,
um darüber drohend und verdrossen
zuzuschauern und damit zu schlafen.
Doch auf einmal kehrt sie, wie geweckt,
ihr Gesicht und mitten in das deine:
und da triffst du deinen Blick im geelen
Amber ihrer runden Augensteine
unerwartet wieder: eingeschlossen
wie ein augestorbenes Insekt.[81]

The first and second verses of "Schwarze Katze" dramatically present aspects of a phenomenology of perception. These stanzas thematize the qualitative perception of the *blackness* of the cat's fur. In his *Farbenlehre* (*Theory of Colours*), which has more recently been interpreted as a phenomenology of perception, Goethe describes the tendency of dark

---

81 Black Cat// A ghost is still like a place/ your glance bumps into with a sound;/ but there, in this black fur,/ your intensest gaze is dissolved:// as a madman, when he pounds/ into the darkness in complete rage,/ abruptly ceases and evaporates/ in the absorptive padding of a cell.// Thus all the glances that have ever met her/ she seems to conceal in herself/ so that, menacingly and disgruntledly,/ she can watch over them, and therewith sleep. But all at once, as if roused,/ she turns her face directly to your own:/ and there, unexpectedly, you meet your gaze again/ in the yellow amber of her round eye-stones:/ trapped like an extinct insect." KA 1, 545.

The *Neue Gedichte* as a Twofold Imagining of Things 251

objects to appear smaller and recede from the viewer and the tendency of bright objects to stand out.[82] The first two verses dramatically convey this tendency of dark appearances to absorb the gaze. The most active or aggressive look ("stärkstes Schauen") is dissolved by the black fur of the cat; this perceptual experience is vividly characterized by the simile of a raging madman pounding into the padded, absorbent walls of his cell.

These stanzas not only offer a dramatically elaborated phenomenology of color-perception, but also lead into a physiognomic and imaginal disclosure of the cat. They serve in the articulation of the cat-ness of the cat. However, this catness is not an abstract Platonic idea, but rather *manifests* or *presences* in the behavior of cats. One need only compare the behavior of a Labrador dog to that of a cat to glimpse their respective phenomenological essences.[83] The former is entirely outgoing, entirely given over to its master, which strongly contrasts with the self-absorbed nature of the cat. The first two verses, in their characterization of an *absorbed* perception, lead into an articulation of the self-*absorbed* character of the cat's manner of being. The image of the cat conjured by the poem matches Rilke's characterization of cats in a recorded conversation with Maurice Betz, in which he stated that cats relate to humans as though we "were only present in our imagination, a shadow, that their pupils do not perceive at all."[84]

While the first verse speaks of *a* look or glance, the third verse speaks of *all glances* ("alle Blicke"). Every glance that has ever met the cat, the cat seems to conceal ("Alle Blicke, die sie jemals trafen,/ scheint sie also an sich zu verhehlen …"). The cat does not expose itself to the other and while sleeping seems to watch over all these looks menacingly. The first four lines of the third verse enact a physiognomic portrayal of the animal that cannot be surpassed or paraphrased. When imaginatively actualized they bring a cat's typical mode of behavior to the most expressive disclosure.

Although the fifth line of the third verse begins with "doch" ("but" or "yet"), thereby announcing a transition or *volta*, what follows in many ways involves an intensification rather than a divergence from the prior

---

82 Gernot Böhme discusses Goethe's *Farbenlehre* as paradigmatic for a *phenomenological* natural science, in *Phänomenologie der Natur*, ed. Gernot Böhme and Gregor Schiemann (Frankfurt am Main: Suhrkamp, 1997), 19ff. Goethe, *Theory of Colours*, 5ff., 276.
83 Rilke made very insightful remarks concerning the specific characters of, and differences between, cats and dogs. See, for instance, Maurice Betz, *Rilke in Frankreich: Erinnerungen, Briefe, Dokumente* (Vienna: Herbert Reichner Verlag, 1938), 160ff.
84 Ibid., 162. See also Rainer Maria Rilke, "Préface à 'Mitsou'," *Sämtliche Werke in zwölf Bänden*, ed. Ruth Sieber-Rilke and Ernst Zinn, vol. 6 (Frankfurt am Main: Insel Verlag, 1976), 1099–1103.

course of the poem. The cat first absorbs the gaze of the seer (first and second quatrains), it then appears to be asleep and watching over the looks others have directed toward it (first four lines of the third verse); in these instances the cat neither allows itself to become the object of another's gaze nor exposes itself to others. When the cat wakes up and suddenly turns its head to face the viewer a further step in this development is accomplished, in a manner which draws on a motif from the last two verses of Baudelaire's poem "Le Chat."[85] The cat, which never suffered to become the constituted object of another's gaze, now proceeds to constitute the other, the viewer, with its gaze ("da triffst du deinen Blick im geelen/ Amber ... eingeschlossen/ wie ein ausgestorbenes Insekt"). This moment serves as a further intensification in the disclosure of the *Wesen* of the cat. Rather than the viewer constituting the cat as an object, the cat, in its phenomenality, articulates its essence in the viewer. In the previous chapter the end of "Schwarze Katze" was discussed as illustrative of a reversal of intentional-directionality in perception.[86] In the present context it can be added that the poem not only thematizes a reversal in the common understanding of perception, but also imaginally enacts this reversal in the mind of the reader.

"Schwarze Katze" clearly demonstrates the manner in which poetry can disclose the primordial unity of essence and existence, the universal in the particular. The poem accomplishes a phenomenological disclosure of the cat in its concrete universality. Through its evocation of typifying gestures, features, and behaviors, it imaginally reveals the cat's embodied, which means particularized, *Wesen*. Furthermore, it articulates a distinctive phenomenological *relation* between seer and seen, knower and known, a relation which must be included, in principle, in any conception of being.

The above readings of Rilke's animal poems have sought to demonstrate how these specific *Dinggedichte* can foster and accomplish a twofold disclosure for their appreciators. The poems realize this twofold disclosure through their imaginative and sonorous language and through the imaginative thinking that they require of the reader. This imaginative and poetic understanding is itself a mode of twofold vision. More specifically, it is a further elaboration in thinking of the twofold *perception* of animals that was articulated in the previous

---

85 Charles Baudelaire, *The Flowers of Evil: A Selection*, ed. Marthiel and Jackson Mathews (New York: New Directions Publishing Corporation, 1955), 48–53.
86 A similar reversal is presented at the end of the poem that precedes "Schwarze Katze," "Schlangen-Beschwörer," in connection to a person watching a snake charmer. For a discussion of this motif of reversal in connection to poetic address, see William Waters, *Poetry's Touch: On Lyric Address* (Ithaca, NY: Cornell University Press, 2003), 86ff.

chapter. In Rilke's twofold perception of animals and in the animal poetry in the *Neue Gedichte*, a physiognomic seeing, which discloses the sensible and the intelligible in their wholeness, can be found. This twofold seeing, which includes an epiphanic dimension, facilitates the overcoming of a dualistic relationship to the world.

Flower Poems

My aim in this and the subsequent sub-section is to indicate the twofold manner in which further aspects of Nature are revealed in the *Neue Gedichte*. There are numerous "flower poems" in the two parts of the *Neue Gedichte* and flowers form a significant motif in Rilke's oeuvre. As this theme is a logical progression from the previous discussion of animals, I will now discuss a selection of these poems.

In the *Neue Gedichte* there are many complementary and mutually illuminating poems. As far as flowers are concerned, one finds "Blaue Hortensie [Blue Hydrangea]" in the first part and "Rosa Hortensie [Pink Hydrangea]" in the second part of the collection. Similarly there are two "rose poems," "Die Rosenschale" and "Das Rosen-Innere," in the first part and second part respectively. Before the publication of *Der neuen Gedichte anderer Teil*, Rilke entertained the idea of renaming the first part of the *Neue Gedichte*, "Blaue Hortensie," and naming the second part, "Rosa Hortensie."[87] This is indicative of the importance of these poems in Rilke's mind and supports the view that there are significant hermeneutic connections between them. We will first turn to "Blaue Hortensie," as it is the earlier poem and Hamburger and Müller discuss its phenomenological character and status.

Blaue Hortensie

So wie das letzte Grün in Farbentiegeln
sind diese Blätter, trocken, stumpf und rauh,
hinter den Blütendolden, die ein Blau
nicht auf sich tragen, nur von ferne spiegeln.

Sie spiegeln es verweint und ungenau,
als wollten sie es wiederum verlieren,
und wie in alten blauen Briefpapieren
ist Gelb in ihnen, Violett und Grau;

Verwaschnes wie an einer Kinderschürze,
Nichtmehrgetragnes, dem nichts mehr geschieht:
wie fühlt man eines kleinen Lebens Kürze.

---

87   See *KA 1*, 901.

Doch plötzlich scheint das Blau sich zu verneuen
in einer von den Dolden, und man sieht
ein rührend Blaues sich vor Grünem freuen.[88]

Hamburger offers a synopsis of her interpretation of "Blaue Hortensie" in the following words:

> The lack of an article in the title—not by chance reminiscent of painting titles—already suggests that it is the blue of the hydrangea that is thematized in the poem: "a blue," whose nuance, or exact nuances, the description seeks to convey, and designates as ultimately indescribable.[89]

I regard Hamburger's interpretation as ultimately untenable and reductive. To begin with, the proposition that the lack of an article indicates that the theme of the poem is the *blue* of the hydrangea is unconvincing. The poem "Spanische Tänzerin" in the *Neue Gedichte* also lacks an article but no one would claim that the theme of the poem is the "Spanishness" of the dancer. Hamburger describes the procedure of the poem as a preparation for the final depiction of the blue in the final tercet of the sonnet, which she interprets as "das Eidos Blau dieser Hortensie [the eidos blue of this hydrangea]." According to Hamburger, the poem isolates a specific instance of the eidos blue and thereby accomplishes a Husserlian eidetic seeing.[90] While the color of the hydrangea is certainly a central theme of the poem, Müller rightly sees that much is overlooked by Hamburger's interpretation: the feeling elements in the poem, the contrast of colors belonging to the hydrangea that is not a pure Husserlian *Wesensschau*, and the conclusion of the poem as an instance of the literary concept of epiphany.[91] However, I cannot share Müller's view that these factors ultimately refute the idea that the poem is phenomenological, and for a number of reasons I cannot agree with his claim that "the poem is not in the least a description of a plant.

---

88 "Blue Hydrangea// Just like the last green in paint pots/ these leaves are dry, dull, and rough,/ behind the flower umbels, that do not/ wear a blue, only mirror it from afar.// They mirror it tearily and vaguely,/ as though they wanted to lose it again,/ and as in an old blue writing paper,/ there is yellow in them, violet and grey;// something washed out as on a child's apron,/ no longer worn, to which nothing more occurs:/ how one feels a small life's brevity.// Yet suddenly the blue appears to renew itself/ in one of the umbels, and one sees/ a touching blue rejoice before green." Translated by Luke Fischer and Lutz Näfelt. KA 1, 481.
89 Hamburger, "Die phänomenologische Struktur der Dichtung Rilkes," 198.
90 Ibid., 199.
91 Müller, "Rilke, Husserl und die Dinglyrik der Moderne," 15–26.

The *Neue Gedichte* as a Twofold Imagining of Things   255

It basically presents only the contrast between two colors perceived in the flower."[92] First, this statement contradicts Müller's other claim that the poem is not phenomenological because it does not present a pure *Wesensschau* but a perception that is connected to "a process" of renewal "that occurs in the thing."[93] In other words, it contradicts his claim that the poem does not abstract from, and suspend the positing of, the thing's existence in a Husserlian manner. Second, the colors presented are the precise colors of the plant itself; in so far as the colors are essential features of a plant it is plainly false to state that the poem is not in the least a description of the plant. More specifically, Rilke's poem captures the distinctive, mottled colors of hydrangea petals in an exceptionally vivid and evocative way. Third, Müller operates with a strong distinction between the thing itself and the perception of the thing, while one of the ontological tenets of phenomenology is that the two cannot ultimately be understood except *in relation* to one another. This phenomenological point of view is expressed most succinctly in the first sentence of Merleau-Ponty's *The Visible and the Invisible*: "We see the things themselves, the world is what we see."[94] Müller's interpretation wavers between the acknowledgment of objective and subjective elements in the poem in ways that seem contradictory. In a sense he justifies this oscillation in his conclusion that the poem hovers between the subjective and the objective (which he regards as typical of Rilke's *Dinggedichte* in general):

> In the poem a middle position [*Mittellage*] between objective givenness of the thing and its absorption through the perceiving subject is, in fact, revealed ... Thingly reality enters ... into the poem only by way of perception, i.e., as perceived-object, and includes the expression of subjective experiences, which are had during the process of perceiving.[95]

---

92 Ibid., 299. In contrast, Brigitte Forsting, in a short analysis of the poem, acknowledges the focus on the colors but at the same time views the poem as an expression of "the plant in its objectivity [*Gegenständlichkeit*]," in a way that relates to my interpretation of Rilke's "sachliches Sagen." Brigitte Forsting, "Rainer Maria Rilke: Blaue Hortensie," in *Wege zum Gedicht*, ed. Rupert Hirschenauer and Albrecht Weber (Munich: Schnell und Steiner, 1956), 285.
93 Ibid., 225.
94 Merleau-Ponty, *The Visible and the Invisible*, 3.
95 Wolfgang Müller, "*Neue Gedichte/Der Neuen Gedichte anderer Teil*," in *Rilke-Handbuch*, 301. While I have previously only cited Müller's essay "Rilke, Husserl, und die Dinglyrik der Moderne" with respect to his interpretation of "Blaue Hortensie," what he states in his introduction to the *Neue Gedichte* in the *Rilke-Handbuch* is continuous with the earlier essay.

Müller is right to emphasize the fact that Rilkean seeing involves specific inner experiences which take place in the very process of perceiving something; to a certain extent he is articulating what Merleau-Ponty calls the "chiasm." However, Müller ultimately *subjectifies* these experiences, rather than redefining the very concept of the "thing itself." In the end, Müller remains within an intellectual framework that opposes the things themselves to the perception of things and for this reason he can maintain that "Blaue Hortensie" is not in the least a description of the plant. His intermediate position or "Mittellage" is ultimately a *subjectified* object and is certainly not adequate to the monistic meaning of *Weltinnenraum* (this later Rilkean term as we saw in the previous chapter is also applicable to Rilke's work in the middle period). In contrast to Müller, I regard the best of Rilke's *Dinggedichte* as thematizing and enacting a deeper disclosure of the things themselves, such that inner events belong to the very phenomenality of things. The interior revealed in Rilke's *sachliches Sagen* is not only intimately bound to perception, but also an interior revelation of the thing itself. The one world reveals itself inwardly and outwardly. In line with these reflections, I will elucidate a more complex unity and richness in "Blaue Hortensie" than is to be found in both Hamburger's and Müller's interpretations.

The central theme of both "Blaue Hortensie" and "Rosa Hortensie" is the mystery of the appearance, disappearance, and transformation of color in the plant. The presence of color is a fundamental feature of the plant world. Almost everywhere in the plant world we find green foliage and one of the most distinctive features of blossoms is their infinite variety of colors. Moreover, these colors are not static. The shoots and leaves of a plant generally move through shades of green and as they gradually decay they turn yellow or brown, etc. Similarly, many petals first have a particular hue that transforms in the process of blossoming and their colors change as they wilt. The transformation of color is thus intimately connected to processes of growth and decay, life and death. More specifically, the colors of hydrangea flowers vary greatly and are highly influenced by environmental factors and minerals in the soil. The central themes of "Blaue Hortensie" and "Rosa Hortensie" are the distinctive colors of the plants as physiognomic expressions of their being, and the transient appearance of the colors within the transformative processes of life and death. These processes concern the plants as living beings and are not reducible to subjective perceptions. As in many of Rilke's poems there is also an epiphanic dimension (in the strong sense) to the flower poems. Rilke's flowers are spiritual physiognomies and in this sense he is continuous with the Romantic tradition and William Blake's imperative, "to see ... a heaven in a wild flower."[96] However, whereas Blake's

---

96 William Blake, "Auguries of Innocence," in *Selected Poetry* (Oxford: Oxford University Press, 1998), 173.

The *Neue Gedichte* as a Twofold Imagining of Things   257

statement, in this instance, remains rather general, Rilke's poems vividly portray specific flowers as distinctive physiognomies of the heavenly or spiritual. In "Blaue Hortensie" and "Rosa Hortensie," it is especially the colors of the blossoms that are disclosed in an epiphanic light.

Both "Blaue Hortensie" and "Rosa Hortensie" thematize the transience and loss of the blossom's color—the blue of the blue hydrangea and the pink of the pink hydrangea. However, while "Blaue Hortensie" ends with an affirmation of new color and life, "Rosa Hortensie" is affirmative of loss and death.[97] Both poems inscribe these processes in a context of interaction between the earthly and the divine.

The sonnet, "Blaue Hortensie," first depicts the specific color and texture of some of the hydrangea's leaves through a comparison to paint left in pots and through the adjectives, "dry, dull, and rough" ("trocken, stumpf und rauh"). These ascriptions already contain more than a mere color-description or subjective perception ("dry" implies a want of water in the leaves; "rough" conveys texture in addition to color; these qualities could also be interpreted as hints that the leaves are approaching decay). Following the description of these leaves, the pale blue color of the hydrangea flowers is richly and subtly conveyed. The umbels in front of the dry, dull leaves seem only to mirror the blue ("nur von ferne spiegeln"); the blue color does not seem to be the flowers' own possession. That they only mirror the blue from afar evokes the paleness and aesthetic atmosphere of their blue. Moreover, it suggests the transience and fragility of their life; there is no fresh generation of color in the flowers and thus they are also approaching decay. This strongly contrasts with the final verse in which the blue appears to be renewing itself ("scheint das Blau sich zu verneuen"); the blue described at the end of the poem is not fragile or as if merely reflected; the final lines suggest a more intense blue that is newly emerging in the growth of the blossoms.

However, further levels of meaning are implied by the image of mirroring in the opening quatrain. An epiphanic dimension is subtly evoked by this characterization. Where is the original of the color that the flowers are only reflecting or mirroring? The clear answer in "Blaue Hortensie" is the sky or the heavens; the flowers seem to mirror the distant blue of the sky. Another flower poem, "Das Rosen-Innere [The Interior of the Rose]," provides a further clue for deciphering this image, in that a correspondence between the earthly and the heavenly

---

97 The difference between "Rosa Hortensie" and "Blaue Hortensie" is summed up well in the commentary by Manfred Engel and Ulrich Fülleborn: "Das Rosa, das die Blume hervorgebracht und sie verlassen hat, wird von vornherein als vergangen gedacht, ohne jede Hoffnung auf eine Wiederkehr im Sinne der *Blauen Hortensie*." KA 1, 999.

is expressed more explicitly and connected to a certain interiority. The poem begins as follows:

> Wo ist zu diesem Innen
> Ein Außen? ...
> Welche Himmel spiegeln sich drinnen
> in dem Binnensee
> dieser offenen Rosen ...[98]

"Das Rosen-Innere" opens by asking the question as to where an outer equivalent can be found to a certain interiority—an interiority in the sense of the "inner-space" or "Innenraum" (this word is used later in the poem) of the roses. This interiority is then connected to the skies or heavens which the poem suggests are mirrored in the roses as in a lake. Thus the flowers are similarly depicted in "Das Rosen-Innere" and "Blaue Hortensie"; in both cases they are evoked as physiognomic reflections of the heavenly. (Similar correspondences between flowers and the heavens, and more specifically the stars, are suggested by other poems. The end of "Die Rosenschale [The Bowl of Roses]" portrays the roses as embodying the "vague influence of distant stars [den vagen Einfluß ferner Sterne]" and the end of "Persisches Heliotrop [Persian Heliotrope]" depicts the scent of the heliotrope as a synaesthetic experience that merges with the stars—"so schließen sich .../ deutliche Sterne zu der seidnen Traube und mischen .../ die Stille mit Vanille und mit Zimmt."[99])

That the color seems only to be mirrored in the umbels in "Blaue Hortensie" raises the question concerning its origin. If the flower and its color reflect the heavenly then the original which comes to manifestation in them must be the divine or spiritual itself. Fortunately, this need not remain a mere conjecture; lines in "Rosa Hortensie" offer direct support for this view. "Rosa Hortensie" explicitly thematizes the loss of the pink color in the flowers. Ordinarily we do not think of the fading of a color in a plant as implying that the color goes somewhere else; this loss is understood as a simple disappearance and change. In contrast, "Rosa Hortensie" explores and plays with the idea that the color is transported to another place. Moreover, the loss of the pink is clearly inscribed in a relation to the divine, and, in light of what we have previously illustrated, this relation should not be reduced to a merely aesthetic meaning. The second quatrain of the poem is as follows:

---

98 "Where is there an exterior/ to this interior? .../ Which heavens mirror themselves inside/ in the inland lake/ of these open roses ..." KA 1, 569.
99 KA 1, 510, 576.

The *Neue Gedichte* as a Twofold Imagining of Things 259

Daß sie für solches Rosa nichts verlangen.
Bleibt es für sie und lächelt aus der Luft?
Sind Engel da, es zärtlich zu empfangen,
wenn es vergeht, großmütig wie ein Duft?[100]

The second half of this quatrain asks whether there are angels who receive the color as it disappears from the blossoms; this invites the reader to see the loss of color in the flower (and wilting) as inscribed in a relation to the divine. The second line of this verse asks whether the color remains for the blossoms ("Bleibt es für sie ...") even once it is no longer present in their sensible appearance. If it does remain, and if the flowers in this case can also be understood as "mirrors," then the color must be in the sphere from which it originally came, of which its sensible appearance is a manifestation—a sphere not subject to the transience of individual flowers. Although most of "Rosa Hortensie" consists of suggestive questions, the poem ends with a strong statement. In the third and final quatrain the question is raised as to whether the blossoms give up the pink so that this color may never have to undergo decay. This question is contrasted ("doch") with the direct claim that the green leaf which wilts and thus loses its color now knows everything ("ein Grün/ ... das jetzt verwelkt und alles weiß").[101] In the fading and decaying of the leaf, the green has returned to the realm from which it *originates* (and thereby "knows" the answers to the previous questions). Whereas "Blaue Hortensie" ends with an affirmation of new color and life, "Rosa Hortensie" affirms the death of the blossom and leaf. This affirmation of death is at the same time an affirmation of the spiritual or heavenly (which is not subject in the same way as the particular blossoms to the transient realm), of which the plant's colors are a manifestation and reflection (mirror).[102]

---

100 "That they demand nothing for such a pink./ Does it remain for them, smiling out of the air?/ Are angels there, to receive it tenderly,/ when it fades, magnanimously like a scent?" Translated by Luke Fischer and Lutz Näfelt. *KA* 1, 579.
101 *KA 1*, 579.
102 There are strong connections between the affirmation of the spiritual as deathless (or as the deeper truth of death) in "Rosa Hortensie," the mirror motif in the flower poems in the *Neue Gedichte*, and one of the poems in *Die Sonette an Orpheus*, which also presents the earthly as a mirror of the spiritual. The ninth sonnet in the first part of *Die Sonette an Orpheus* reads as follows: "Nur wer die Leier schon hob/ auch unter Schatten,/ darf das unendliche Lob/ ahnend erstatten.// Nur wer mit Toten vom Mohn/ aß, von dem ihren,/ wird nicht den leisesten Ton/ wieder verlieren.// Mag auch die Spiegelung im Teich/ oft uns verschwimmen:/ *Wisse das Bild*./ Erst in dem Doppelbereich/ werden die Stimmen/ ewig und mild." *KA 2*, 245. In knowing the spiritual "image" ("Bild") and its reflection ("Spiegelung"), one at the same time knows

While the central aim at present is to explicate "Blaue Hortensie," these divergent considerations of several flower poems have provided essential clues for this task and have also served to establish a general horizon for an adequate interpretation of the flowers in Rilke's *Neue Gedichte*. The first line of the second quatrain of "Blaue Hortensie" could stimulate an objection to the phenomenological spirit of my interpretation, in that the umbels are described as mirroring the blue in a tear-stained manner ("verweint") and inexactly ("ungenau"). In the first instance, this offers a brilliant depiction of the blurry appearance of the blue in the mottled colors of the petals, which is not unlike the look of make-up (eyeliner, for instance) smudged by tears. Along with "ungenau" this description vividly paints, for the reader's imagination, the precise look of the blossoms—the variety of hues contained in them. However, the word "verweint" is also charged with a distinctive tone of feeling. Is this feeling not merely an inappropriate projection of human emotions onto a plant? Is Müller not correct in affirming that such feelings would need to be excluded from a strictly phenomenological poetics?

The answers to these questions will be gradually elaborated. However, a couple of responses can be formulated at this point. "Das Rosen-Innere," for instance, articulates the flower as a manifestation of a certain inwardness, an inwardness which is connected to the heavenly. In this sense, tones of feeling in "Blaue Hortensie" can also be understood as aspects of an epiphanic disclosure. Furthermore, there are more precise connections between the feeling elements and the process described in the poem. The first three verses of "Blaue Hortensie" focus on the process of loss and suggest decay and death. The last verse thematizes the generation of new color and life. The tones of feeling, as will be seen, directly correspond to the revelation of these two processes in the plant.

The second line of the second quatrain characterizes the umbels as if they wanted to lose the blue again ("als wollten sie es wiederum verlieren"). This suggests the paleness of their blue and also that they are fading. It also parallels the thematization in "Rosa Hortensie" of the place where the color might go once it leaves the blossoms. The third and fourth lines of the second verse offer an obvious confirmation of my interpretation and in these lines Rilke shows himself as a master

---

the "double-realm" or "twin-realm" ("Doppelbereich") which reconciles life and death (or the other side of life, according to Rilke). In accordance with my chosen terminology, the "double-realm" could also be called the "twofold-realm." It is, of course, far from insignificant that Rilke writes this whole cycle of poems in the name of Orpheus, Orpheus being one who is permitted to enter the realm of the dead already in this life.

The *Neue Gedichte* as a Twofold Imagining of Things 261

of the *phanopoeic* possibilities of poetry.[103] The blue of the flowers is depicted through the simile of *old* blue writing paper, which has yellow, purple, and grey in it. This brilliant and vivid evocation further elaborates the earlier characterization of the blossoms as "verweint und ungenau." In addition, the lines intimate that the blue is no longer fresh or new and that the umbels are approaching decay.

The third verse (first tercet) of the sonnet further develops in the same direction. Another superb simile vividly articulates the flower's colors and suggests the theme of death. The flowers appear like a patch of washed-out colors on a child's apron which is no longer worn ("Nichtmehrgetragnes") and to which nothing happens anymore ("dem nichts mehr geschieht"). That nothing happens to it anymore implies that previously something did happen to it. What no longer happens is the generation of fresh color (blue) in the flowers. The "getragenes" of "Nichtmehrgetragnes" is clearly an echo of the description of the umbels in the first verse as not wearing or carrying ("tragen") the blue but only mirroring it from afar. The flowers appear to be fading. The umbels are like a child's apron (presumably a painting apron) which is no longer worn, and no longer in a position to receive new color or paint (recall "Farbentiegeln" in the first line). These descriptions intimate that the umbels are approaching, or already beginning to, decay. The link to decay and death is made explicit in the third line of the third verse when it is said, "wie fühlt man eines kleinen Lebens Kürze [how one feels a small life's brevity]." This line is a generalizing statement. While it connotes the death of a small child and the blossoms, it mentions neither the child nor the flowers specifically, but *a* small life's brevity or shortness. This generalizing also occurs in the first part of the line which thematizes the act of feeling and how *one* ("man") feels. The use of "man" here implies the universality or supra-subjective character of this feeling, in contrast to what we commonly understand and experience as the merely subjective character of feeling. Thus feeling is explicitly thematized by the poem and specifically with regard to how a brief life is felt. At this point it is instructive to recall that Rilke described the *Neue Gedichte* as poems not about his feelings toward things but as "*things* felt."[104] Equally instructive is the passage from *Malte* that speaks of feeling how birds fly, which I previously explicated as indicative of a cognitive type of feeling.[105] Following Gernot Böhme's environmental aesthetics, the feelings evoked by "Blaue Hortensie" could also be described as "atmospheres" (see Chapter 2) connected to the flowers and their colors. In addition, it is worth mentioning that

---

103 The term "phanopoeia" derives from Ezra Pound. Pound, "How to Read."
104 Letter of February 3, 1923, "À une Amie," in Rilke, *Briefe*, vol. 2, 1914–26, 389.
105 See Chapter 3, "Conclusion of Chapter."

a numinous significance of the affects in this poem is suggested by its placement. "Blaue Hortensie" is preceded and followed by poems ("Todes-Erfahrung" and "Vor dem Sommerregen" respectively) that thematize feelings of absence. More specifically, the theme of "Todes-Erfahrung" ("Experience of Death") is, so to speak, the way in which another's death is felt.[106] Significantly, however, the poem ultimately emphasizes a genuine experience of the spiritual presence of the departed person (and not the feeling of absence and loss). Hence, as in "Rosa Hortensie," the loss of color (and its corresponding feeling) in "Blaue Hortensie" is inscribed in a relationship to the spiritual.

The *volta* or turn in the sonnet occurs in the final tercet and is characteristically announced with "Doch [yet or but]," immediately followed by "plötzlich [suddenly]." Müller is right in his identification of a small epiphany—the instant of an exceptionally vivid perception—in the final lines; however, it should be emphasized that this epiphany is connected to a sudden perception of color in the flower that is also an intimation of new life. The blue of one of the umbels appears to be renewing itself ("sich verneuen"). Previously, the blue in the umbels was portrayed as akin to a reflection. This blue, in contrast, is active, is possessed by the flower (is "carried" [*getragen*] by the flower), is *renewing* itself; it is, we can assume, a deeper blue, which differs from the previously described petals that seem to want to lose their color ("als wollten sie es wiederum verlieren"). The penultimate and final lines clearly convey an aesthetic moment of an exceptionally vivid color harmony of the fresh blue of hydrangea petals before a background of green, and reverse the pallid contrast of the green and the blue in the opening verse. This color phenomenon is also linked to certain feelings—a touching blue ("rührend Blaues") and a specific sense of joy ("vor Grünem freuen"). However, this appearance of new color is expressive of the total phenomenon, namely, the color-transformation of petals (and, perhaps, leaves) as a manifestation of life.

At this point the question of feeling and phenomenology can be more comprehensively addressed. Are the feelings evoked by "Blaue Hortensie" simply anthropomorphic projections, cases of the pathetic fallacy, or an aestheticization which has nothing to do with truth? It has been demonstrated that the "interiority" of Rilke's flower poems is part of the epiphanic revelation of the flowers themselves. In so far as this involves "feelings," these feelings belong to the epiphanic disclosure. However, in "Blaue Hortensie" there are yet more specific feeling-tones that are connected to the loss and generation of color in the plant. In closely attending to the trajectory of these affective nuances, one perceives their cognitive status.

---

106 KA 1, 480.

The first three verses of the poem convey a unified tone of feeling. To use a musical analogy, this feeling is akin to a minor key. In the third line of the third verse, it is explicitly stated that the brevity of life is something felt; the process of fading, decay, and death is felt. Just as this process is expressed in the changing colors of a plant (or any other visible manifestation of dying) so too it is inwardly expressed in a tone of feeling to the one who attends to it in the requisite manner. The specific feeling which arises only in connection to the phenomenon of decay is a dimension of the phenomenon's self-revelation, as much a revelation as the more externally perceptible changes. The same holds for the opposite feeling, which can be compared to a major key and is evoked by attending to phenomena expressive of new life, such as the fresh colors depicted in the final verse. Thus, "Blaue Hortensie" as a whole offers a striking and vivid portrait of the sensible qualities of a blue hydrangea as expressive of processes of decay, growth, and transformation, in such a way that the inner life and feelings are stirred in conjunction with these subtle processes.[107] Through its musicality, descriptions, similes, etc., the poem enacts this total phenomenon for the feeling imagination. In conclusion it can be stated that I share Müller's view that the affective elements should be incorporated into any interpretation of the poem, but, in contrast to him, I nonetheless affirm its phenomenological status.

While the reader might grant that the feeling elements of the poem can be adequately understood in phenomenological terms (at the very least they can be connected to a phenomenology of affects), doubts might be raised in relation to the epiphanic aspects (epiphanic in the strong sense of an appearance of the divine or heavenly) of Rilke's flower poems. The epiphanic aspects might be regarded as metaphysical and merely speculative, rather than as phenomenological. In the previous chapter, however, the epiphanic dimension of Rilke's experience and vision was clearly demonstrated and thus the continuity of his poetry with such a vision should be almost self-explanatory. In his flower poems Rilke was as equally concerned with a direct vision of the holy in the things themselves, as William Blake was when he wrote, "to *see* ... heaven in a wild flower" and not "to conjecture that heaven is manifest in a wild flower." Furthermore, the

---

107 Cf. Günter Stephan, "Die Verwandlung der sichtbaren Natur: Rainer Maria Rilke," in *Lektürehilfen Naturlyrik: Gattungs- und epochenspezifische Aspekte* (Stuttgart: Klett, 1989), 98–108; Anthony Phelan, *Rilke: Neue Gedichte*, 47–51. Elsewhere, I have further explored ways in which human affects can be conceived as continuous with natural phenomena (with specific regard to the seasons). Luke Fischer, "A Poetic Phenomenology of the Temperate Seasons," *Environment, Space, Place* 6, no. 1 (2014): 7–32.

opening of another flower poem, namely "Die Rosenschale," clearly reveals the *phenomenological* character of this twofold vision of flowers. The poem begins as follows (a detailed consideration of this long poem and the rose motif in Rilke's work is beyond the scope of this book):

Die Rosenschale

Zornige sahst du flackern, sahst zwei Knaben
zu einem Etwas sich zusammenballen,
das Haß war und sich auf der Erde wälzte
wie von Bienen überfallnes Tier;
Schauspieler, aufgetürmte Übertreiber,
rasende Pferde, die zusammenbrachen,
den Blick wegwerfend, bläkend das Gebiß
als schälte sich der Schädel aus dem Maule.

Nun aber weißt du, wie sich das vergißt:
denn vor dir steht die volle Rosenschale ...[108]

The first verse surprises the reader as ostensibly it has nothing to do with roses. The length of the verse and the dramatic and literally convoluted depiction also make the reader forget the title and main subject of the poem, "Die Rosenschale" ("The Bowl of Roses"). An aggressive scene, involving two boys full of hate and wrestling one another, is compared to an animal under attack by bees and frenzied horses. The verse enacts a scene filled with frantic activity, aggression, and rage.

It is the striking contrast, announced by the opening of the second verse, that enables the roses to take the center stage in such an evocative way.[109] Just as in chiaroscuro the darkness and the light intensify one another through their contrasts and thus manifest their

---

108 "The Bowl of Roses// You saw them flare in anger, saw two lads/ contort themselves into some-thing,/ that was hate and roll over the earth/ like an animal attacked by bees;/ actors, piled exaggerators,/ raving horses, which crashed down,/ tossing away a glance, baring teeth/ as though the skull peeled itself from the mouth.// But now you know, how that is forgotten:/ as before you stands the full bowl of roses ..." Translated by Luke Fischer and Lutz Näfelt. KA 1, 508.

109 The scenes presented in the first verse and the opening of the second verse, as with so many of Rilke's poems, have an experiential source. In Naples Rilke saw a fight break out between two young men and fled to his home, where he was struck by the appearance of a bowl of roses standing on his table. KA 1, 956.

distinctive qualities, so the contrast between the first and second verse intensifies their specific themes. After the dramatic opening of the poem, the second verse is almost loud in its quietness. The poem addresses the reader, whose imaginative gaze has just been consumed by a violent scene, in the second person: "Nun aber weißt du, wie sich das vergisst [But now you know, how that is forgotten]." The reason this scene of aggression is forgotten is uttered in the second line: "denn vor dir steht die volle Rosenschale [because before you stands the full bowl of roses]." Thus the catalyst of this sudden change in mood is the very appearance or *phenomenality* of the roses themselves. The roses physiognomically manifest an inwardness and peacefulness which are the antithesis of the drama enacted by the first verse. This inwardness is not a quality imposed on the roses by the viewer; rather it is their very appearing to the human subject that institutes a radically different meaning and atmosphere. The phenomenality of the roses is in the mode of excess. The line speaks of the "volle" ("full") bowl of roses; in Chapter 2 various examples were already discussed in which Rilke uses this word to evoke phenomena that give themselves with a superabundance or inexhaustibility of meaning. The roses reveal themselves as "saturated phenomena." "Die Rosenschale" also reminds us of the aforementioned quotation in which Rilke reports the transformation that has occurred in his vision of things and specifically speaks of flowers: "Ich fange an, Neues zu sehen: schon sind mir Blumen oft so unendlich viel [I am beginning to see newly: already flowers are often so infinitely much to me]." In short, flowers revealed themselves to him with a fullness or plenitude of meaning and his flower poems seek to articulate an exceptional disclosure for the imagination of the reader.

One flower poem that has not yet been mentioned is "Schlaf-Mohn" ("Opium Poppy"). A consideration of the way in which this poem presents and thematizes the opium poppy will facilitate further insights into Rilke's physiognomic vision of flowers.

Schlaf-Mohn

Abseits im Garten blüht der böse Schlaf,
in welchem die, die heimlich eingedrungen,
die Liebe fanden junger Spiegelungen,
die willig waren, offen und konkav,

und Träume, die mit aufgeregten Masken
auftraten, riesiger durch die Kothurne – :
das alles stockt in diesen oben flasken
weichlichen Stengeln, die die Samenurne

(nachdem sie lang, die Knospe abwärts tragend,
zu welken meinten) festverschlossen heben:
gefranste Kelche auseinanderschlagend,
die fieberhaft das Mohngefäß umgeben.[110]

It is important to discern the overall structure of this poem. It opens with the statement that the opium poppy is growing in a remote part of the garden and the flower is introduced as "the evil sleep" ("der böse Schlaf"). This characterization links directly to the title of the poem and the German word for opium poppy (as well as the Latin, *papaver somniferum*), *Schlaf-Mohn* (sleep-poppy), a connection that is lost in any English translation of the title. Through this description and these linguistic connections the flower is immediately identified with the soporific and intoxicating effects of ingesting opium. A somewhat, yet appropriately, surreal depiction of the hallucinatory state of intoxication forms the focus until the very middle of the poem. However, already in the first half of the poem the description of an intoxicated state of consciousness and a depiction of the flower's appearance blur into one another. The second half of the poem explicitly accomplishes the typically Rilkean correspondence between inner and outer. The third line of the second verse makes the transition with the statement that this narcotized state of mind congeals in the plant ("das alles stockt in diesen oben flasken/ weichlichen Stengeln ..."); this statement points especially, but not solely, to the sap or latex that ultimately gathers in the seed capsules on top of the stems. In other words, the plant in its visual form is already a manifestation of a certain mental or spiritual quality, which later comes to expression in its narcotic and hallucinatory effects. The poem proceeds to depict accurately and expressively the appearance of the plant's growth and its various parts: the stems, the drooping of the bud before it blossoms, the flower, and the capsule. The structure and depictions of "Schlaf-Mohn" vividly evoke the physiognomy of the plant as expressive of its toxicity, and connect an accurate description of the plant's appearance to the mental states with which the opium poppy is intrinsically associated. After explicitly stating a connection between the mental qualities of intoxication and the plant's appearance in the second half of the second verse, the

---

110 "Opium-Poppy// In a remote part of the garden blooms the evil sleep,/ in which those, who secretly gained entrance,/ found the love of young reflections,/ which were willing, open and concave,// and dreams, which with excited masks/ appeared, more gigantic through the cothurnus – :/ all of this congeals in these, at the top, droopy/ soft stems, which raise the seed-urn// (after they, holding the bud downwards,/ long implied wilting) tightly closed:/ unfurling fringed calyxes,/ which feverishly surround the poppy-vessel." KA 1, 574–5.

poem seeks to illustrate this connection for the reader's imagination. The merging of inner and outer, the plant's visual appearance and the narcotic effects derived from the latex in the seed capsule (or the "seed-urn [Samenurne]" as it is fittingly and metaphorically described), reveals that the entire plant—including its form, color, and manner of growing—is expressive of its toxicity and the mental state induced by opium. Although only an outline of the poem has been provided, this gives sufficient orientation for an adequate closer reading.

Other Aspects of Nature
Having elucidated the twofold disclosure of animals and plants, I will now discuss a few other examples of the non-dualistic presentation of natural phenomena in the *Neue Gedichte*. As a whole, the aim of these three sub-sections is to show the distinctive ways in which individual poems facilitate non-dualistic, holistic, and imaginal presentations of things, and, at the same time, to establish a general interpretative horizon for the diverse thematizations of Nature in the *Neue Gedichte*.

The sonnet "Vor dem Sommerregen" portrays a period of time just before a downpour. This natural process is simultaneously conveyed as an inner and outer event. I share Müller's interpretation that the poem evokes "the uncanny atmosphere [*unheimliche Atmosphäre*] before a downpour in summer."[111] The word "atmosphere" should here be understood in a twofold sense, in the sense of both an ambience or mood and its meteorological meaning.[112]

Vor dem Sommerregen

Auf einmal ist aus allem Grün im Park
man weiß nicht was, ein Etwas, fortgenommen;
man fühlt ihn näher an die Fenster kommen
und schweigsam sein. Inständig nur und stark

ertönt aus dem Gehölz der Regenpfeifer,
man denkt an einen Hieronymus:
so sehr steigt irgend Einsamkeit und Eifer
aus dieser einen Stimme, die der Guß

erhören wird. Des Saales Wände sind
mit ihren Bildern von uns fortgetreten,
als dürften sie nicht hören was wir sagen.

---
111 Wolfgang Müller, *Rainer Maria Rilkes "Neue Gedichte,"* 172–3.
112 See the discussion of atmospheres and moods in Chapter 2.

Es spiegeln die verblichenen Tapeten
das ungewisse Licht von Nachmittagen,
in denen man sich fürchtete als Kind.[113]

From the second line of the fourth verse (final tercet) of the sonnet we know that a group ("von *uns*") of people are in the interior space of a hall. The first quatrain describes a mysterious and sudden sense of absence connected with the coming downpour. Something—"ein Etwas"—has been taken out of all the greenery in the park—the leaves and grass. This intuitive sense that something has been subtracted is further developed in the third and fourth lines of the first verse (which are preceded by a semi-colon at the end of the second line). The speaker states that one feels the park ("man fühlt ihn") come closer to the windows and one senses its silence. That this felt change in the atmosphere has more than a merely subjective character is indicated by the use of the third person neuter, "man" ("one"), in the second and third lines ("man weiß" and "man fühlt"). The approaching rainstorm is announced by a sense of lack or absence, a stillness or silence, which is connected to the plants outside and involves a felt change in the relation between the outside world and the interior space of the hall. It is striking to compare the opening of "Vor dem Sommerregen" with the opening of the poem "Last Tryst" by Rabindranath Tagore, which also describes trees in relation to an approaching storm. Both poems are clearly variations on the same insight.

> Ink-black clouds banked in the north-east:
> The force of the coming storm latent in the forest,
>   Waiting as quietly as the bats hanging
>   In the branches. Darkness blanketing
>   Dense leaves that are still and silent
>   As a crouching tiger intent
>   On its prey ...[114]

---

113 "Before the Summer Rain// Suddenly out of all the green in the park/ one knows not what, something, is taken away;/ one feels it [the park] come nearer to the windows/ and keep silent. Imploringly and strongly// a plover calls from the copse,/ one thinks of a Hieronymus:/ so greatly intensifies some loneliness and zeal/ from this one voice that the downpour// will answer. The walls of the hall/ with their pictures have stepped back from us,/ as if they were not allowed to hear what we say.// The faded hangings mirror/ the uncertain light of afternoons,/ in which one was frightened as a child." KA 1, 481–2.

114 Rabindranath Tagore, *Selected Poems*, trans. William Radice (London: Penguin Books, 1994), 117.

The *Neue Gedichte* as a Twofold Imagining of Things   269

Tagore and Rilke convey the same poetic insight into the natural event of an approaching storm. Both poems evoke how the nearing of a rainstorm is announced by an uncanny silence or stillness in the trees. Tagore, in a certain respect, goes further than Rilke in that he actually names this silence as "the force of the coming storm." In "Vor dem Sommerregen" this is suggested rather than explicitly stated.

The second quatrain of "Vor dem Sommerregen" describes the call of a bird, "der Regenpfeifer," whose tone also seems to portend the rain. Although "Regenpfeifer" is the name of the bird family known as plover in English, there is a pertinent sense to the German word that does not translate; the two parts of the compound noun literally mean "rain-whistler." Rilke's diction is thus particularly apt in suggesting that the "Regenpfeifer" intimates the coming rain. The resonant call of the plover is first conveyed as only imploring and strong ("Inständig nur und stark"), while the surrounding environment is silent. The speaker then states that the plover's call makes one think of a Hieronymus ("einen Hieronymus") or St. Jerome, the early church father, ascetic, translator of the bible, and polemicist. The meaning of this allusion is elaborated by the remainder of the second quatrain. The character of the plover's solitary voice in the surrounding silence suggests "loneliness and zeal" ("irgend Einsamkeit und Eifer"). It is then said that the downpour ("Guß") will answer this voice. The tone of the plover's call is a further portent of the coming rain, for one ("man") who experiences this scene. The sense of loneliness and fervor in the plover's call from the copse is clearly an elaboration of the subtracted "Etwas" of the first verse; the voice is an intensification of "*irgend* Einsamkeit und Eifer," "irgend" ("some") carrying the same indefinite sense as "Etwas." The call of the plover, moreover, is directly correlated to the coming rain that will answer it ("der Guß erhören wird"). Hans Berendt regards the ecclesiastical allusion as an identification of the voice of the plover with the praying Hieronymus and the rain with the God who answers his prayers.[115] Whether the text grants such a specific identification is questionable. At the least, however, the specific tone or atmosphere of the plover's call can be said to be *suggestive* of qualities possessed by someone like ("*einen* Hieronymus") the fervent hermit and that the coming rain and the call are in relation to one another (as are prayer and God). However, as in other poems, these allusions are better understood as characterizations of the phenomenon itself—the time before summer rain—rather than as symbols of something else. The *sound of the plover* makes one think of a Hieronymus; the allusion serves to characterize the tone of the call, rather than symbolizing a separate religious state of

---

115   Hans Berendt, *Rainer Maria Rilkes Neue Gedichte: Versuch einer Deutung* (Bonn: H. Bouvier u. Co. Verlag, 1957), 141.

affairs. In the first two verses (quatrains) aspects of Nature—the trees outside, the call of a bird, the sense of the coming rain—and the poetic awareness of these phenomena are articulated within an encompassing whole. They participate in a single happening, in what might be called *Naturinnenraum* or a single atmosphere.[116]

The sense of absence (first verse) and the change in the felt relation between the interior and exterior space are further developed in the third verse (the first tercet). While there is a felt diminishing of distance between the inside and the outside in the first verse, in the third verse all sense of distance is abolished. The walls of the hall and their paintings step back ("Des Saales Wände sind mit ihren Bildern von uns fortgetreten"). This removal—the feeling of sudden lack—involves the loss of any feeling of spatial containment. Although the group is inside, the change in the atmosphere does not know the boundary between inside and outside, interior and exterior. While there is no direct mention of an alteration in light or darkness in the first tercet, this description could, in addition, be understood to mean that the pictures and walls are plunged into darkness by the shadow cast by the dense rain clouds. The paintings recede into darkness as if they were not allowed to hear the conversation ("als dürften sie nicht hören was wir sagen"). No matter how one reads this verse, it is clear that there is no longer any felt distance between the external natural occurrence and inner space, the outside and the inside, interior and exterior.

In the final tercet the quality of the light, which reflects off the wall-hangings, provokes memories in the speaker of other afternoons when rainstorms approached. The phenomenality of the light has an uncanny and indefinite atmosphere; the light is "uncertain" ("ungewiss"). This adjective is another member in the series of expressions that evoke the mysterious, the indefinite, the uncanny—"man weiß nicht was," "ein Etwas," "man fühlt," "einen Hieronymus," "irgend," etc.[117] The sibilance of the stressed "s" in "ungewisse" contributes to the evocation of this strange mood (the assonance on the high-pitched vowel, "i," throughout the final verse also plays a significant role). The final line of the poem specifies that the light recalls afternoons when one was scared as a child ("in denen man sich fürchtete als Kind"), presumably because its quality boded a frightening storm. It is not surprising that

---

116 In the article "A Poetic Phenomenology of the Temperate Seasons" I have argued for a related view of the connection between human affects and natural phenomena. While there I do not use the term *Naturinnenraum* (or *Weltinnenraum*), this term is thoroughly in keeping with the article's central argument concerning the human experience of the seasons.

117 This indeterminacy accords with Böhme's understanding of atmospheres. See, for instance, his discussion of twilight as exemplary of "the atmospheric" ("das Atmosphärische") in *Anmutungen: Über das Atmosphärische*, 13–34.

The *Neue Gedichte* as a Twofold Imagining of Things 271

the child appears at the end of the poem if we recall that the child in Rilke's work is a figure of pre-dualism and participation. The coming downpour is invoked in the poem not as an indifferent objective process but as an event that claims the speaker's participation; a child is frightened by such a state of affairs because he or she does not experience it as a detached natural occurrence. The adult speaker in the poem is reminded of childhood experiences of the same phenomenon because the adult is experiencing the natural event in a similarly participative way. In "Vor dem Sommerregen," mind and Nature, inner and outer, take part in a single event and atmosphere.

The first poem in the *Neue Gedichte*, the sonnet "Früher Apollo," thematizes poetic inspiration through the figure of Apollo, the god of poetry, and thus fittingly introduces the entire collection. This poem revolves around an extended analogy between early spring and later spring (and summer) on the one hand, and poetic inspiration and the writing of poems on the other. While its central theme is not directly relevant to our present concern, not incidentally the poem conveys the pertinent phenomenon of sunlight as a manifestation of early spring. This is not incidental as Apollo is not only a god of poetry but also of the sun. The complementary poem in *Der Neuen Gedichte anderer Teil*, "Archaïscher Torso Apollos," also appropriately contains many metaphors relating to light. "Früher Apollo" begins as follows:

Früher Apollo

Wie manches Mal durch das noch unbelaubte
Gezweig ein Morgen durchsieht, der schon ganz
im Frühling ist: so ist in seinem Haupte
nichts was verhindern könnte, daß der Glanz

aller Gedichte uns fast tödlich träfe ...[118]

As in many of Rilke's poems the members of the analogy or simile are mutually illuminating. Here the analogues are Apollo and spring. Although the former is the central theme or tenor of the poem, it is the latter which most interests us. The sonnet presents a qualitative shift in the year, the transition from one season to another, as it is announced by a change in the phenomenality of the light.[119] The branches are still

---

[118] "Early Apollo// As sometimes through the branches still void/ of foliage a morning looks, which already/ is wholly in spring: so is there nothing/ in his head's bearing which could prevent the luster// of all poems from striking us almost fatally ..." Translated by Luke Fischer and Lutz Näfelt. *KA 1*, 449.

[119] See also Luke Fischer, "A Poetic Phenomenology of the Temperate Seasons."

bare, spring has not yet manifested itself in new vegetation; however, the quality of the morning light suggests the spring; it seems to harbor in potency the fullness of spring that will only later unfold in an abundance of new growth and vegetation. Just as the light seems to harbor in advance the fullness of spring, so the gaze of Apollo seems to hold the inspiration of all the poems to come. Light does not appear here as an indifferent physical property but as a qualitative phenomenon; the shift in the light's character is the first word of spring.

The poem "Landschaft" also depicts the alteration of light between two times, but in this case, the transition from sunset into night. The changing appearance of a townscape is shown in its natural setting and the portrayal clearly suggests an epiphanic dimension.

Landschaft

Wie zuletzt, in einem Augenblick
aufgehäuft aus Hängen, Häusern, Stücken
alter Himmel und zerbrochnen Brücken,
und von drüben her, wie vom Geschick,
von dem Sonnenuntergang getroffen,
angeschuldigt, aufgerissen, offen –
ginge dort die Ortschaft tragisch aus:

fiele nicht auf einmal in das Wunde,
drin zerfließend, aus der nächsten Stunde
jener Tropfen kühlen Blaus,
der die Nacht schon in den Abend mischt,
so daß das von ferne Angefachte
sachte, wie erlöst, erlischt.

Ruhig sind die Tore und die Bogen,
durchsichtige Wolken wogen
über blasser Häuserreihn
die schon Dunkel in sich eingesogen;
aber plötzlich ist vom Mond ein Schein
durchgeglitten, licht, als hätte ein
Erzengel irgendwo sein Schwert gezogen.[120]

---

120 "Landscape// How finally, in an instant/ amassed from hillsides, houses, pieces/ of old sky and broken bridges,/ and from over there, as by fate,/ struck by the sunset,/ accused, torn open, disclosed –/ this locality would tragically go out:// if there did not fall, at once, into the wound,/ deliquescent, from the next hour/ this drop of cool blue,/ which already mixes the night into the evening,/ so that that which was kindled from a distance/ gently, as

A landscape and townscape are presented during their passage from sunset to night. Already in the first two verses religious imagery and allusions are to be found. The town was struck by the light of the setting sun as by fate ("vom Geschick … getroffen"). A religious, and more specifically Christian, symbolism is implied by the word "accused" ("angeschuldigt") in the first verse, and the mention of redemption ("erlöst") at the end of the second verse. This religious language, along with the statement that the township could go out tragically ("ginge … Ortschaft tragisch aus"), leads the reader to think of a passion play. Due to these religious allusions a modern reader with a dualistic metaphysics is likely to reinterpret the whole poem as a symbol: the image of the shifting appearance of the townscape is a symbol for the passion of Christ or some other religious content. However, there is another interpretative possibility, which takes into account the poem as a whole and regards the religious allusions as serving to evoke an epiphanic disclosure of a situated natural event. According to this reading, the allusions serve to depict the fullness of the scene, rather than to indicate that the ostensible content of the poem is only a symbol or allegory for something else.

As in many other cases, there is a letter which sheds light on the experience that inspired this poem. In considering the letter, I am not suggesting that the meaning of the linguistic work of art should be substituted with a personal account from the author. A poem is composed for the appreciation of a reader and its imaginative language must demonstrate a self-evident validity; it does not merely recount a perception in all of its contingencies (even in the case of Rilke's *Dinggedichte*, which were inspired by perceptions). My reason for turning to this letter lies in the fact that it challenges a metaphysics that refuses to allow that the world can reveal itself with an inner depth, that a landscape, for instance, can disclose itself epiphanically. The religious and even mystical significance of place and landscape for Rilke is most emphatically revealed in his letters from 1913 written in Spain. However, due to its connection to the poem "Landschaft" it is apt to consider here a passage from the letter to Clara Rilke, written on Capri on January 1, 1907. Rilke describes the previous night of New Year's Eve as follows:

> The night was bright and distant, a night which seemed to rest above far more than only the earth; one felt that it lay above seas

---

though redeemed, expires.// Peaceful are the gates and the arches,/ transparent clouds undulate/ over pale rows of houses/ which already absorbed darkness into themselves;/ but suddenly from the moon a beam/ glided through, light, as though an/ archangel somewhere had drawn his sword." *KA 1*, 548–9.

and far beyond them above space, above itself, above stars, which looked upon their stars from an infinite depth. All of this was mirrored in it and held by it above the earth: because it was like a continual overflowing of the heavens.[121]

In Rilke's description of a night that seemed to rest over much more than merely the earth, a "heavenly" or religious dimension is already intimated. Later in this excerpt he speaks of an "infinite depth" and by the end of the passage the language becomes explicitly religious or mystical, in his description of an experience that was like a constant "overflowing of the heavens" ("Überfließen von Himmeln"). Berendt relates this statement to the drop of cool blue which the night mixes into the evening ("jener Tropfen kühlen Blaus,/ der die Nacht schon in der Abend mischt") as well as to the reference to the archangel at the end of the poem, "Landschaft."[122] While there are other parallels between the poem and the letter, the quoted passage suffices to support an epi-phanic reading of the poem.

"Landschaft" opens with a portrait of an old town and landscape—of accumulated houses and broken bridges—that are struck by the colors of the sunset. The sense of ruin and fragmentation is evoked both on a semantic and a sonorous level. With regard to the latter, the consonance of the phonemes, "t," "ch," and "ck," plays an important role: "Wie zuletzt, in einem Augenblick/ aufgehäuft aus Hängen, Häusern, Stücken/ alter Himmel und zerbrochnen Brücken…" The first and second verses are organized around subjunctive formulations: were the day to go out simply like a light, the village and landscape would go out tragically ("ginge die Ortschaft tragisch aus"). In the second verse the town and landscape are described as a sore wound,[123] which emphatically elaborates the broken and ruined appearance of the scene. More significantly, however, these metaphors and allusions are set up to convey an epi-phanic phenomenality. The blue light of dusk spreads over the landscape and is wonderfully portrayed by the expression that a cool drop of blue already mixes the night into the evening. This light of dusk is a transitionary phase and the townscape is not suddenly plunged into darkness or night. The expression, "this drop of cool blue" ("jener Tropfen kühlen Blaus"), synaesthetically suggests the quality of the evening light, the cooler air, and the

---

121 Rainer Maria Rilke, *Briefe aus den Jahren 1906–1907*, vol. 2 (Leipzig: Insel Verlag, 1930), 153.
122 Berendt, *Rainer Maria Rilkes Neue Gedichte: Versuch einer Deutung*, 282.
123 Rilke coins the noun "*das* Wunde"; the normal word for "wound" in German is "*die* Wunde." "Das Wunde" is derived from the adjective "wund" (sore) but is also suggestive of "die Wunde" (wound).

The *Neue Gedichte* as a Twofold Imagining of Things   275

metaphor of a healing lotion applied to the "wounded" town. The light of day fades away gently ("sachte") as if the town were redeemed or saved ("erlischt"). As a dimension of its phenomenality the blue light of evening assumes the depth of the holy.

In the third verse a peaceful mood settles over the town ("Ruhig sind die Tore und die Bogen ..."). Transparent clouds undulate over the rows of houses which are already dark ("die schon Dunkel in sich eingesogen"). Then a shaft of moonlight suddenly shines through the darkness; the momentous and epiphanic character of this event is made obvious by the final analogy; the sudden beam of light appears as though an archangel somewhere had drawn his sword ("als hätte ein/ Erzengel irgendwo sein Schwert gezogen"). While the meaning of this poem could be further elaborated in wider symbolic terms, it is centered in an atmospheric and epiphanic disclosure of place and the appearance of natural time.

Conclusion of Section
From the above discussion of the presentations of Nature—animals, flowers, weather, light, and landscape—in the *Neue Gedichte*, the continuity between Rilke's twofold perception, as explicated in the preceding chapter, and his poetry should be evident. The poems enact for the reader's imagination a physiognomic and epiphanic disclosure of natural things and events. In distinctive and appropriate ways, they perform a twofold meaning, in which inner and outer, the spiritual and the sensible, nature and mind, are revealed as aspects of the total phenomenon. The interiority evoked in Rilke's poems is not that of a self-contained subjectivity, but an interiority that transcends solipsistic confinement and its correlative sense of Nature as an inanimate exterior. Moreover, in their vivid imagery and "objectivity" (*Sachlichkeit*) the poems bear a clear relation to the visual art of Rodin and Cézanne. They "realize" a twofold imaginative vision of natural phenomena for the attentive and sensitive reader.

Other *Dinggedichte*
While thus far we have focused on the appearance of Nature in the *Neue Gedichte*, numerous *Dinggedichte* are concerned with human figures, works of art, places, artifacts, and other things. This section aims to demonstrate the close affinity between these other *Dinggedichte* and the disclosure of "natural things." The following considerations illustrate the broader scope of Rilke's twofold poetry. Moreover, the attention to human figures will reveal illuminating connections to the earlier discussion of the human Other in Chapters 1 and 2.

Human figures in the *Neue Gedichte* are presented in a gestural and physiognomic manner (not dissimilar from the presentation of animals). As in other poems (such as "Der Schwan"—the swan's transition from land to water), time and temporal sequences play an essential role in the disclosure of human figures. The time of the poem enacts the temporal unfolding of an event. This coincidence of the temporal structure of the poem with the temporal structure of its theme is perhaps most strikingly realized in "Spanische Tänzerin" (see below).

The *Neue Gedichte* includes two poems which thematize blind people, "Die Erblindende" in the first part of the collection and "Der Blinde" in *Der neuen Gedichte anderer Teil*. The latter poem, which will be the focus of our consideration, belongs in a sequence of poems about outcasts and figures on the fringes of society—the old, the mad, the poor, etc.—and clearly relates to the presentation of outcasts in *Malte*.

Der Blinde
Paris

Sieh, er geht und unterbricht die Stadt,
die nicht ist auf seiner dunkeln Stelle,
wie ein dunkler Sprung durch eine helle
Tasse geht. Und wie auf einem Blatt

ist auf ihm der Widerschein der Dinge
aufgemalt; er nimmt ihn nicht hinein.
Nur sein Fühlen rührt sich, so als finge
es die Welt in kleinen Wellen ein:

eine Stille, einen Widerstand –,
und dann scheint er wartend wen zu wählen:
hingegeben hebt er seine Hand,
festlich fast, wie um sich zu vermählen.[124]

"Der Blinde" begins with an imperative typical of the *Neue Gedichte*; it asks the reader to watch or see ("Sieh") the blind man as he goes through the city of Paris. Of course, we cannot literally see the blind person, but this request calls the reader to perceive the blind man imaginatively or

---

124 "The Blind Man/ *Paris*// See, he moves and interrupts the city,/ which does not exist in his dark place,/ like a dark crack moving through a bright/ cup. And as on a sheet of paper// the reflection of things is painted/ on him; he doesn't take it in./ Only his feeling is astir, as if/ capturing the world in small waves:// a silence, a resistance –,/ and then he seems waiting whom to choose:/ consigned he raises his hand,/ almost solemnly, as if to marry." Translated by Luke Fischer and Lutz Näfelt. KA 1, 541.

with the mind's eye. The blind man "interrupts the city" ("unterbricht die Stadt") because he cannot navigate his way with the same ease as others, and thus gets in the way. This expression conveys the dialectical relationship between the blind man and the other inhabitants; on the one hand, his inability to participate in the general life of the city, and on the other, the rejection of the blind person evinced in the behavior of others—his status as an outcast. The difference between the city for a person with sight and the city for a blind person is strikingly conveyed in the statement that the city does not exist ("nicht ist") in his dark place and in the simile of his path being like a dark crack that moves through a bright cup ("wie ein dunkler Sprung durch eine helle/ Tasse geht"). The relation between light and vision is introduced here and, as in the counterpart poem, "Die Erblindende," the condition of blindness is associated with a distinctive inwardness—the blind person possesses an interior space that contrasts with the bright and busy metropolis.[125] The absence of visual phenomena for the blind person is brilliantly conveyed by the image of his body as a sheet of paper, on which the reflections ("der Widerschein") of things, which he cannot see ("er nimmt ihn nicht hinein"), paint themselves. He is as indifferent to this play of light as a sheet of paper is to that which is painted on it. In "Die Erblindende" a similar idea is conveyed by an even richer image. There it is said that "auf ihren hellen Augen die sich freuten/ war Licht von außen wie auf einem Teich [on her bright eyes that rejoiced/ was light from outside as on a pond]."[126] Light shone onto the eyes of the woman who was going blind (*die Erblindende*) as onto a pond. This description of the indifference of her *eyes* to the light (a pond cannot see) is a more explicit image of the relation between blindness, the eyes, light, and sight than the image in "Der Blinde." The distinctive interiority of the woman is also encapsulated in this image; although her eyes cannot see into outer space, an inner joy is physiognomically expressed in them ("Augen die sich freuten"). On the one hand, eyes—"windows of the soul"—are one of the most expressive aspects of a person's appearance. On the other hand, they are organs of vision. While the blind woman's eyes are no longer organs of vision, they are still telling of her inner life. Much more could be unpacked from this incredibly rich image in "Die Erblindende," but what has been stated suffices to indicate some of its core semantic aspects.

For a person with normal vision, sight is the most encompassing of the senses for an awareness of the surroundings. The sense of touch can only give us knowledge of objects directly within our bodily reach.

---

125 Blind figures in earlier collections of Rilke's poetry are also presented as possessing a specific interiority and sensitivity. See, for instance, "Pont du Carrousel" and "Die Blinde," in *Das Buch der Bilder*, KA 1, 277, 337–40.
126 KA 1, 478.

While hearing can give us some awareness of objects at a distance, sight is by far the most ec-static and expansive sense. The reach of our eyes extends to distant mountains and to the stars. Sight turns us outward. To be deprived of sight is, in a certain sense, to be deprived of this ec-stasy or outwardness. Thus, the blind person is cast inward to a greater degree. "Der Blinde" illustrates this brilliantly in the aforementioned image and in what follows.

As far as vision is concerned the blind man is inactive; however, he is active in his inner sensing or "feeling" ("Fühlen"); his feeling is astir ("Nur sein Fühlen rührt sich"). Unable to depend on the sense of sight, he needs to be more inwardly active in order to navigate his way through space. It is through "feeling" (and the heightening of other senses, of course) that he manages to attain a spatial awareness that compensates for his lack of vision. These lines about the blind man's "feeling" can be interpreted as descriptions of his intuitive perception of space; he senses a "silence" or a "resistance." The lines have also been interpreted as referring to a cane that the blind man uses in order to feel his way.[127] However, as no obvious reference is made to a cane and the poem uses "Fühlen" rather than "Tasten" (touching), the latter reading is not entirely warranted by the text. Either way, "Fühlen ..." is suggestive of the blind person's intuitive sensitivity to his surroundings.

After having walked a certain distance through the city, the blind man waits, presumably for someone to help him cross a road. The last two lines reveal the blind man's dependence on the hand of another— "hingegeben hebt er seine Hand [consigned he raises his hand]." The word "hingegeben" implies the blind person's difficult fate. Although in a certain sense he freely raises his hand, in another sense he has been consigned to this condition of dependence on others. "Hingegeben," in the first instance, suggests that the blind person is given over ("hin-gegeben") to this fate—the raising of his hand as a sign for help is determined by his condition and is thus not an entirely free act. However, "hingegeben" concomitantly suggests that the blind man gives himself over or entrusts himself to another. The latter is gesturally encapsulated in the simile of the blind man giving his hand, almost solemnly or festively ("festlich"), as if in marriage. This final image is characteristic of Rilke's poetic genius in the way it indissolubly unites gesture and meaning. Through its complex similes, metaphors, and diction, which call for a gestural, physiognomic imagining on the part of the reader, "Der Blinde" portrays a scene that exemplifies the condition of human blindness and its correlative manner of being-in-the-world. The poem presents a particular scene that is expressive of a universal significance; it weds the sensible and the intelligible in a holistic manner.

---

127 Lawrence Ryan, "Rilke's *Dinggedichte*: The 'Thing' as 'Poem in Itself,'" 34ff.

"Das Karussell" ("The Carousel") is one of Rilke's most striking *Dinggedichte*, in its tight construction, temporal unfolding, and vivid description.

Das Karussell
Jardin du Luxembourg

Mit einem Dach und seinem Schatten dreht
sich eine kleine Weile der Bestand
von bunten Pferden, alle aus dem Land,
das lange zögert, eh es untergeht.
Zwar manche sind an Wagen angespannt,
doch alle haben Mut in ihren Mienen;
ein böser roter Löwe geht mit ihnen
und dann und wann ein weißer Elefant.

Sogar ein Hirsch ist da, ganz wie im Wald,
nur daß er einen Sattel trägt und drüber
ein kleines blaues Mädchen aufgeschnallt.

Und auf dem Löwen reitet weiß ein Junge
und hält sich mit der kleinen heißen Hand,
dieweil der Löwe Zähne zeigt und Zunge.

Und dann und wann ein weißer Elefant.

Und auf den Pferden kommen sie vorüber,
auch Mädchen, helle, diesem Pferdesprunge
fast schon entwachsen, mitten in dem Schwunge
schauen sie auf, irgendwohin, herüber –

Und dann und wann ein weißer Elefant.

Und das geht hin und eilt sich, daß es endet,
und kreist und dreht sich nur und hat kein Ziel.
Ein Rot, ein Grün, ein Grau vorbeigesendet,
ein kleines kaum begonnenes Profil – .
Und manchesmal ein Lächeln, hergewendet,
ein seliges, das blendet und verschwendet
an dieses atemlose blinde Spiel ...[128]

---

128 "The Carousel/ *Jardin du Luxembourg*// With a roof and its shadow/ the stock of colorful horses/ for a short while revolves, all from the country,/ which long hesitates, before it goes under./ Indeed many are hitched to wagons,/ but

"Das Karussell" is a paradigmatic *Dinggedicht*. Like many *Dinggedichte*, its subtitle names the location that occasioned the poem (the Jardin du Luxembourg in Paris). While language and a turning object such as a carousel seem to bear no obvious similarities, the temporal unfolding of Rilke's verse—in its formal structure and images—itself seems to revolve like a merry-go-round. Berendt characterizes this well in his description of all the optical impressions which "paint the circling movement in such a lively manner that the reader is virtually pulled into it." [129] Along with the vivid portrayal of numerous visual impressions and movements the repetition of "Und dann und wann ein weißer Elefant" signals the revolutions of the carousel for the reader, in announcing that the elephant is coming round again. Durs Grünbein suggestively draws attention to the numerous repetitions of "und" ("and"): the conjunction appears "at the beginning of lines, musical as a bar sign, and then as a copula, in order to bind the various elements of the carousel, as though the poet were at the same time its constructor. Toward the end it is used almost solely in service of acceleration until with the final word 'game' the whole thing comes to a jerky halt."[130]

The poem holistically conveys the scene and its atmosphere or mood. This mood is not a merely subjective characteristic; it is not a colored light projected onto the white canvas of things. The supra-subjective significance of moods and atmospheres was already illustrated in the discussion of aspects of Nature in the *Neue Gedichte* and in the articulation of artistic dispositions and atmospheres in Chapter 2. However, it is worthwhile to recall some of the earlier points and to say a bit more about how this conception of moods applies to the human realm.

Heidegger, in *Sein und Zeit*, rightly points out that we always find ourselves in a particular mood or disposition (even "indifference" is a

---

all have courage in their miens;/ a vicious red lion goes with them/ and now and then a white elephant.// Even a stag is there, just as in the forest,/ only it bears a saddle and upon it/ a little blue girl is strapped.// And upon the lion rides a boy in white,/ and holds himself on with a small hot hand,/ while the lion bares its teeth and tongue.// And now and then a white elephant.// And on the horses also pass by,/ bright girls, who've already almost outgrown/ these horses' leaps; in the middle of the arc/ they look up and around, somewhere over here –// And now and then a white elephant.// And it continues and rushes toward its end,/ and only circles and revolves and has no goal./ A red, a green, a gray sent by,/ a small scarcely begun profile – ./ And sometimes a smile, turned this way,/ something blessed, that dazzles and lavishes/ on this breathless blind game …" KA 1, 490–1.

129 Berendt, *Rainer Maria Rilkes Neue Gedichte: Versuch einer Deutung*, 157.
130 Durs Grünbein, "Ein kleines blaues Mädchen 'Das Karussell': Ein Rilke-Manuskript im Marbacher Literaturarchiv," in *Denkbilder und Schaustücke: Das Literaturmuseum der Moderne: Marbacher Katalog 60* (Marbach: Deutsches Literaturarchiv, 2006), 104.

The *Neue Gedichte* as a Twofold Imagining of Things   281

mood).[131] He also demonstrates that moods are distinctive "attunements" to reality; they allow the world and ourselves to appear in a certain manner and are not mere subjective projections or states.[132] The sense of mood as "attunement" is suggested by the German word ("Stimmung") which can mean "tuning" and is connected to the verb "stimmen"—"to attune" or "to tune." Poetry (as well as music) is especially significant in that it not only has the capacity to describe or refer to a mood but through the musicality of its language can put the listener into a specific mood; it is thus able to "attune" the reader to the world in a certain way.

Prior to Heidegger, Scheler already made significant advances in explicating a phenomenology of affects (in ways that relate to the more recent phenomenology of atmospheres in Gernot Böhme's aesthetics[133]). Scheler's philosophy of affects (which influenced Heidegger) also cannot be understood in subjectivistic terms.[134] Scheler convincingly illustrates that things and scenes bear intrinsic moods that are every bit as "objective" or supra-subjective as a thing's color or shape.[135] Scheler offers, for instance, the example of the mood of a party, with which I am "infected" and which differs from my preceding state of mind.[136] This mood is not projected but in a certain sense takes hold of me and is an intersubjective and supra-subjective reality. Affects of this kind are indicated by our everyday habits of speech; we speak of "mood," "atmosphere," "ambience," "feel," or "vibe" in relation to persons, places, and events.

The language of "Das Karussell" simultaneously attunes the reader to the depicted phenomenon and conveys the atmosphere of the scene. The poem thereby presents the phenomenon with an affective depth rather than as a mere exterior surface (a related evocation of supra-subjective atmospheres is evident in Rilke's "place poems," such as "Quai du Rosaire" and "Béguinage").[137] There is a childlike quality to the diction and a playful irony that evokes the mood of the scene and is inseparable from the overall context—children riding a carousel or merry-go-round. This playfulness is evident, for instance, in the claim that the carousel horses are all from the country ("alle aus dem Land"), as well as in the second verse, where the stag is characterized as identical to a stag

---

131 Heidegger states, "Daß Stimmungen verdorben werden und umschlagen können, sagt nur, daß das Dasein je schon immer gestimmt ist." *Sein und Zeit*, 134.
132 See the whole discussion of "Befindlichkeit," in *Sein und Zeit*, 134ff. "Die Stimmung überfällt. Sie kommt weder von "Außen" noch von "Innen", sondern steigt als Weise des In-der-Welt-seins aus diesem selbst auf" (p. 136).
133 See the discussion of Böhme's conception of atmospheres in Chapter 2.
134 Coriando, *Affektenlehre und Phänomenologie der Stimmungen*, 17ff.
135 Max Scheler, *Wesen und Formen der Sympathie* (Bern: Francke Verlag, 1973), 17ff.
136 Scheler, *Wesen und Formen der Sympathie*, 25ff.
137 KA 1, 493–5.

in the forest. The playful mood is also evoked by the monosyllabic, simple-sounding words, and a gentle irony is conveyed by the obvious absurdity of the statements. This ironic inflection implies an adult perception of the carousel, which pursues no goal and simply turns on the spot—"kreist und dreht sich nur und hat kein Ziel"—but a childlike wonder is also communicated in the descriptions. The line that is most childlike in its mood is the aforementioned refrain, "Und dann und wann ein weißer Elefant [And now and then a white elephant]." It has the ring of a nursery rhyme through its use of the colloquial expression "dann und wann" ("now and then"), simple rhythm, predominance of monosyllabic words, internal rhyme, assonance and consonance—the simple "a" assonance and "n" consonance ("d*a*nn," "w*a*nn," "Elef*a*nt," and "u*n*d," "da*nn*," "wa*nn*," "ei*n*," "Elefa*n*t"), for instance.

The comportment of the children within the entire state of affairs is also expressively conveyed. The "blue girl" ("blaues Mädchen") strapped on a stag, and the boy in white who holds onto a lion with his "small hot hand" ("mit der kleinen heißen Hand") are thoroughly absorbed in the ride. In contrast, some older girls, evidently in or approaching puberty, no longer wholly participate in the experience; when their horses leap, without a doubt the most exciting moments of the ride, they look elsewhere—they are no longer immersed.

The last verse brilliantly conveys the carousel's movement as it speeds up: colors start to blur; as soon as the profile of a face emerges it vanishes again; and the occasional smile is glimpsed—a momentary epiphany amid the whirl of colors. The poem presents the scene holistically (or hermeneutically) and atmospherically. It exemplifies the claim made in Chapter 1 that the meaning of a specific human event is contextually situated and is best communicated by language that invites the imagination to picture its sensible-intelligible wholeness. While the carousel-scene is presented from the point of view of an adult onlooker, this view has a chiasmic structure and enables the scene to show itself.

"Spanische Tänzerin" exemplifies in a superlative manner much of what has been previously discussed. It presents the temporal unfolding of a Spanish dance in an expressive (physiognomic), dynamic, and exact way. The various verses portray the successive stages of the dance from its beginning to its end.

Spanische Tänzerin

Wie in der Hand ein Schwefelzündholz, weiß,
eh es zur Flamme kommt, nach allen Seiten
zuckende Zungen streckt – : beginnt im Kreis
naher Beschauer hastig, hell und heiß
ihr runder Tanz sich zuckend auszubreiten.

Und plötzlich ist er Flamme, ganz und gar.

Mit einem Blick entzündet sie ihr Haar
und dreht auf einmal mit gewagter Kunst
ihr ganzes Kleid in dieser Feuerbrunst,
aus welcher sich, wie Schlangen die erschrecken,
die nackten Arme wach und klappernd strecken.

Und dann: als würde ihr das Feuer knapp,
nimmt sie es ganz zusamm und wirft es ab
sehr herrisch, mit hochmütiger Gebärde
und schaut: da liegt es rasend auf der Erde
und flammt noch immer und ergiebt sich nicht –.
Doch sieghaft, sicher und mit einem süßen
grüßenden Lächeln hebt sie ihr Gesicht
und stampft es aus mit kleinen festen Füßen.[138]

The poem is organized around the image of fire, which begins as a simile ("wie ... ein Schwefelzündholz [like ... a match]") and after the first verse functions as a metaphor for the remainder of the poem. Even at the most general level this image is suggestive and fitting, in that it evokes the passionate character of the dance as an expression of the Southern European culture of Spain. However, it also serves in the portrayal of gestural movements of the dancer in the most exact physiognomic manner.

The first verse performs the opening of the dance, which is compared to the way an igniting match flickers tongues of flame in various directions. The dancer is surrounded by an audience, or a circle of spectators, but all explicit reference to the audience disappears after the first verse. There are at least two reasons for this. The solitary line succeeding the first verse, which elaborates the image of the igniting match, declares that the dance *is* suddenly entirely flame ("ganz und gar"). At this point the simile becomes a metaphor; the flame and the dance

---

138 "Spanish Dancer// As in the hand a struck-match, white,/ before it is aflame," on all sides/ stretches flickering tongues – : beginning in the circle/ of near viewers, hasty, hot and bright,/ her round dance flickering extends itself.// And suddenly it is entirely flame.// With a glance she ignites her hair/ and whirls at once with daring art/ her whole dress into this conflagration,/ from which, like snakes, frightened,/ the naked arms roused and rattling stretch.// And then: as if the fire were getting too tight for her,/ she gathers it all together and discards it/ imperiously, with a haughty gesture/ and looks: there it lies raving on the ground/ and still continues to flame and does not yield –./ But triumphantly, sure, and with a sweet/ greeting smile she lifts her face/ and stamps it out with small firm feet." KA 1, 491.

are identified; the dancer is no longer finding her way into the dance but is completely immersed in the performance or fire. In any performance there is an intimate correlation between the engagement of the performer and the engagement of the audience. In the present case, the solitary line marks the moment in which the dancer has become immersed in the dance and the audience has become captivated by the performance. Thus, one reason why the audience disappears is because their attention is now given over to the dance. The second reason for this disappearance pertains to the fact that the poem portrays the dance with such vividness for the reader's (or listener's) imagination that the reader, virtually speaking, becomes a member of the audience; like an audience member the reader does not observe the other spectators but attends to the performance.

In the second major verse (following the solitary line), typifying gestures of the dance are expressively conveyed—with a look the dancer ignites her hair and twirls her dress into the fire. The last two lines of this verse are unsurpassable in their visual and aural evocation of the dancer's arms. The movement and shape of the arms are compared to aroused snakes frightened by the fire, and the clicking of the hands is conveyed by "klappernd." This combination of descriptions alludes to "rattle snakes"—"Klapperschlangen." Furthermore, the hard consonant "ck" in the end rhyme of "erschrecken" and "strecken," and the "ckt" of "nackten" and "kl" and "pp" of "klappernd" evoke the distinctive sound made by the dancer's hands.

The exact, dynamic, and physiognomic portrayal attains a further stage in the last verse. If in the second major verse it seemed like the dancer was being consumed by the fire, she now shows that she has complete mastery over the whole state of affairs. She gathers the whole fire into her hands and casts it onto the ground with a haughty gesture ("mit hochmütiger Gebärde") and looks down upon the flames which continue to burn on the ground.

The final stage of the dance and the dancer's supreme virtuosity are strikingly conveyed in the concluding three lines. She lifts her face with a smile, as if already certain of her victory, and stamps out the final flames with small firm feet—"und stampft es aus mit kleinen festen Füßen." The *melopoeia* of the final line synaesthetically and kinaesthetically conveys the action. The *f*orceful character of the "f" accented in "festen" and "Füßen," along with the preceding stress on "*klein*en," conveys the *action* of the feet stomping on the ground. *St*rength and firmness, as well as the "inner" surety of the dancer, are evoked by the near consonance of "sht" and "st" of "*st*ampft" and "fes*t*en." The imaginal significance of poetic language is here clearly discernible. The synaesthetic suggestiveness of the rhythm and sound of the words influences our imagination of the scene (the synaesthetic character of artistic expression was also discussed earlier in relation to the visual art of Rodin and Cézanne).

A dance is an artistic, expressive form of human movement that is seen and heard by the viewer. If its wholeness is to be said in language, then the only manner in which this is possible is through conveying its visual, aural, and expressive character imaginally. This is precisely what "Spanische Tänzerin" achieves. A dance is also essentially temporal, and the poem enacts this temporality in its own temporal unfolding. "Spanische Tänzerin" "performs" the sequences of a dance for the imagination, in a way which enables its expressive, physiognomic essence or *Wesen* ("How can we know the dancer from the dance?"[139]) to be disclosed and recognized. It says the Spanish dance in the fullness of its phenomenality, "realizes" it as a linguistic and imaginal event. A critical commentary can do little more than point out significant features, which might assist the reader in allowing *the poem* to work more effectively.

The above discussion focused on a few poems that exemplify the portrayal of human figures and scenes in the *Neue Gedichte*. In addition to the obvious connections between these poems and Rodin's perception of his models, there is an evident continuity between the phenomenological account of the givenness of the Other in Chapter 1 and these portrayals of human figures. The human figures in the *Neue Gedichte* are contextually situated and the linguistic depictions of the expressive *Leib* (animate-body) play a central role in the disclosure of meaning. However, whereas a conceptual treatment of the givenness of the human Other remains somewhat generic, poetic language is better able to conjure, evoke, and convey the wholeness and haecceity of phenomena.[140]

---

139 William Butler Yeats, "Among School Children," in *Collected Poems of W. B. Yeats* (New York: Simon & Schuster, 1996), 217.

140 The virtue of philosophical language lies in its capacity to articulate general or universal *types* and *structures*. The virtue of poetic language is its capacity to disclose things in their haecceity, to reveal the universal *in the particular*, to disclose *concrete* essences. Poetic language discloses a *content* which is not readily accessible to philosophy, in the latter's tendency toward a more abstract conceptualization of the world. The poetic delivers insights which *enrich* thought; in attending to poetry and seeking a way into *the poetic* the "philosopher" or thinker is *extended*. Conceptual thought certainly has the advantage when it comes to articulating the general. However, what is ultimately required is surely not just any "universal" characterization but a form of insight which discloses essence and existence in their primordial belonging together. It seems to me, therefore, that the *true universal* is discovered through the *poetic* mind. This means that if philosophy is genuinely devoted to the truth, then it has to become more poetic and concern itself with poetry, otherwise certain insights will remain inaccessible. This is one of my main disagreements with Hegel; philosophy does not sublate poetry. See also, Luke Fischer, "Goethe contra Hegel: The Question of the End of Art."

The consideration of "Spanische Tänzerin" made a transition into the realm of art, but an art whose medium is the expressive human body. The *Neue Gedichte* not only contains many poems that reveal strong intermedial connections to non-literary art forms, the collection also includes numerous ekphrastic poems. That a number of poems focus, in particular, on sculptural works is not surprising considering the influence of Rodin on Rilke's aesthetics in the middle period. We will turn again to the most famous of these poems—the premier poem in *Der Neuen Gedichte anderer Teil* (which is dedicated to Rodin) and the complement to "Früher Apollo"—"Archaïscher Torso Apollos," as a paradigmatic example of the twofold disclosure facilitated by Rilke's ekphrastic poetry. In Chapter 2 this sonnet was discussed with reference to Rilke's aesthetics and to his conception of the part–whole relationship manifest in Rodin's sculptures. It was shown how aspects of a philosophy of art are embodied in the poem: the way art can institute a new horizon of meaning; an ethical imperative connected to the latter; and the necessary wholeness of the work of art. This recollection of the earlier discussion raises the question as to the purpose of reconsidering this sonnet. Why not analyze, for instance, one of the three Buddha poems or "L'Ange du Méridien"? The answer is that the explication of the conceptual or philosophical content of the text far from exhausts its meaning. A work of poetry offers something more than the universality of thought. It is precisely through the reconsideration of "Archaïscher Torso Apollos" that essential differences between *wissenschaftliche Sprache* and *dichterische Sprache* can be brought into relief.

If there is one thing that a work of art demonstrates, it is that the sensible is not meaningless, is not, in other words, the opposite of the intelligible. Of all the arts, music manifests this most clearly in its capacity to communicate sense by virtue of its sensible (and temporal) form in a manner that is not reducible to conventionalized or referential meaning. Nevertheless, the same is true of all the arts—the contours of a sculpture, the color-composition of a painting, the musicality of poetic language. The work of art *is* the most extreme overcoming of an opposition between the sensible and the intelligible. In saying this, a merit of poetic language (above conceptual language) in linguistically articulating the specific character of a work of art has been intimated. Poetic language, in calling on the imagination, can present the very unity of the sensible and the intelligible in its thematization of a work of art. If "Archaïscher Torso Apollos" embodies a philosophical aesthetics, it is not in the form of abstract concepts; rather it conveys the phenomenality of a specific work of art in a way that allows the work's essence to shine—this essence or universal, however, is not distinct from the particular, but manifest in the haecceity of the individual work (in the terminology of Goethe it is an *Urphänomen* or archetypal phenomenon[141]). "Archaïscher Torso Apollos" simultaneously conveys the radically singular and the universal; it reveals the fundamental unity of the sensible and the intelligible, the phenomenon of a work of art in its wholeness. Thus contrary to Hegel, I regard art as the best and most adequate medium for interpreting art.[142] More specifically, ekphrastic poetry can evoke the essence of an artwork more profoundly than conceptual criticism.

Archaïscher Torso Apollos

Wir kannten nicht sein unerhörtes Haupt,
darin die Augenäpfel reiften. Aber
sein Torso glüht noch wie ein Kandelaber,
in dem sein Schauen, nur zurückgeschraubt,

sich hält und glänzt. Sonst könnte nicht der Bug
der Brust dich blenden, und im leisen Drehen
der Lenden könnte nicht ein Lächeln gehen
zu jener Mitte, die die Zeugung trug.

Sonst stünde dieser Stein enstellt und kurz
unter der Schultern durchsichtigem Sturz
und flimmerte nicht so wie Raubtierfelle;

und bräche nicht aus allen seinen Rändern
aus wie ein Stern: denn da ist keine Stelle,
die dich nicht sieht. Du mußt dein Leben ändern.[143]

---

141 The following aphorism by Goethe encapsulates a central aspect of his understanding of the *Urphänomen*: "Das Allgemeine und Besondere fallen zusammen: Das Besondere ist das Allgemeine, unter verschiedenen Bedingungen erscheinend [The particular and the universal coincide: The particular is the universal appearing under various conditions]." This also pertains to Goethe's understanding of "true symbolism" as the particular that implicitly conveys the universal. Goethe, *Sämtliche Werke nach Epochen seines Schaffens: Wilhelm Meisters Wanderjahre, Maximen und Reflexionen*, ed. Karl Richter et al., vol. 17 (Munich: Carl Hanser Verlag, 1991), 569, 775, 767. See also Luke Fischer, "Goethe contra Hegel: The Question of the End of Art," 135ff.
142 See n. 24 and n. 140.
143 "Archaic Torso of Apollo// We never knew his tremendous head,/ in which the eyeballs [*Augenäpfel*] ripened. Yet/ his torso still glows like a lamp,/ in which his gaze, only turned low,// persists and gleams. Otherwise the bow/ of the breast could not dazzle you, and in the quiet turning/ of the loins a

Like many of Rilke's sonnets in the *Neue Gedichte*, "Archaïscher Torso Apollos" employs this compact form in the service of a concentrated depiction, which in concert with the tightly interlocked sentences and clauses grants the poem the feel of an almost sculptural self-containment.

The first two lines thematize the sculpture's missing head in a way that sets up the images for the remainder of the poem. It is important to note that Rilke employs the word "Haupt" rather than "Kopf." The latter is the more common German word for "head," but "Haupt" refers more specifically to the expressive bearing of a head, and is also used in "Früher Apollo"—the earlier counterpart to "Archaïscher Torso Apollos." Both sonnets also fittingly employ images of light to describe the statues of the sun god, Apollo.[144] However, the later sonnet is a far more concentrated depiction of the sculpture itself.

We never knew the tremendous expression of the head, as the statue, like many ancient sculptures, has not remained intact. The head is inconceivable or literally "unheard-of" (Rilke plays on the etymological sense of "unerhört"). As noted in Chapter 2, the use of the word "Augenäpfel" as a description of the eyes also poses serious difficulties for translators.[145] "Augenäpfel" ("eye-apples") relates to the normal German word for eyeball ("Augapfel") but the poem draws on its implicit metaphoricity: the "Augenäpfel" ("eye-apples") "ripened" ("reiften") in the former head. This metaphor weaves a relation between the god and Nature which is both historically appropriate and typically Rilkean; the Greek gods embody natural (and divine) powers and Rilke consistently regards the work of art as a higher revelation of Nature. A further relation to Nature is depicted in the third line of the first tercet where the gleam of the marble is likened to the shimmering fur of a wild animal or predator. Similarly to "Früher Apollo," this sonnet blends the description of the god and Nature.

"Archaïscher Torso Apollos" does not describe the torso in abstract terms, but conjures its aesthetic (though not merely aesthetic) appearance. The rich and concrete evocation of the sculpture's form is facilitated by the central metaphors of light and vision. The torso glows

---

smile could not travel/ to that center, which bore procreation.// Otherwise this stone would stand disfigured and short/ under the shoulders' transparent fall/ and not shimmer like a predator's coat;// and not break out from all its borders/ like a star: because there is no place/ that does not see you. You must change your life." *KA 1*, 513.

144 For a discussion of these poems as encounters with the Greek god, see Wolfgang Schadewaldt, *Winckelmann und Rilke: Zwei Beschreibungen des Apollon* (Pfullingen: Verlag Günther Neske, 1968).

145 For a more detailed discussion of the challenges of translating the *Neue Gedichte*, see Luke Fischer, "Understanding through Translation: Rilke's *New Poems*."

("glüht") like a "Kandelaber"—another untranslatable word due to its double meaning in German. "Kandelaber" is cognate with the English "candelabrum"; however, in addition to naming a branched candleholder it can also refer to a certain kind of gas lamp that was prevalent in the streets of Paris during Rilke's time, and the subsequent lines of the poem primarily draw upon this latter meaning. Although the head is absent, the torso continues to shine like a lamp that is turned down— "zurückgeschraubt." The radiant gaze of the head is lost, but even so the torso still gazes, only a little less brightly. This image intensifies into an epiphany in the poem's conclusion.

Much of the remainder of the poem involves subjunctive formulations justifying the idea that the torso gazes (despite the missing head). However, this poetic argument is not abstract, but rather proceeds by way of incredibly vivid depictions of the specific curve and expressive character of the chest and loins. The radiant imagery serves to evoke the way in which the contours of the sculpture literally catch and deflect the light (Schmoll identifies in these descriptions the influence of Rodin's conception of *modelé*[146]). The reader, in attempting to imagine this torso, draws on recollected perceptions of Archaic and Classical sculptures that exhibit a similar expressivity and mastery of form.[147] The characterization of the smiling bend of the loins and dazzling curve of the chest recalls Rilke's statement in his monograph on Rodin that a hand can bark.[148] These descriptions also further explicate the manner in which the torso and the (missing) head are aspects of a single expression; the loins can smile because they express what was also expressed by Apollo's smiling mouth. In addition, a certain affirmation of sexuality and procreative powers is indicated, in that the smile moves toward the (missing) center of procreation ("zu jener Mitte, die die Zeugung trug"). The third verse (first tercet) further conveys the sculpture's intrinsic wholeness ("sonst stünde dieser Stein entstellt ...") and vividly portrays other aspects of its appearance—the shoulders' transparent ("durchsichtig") fall and the stone shimmering like a predator's coat.

The final tercet of this tightly constructed sonnet draws everything together. The work of art's capacity to manifest meaning through its

---

146 J. A. Schmoll, *Rodin-Studien*, 105ff. See the discussion of *modelé* in Chapter 2.
147 Ulrich Hausmann regards an Early Classical (previously not distinguished from the Archaic and bearing features of the Late Archaic style) torso of a youth (from Miletus, c. 480–470 BC) exhibited in the Louvre as a likely inspiration for Rilke's poem. Ulrich Hausmann, *Die Apollosonette Rilkes und ihre plastischen Urbilder*. Paul Böckmann disagrees with Hausmann and mentions alternative possibilities. See Böckmann, *Dichterische Wege der Subjektivierung*, 338, n. 50.
148 KA 4, 422.

sensible form has already been so masterfully conveyed that as a reader one feels as if one is standing directly before the sculpture. In *Wahrheit und Methode*, Gadamer discusses the concept of play as an aesthetic category (more accurately, as a category for a philosophy of art) and the power of the work of art to transform its appreciator.[149] In giving our attention to a work of art—in letting it work—new meanings, insights, and horizons are opened up. This transformative capacity of art is conveyed in striking terms in the final tercet of "Archaïscher Torso Apollos." The sculpture breaks out at every point like a star. This image gathers all the earlier images of light and further elaborates the wholeness of the work—its meaning is articulated and shines through every feature and place. Here it also becomes most evident that the descriptions of light do not solely concern the manner in which the carved stone catches and reflects light; the sculpture is characterized as productive of its own light like a star. In other words, the work of art institutes its own meaning, is illuminating. This capacity to transmit meaning is encapsulated in the final line through a reversal of intentional-directionality (a similar reversal was discussed earlier with respect to Rilke's animal poem, "Schwarze Katze" and these reversals are present in other ekphrastic poems such as "Die Fensterrose").[150] The sculpture looks at the viewer rather than vice versa, or, as Müller states, "the relationship between the viewer and the viewed artwork is reversed."[151] This is also the climactic formulation of the torso as revelatory of the gaze of the missing head. After a pregnant pause in the last line, the entire poem finds its culmination in the final terse sentence: "Du mußt dein Leben ändern [You must change your life]." In the artwork's mediation of an unprecedented meaning and horizon the viewer is brought to re-evaluate his or her life.[152] The sculpture mediates a *metanoia* or a deep change of mind. Moreover, it is the sculpture itself that seems to address the viewer ("du")—the "unheard-of" head of the first line "speaks" to the viewer through the torso—and to transport the viewer to a standpoint beyond the horizon of the everyday self. Finally, if the *poem* works for the reader, the reader in

---

149 Gadamer, *Wahrheit und Methode*, 116ff.; *Truth and Method*, 110ff.
150 Similar reversals also occur in poems that thematize human figures, such as the ending of "Begegnung in der Kastanien-Allee" (*KA 1*, 566). This theme of perceptual reversal is common to many of the "new poems" and, as was suggested in the previous chapter, is a thematization of an exceptional perception of things.
151 Müller, *Rainer Maria Rilkes "Neue Gedichte,"* 128.
152 For a philosophical evaluation of the poem as a personal call to live a richer and more meaningful existence in the context of the fragmented modern world, see Richard Eldridge, *Literature, Life, and Modernity* (New York: Columbia University Press, 2008), 114ff.

The *Neue Gedichte* as a Twofold Imagining of Things 291

turn becomes the "du."[153] In this case, Rilke's ekphrastic poem itself becomes an experience of the transformative power of art and that many readers feel this way about the poem is evinced by its enduring renown. The poetic sculpture dazzles the eye of the mind. It should almost go without saying that "Archaïscher Torso Apollos" conveys the twofoldness of the work of art in a manner that is impossible for generic abstract concepts.

Having considered human figures, natural beings and events, and works of art, it is fitting to conclude the discussion of Rilke's *Neue Gedichte* with a poem that thematizes a "thing" in the more limited sense of the word (in contrast to the broader meanings of a "being" or a "model" [in Rilke's sense] that have been primary) and more specifically, a human-made artifact or "object" of *technē*—a *Zeug*.

Rilke regarded "Der Ball" as the most accomplished of his *Dinggedichte* and it will be seen that even with regard to a plaything, a ball, it is not inappropriate to speak of a holistic twofold disclosure.[154] Although a ball, unlike a person or animal, is not self-expressive or animated, the poem vividly reveals the ball's meaning, function, and human significance. It discloses the ball's intrinsic characteristics as a work of *technē* or a *Zeug* (a tool or piece of equipment). The being of a chair, a table, a bike, a ball, can, in principle, only be understood if their human significance is taken into account—a bike is made for humans to ride, a table is for humans to place things on, etc. My interpretation of "Der Ball" is in the same spirit as Hamburger's view that the poem thematizes the "thing-character [*Dingsein*] of the ball, the ball-character [*Ballsein*] of the thing."[155] In contrast, however, I regard Heidegger's hermeneutic phenomenology of *das Zeug* as a more adequate horizon of interpretation than Husserl's phenomenological analyses, which often overlook the "*Zeug*-character" of *Zeuge* through limiting them to examples of perceptual objects.

The ball is not any kind of *Zeug*, it is a very specific kind of *Zeug*, namely a *Spielzeug* (a plaything or toy). To my knowledge, the best philosophical elucidation of the nature of play or *das Spiel* is Gadamer's hermeneutic-phenomenological analysis in *Wahrheit und Methode*. I will draw on Gadamer's conceptualization of *das Spiel* and Heidegger's understanding of *das Zeug*, in order to demonstrate how Rilke's poem accomplishes a revelation of the ball as a specific kind of *Spiel-Zeug*. I do not regard this approach as an imposition of foreign philosophical concepts onto Rilke's poetry; rather the poetry itself (as in the earlier examples) is intrinsically

---

153 See also William Waters' discussion of Rilke's use of pronouns and address. William Waters, *Poetry's Touch: On Lyric Address*, 86ff.
154 Elisabeth von Schmidt-Pauli, *Rainer Maria Rilke: Ein Gedenkbuch* (Stuttgart: Bürger Verlag, 1946), 20. See n. 157.
155 Hamburger, "Die phänomenologische Struktur der Dichtung Rilkes," 201.

phenomenological. My reading also shares much in common with Otto Olzien's ontological interpretation of "Der Ball" in his article, "R. M. Rilke: 'Der Ball.' Sprache und Ontologie." However, Olzien does not interpret the ball in hermeneutic-phenomenological terms.[156]

My hermeneutic-phenomenological interpretation contrasts strongly with many interpretations of "Der Ball," which treat the ball as a symbol. These readings almost totally overlook the poem's phenomenological character and thus evince a kind of hermeneutic violence. This is evident, for instance, in Berendt's interpretation and his disagreement with Rilke's own reading of the poem. Rilke says of "Der Ball," "Da habe ich gar nichts als das fast Unaussprechbare einer reinen Bewegung ausgesprochen [There I have articulated nothing but the almost unsayable character of a pure movement]."[157] Berendt treats this statement suspiciously, as though Rilke did not really mean what he says, and proceeds to interpret the ball as a "symbol ... of a human being."[158]

Although I think the poem does say more than the almost inexpressible character of a pure movement, the thematization of movement is central to the text and my interpretation is in the spirit of Rilke's *literal* interpretation. Moreover, the larger context of Rilke's statement also suggests that he viewed the poem as a thematization of the ball itself.[159] As a general outline of my interpretation, it can be stated that the poem presents the movement of a ball in a manner and context that reveal its essence as a throwable plaything. Gadamer speaks of the essentiality of *Bewegung* or movement in playing a game.[160] Rilke's poem enacts for the imagination the movement of the

---

156 Otto H. Olzien, "R. M. Rilke: 'Der Ball.' Sprache und Ontologie," *Germanisch-Romanische Monatsschrift* 28 (1978): 183–93.
157 Elisabeth von Schmidt-Pauli, *Rainer Maria Rilke: Ein Gedenkbuch*, 20. This statement is recorded by Elisabeth von Schmidt-Pauli from a conversation she had with Rilke while walking through English gardens in the autumn of 1918. The whole passage is of interest with regard to Rilke's *sachliches Sagen* and further speaks against Berendt's symbolic interpretation. Rilke is quoted as saying the following while pointing to a tree: "Sehen Sie – das ist es, was ich will und nichts anderes: ich möchte diesen Baum so sagen, daß nur noch der Baum in meinen Worten spräche, so wie er ist, ohne irgend etwas von Rilke hinzuzufügen. Mein Gedicht "Der Ball" ist mir in dieser Weise ganz gelungen. Da habe ich gar nichts als das fast Unaussprechbare einer reinen Bewegung ausgesprochen – und darum ist es mein bestes Gedicht."
158 Berendt, *Rainer Maria Rilkes Neue Gedichte: Versuch einer Deutung*, 345. There are, of course, "ball poems" by Rilke which must be read symbolically, such as the later poem Gadamer chose as an epigraph for *Wahrheit und Methode*, "Solang du Selbstgeworfnes fängst, ist alles ..." However, this does not hold for "Der Ball" in the *Neue Gedichte*.
159 See n. 157.
160 Gadamer, *Truth and Method*, 104ff.; *Wahrheit und Methode*, 109ff.

ball *im Spiel* (in play), and this movement of the ball is, in fact, what lies at the heart of a *Ballspiel* (ball-play). Moreover, as an axe is most itself when being used to chop, a ball is most itself when it is "in play" or *im Spiel*. As a *Spielzeug*, playing is its *raison d'être* or final cause. In describing the ball in the state and context of play or *im Spiel* the poem discloses the essence of the ball as a *Spielzeug*.

"Der Ball" opens with the ball being thrown and closes with it being caught. These two moments frame the text and, as in other *Dinggedichte*, the poem's temporal unfolding imitates the thing's movement. The text is basically one long sentence that traces the movement of the ball.

Der Ball

Du Runder, der das Warme aus zwei Händen
im Fliegen, oben, fortgiebt, sorglos wie
sein Eigenes; was in den Gegenständen
nicht bleiben kann, zu unbeschwert für sie,

zu wenig Ding und doch noch Ding genug,
um nicht aus allem draußen Aufgereihten
unsichtbar plötzlich in uns einzugleiten:
das glitt in dich, du zwischen Fall und Flug

noch Unentschlossener: der, wenn er steigt,
als hätte er ihn mit hinaufgehoben,
den Wurf entführt und freiläßt –, und sich neigt
und einhält und den Spielenden von oben
auf einmal eine neue Stelle zeigt,
sie ordnend wie zu einer Tanzfigur,

um dann, erwartet und erwünscht von allen,
rasch, einfach, kunstlos, ganz Natur,
dem Becher hoher Hände zuzufallen.[161]

---

[161] "The Ball// You round-one, which gives away in its flight/ above, the warmth from two hands, carefreely as/ if its own; that which in objects/ cannot remain, too unburdened for them,// hardly a thing and yet still thing enough/ for it not, from all that is ordered outside,/ to slip into us invisibly:/ that slipped into you, who between fall and flight// are still undecided: which, when it climbs,/ as though it had lifted the throw as well,/ abducts and sets free –, and inclines/ and holds and shows the players from above/ all at once a new position,/ coordinating them like a choreography,// in order then, expected and desired by all,/ swift, simple, artless, completely nature,/ to fall to the cup of high hands." *KA 1*, 583–4.

To begin with (following the title) the ball is addressed in the second person. This may appear inappropriate or strange as a ball is an inanimate thing. Is this then a form of anthropomorphism? Is the ball a symbol for the human? No, in its function as a plaything for people, a human significance is intrinsic to its being. Roundness is a characteristic of many balls; this property is connected to a ball's "throwability" and "catchability"; it makes the ball easy to hold, throw, and catch. Thus, the poem appropriately names the ball, the "round one" ("Runder"). As throwable and catchable the ball is shaped for human hands. It absorbs the warmth of the hands that throw it and loses this warmth in flight, as is described by the first two lines. While the poem thus depicts a physical process, there is an additional dimension to the poetic evocation. The ball gives away this warmth "carefreely as if its own" ("sorglos wie sein Eigenes"). This release of warmth is not only physical but also affective, as, for example, in the description of a person as "warm-hearted." Is this not a case of anthropomorphic projection? A ball, as aforementioned, bears an intrinsic human significance; its very being derives from a human need, namely, the need for play. A ball is thus not an indifferent object; rather as a *play*thing it is part of the tissue of human lives and is essentially connected to *the spirit of playing* that it facilitates. The ball acquires a psychological or affective significance that is not merely a projection onto an indifferent object but connected to the fact that the ball plays an essential role in joining human beings in the activity and mood of playing. The ball is not an object or a simple correlate of consciousness, but a being whose significance lies in its references to many other things (in its *Verweisungszusammenhang* or referential nexus[162]) and in its place and role in the context of *playing*.

The remainder of the first verse and the second verse thematize the lightness of the ball in a twofold sense—physical lightness and inner lightness ("light-hearted"—"unbeschwert"). The ball's physical lightness is essential to its being. Were a ball too heavy, it could not be thrown and would thereby no longer be a ball. Were it too light, it would float like a helium balloon and also cease to be a ball. The ball is relatively light; it is light enough to be thrown but heavy enough to fall; it is substantial enough to be a "thing" but unlike heavier, earth-bound *Zeuge* and things (chairs, tables, brooms, stones, trees, etc.) it is almost insubstantial. It embodies what is "zu wenig Ding und doch noch Ding genug ... [hardly a thing and yet still thing enough]." In reference to Rilke's emphasis on the poem's presentation of movement, it can also be specified that this relative lightness grants the ball its distinctive mobility or *Beweglichkeit*, which enables it to "fly" and to fall—to move,

---

162 Heidegger, *Sein und Zeit*, 66ff.

The *Neue Gedichte* as a Twofold Imagining of Things   295

so to speak, between earth and sky (see the discussion of the third verse below).

The thematization of the lightness of the ball is also an elaboration of its "carefree [sorglos]" nature, as indicated by the semi-colon in the third line of the first verse. This affective dimension pertaining to the ball is intimately connected to the ball's physical lightness (the two senses of lightness are not distinguished by the poem but presented as a unity) and its significance in the context of playing or what Gadamer calls "the ease of play [*die Leichtigkeit des Spiels*]" and literally the "lightness" ("Leichtigkeit") of play.[163] Playing is an activity that has a feeling of effortlessness. It does not involve the ardor of work, nor is it a mere passivity or laziness. According to Gadamer, play is experienced as a kind of "Entlastung" or release.[164] In other words, it is a leisure.

The second and third lines of the second verse are especially cryptic. They can, however, be deciphered in relation to the polarities already mentioned. It should be recalled that these lines are a further elaboration of the unnamed "something" ("was") that is announced in the first verse. More specifically, these lines indicate how this "something" is "still thing enough" ("noch Ding genug"). In other words, they elaborate the relation of this "something" to the "earthly" or "thingly" pole. We are told that this "something" is thingly enough such that it could not pass into us "invisibly" ("unsichtbar") "from all that is ordered outside" ("aus allem draußen Aufgereihten"). Thus, it is neither purely spiritual or invisible nor is it entirely physical. It is present in other things and the surrounding natural world (I think it makes sense to interpret the "draußen Aufgereihten" as a reference to Nature) but it is almost insubstantial. Olzien's interpretation of the unnamed "something" as ultimately a reference to "movement" as a quality of things in relation to gravity (in line with the older Aristotelian view of movement) seems convincing to me.[165] However, it would perhaps be even more fitting to speak of "mobility" (the capacity for movement) rather than "movement" (*Beweglichkeit* rather than *Bewegung*). To say that the unnamed "something" is a capacity for movement (connected to the aforementioned relative lightness) that is present in other things but cannot remain in them ("nicht bleiben kann") and is manifest in a special way in the ball makes sense of the various characterizations of the unnamed "something." While this mobility could not remain in other things or pass into us invisibly, the final line of the second stanza states that it passed into the ball ("das glitt in dich"). The ball is thus related to the wider natural order but is an especial expression

---

163 Gadamer, *Truth and Method*, 105; *Wahrheit und Methode*, 110.
164 Ibid.
165 Otto H. Olzien, "R. M. Rilke: 'Der Ball.' Sprache und Ontologie," 189ff.

of a shared mobility. In so far as the ball manifests something that also belongs to the order and lawfulness of Nature, these lines suggest an esoteric connection between the ball as a work of *technē* and *physis* (this view is supported by the final lines of the poem; see below).[166]

The enjambment between the second and third stanza brilliantly conveys the essential mobility of the ball in relation to the polarity of rising and falling—"du zwischen Fall und Flug// noch Unentschlossener [you, who between fall and flight// are still undecided]." Here the ball's necessary lightness and heaviness, in connection to its capacity to be thrown and to fall, are thematized more explicitly. The ball is continually transitioning from a state of flying (rising) to falling. The unpredictability in the ball's direction of flight and its ultimate landing place, which is connected to the freedom of the thrower and the role of the wind and other factors, is brilliantly articulated. This unpredictability is also essential to a game or play. While playing the players do not know how things will play themselves out. The ball in its dynamic unpredictability is thus described as the "still undecided" or "still unresolved one" ("noch Unentschlossener"). Due to this essential unpredictability, there is a sense in which the players not only play with the ball but are played by the ball. The ball lifts up, so to speak, the "throw" in its flight ("wenn er steigt,/ als hätte er ihn mit hinaufgehoben …"); the players follow the ball upward, as if carried by it, and are drawn to anticipate its uncertain landing place. Once it is in flight the ball in a sense directs the players; they anticipate its movement and *follow it*. This is wonderfully articulated in the statement that the ball shows the players a new position ("eine neue Stelle zeigt"). The participation of all the players in the game (their continuous anticipation of the ball's movement) and its dynamic character are vividly portrayed in the image of the players being directed by the ball as in a dance choreography ("Tanzfigur"). What the poem here enacts for the imagination corresponds exactly to Gadamer's hermeneutic analysis of *das Spiel*. First, Gadamer states, "all playing is a being-played. The attraction of a game, the fascination it exerts, consists precisely in the fact that the game masters the players."[167] That the ball, or play of the ball, masters the players is precisely what is conveyed by the aforementioned lines. Second, Gadamer relates this point to the exemplary character of the ball and states that, "ball games will be with us forever because the ball is freely mobile in every direction, appearing to do surprising things

---

166 This might be fruitfully compared to Heidegger's interpretation of the ancient Greek conception of *technē* and *physis* as two kinds of *poiesis*. See Heidegger, "Die Frage nach der Technik," in *GA* 7 (2000 [1953]), 7–36.
167 Gadamer, *Truth and Method*, 106; *Wahrheit und Methode*, 112.

The *Neue Gedichte* as a Twofold Imagining of Things   297

of its own accord."[168] This characterization is so apt that Gadamer could have even been thinking of Rilke's poem "Der Ball" when he wrote these words. At this point, it is also worthwhile to mention some distinctive formal characteristics of "Der Ball." The poem is basically an expanded sonnet. It begins with the octet of two quatrains and is followed by a sestet (the verse currently under discussion). However, the poem does not end here as a traditional sonnet would. The sestet is followed by an additional tercet. The fact that the poem does not follow the predictable sonnet form matches the unpredictability of the ball's flight.

The final verse (tercet) describes all the players as captivated by the game and wanting the ball ("erwartet und erwünscht von allen"). The ball is the center of the game and to play a game is to be drawn into it. The poem's single long sentence, which suggests the continuity of the ball's movement, begins with the ball being launched and now ends with a catch. Both moments involve an essential connection between the hands and the shape and weight of the ball. The time in which a ball is caught is incredibly swift. The end of the poem slows down this time, so to speak, such that it is revealed more clearly (even though the tercet is suitably short and quick in relation to the text as a whole). The ball swiftly and simply falls to the cup—the receptive gesture—of two hands and is described as wholly nature—"kunstlos, ganz Natur." These lines suggest the perfect manner in which the ball and the hands are fitted to one another and the ball's observation of the natural law of gravity.

"Der Ball" presents the ball in a state of play, enacts its typical movement from being thrown to being caught, and thematizes the ball's essential mobility. Moreover, the ball is revealed in its relational context—what Heidegger calls the *Verweisungszusammenhang* that is intrinsic to the Being of a *Zeug*; the ball is articulated in its relation to the players, to the air, to gravity, and to human hands. The ball's *raison d'être* as a *play*thing is revealed in a manner that corresponds directly to Gadamer's analysis of *das Spiel*. The poem performs for the reader's imagination the significance of the ball as a distinctive *Spielzeug*; the ball's essence is disclosed in a dynamic and integral way.

Conclusion of Chapter

This chapter has demonstrated the distinctive ways in which Rilke's *Dinggedichte* foster a twofold disclosure of things for the reader's imagination. This twofold disclosure is continuous with the twofold perception that was articulated in Chapters 2 and 3 and is its ultimate linguistic articulation. In other words, the poems facilitate a twofold

---

168 Gadamer, *Truth and Method*, 106; *Wahrheit und Methode*, 111.

imaginative vision. The consideration of Nature in Rilke's *Neue Gedichte* followed most directly from the main discussion in the preceding chapters. In addition, it was revealed how human figures, artworks, and artifacts are linguistically "realized" in Rilke's poems as distinctive variations of a twofold seeing. Ultimately, the diverse poems can be regarded as individuated articulations of *Weltinnenraum*; they reveal both the broad scope and the specificity of twofold vision.

Conclusion

By way of conclusion I will first recapitulate in broad outlines the central argument that runs through the present work.

Chapter 1 demonstrated that the problem of dualism is more than a merely theoretical problem. A merely theoretical response to dualism fails to address the existential and experiential dimension of this problem. After revealing the necessity of an experiential resolution of dualism, it was shown that only a phenomenological approach can adequately articulate the character of experience, and thus an experiential approach to the problem of dualism must proceed phenomenologically. The second main section of Chapter 1 was devoted to a phenomenological analysis of the everyday perception of the individual human Other. This explication served a number of purposes. First, it distinguished a structure of seeing (and understanding), in which the sensible and the intelligible, passivity and activity, are closely intertwined. Concretely, it was demonstrated that the individual Other is disclosed as a twofold haecceity (an individuated unity of the sensible and the intelligible). Second, this explication served a propaedeutic purpose. It undermined and corrected common dualistic conceptions and thus opened up the possibility of a deeper and wider non-dualistic disclosure. This phenomenological consideration was directed toward a non-dualistic disclosure that is close and familiar, that is implicit to our everyday encounters with Others but often misrepresented and misunderstood.

Chapters 2 and 3 broadened and deepened the discussion in Chapter 1. In the consideration of Rilke's approach to dualism, a poetic and artistic manner of being-in-the-world, and an *exceptional* vision of things, in particular of Nature, were explicated. Inspired by the example of visual artists, Rilke undertook a *praxis* of seeing that is not common or implicit to everyday life (and differs from a philosophical methodology), and this *praxis* facilitated a twofold disclosure that includes mystical aspects. Mystical experience is *uncommon* or *extra-mundane* as it involves a revelation of the numinous or spiritual that is not ordinarily given. However, Rilke's vision is not mystical in an other-worldly sense; rather it is non-dualistic. This consideration of Rilke demonstrated a kind of seeing, in which the visible and the invisible are disclosed in a holistic manner.

Chapter 4 discussed a number of poems from Rilke's *Neue Gedichte*. Poetic language was contrasted with conceptual language—the distinctive language of philosophy and *Wissenschaft*. A number of ways were demonstrated, in which poetic language surpasses conceptual language in its ability to facilitate a twofold disclosure. The poems foster a twofold disclosure of things for the *imagination*, which is able to present the sensible (virtually or for the mind's eye) and the intelligible in their unity. In contrast, conceptual language remains abstractly universal. Rilke's *Dinggedichte* cultivate a twofold imaginative vision that is continuous with the twofold perception articulated in Chapters 2 and 3 and its ultimate linguistic translation and expression. (In broader terms, twofold perception and twofold imagination mutually inform one another and are two sides of twofold seeing.)

At this point a qualification should be made regarding the twofold vision of things in the poems of the *Neue Gedichte*. It is possible (even likely) that not all of the *Dinggedichte* maintain the standard of a *sachliches Sagen* and twofold disclosure as articulated in the present work. Nevertheless, *The Poet as Phenomenologist* has explicated numerous examples in which Rilke's vision and poetry do meet this standard. In principle, only one instance of a twofold vision is required in order to prove its genuine possibility. However, as twofold vision is individuated, the demonstration of diverse instances enriches understanding in essential ways. According to my estimation, Rilke's *Neue Gedichte* remains unsurpassed in the variety and simultaneous depth and specificity of its twofold poetry.

The present work was introduced through a discussion of the crisis of philosophy, particularly with reference to the Heideggerian view of the "end of metaphysics" and the "end of philosophy." Turning to a poet in order to address this crisis is also in keeping with Heidegger's later project. However, I have turned to Rilke (rather than Hölderlin) and my interpretation of Rilke's vision is distinctive and self-legitimating. In particular, I have demonstrated the significance of Rilke's vision in his middle period as a response to the "philosophical" problem of dualism.

A number of ways have been indicated and elaborated in which this poetic vision surpasses ordinary conceptual thought and phenomenological reflection on mundane experience. While phenomenology is not limited to the horizon of the everyday, and already, in the case of Husserl, phenomenology involves an *exceptional* standpoint that reveals the world in an entirely new light, much of the "material" for phenomenological reflections on perception is derived from the everyday world of perception. A phenomenological articulation of the appearance of objects or even of the *Verweisungszusammenhang* of *Zeuge* (*Sein und Zeit*) sheds new light on the familiar world. In contrast, Rilke's poetic vision, especially in its epiphanic and mystical aspects, opens up the horizon of a "phenomenology of the exceptional" or, more specifically, a phenomenology of epiphanic vision. This kind of vision involves a *praxis* that facilitates a transformation of the entire character of perception and overcomes dualism in a manner that is not otherwise possible. It was also demonstrated that the poetic imagination, the thinking articulated in poetic language, surpasses conceptual thought in its capacity to evoke a twofold disclosure of things. In these two ways, *The Poet as Phenomenologist* has shown how poetic vision exceeds the traditional means of philosophy (conceptual thought) for addressing the problem of dualism. In a certain respect, the conclusion to the present work can be compared to the conclusion of Schelling's *System of Transcendental Idealism* (*System des transscendentalen Idealismus*), in which Schelling demonstrates that art offers the final resolution of a philosophical problem. More specifically, I have argued that poetry and poetic vision resolve a core aspect of the philosophical problem of dualism—that the solution to a philosophical problem is poetic, even if it requires philosophy for its formulation.

It is worthwhile to repeat that I do not regard this poetic approach to the problem of dualism as a comprehensive solution to this problem. It is possible that my approach will give rise to more questions than answers. If this turns out to be the case, this would only please me, as questions invite original thinking. Nevertheless, I will reiterate the claim that *The Poet as Phenomenologist* positively demonstrates the experiential dimension of dualism as well as an experiential answer to this problem. In the non-dualistic experience of twofold vision the world reveals itself in a new light; the relation between the sensible and the intelligible, the visible and the invisible, the inner and the outer, passivity and activity, is transformed. This transformed experience of the world implies and calls for a non-dualistic way of thinking. This exceptional disclosure, which is not made possible through a philosophical methodology (in any traditional sense), is thereby philosophically significant.

Philosophy is thus called to transform itself in order to resolve its own problems. I have not sought to assess the extent in which this transmutation has already taken place, either in the thought of the later Heidegger or in the works of post-modern thinkers that have challenged and blurred traditional distinctions between philosophical and poetic language.[1] Such an inquiry would require a separate monograph (or

---

1   See, for instance, Jacques Derrida, "White Mythology," in *Margins of Philosophy* [*Marges de la philosophie*], trans. Alan Bass (Chicago: University of Chicago Press, 1982 [1971]), 207–72.

two). I sought to undertake a dialogue between philosophy and poetry, in which conceptual language (the traditional language of philosophy) and poetic language confront and mutually illuminate one another. Here I do not wish to elaborate in detail how I think philosophy is called to transform itself. However, philosophy can certainly learn from *poetic and artistic vision* and from *poetic language*. The discussion of moods and atmospheres also drew further attention (in line with the work of other phenomenologists) to the importance of "extra-rational" factors for understanding and insight.

Nevertheless, philosophy (or "post-philosophy") cannot simply become poetry, otherwise it loses an independent identity and ceases to exist. Moreover, philosophy clearly offers insights that cannot be substituted by poetry. This can be indicated through a reflection on the present work. The approach to Rilke was premised on the idea that his poetry contains an *implicit* philosophical significance and importantly, a philosophical significance that is at the same time intrinsically *poetic*. For the latter reason its "philosophical" significance cannot be translated into concepts without remainder. A methodology was required that recognizes the untranslatability and irreducibility of poetic vision and is at the same time *philosophically* informed. Thus, the present work executed a *philosophically* informed criticism of *poetry*. In taking this approach it was possible to make *explicit* the *implicit philosophical* significance of Rilke's *poetry*. Hence, at this point the value of a *philosophically* informed poetry criticism can be affirmed. While the main endeavor was to indicate the philosophical value of Rilke's poetry for the overcoming of dualism, in practice it has also been demonstrated that philosophy plays a crucial role in making this significance explicit.

Moreover, poetry and the arts are also in a time of crisis as indicated by the popularity of the thesis of the "end of art," which originates with Hegel but has been adapted to the contemporary context.[2] The value and role of the arts are no longer self-evident and philosophical reflection on art thus assumes an important role. Although my main aim has been to demonstrate the importance of poetry for "philosophy," philosophy and poetry clearly require one another in distinctive ways.

At the very least I hope that *The Poet as Phenomenologist* has served to demonstrate the importance of undertaking and maintaining a genuine dialogue between poetry and philosophy—a dialogue in which both partners in the conversation are open to being extended and transformed by the other. In terms of the dialogue carried out in this work, it has been shown (with respect to the problem of dualism)

---

2   See, for instance, Arthur C. Danto, "The End of Art," in *The Philosophical Disenfranchisement of Art* (New York: Columbia University Press, 1986). See also Luke Fischer, "Goethe contra Hegel: The Question of the End of Art."

that if philosophy is to remain true to its constitutive eros for truth, then it must undergo a transformation in its essence, with regard to which poetry has something to say. This was demonstrated through the example of the middle work of Rainer Maria Rilke.

Epilogue

> ... the separation of poet and thinker is only apparent and to the disadvantage of both ...[1]
> —Novalis

While *The Poet as Phenomenologist* has focused on the significance of poetry for philosophy, it is worthwhile to add a few remarks on the significance of philosophy for poetry (as a creative praxis). Philosophy is in certain respects inconducive to the art of writing poetry. Philosophical language tends to be abstract and universal, whereas poetry has need of the particular. For this reason, history, anthropology, science, etc. may be of more value to poetry than philosophy, as they offer more *specific empirical* content. Philosophy in contrast focuses on *formal* or *abstract universality*, and *abstract universality* does not for the most part make good poetry.[2] Poetry, in my opinion, is alive in the *details*. However, while this is the case, poetry and art become fairly insignificant from a broader perspective if they *solely* focus on the *details*. Without a broader and more universal orientation the details become random and contingent. Poetry that is only concerned with the particular is as remote from great poetry as didactic or abstract poetry that reproduces philosophical content in an inferior manner to philosophy. To my mind, great poetry *lives in the particulars* but in particulars that are presented in such a way that they reveal a *substantial and universal content*—details that in concert reveal a larger vision. Philosophy is of significance to poetry in precisely this respect as philosophy concerns itself with the large and important themes. A

---

1 Novalis, *Novalis Schriften: Die Werke von Friedrich von Hardenberg*, vol. 3, 406, Nr. 717.
2 This is not to say that poetry should not take on grand themes or address philosophical matters. It is the distinctive way in which poetry explores these themes that is crucial. Rilke's *Duineser Elegien*, Dante's *Divina Commedia*, and Goethe's *Faust* are three examples of supreme works of poetry that address large ideas.

poet need not *be* a philosopher, but poetry benefits from a broader, at least implicit, philosophical orientation. Without such an orientation poetry can be carried away by the mere contingency of particulars. Rather than revealing the *universal in the particular, the intelligible in the sensible*, poetry without any "philosophical" orientation can incline toward *mere particularity* and *idiosyncrasy*.

Although Rilke is a widely appreciated poet, it is worthwhile to mention his significance with respect to the poetic value of philosophy. In her book *Philosophie der Dichter* (*Philosophy of Poets*) Hamburger rightly refers to Rilke's poetry as occupying the place of a philosophy.[3] In other words, Rilke's poetry is philosophical while never ceasing to be poetry. Rilke has no separate philosophy but his poetry is philosophical. For this reason, Rilke's poetry contains a philosophical breadth and depth, without which it would be less significant. A poet need not be a poet as well as a philosopher (such as Coleridge or Novalis), but an implicitly philosophical orientation or an interest in important philosophical questions benefits poetry. In short, while the overall argument of this book concerns the philosophical importance of poetry, I am of the view that philosophy, broadly speaking, is also of benefit to poetry.

---

3 Käte Hamburger, *Philosophie der Dichter: Novalis, Schiller, Rilke*, 268.

Bibliography

Agamben, Giorgio. *The Open: Man and Animal*. Translated by Kevin Attell. Stanford, CA: Stanford University Press, 2004.
Amrine, Frederick. "The Music of the Organism: Uexküll, Merleau-Ponty, Zuckerkandl, and Deleuze as Goethean Ecologists in Search of a New Paradigm." *Goethe Yearbook* 21 (2015).
Bachelard, Gaston. *The Poetics of Reverie: Childhood, Language, and the Cosmos*. Translated by Daniel Russell. Boston, MA: Beacon Press, 1971.
Badt, Kurt. *Die Kunst Cézannes*. Munich: Prestel-Verlag, 1956.
Barfield, Owen. *Poetic Diction: A Study in Meaning*. Middletown, CT: Wesleyan University Press, 1973 [1928].
—*Saving the Appearances: A Study in Idolatry*. Middletown, CT: Wesleyan University Press, 1988 [1957].
—*Speaker's Meaning*. Middletown, CT: Wesleyan University Press, 1967.
Bate, Jonathan. *Romantic Ecology: Wordsworth and the Environmental Tradition*. London: Routledge, 1991.
Baudelaire, Charles. *The Flowers of Evil: A Selection*. Edited by Marthiel Mathews and Jackson Mathews. New York: New Directions Publishing Corporation, 1955.
Beiser, Frederick. *The Romantic Imperative: The Concept of Early German Romanticism*. Cambridge, MA: Harvard University Press, 2003.
Berendt, Hans. *Rainer Maria Rilkes Neue Gedichte: Versuch einer Deutung*. Bonn: H. Bouvier u. Co. Verlag, 1957.
Bermes, Christian, Wolfhart Henckmann, and Heinz Leonardy, eds. *Vernunft und Gefühl: Schelers Phänomenologie des emotionalen Lebens*. Würzburg: Königshausen & Neumann, 2003.
Betz, Maurice. *Rilke in Frankreich: Erinnerungen, Briefe, Dokumente*. Vienna: Herbert Reichner Verlag, 1938.
Bishop, Paul. "Rilke: Thought and Mysticism." In *The Cambridge Companion to Rilke*, edited by Karen Leeder and Robert Vilain, 159–73. Cambridge: Cambridge University Press, 2010.
Blake, William. *Selected Poetry*. Oxford: Oxford University Press, 1998.
Böckmann, Paul. *Dichterische Wege der Subjektivität: Studien zur deutschen Literatur im 19. und 20. Jahrhundert*. Tübingen: Max Niemeyer Verlag, 1999.
Boehm, Gottfried. *Paul Cézanne: Montagne Sainte-Victoire*. Frankfurt am Main: Insel Verlag, 1988.
Böhme, Gernot. *Für eine ökologische Naturästhetik*. Frankfurt am Main: Suhrkamp, 1989.

Bibliography

—*Atmosphäre: Essays zur neuen Ästhetik*. Frankfurt am Main: Suhrkamp, 1995.
—*Anmutungen: Über das Atmosphärische*. Ostfildern vor Stuttgart: Edition Tertium Arcaden, 1998.
—*Aisthetik: Vorlesungen über Ästhetik als allgemeine Wahrnehmungslehre*. Munich: Wilhelm Fink Verlag, 2001.
Böhme, Gernot and Gregor Schiemann, eds. *Phänomenologie der Natur*. Frankfurt am Main: Suhrkamp, 1997.
Böschenstein, Bernhard. "R. M . R.s französische Gedichte." In *Rilke – ein europäischer Dichter aus Prag*, edited by Peter Demetz, Joachim W. Storck, and Hans Dieter Zimmermann, 191–200. Würzburg: Königshausen & Neumann, 1998.
Bradley, Brigitte L. *R. M. Rilkes Neue Gedichte: Ihr zyklisches Gefüge*. Bern: Francke Verlag, 1967.
Buchanan, Brett. *Onto-Ethologies: The Animal Environments of Uexküll, Heidegger, Merleau-Ponty, and Deleuze*. Albany, NY: SUNY Press, 2008.
Caputo, John D. *The Mystical Element in Heidegger's Thought*. New York: Fordham University Press, 1986.
Carbone, Mauro. *The Thinking of the Sensible: Merleau-Ponty's A-Philosophy*. Evanston, IL: Northwestern University Press, 2004.
Cassirer, Ernst. *The Philosophy of Symbolic Forms: Volume III: The Phenomenology of Knowledge*. Translated by Ralph Manheim. New Haven, CT: Yale University Press, 1957.
Coriando, Paola-Ludovika. *Affektenlehre und Phänomenologie der Stimmungen: Wege einer Ontologie und Ethik des Emotionalen*. Frankfurt am Main: Vittorio Klostermann, 2002.
Cox, Richard Francis. *Figures of Transformation: Rilke and the Example of Valéry*. London: University of London, 1979.
Danto, Arthur C. "The End of Art." In *The Philosophical Disenfranchisement of Art*. New York: Columbia University Press, 1986.
Derrida, Jacques. "White Mythology." In *Margins of Philosophy* [*Marges de la philosophie*], trans. Alan Bass, 207–72. Chicago: University of Chicago Press, 1982 [1971].
Doran, Michael, ed. *Conversations with Cézanne*. Translated by Julie Lawrence Cochran. Introduction by Richard Shiff. Berkeley, CA: University of California Press, 2001.
Driscoll, Kári. *Toward a Poetics of Animality: Hofmannsthal, Rilke, Pirandello, Kafka*. PhD diss., Columbia University, New York, 2014.
Eckhart, Meister. *Die deutschen Werke*. Volume 1. Translated by Josef Quint. Stuttgart: 1958.
Eldridge, Richard. *Literature, Life, and Modernity*. New York: Columbia University Press, 2008.
Eliot, T. S. *The Complete Poems and Plays*. London: Faber and Faber, 1969.
Engel, Manfred. "Nachwort [Afterword]." In *Die Aufzeichnungen des Malte Laurids Brigge*, by Rainer Maria Rilke, 319–50. Stuttgart: Philipp Reclam, 1997.
Engel, Manfred, ed. *Rilke-Handbuch*. Stuttgart: J. B. Metzler, 2004.
Engel, Manfred and Dieter Lamping, eds. *Rilke und die Weltliteratur*. Düsseldorf: Artemis und Winkler, 1999.
Engelhardt, Hartmut. *Der Versuch, wirklich zu sein: Zu Rilkes sachlichem Sagen*. Frankfurt am Main: Suhrkamp, 1973.
Eppelsheimer, Rudolf. *Rilkes larische Landschaft: Eine Deutung des Gesamtwerkes mit besonderem Bezug auf die mittlere Periode*. Stuttgart: Verlag Freies Geistes Leben, 1975.

Faivre, Antoine. *Access to Western Esotericism.* Albany, NY: SUNY Press, 1994.
Fick, Monicka. *Sinnenwelt und Weltseele: Der psychophysische Monismus in der Literatur der Jahrhundertwende.* Tübingen: Max Niemeyer Verlag, 1993.
Fiedler, Konrad. *Schriften zur Kunst.* Volume 1. Edited by Gottfried Boehm and Karlheinz Stierle. Munich: Wilhelm Fink Verlag, 1991.
Fingerhut, Karl-Heinz. *Das Kreatürliche im Werke Rainer Maria Rilkes: Untersuchung zur Figur des Tieres.* Bonn: H. Bouvier u. Co. Verlag, 1970.
Fischer, Luke. "Perception as Inspiration: Rilke and the *New Poems.*" *Agenda* (Special Rilke Issue) 42, nos. 3–4 (2007): 170–83.
—"Goethe contra Hegel: The Question of the End of Art." *Goethe Yearbook* 18 (2011): 127–58.
—"Owen Barfield and Rudolf Steiner: The Poetic and Esoteric Imagination." *Literature and Aesthetics* 21, no. 1 (2011): 136–58.
—"Animalising Art: Rainer Maria Rilke and Franz Marc." *Australasian Journal of Ecocriticism and Cultural Ecology* 3 (2013): 45–60; http://www.nla.gov.au/openpublish/index.php/aslec-anz/article/view/2884/3820
—"Die Animalisierung der Kunst: Rainer Maria Rilke und Franz Marc." In *Mythos-Geist-Kultur: Festschrift zum 60. Geburtstag von Christoph Jamme*, edited by Kerstin Andermann and Andreas Jürgens, 335–48. Munich: Wilhelm Fink Verlag, 2013.
—"Understanding through Translation: Rilke's *New Poems.*" In *Perspectives on Literature and Translation: Creation, Circulation, Reception*, edited by Brian Nelson and Brigid Maher, 56–72. New York: Routledge, 2013.
—*Paths of Flight.* North Fitzroy, VIC: Black Pepper Publishing, 2013.
—"A Poetic Phenomenology of the Temperate Seasons." *Environment, Space, Place* 6, no. 1 (2014): 7–32.
—"Metaphor and the Poetic Origin of Meaning." In *On Meaning: The Making of Civic Sense*, edited by Jose Ciprut (under review).
Fischer, Luke and Dalia Nassar, eds. "Goethe and Environmentalism." Special Section of the *Goethe Yearbook* 22 (2015).
Förster, Eckart. *Die 25 Jahre der Philosophie: Eine systematische Rekonstruktion.* Frankfurt am Main: Vittorio Klostermann, 2011.
Forsting, Brigitte. "Rainer Maria Rilke: Blaue Hortensie." In *Wege zum Gedicht*, edited by Rupert Hirschenauer and Albrecht Weber, 283–7. Munich: Schnell und Steiner, 1956.
Frank, Manfred. *Einführung in die frühromantische Ästhetik.* Frankfurt am Main: Suhrkamp, 1989.
—*Unendliche Annäherung: Die Anfänge der philosophischen Frühromantik.* Frankfurt am Main: Suhrkamp, 1997.
Fülleborn, Ulrich. *Besitzen als besässe man nicht: Besitzdenken und seine Alternativen in der Literatur.* Frankfurt am Main: Insel Verlag, 1995.
Gadamer, Hans-Georg. *Wahrheit und Methode.* Tübingen: J. C. B. Mohr (Siebeck), 1990 [1960].
—*Truth and Method.* Translation revised by Joel Weinsheimer and Donald G. Marshall. New York: Continuum, 1999.
Gasquet, Joachim. *Joachim Gasquet's Cézanne: A Memoir with Conversations.* Translated by Christopher Pemberton. London: Thames and Hudson, 1991.
Goethe, Johann Wolfgang von. *Theory of Colours.* Translated by Charles Lock Eastlake. London: Frank Cass & Co., 1967.
—*Sämtliche Werke nach Epochen seines Schaffens.* Edited by Karl Richter et al. Munich: Carl Hanser Verlag, 1985–1998.

—*Scientific Studies*. Translated by Douglas Miller. Princeton, NJ: Princeton University Press, 1994.

Gosetti-Ferencei, Anna Jennifer. *The Ecstatic Quotidian: Phenomenological Sightings in Modern Literature and Art*. University Park, PA: The Pennsylvania State University Press, 2007.

Grünbein, Durs. "Ein kleines blaues Mädchen 'Das Karussell': Ein Rilke-Manuskript im Marbacher Literaturarchiv." In *Denkbilder und Schaustücke: Das Literaturmuseum der Moderne: Marbacher Katalog 60*, 95–134. Marbach: Deutsches Literaturarchiv, 2006.

Hamburger, Käte. *Philosophie der Dichter: Novalis, Schiller, Rilke*. Stuttgart: W. Kohlhammer Verlag, 1966.

—"Die phänomenologische Struktur der Dichtung Rilkes." In *Philosophie der Dichter: Novalis, Schiller, Rilke*, 179–275.

Haney, Kathleen M. *Intersubjectivity Revisited: Phenomenology and the Other*. Athens, OH: Ohio University Press, 1994.

Hanson, Norwood Russell. *Patterns of Discovery: An Inquiry into the Conceptual Foundations of Science*. Cambridge: Cambridge University Press, 1958.

Hausmann, Ulrich. *Die Apollosonette Rilkes und ihre plastischen Urbilder*. Berlin: Verlag Gebr. Mann, 1947.

Hegel, G. W. F. *Aesthetics: Lectures on Fine Art*. Volume 2. Translated by T. M. Knox. Oxford: Clarendon Press, 1975.

Heidegger, Martin. "Phänomenologie und Theologie." In *Gesamtausgabe* [*GA*] 9. Edited by F.-W. von Herrmann, 45–78. 1976 [1927].

—*Sein und Zeit. GA* 2. Edited by F.-W. von Herrmann. 1977 [1927].

—*Kant und das Problem der Metaphysik. GA* 3. Edited by F.-W. von Herrmann. 1991 [1929].

—*Die Grundbegriffe der Metaphysik: Welt – Endlichkeit – Einsamkeit. GA* 29/30. Edited by F.-W. von Herrmann. 2004 [1929/30].

—"Vom Wesen der Wahrheit." In *GA* 9. Edited by F.-W. von Herrmann, 177–202. 1976 [1930].

—"Überwindung der Metaphysik." In *GA* 7. Edited by F.-W. von Herrmann, 67–98. 2000 [1936–1946].

—*Erläuterungen zu Hölderlins Dichtung. GA* 4. Edited by F.-W. von Herrmann. Frankfurt am Main: Vittorio Klostermann, 1996 [1936–1968].

—*Hölderlins Hymne "Der Ister." GA* 53. Edited by W. Biemel. 1993 [1942].

—*Parmenides. GA* 54. Edited by M. S. Frings. 1992 [1942/43].

—"Zur Erörterung der Gelassenheit: Aus einem Feldweggespräch über das Denken." In *GA* 13. Edited by H. Heidegger, 37–74. 1983 [1944/45].

—"Wozu Dichter?" In *GA* 5. Edited by F.-W. von Herrmann, 269–320. 1977 [1946].

—"Die Kehre." In *GA* 79. Edited by Petra Jaeger, 68–77. 2005 [1949].

—"Die Frage nach der Technik." In *GA* 7. Edited by F.-W. von Herrmann, 7–36. 2000 [1953].

—"Der Weg zur Sprache." In *GA* 12. Edited by F.-W. von Herrmann, 227–57. 1985 [1959].

—*Being and Time*. Translated by John Macquarrie and Edward Robinson. Oxford: Blackwell Publishers, 1962.

—"Die Herkunft der Kunst und die Bestimmung des Denkens." In *GA* 80. Edited by H. Heidegger, 135–49. 1983 [1967].

—"What Are Poets For? [Wozu Dichter?]" In *Poetry, Language, Thought*. Translated by Albert Hofstadter, 91–142. New York: Harper & Row, 1971.

—"Seminar in Zähringen 1973." In *GA* 15. Edited by C. Ochwadt, 372–407. 2005 [1973].
—*The End of Philosophy*. Translated by Joan Stambaugh. Norwich: Souvenir Press, 1975.
—"The Turning." In *The Question Concerning Technology and Other Essays*. Translated by William Lovitt, 36–49. New York: Harper, 1977.
—*Basic Writings*. Edited by David Farrell Krell. London: Routledge, 1978.
—*Parmenides*. Translated by André Schuwer and Richard Rojcewicz. Bloomington, IN: Indiana University Press, 1992.
—*Hölderlin's Hymn "The Ister."* Translated by William McNeill and Julia Davis. Bloomington, IN: Indiana University Press, 1996.
—*Introduction to Metaphysics*. Translated by Gregory Fried and Richard Polt. New Haven, CT: Yale University Press, 2000.
—*Identity and Difference*. Translated by Joan Stambaugh. Chicago: University of Chicago Press, 2002.
Hermann, Ruth. *Im Zwischenraum zwischen Welt und Spielzeug: Eine Poetik der Kindheit bei Rilke*. Königshausen & Neumann, 2001.
Herwig, Malte. "The Unwitting Muse: Jakob von Uexküll's Theory of Umwelt and Twentieth-Century Literature." *Semiotica* 134 (2001): 553–92.
Holdrege, Craig. *Thinking Like a Plant: A Living Science for Life*. Great Barrington, MA: Lindisfarne Books, 2013.
Holdrege, Craig and Steve Talbott. *Beyond Biotechnology: The Barren Promise of Genetic Engineering*. Lexington, KY: The University Press of Kentucky, 2008.
Hübener, Andrea, Rätus Luck, Renate Scharffenberg, Erich Unglaub, and William Waters, eds. *Rilkes Welt: Festschrift für August Stahl zum 75. Geburtstag*. Frankfurt am Main: Peter Lang, 2009.
Husserl, Edmund. *Ideas Pertaining to a Pure Phenomenology and to a Phenomenological Philosophy*. First Book. Translated by F. Kersten. The Hague: Martinus Nijhoff, 1982 [1913].
—*Cartesian Meditations*. Translated by Dorion Cairns. The Hague: Martinus Nijhoff, 1960 [1931].
—*The Crisis of European Sciences and Transcendental Phenomenology*. Translated by David Carr. Evanston, IL: Northwestern University Press, 1970 [1936].
—*Ideas Pertaining to a Pure Phenomenology and to a Phenomenological Philosophy*. Second Book. Translated by Richard Rojcewicz and André Schuwer. Dordrecht: Kluwer Academic Publishers, 1989 [1952].
—*Analyses concerning Passive and Active Synthesis: Lectures on Transcendental Logic*. Translated by Anthony J. Steinbock. Dordrecht: Kluwer Academic Publishers, 2001 [1966].
Imdahl, Max. *Bildautonomie und Wirklichkeit: Zur theoretischen Begründung moderner Malerei*. Mittenwald: Mäander-Kunstverlag, 1981.
—*Farbe: Kunsttheoretische Reflexionen in Frankreich*. Munich: Wilhelm Fink Verlag, 2003.
Jackson, Frank. "Epiphenomenal Qualia." *Philosophical Quarterly* 32 (1982): 127–36.
Jamme, Christoph. "'Zwiefalt' und 'Einfalt': Heidegger's Deutung der Kunst Cézannes." In *Wege und Irrwege des neueren Umganges mit Heideggers Werk: ein deutsch-ungarisches Symposium*, 99–108. Berlin: Duncker & Humblot, 1991.
—"Der Verlust der Dinge: Cézanne – Rilke – Heidegger." *Deutsche Zeitschrift für Philosophie* 40 (1992): 385–97.

—"'Doppelbotschaft vom wirklichen Liebenkönnen und vom Sterbenmüssen': Gadamer und Rilke." In *Wege zur Wahrheit. Festschrift für Otto Pöggeler zum 80.Geburtstag*, edited by Annemarie Gethmann-Siefert and Elisabeth Weisser-Lohmann, 145–56. Munich: Wilhelm Fink Verlag, 2009.

—"Being Able to Love and Having to Die': Gadamer and Rilke," translated by Michael Eldred and Luke Fischer. In *Consequences of Hermeneutics: Fifty Years after Truth and Method*, edited by Jeff Malpas and Santiago Zabala, 177–89. Evanston, IL: Northwestern University Press, 2010.

Jephcott, E. F. N. *Proust and Rilke: The Literature of Expanded Consciousness*. London: Chatto & Windus, 1972.

Johnson, Galen A., "Phenomenology and Painting: 'Cézanne's Doubt.'" In *The Merleau-Ponty Aesthetics Reader: Philosophy and Painting*, edited by Galen A. Johnson and Michael B. Smith, 3–14. Evanston, IL: Northwestern University Press, 1993.

Kahl, Michael. *Lebensphilosophie und Ästhetik: Zu Rilkes Werk 1902–1910*. Freiburg: Rombach Verlag, 1999.

Kant, Immanuel. *Critique of Pure Reason*. Translated by Norman Kemp Smith. London: Macmillan Press, 1929.

—*Critique of Judgment*. Translated by Werner Pluhar. Indianapolis, IN: Hackett Publishing Company, 1984.

Kassner, Rudolf. *Rilke: Gesammelte Erinnerungen 1926–1956*. Edited by Klaus E. Bohnenkamp. Pfullingen: Neske Verlag, 1976.

Kearney, Richard. *Poetics of Imagining: Modern to Post-modern*. New York: Fordham University Press, 1998.

Keats, John. *Letters of John Keats*. Edited by Stanley Gardner. London: University of London Press, 1965.

Klieneberger, H. R. "Rilke and the 'Change of Sensibility': An Introduction." In *Rilke und der Wandel der Sensibilität*, edited by Herbert Herzmann and Hugh Ridler, 9–18. Essen: Die Blaue Eule, 1990.

—*George, Rilke, Hofmannsthal and the Romantic Tradition*. Stuttgart: Hans-Dieter Heinz Akademischer Verlag, 1991.

Krießbach-Thomasberger, Martina. "Rilke und Rodin." In *Rilke – ein europäischer Dichter aus Prag*, edited by Peter Demetz, Joachim W. Storck, and Hans Dieter Zimmermann, 149–163. Würzburg: Königshausen & Neumann, 1998.

Köhnen, Ralph. *Sehen als Textkultur: Intermediale Beziehungen zwischen Rilke und Cézanne*. Bielefeld: Aisthesis Verlag, 1995.

Kuh, Kih-Seong. *Die Tiersymbolik bei Rainer Maria Rilke*. Berlin: Ernst-Reuter-Gesellschaft, 1967.

Kwant, Remy C. *Phenomenology of Expression*. Pittsburgh, PA: Duquesne University Press, 1969.

Lee, Yen-Hui. *Gelassenheit und Wu-Wei: Nähe und Ferne zwischen dem späten Heidegger und dem Taoismus*. PhD diss., Albert-Ludwigs-Universität, Freiburg, 2001.

Leeder, Karen and Robert Vilain, eds. *The Cambridge Companion to Rilke*. Cambridge: Cambridge University Press, 2010.

Luther, Arthur R. "The Articulated Unity of Being in Scheler's Phenomenology. Basic Drive and Spirit." In *Max Scheler (1874–1928): Centennial Essays*, edited by Manfred S. Frings, 1–42. The Hague: Martinus Nijhoff, 1974.

Lysaker, John. *You Must Change Your Life: Poetry, Philosophy, and the Birth of Sense*. University Park, PA: The Pennsylvania State University Press, 2002.

Magnússon, Gísli. "Rilke und der Okkultismus." In *Metaphysik und Moderne: Von*

Wilhelm Raabe bis Thomas Mann, edited by Andreas Blödorn and Søren R. Fauth, 144–72. Wuppertal: Arco, 2006.
—*Dichtung als Erfahrungsmetaphysik: Esoterische und okkultistische Modernität bei R. M. Rilke*. Würzburg: Königshausen & Neumann, 2009.
Makkreel, Rudolf. "How is Empathy Related to Understanding?" In *Issues in Husserl's Ideas II*, edited by Thomas Nenon and Lester Embree, 199–212. Dordrecht: Kluwer Academic Publishers, 1996.
Man, Paul de. *Allegories of Reading: Figural Language in Rousseau, Nietzsche, Rilke, and Proust*. New Haven, CT: Yale University Press, 1979.
Marion, Jean-Luc. *Reduction and Givenness*. Translated by Thomas A. Carlson. Evanston, IL: Northwestern University Press, 1998.
—*Being Given: Toward a Phenomenology of Givenness*. Translated by Jeffrey L. Kosky. Stanford, CA: Stanford University Press, 2002.
—*In Excess: Studies of Saturated Phenomena*. Translated by Robyn Horner. New York: Fordham University Press, 2004.
Mayer, Gerhart. *Rilke und Kassner: eine geistige Begegnung*. Bonn: H. Bouvier u. Co. Verlag, 1960.
Merchant, Carolyn. *The Death of Nature: Women, Ecology, and the Scientific Revolution*. San Francisco, CA: HarperCollins, 1983 [1980].
Merleau-Ponty, Maurice. "Cézanne's Doubt." In *The Merleau-Ponty Aesthetics Reader: Philosophy and Painting*, edited by Galen A. Johnson and Michael B. Smith, 59–75. Evanston, IL: Northwestern University Press, 1993 [1945].
—*Phenomenology of Perception*. Translated by Colin Smith. London: Routledge Classics, 2002 [1945].
—"The Philosopher and His Shadow." In *Signs*. Translated by Richard C. McCleary, 159–81. Evanston, IL: Northwestern University Press, 1964 [1960].
—"Eye and Mind." In *The Merleau-Ponty Aesthetics Reader: Philosophy and Painting*, [1961] 121–49.
—*The Visible and the Invisible*. Edited by Claude Lefort. Translated by Alphonso Lingis. Evanston, IL: Northwestern University Press, 1968 [1964].
—*Nature: Course Notes from the Collège de France*. Translated by Robert Vallier. Evanston, IL: Northwestern University Press, 2003 [1995].
Métraux, Alexandre and Bernhard Waldenfels, eds. *Leibhaftige Vernunft: Spuren von Merleau-Pontys Denken*. Munich: Wilhelm Fink Verlag, 1986.
Meyer, Hermann. "Rilkes Cézanne-Erlebnis." In *Zarte Empirie: Studien zur Literaturgeschichte*, 244–86. Stuttgart: J. B. Metzlersche Verlagsbuchhandlung, 1963.
—"Die Verwandlung des Sichtbaren: Die Bedeutung der modernen bildenen Kunst für Rilkes späte Dichtung." In *Zarte Empirie: Studien zur Literaturgeschichte*, 287–336.
Mislin, Hans. "Rilkes Partnerschaft mit der Natur." *Blätter der Rilke-Gesellschaft* 3 (1974): 39–49.
Morton, Timothy. *Ecology without Nature: Rethinking Environmental Aesthetics*. Cambridge, MA: Harvard University Press, 2007.
Müller, Wolfgang. *Rainer Maria Rilkes "Neue Gedichte": Vielfältigkeit eines Gedichttypus*. Meisenheim am Glan: Verlag Anton Hain, 1971.
—"Rilke und die Dinglyrik der Moderne." In *Rilke und die Weltliteratur*, edited by Manfred Engel and Dieter Lamping, 214–35. Düsseldorf: Artemis und Winkler, 1999.
—"Neue Gedichte/Der Neuen Gedichte anderer Teil." In *Rilke-Handbuch*, edited by Manfred Engel, 296–318. Stuttgart: J. B. Metzler, 2004.

—"Rilkes *Neue Gedichte* und der Imagismus." *Blätter der Rilke-Gesellschaft* 30 (2010): 231–45.
Naess, Arne. "The Shallow and the Deep, Long-range Ecology Movement." *Inquiry* 16 (1973): 95–100.
Nassar, Dalia. *The Romantic Absolute: Being and Knowing in Early German Romantic Philosophy, 1795–1804*. Chicago: University of Chicago Press, 2013.
—ed. *The Relevance of Romanticism: Essays on German Romantic Philosophy*. New York: Oxford University Press, 2014.
Nitta, Yoshihiro. "Der Weg zu einer Phänomenologie des Unscheinbaren." In *Zur philosophischen Aktualität Heideggers*, vol. 2, edited by Dietrich Papenfuss and Otto Pöggeler, 43–54. Frankfurt am Main: Vittorio Klostermann, 1990.
Nostitz, Helene. *Rodin: In Gesprächen und Briefen*. Dresden: Wolfgang Jess Verlag, 1949.
Novalis [Friedrich von Hardenberg]. *Novalis Schriften: Die Werke von Friedrich von Hardenberg*. Edited by Richard Samuel, H.-J. Mähl, Paul Kluckhorn, and G. Schulz. Stuttgart: W. Kohlhammer, 1960–1988.
Olzien, Otto H. "R. M. Rilke: 'Der Ball.' Sprache und Ontologie." *Germanisch-Romanische Monatsschrift* 28 (1978): 183–93.
Oppert, Kurt. "Das Dinggedicht. Eine Kunstform bei Mörike, Meyer und Rilke." *Deutsche Vierteljahrsschrift für Literaturwissenschaft und Geistesgeschichte* 4 (1926): 747–83.
Petzet, Heinrich Wiegand. "Nachwort [Afterword]." In *Briefe über Cézanne*, by Rainer Maria Rilke. Edited by Clara Rilke. Frankfurt am Main: Insel Verlag, 1962.
—"Foreword." In *Letters on Cézanne*, by Rainer Maria Rilke. Translated by Joel Agee, vii–xxvi. New York: Fromm International Publishing Corporation, 1985.
—*Encounters and Dialogues with Martin Heidegger 1929–1976*. Translated by Parvis Emad and Kenneth Maly. Chicago: University of Chicago Press, 1993.
Phelan, Anthony. *Rilke: Neue Gedichte*. London: Grant & Cutler Ltd, 1992.
—"Rilke and His Philosophical Critics." In *The Cambridge Companion to Rilke*, edited by Karen Leeder and Robert Vilain, 174–88. Cambridge: Cambridge University Press, 2010.
Plumwood, Val. *Feminism and the Mastery of Nature*. London: Routledge, 1993.
Pound, Ezra. "How to Read." In *Literary Essays*. Edited by T. S. Eliot, 15–40. New York: New Directions, 1968 [1929].
Rigby, Kate. "Ecocriticism." In *Introducing Criticism at the 21st Century*, edited by Julian Wolfreys, 151–78. Edinburgh: Edinburgh University Press, 2002.
—*Topographies of the Sacred: The Poetics of Place in European Romanticism*. Charlottesville, VA: University of Virginia Press, 2004.
—"Gernot Böhme's Ecological Aesthetics of Atmosphere." In *Ecocritical Theory: New European Approaches*, edited by Axel Goodbody and Kate Rigby, 139–52. Charlottesville, VA: University of Virginia Press, 2011.
Rilke, Rainer Maria. *Briefe aus den Jahren 1902–1906*. Vol. 1. Leipzig: Insel Verlag, 1930.
—*Briefe aus den Jahren 1906–1907*. Vol. 2. Leipzig: Insel Verlag, 1930.
—*Briefe aus den Jahren 1907–1914*. Vol. 3. Leipzig: Insel Verlag, 1930.
—*Tagebücher aus der Frühzeit*. Edited by Ruth Sieber-Rilke and Carl Sieber. Leipzig: Insel Verlag, 1942.
—*Briefe*. Vol. 2, 1914–26. Wiesbaden: Insel Verlag, 1950.
—*Sämtliche Werke in zwölf Bänden*. Edited by Ruth Sieber-Rilke and Ernst Zinn. Frankfurt am Main: Insel Verlag, 1976.

—"An Experience (I)." In *Where Silence Reigns*. Translated by G. Craig Houston, 34–6. New York: New Directions Books, 1978.
—"An Experience (II)." In *Where Silence Reigns*, 36–8.
—"Worpswede" [Translation of the Introduction to *Worpswede*]. In *Where Silence Reigns*, 6–22.
—*Letters on Cézanne*. Translated by Joel Agee. Foreword by Heinrich Wiegand Petzet. New York: Fromm International Publishing Corporation, 1985.
—*Selected Letters 1902–1926*. Translated by R. F. C. Hull. London: Quartet Books, 1988.
—*Werke: Kommentierte Ausgabe in vier Bänden*. Edited by Manfred Engel, Ulrich Fülleborn, Horst Nalewski, and August Stahl. Frankfurt am Main: Insel Verlag, 1996.
—*Briefwechsel mit Magda von Hattingberg "Benvenuta."* Edited by Ingeborg Schnack and Renate Scharffenberg. Frankfurt am Main: Insel Verlag, 2000.
—*Rainer Maria Rilke: Über moderne Malerei*. Edited by Martina Krießbach-Thomasberger. Frankfurt am Main: Insel Verlag, 2000.
—*New Poems: A Revised Bilingual Edition*. Translated by Edward Snow. New York: North Point Press, 2001.
—*Werke: Kommentierte Ausgabe. Supplement Band: Gedichte in französischer Sprache. Mit deutschen Prosafassungen*. Edited by Manfred Engel and Dorothea Lauterbach. Frankfurt am Main: Insel Verlag, 2003.
—*Auguste Rodin*. Translated by G. Craig Houston. Mineola, NY: Dover Publications, 2006.
Rilke, Rainer Maria and Auguste Rodin. *Der Briefwechsel und andere Dokumente zu Rilkes Begegnung mit Rodin*. Edited by Rätus Luck. Frankfurt am Main: Insel Verlag, 2001.
Rodin, Auguste. *Das Testament* [*Le Testament*]. Überlingen: Werner Wulff Verlag, 1946.
—"Rodin's Reflections on Art." Recorded by Henri Charles Etienne Dujardin-Beaumetz. Translated by Ann McGarrell. In *Auguste Rodin: Readings on his Life and Work*, edited by Albert Elsen. Englewood Cliffs, NJ: Prentice Hall, 1965.
—*Rodin on Art and Artists: Conversations with Paul Gsell*. New York: Dover Publications, 1983.
Ryan, Judith. *Umschlag und Verwandlung: Poetische Struktur und Dichtungstheorie in R. M. Rilkes Lyrik der mittleren Periode (1907–1914)*. Munich: Winkler Verlag, 1972.
—*Rilke, Modernism and Poetic Tradition*. Cambridge: Cambridge University Press, 1999.
Ryan, Lawrence. "Rilke's *Dinggedichte*: The 'Thing' as 'Poem in Itself.'" In *Rilke-Rezeptionen*, edited by Susan L. Cocalis, Karin Obermeier, and Sigrid Bauschinger, 27–35. Tübingen: Francke Verlag, 1995.
Sallis, John. *Delimitations: Phenomenology and the End of Metaphysics*. Bloomington, IN: Indiana University Press, 1995 [2nd edn].
Sanchez, Pierre. *Dictionnaire du Salon d'Automne. Répertoire des exposants et liste des œuvres présentées 1903–1945*, Vol. 1. Dijon: Échelle de Jacob, 2006.
Schadewaldt, Wolfgang. *Winckelmann und Rilke: Zwei Beschreibungen des Apollon*. Pfullingen: Verlag Günther Neske, 1968.
Scheler, Max. *Wesen und Formen der Sympathie*. Edited by Manfred S. Frings. Bern: Francke Verlag, 1973 [1923].

316 Bibliography

—*The Nature of Sympathy*. Translated by Peter Heath. London: Routledge & Kegan Paul, 1954.
—"Liebe und Erkenntnis." In *Liebe und Erkenntnis*. Munich: Lehnen Verlag, 1955.
Schlegel, Friedrich. *Kritische Friedrich Schlegel Ausgabe*. Vol. 2. Edited by Ernst Behler. Paderborn: Schöningh, 1958.
Schmidt-Pauli, Elisabeth von. *Rainer Maria Rilke: Ein Gedenkbuch*. Stuttgart: Bürger Verlag, 1946.
Schmoll gen. Eisenwerth, J. A. *Rodin-Studien: Persönlichkeit – Werke – Wirkung – Biographie*. Munich: Prestel-Verlag, 1983.
Schnell, Werner. *Der Torso als Problem der modernen Kunst*. Berlin: Gebr. Mann Verlag, 1980.
Seamon, David and Arthur Zajonc, eds. *Goethe's Way of Science: A Phenomenology of Nature*. Albany, NY: SUNY Press, 1998.
Seubold, Günter. *Kunst als Enteignis: Heideggers Weg zu einer nicht mehr metaphysischen Kunst*. Bonn: Bouvier Verlag, 1996.
Snell, Bruno. *The Discovery of the Mind: In Greek Philosophy and Literature*. Translated by T. G. Rosenmeyer. New York: Dover Publications, 1982.
Stein, Edith. *On the Problem of Empathy*. Translated by Waltraut Stein. Washington, D.C.: ICS Publications, 1989.
Steinbock, Anthony J. "Spirit and Generativity: The Role and Contribution of the Phenomenologist in Hegel and Husserl." In *Alterity and Facticity: New Perspectives on Husserl*, edited by Natalie Depraz and Dan Zahavi, 163–203. Dordrecht: Kluwer Academic Publishers, 1998.
—*Phenomenology and Mysticism: The Verticality of Religious Experience*. Bloomington, IN: Indiana University Press, 2007.
Steiner, Rudolf. *Die Welt der Sinne und die Welt des Geistes. Gesamtausgabe*, vol. 134. Dornach, Switzerland: Verlag der Rudolf Steiner-Nachlassverwaltung, 1979 [1911/12].
Stephan, Günter. "Die Verwandlung der sichtbaren Natur: Rainer Maria Rilke." In *Lektürehilfen Naturlyrik: Gattungs- und epochenspezifische Aspekte*, 98–108. Stuttgart: Klett, 1989.
Tagore, Rabindranath. *Selected Poems*. Translated by William Radice. London: Penguin Books, 1994.
Treanor, Brian. *Aspects of Alterity: Levinas, Marcel, and the Contemporary Debate*. New York: Fordham University Press, 2006.
Uexküll, Gudrun von. *Jakob von Uexküll: seine Welt und Umwelt*. Hamburg: Christian Wegner Verlag, 1964.
Uexküll, Jakob von. *Umwelt und Innenwelt der Tiere*. Berlin: Springer, 1909.
—*Theoretical Biology*. Translated by D. L. Mackinnon. New York: Harcourt, Brace & Company, 1926.
—*A Foray into the Worlds of Animals and Humans* with *A Theory of Meaning*. Translated by Joseph D. O'Neil. Minneapolis, MN: University of Minnesota Press, 2010.
Uexküll, Jakob von and Georg Kriszat. *Streifzüge durch die Umwelten von Tieren und Menschen* [1934]; *Bedeutungslehre* [1940]. Frankfurt am Main: S. Fischer Verlag, 1970.
Uexküll, Thure von. "Die Umweltforschung als subjekt- und objektumgreifende Naturforschung." In *Streifzüge durch die Umwelten von Tieren und Menschen; Bedeutungslehre*, by Jakob von Uexküll and Georg Kriszat.
Valéry, Paul. "Poetry and Abstract Thought." In *The Art of Poetry*. Translated by Denise Folliot, 52–81. Princeton, NJ: Princeton University Press, 1958.

Wagner-Egelhaaf, Martina. *Mystik der Moderne: Die visionäre Ästhetik der deutschen Literatur im 20. Jahrhundert.* Stuttgart: J. B. Metzler, 1989.
Waldenfels, Bernhard. *Das Zwischenreich des Dialogs: Sozialphilosophische Untersuchungen im Anschluss an Edmund Husserl.* Den Haag: Martinus Nijhoff, 1971.
—*Grundmotive einer Phänomenologie des Fremden.* Frankfurt am Main: Suhrkamp, 2006.
Waters, William. *Poetry's Touch: On Lyric Address.* Ithaca, NY: Cornell University Press, 2003.
—"The *New Poems*," in *The Cambridge Companion to Rilke*, edited by Karen Leeder and Robert Vilain, 59–73. Cambridge: Cambridge University Press, 2010.
Wittgenstein, Ludwig. *Philosophische Untersuchungen.* Edited by Joachim Schulte. Frankfurt am Main: Suhrkamp, 2001.
Wordsworth, William. *Poetical Works.* Paris: A. & W. Galignani and Co., 1828.
Yeats, William Butler. *Collected Poems of W. B. Yeats.* New York: Simon & Schuster, 1996.
Zahavi, Dan. "Phenomenology and Metaphysics." In *Metaphysics, Facticity, Interpretation: Phenomenology in the Nordic Countries,* edited by Dan Zahavi, Sara Heinämaa, and Hans Ruin, 3–22. Dordrecht: Kluwer Academic Publishers, 2003.

Index

active-passivity 37, 44, 67–8, 88–90, 100–6, 112–15, 171, 174, 177–81, 187, 190, 193, 207
Andreas-Salomé, Lou 179
animals
    perception of 72n. 4, 128n. 149, 178–98, 200–6, 208
    poems, in 71–2, 182, 185, 191–3, 206, 230n. 6, 231–53
anthropomorphism 183–4, 190, 237–8, 262, 294
Aristotle 6, 244
art
    abstract 127–8, 127n. 149, 161–2, 162n. 247
    end of 2, 224–5n. 24, 285n. 140, 302
    excess of meaning 83, 87–9, 174, 212–14, 226, 244, 265
    form 75, 115–18, 118n. 126, 122, 125, 127, 132–4, 137–8, 145n. 198, 158–65, 210–14, 230, 242, 285–90, 297
    nature, and 76, 90, 99, 103, 127n. 149, 128–9, 129n. 152, 138, 140, 146–69, 151n. 216, 158, 166n. 258, 178–9, 229–30
    phenomenology, and 210–11, 216–31, 301
    relation to world 98–9, 134–5, 154, 154n. 228, 168
    see also Cézanne; Rilke; Rodin

artist
    creative process 69, 74, 98–103, 113–15, 118, 123–41, 150–1, 154, 156–68, 178, 185–6, 207–12
    disposition of 88–90, 92, 100–15, 177, 180–1 *see also* dispositions
    perception 74, 88–90, 98, 100, 110, 113–15, 121–3, 143–50, 170–214
    see also Cézanne; Rilke; Rodin
atmospheres 107–9, 113n. 113, 149–50, 257, 261, 265, 267–71, 280–2, 302 *see also* dispositions

Badt, Kurt 142n. 189, 146n. 205, 154n. 228, 164n. 254
Balzac, Honoré de 132–3, 213
Baudelaire, Charles 110, 152–5, 237, 252
Being *see* ontology
Berendt, Hans 269–70, 274, 280, 292
Bernard, Émile 144n. 194, 159, 161
Betz, Maurice 251
Blake, William 172–3, 221, 256–7, 263
body, human 36, 39, 43, 47–51, 53–8, 61, 65–6, 76, 115, 117–21, 126–31, 136–8, 141, 285–6
see also *Leib*

320 Index

Boehm, Gottfried 142n. 189, 144,
    154n. 228, 158–9, 164–6
Böhme, Gernot 107–9, 112–13n.
    113, 212n. 90, 251n. 82, 261,
    270n. 117, 281
Bradley, Brigitte 237n. 58, 246n. 74
Brentano, Franz 38, 112–13n. 108
Buchanan, Brett 235, 236n. 55

Caputo, John 2–3n. 1, 103n. 83,
    104n. 84
Cassirer, Ernst 53
Cézanne, Paul
    Baudelaire, Charles 110n. 104,
        152–4
    color 144–50, 156–63, 165, 167
    Heidegger on 7, 75, 99–100,
        146n. 205, 151, 153–4, 163,
        167–8
    landscape 41, 57, 98, 141–8, 151,
        156–68
    Merleau-Ponty on 7, 41, 58, 75,
        99–100, 117n. 122, 148, 151,
        154n. 228, 156, 162–3, 166–8,
        217–18
    Mont Sainte-Victoire 57, 143–4,
        146, 151, 158–68
    motif 147–8, 156–7, 164, 167–8
    Nature 141–68
    Nature, Book of 146, 164
    ontological significance of 146n.
        205, 152–4, 162–3, 164n. 254,
        166–8
    painting process 98–100,
        113–15, 151, 155–9 see also
        réalisation, la
    paintings, composition of
        158–62, 165–6
    participative vision 141–50,
        154n. 128, 162–3, 166
    phenomenological status of 144,
        148, 151–4, 162, 167–8
    portraiture 149–52, 160–1
    réalisation, la 146n. 207, 150–8, 217

Rilke
    influence on 74–5, 97–100,
        113–14, 123, 127n. 149,
        141–3, 177–8, 199, 208
    intermedial connections
        (between painting and
        poetry) 9–10, 74–5, 94,
        97–100, 110n. 104, 127–8n.
        149, 146n. 207, 152–5, 154n.
        228, 185, 188, 208–9, 215,
        216–18, 227, 229, 237, 242,
        252–3, 275–6, 284–5, 297–8,
        300
    seeing, similarities in manner
        of 75, 110, 113, 123, 143–6,
        177–8, 185, 217–18
    see also *Briefe über Cézanne*
        under works under Rilke;
        sachliches Sagen; *réalisation,
        la*
Rodin, and 74–5, 96–100, 110n.
    104, 114–15, 105, 113, 139,
    127n. 149, 137, 141–5, 146n.
    206, 148, 150–1, 155–6,
    159–61, 169, 171, 173, 229,
    275, 284–5
sachliches Sagen 150–68
still-life 141–2, 148–52
chiasm 7, 29n. 21, 59–60, 65,
    174, 187–9, 195n. 57,
    213, 218–20, 227, 256,
    282 see also chiasmic
    under phenomenology;
    Merleau-Ponty
childhood see childhood, view of
    under Rilke
Coleridge, Samuel Taylor 95–6,
    103, 306
Coriando, Paola-Ludovika 100n.
    71, 108–9, 110n. 104,
    112–13n. 113

Dante 305n. 2
death 95, 110n. 104, 111, 256–63

Derrida, Jacques 2, 16, 43, 301n. 1
Descartes, René 22, 32–3, 38–9
Ding and *Kunst-Ding* 123–41, 179, 227, 229–30
Dinggedicht 10, 72, 94n. 48, 124n. 140, 215–16, 221–2, 224–5, 227–31, 236, 242–3, 252–3, 255–6, 273, 275, 279–80, 291, 293, 297–8, 300
dispositions
   active-passivity 27, 44, 67–8, 88–90, 100–15, 171, 174, 177–81, 187, 190, 193, 207
   childlikeness 86–9, 92, 100–2, 105–6, 112, 171, 281–2 *see also* childhood, view of *under* Rilke
   disclosive, as 108–9, 112–13, 280–1
   Gelassenheit 35, 89, 102–6, 109–14, 171–7, 179
   impartiality 89, 107–12, 152, 172
   poverty 105–6, 112, 171–3
divine, the *see* God, gods, goddesses; mysticism; epiphany
dualism(s)
   activity/passivity 7, 9, 18, 35, 36–7, 44, 88–90
   Cartesian 22, 39
   experience of 20–2, 69, 78–85
   experiential overcoming of 11–13, 16, 21, 25–6, 31, 34, 41, 66–7, 69–71, 74, 86–9, 97, 99–100, 104–5, 171, 174, 191–3, 199–208, 215, 220–6, 231, 233–51, 267, 299–302 *see also* twofold *under* seeing; *Weltinnenraum*
   human/nature 7, 15, 39, 74–9, 83, 141, 166, 174, 204, 221, 275, 300
   material/spiritual 7, 18, 23–4, 39, 171, 174, 220–1, 232, 275
   metaphysical 15–16, 19, 22–5, 47–9, 77, 231–2, 273
   mind/body 7, 15, 20, 39, 48–9, 56, 61, 76 *see also* body, human
   outer/inner 1, 7, 9–10, 18, 20–1, 49, 54, 81, 85, 97, 166, 191–2, 204, 206–8, 232, 275, 301
   phenomenological approaches to 25–39, 41, 43–4, 67–8, 70–1, 174, 215, 220–1, 299–303
   sensible/intelligible 7, 17–18, 24, 30, 39, 49, 174–5, 275, 301
   visible/invisible 1, 7, 9–10, 22, 122–3, 174, 191, 204, 206–8, 221, 255, 301
   see also dualism *under* Rilke

Eckhart, Meister 103–5, 179, 195
ecocriticism xii, 15n. 1, 70n. 3, 95n. 52, 99, 107n. 97, 129n. 152
Eldridge, Richard 290n. 152
Eliot, T. S. 114–15
empathy 47–51, 55, 183–4 *see also* sympathy
Empiricism 26–7, 30–1, 36, 53, 56, 88
Engel, Manfred 91, 111–12, 257n. 96
environment 15, 99, 151n. 216, 183, 186, 188, 192–3, 233–6, 239–41, 246 see also *Umwelt*
environmental philosophy xii, 15, 19n. 6, 39, 70n. 3, 99, 230n. 36, 261
epiphany 7, 39, 105n. 88, 145–50, 171, 173–4, 189n. 147, 195–8, 201–4, 219–20, 246–56, 260–3, 272–5, 289, 300–1
Eppelsheimer, Rudolf 232–3
esotericism 172n. 2, 228, 232, 232–3n. 42, 296 *see also* mysticism
essence 28, 30–1, 35–6, 56, 65–6,

103, 122, 128–36, 141, 148, 152, 178n. 19, 183, 188–91, 195, 224, 229–31, 241, 252, 285–7, 292–3, 297 see also *Wesensschau*
everyday, the 11, 33, 40–2, 67, 70–1, 171, 174–5, 177, 188, 202, 218, 290, 299–300
exactitude (detail) 94n. 48, 95–6, 111n. 107, 118–23, 143, 152–4, 169, 172, 185–7, 207–8, 239, 275, 305 see also objectivity
exceptional, the 12n. 19, 39, 41–2, 67, 71, 84, 145, 158, 171–7, 185, 196, 218–20, 226, 231, 238, 243, 262, 265, 299–301 see also epiphany

Fick, Monicka 232–3
Fingerhut, Karl-Heinz 231–2
flowers *see* flowers *under* Nature *under* Rilke
Forsting, Brigitte 255n. 92
Fülleborn, Ulrich 146n. 207, 257n. 97

Gadamer, Hans-Georg 5n. 6, 8–9n. 12, 45n. 55, 98n. 65, 222, 290–3, 295–7
Gasquet, Joachim 57n. 74, 143–4, 147, 150n. 213
Gelassenheit see *Gelassenheit under* dispositions
God, gods, goddesses 3–4, 16–17, 24, 104–6, 140, 175–9, 194–5, 244, 246, 269, 271–2, 288
Goethe, Johann Wolfgang von 62, 94–6, 103, 112–13n. 113, 223n. 19, 232, 235–6, 250–1, 287, 305n. 2
Gogh, Vincent van 93n. 46, 105–6, 146, 151–2, 177–8
Gosetti-Ferencei, Anna Jennifer 10

Grünbein, Durs 280

haecceity 44–6, 59, 66, 183, 224n. 24, 285–7, 298, 299–300
Hamburger, Käte 9, 96, 174, 216–19, 232, 248, 253–6, 291, 306
Hardenberg, Friedrich von *see* Novalis
Hausmann, Ulrich 139n. 183, 289n. 147
Hegel, G. W. F. 6, 95–6, 223–5, 232, 240, 285n. 140, 287, 302
Heidegger, Martin
  Being 4, 7, 10, 23n. 10, 33–5, 40, 99–100, 153, 104n. 84, 153–4
  Cézanne, on 75, 99–100, 151, 153–4, 167–8
  Dasein 11n. 18, 29, 34n. 31, 35, 40, 60, 114n. 113, 233, 281n. 131
  dispositions 100, 107, 112, 112–13n. 113, 280–1
  dualism, response to 29n. 21, 34–6, 59–60
  Eckhart, Meister, and 103n. 83, 104
  end of philosophy (metaphysics), on the 2–6, 16, 206, 221, 300–1
  everydayness 11n. 18, 40, 42, 300–1
  finitude 3, 5n. 6
  Gelassenheit 35, 102–4, 174
  holy, the 4, 7, 221n. 16
  Husserl, and 11n. 18, 29n. 21, 33n. 29, 40, 43, 217, 291, 301
  Kant, and 2–4, 5n. 6
  Merleau-Ponty, and 7–9, 11, 29n. 21, 99–100, 151, 167–8, 233
  metaphysics as onto-theo-logy 4, 24
  Mitsein 43, 59–60, 62
  mysticism 103–5, 175–6
phenomenology, conception of

4n. 5, 5n. 6, 12n. 19, 29n. 21,
33n. 29, 34–5, 40, 43, 100,
103, 175–6, 209–10, 216, 223,
280–1, 291
physis 35, 163, 296
poetry, on 8, 210, 221n. 16, 226n.
27, 300
Rilke, and 2, 7–9, 12n. 19, 75,
99–100, 102–13, 150–68,
174–6, 181n. 26, 206, 207–11,
216–18, 221, 223, 226n. 27,
228, 230n. 36, 233, 280–1,
291–7, 300–3
Rilke, on 8, 104n. 84, 153, 221n.
16
Scheler, and 36, 43, 112–13n. 113,
281
technology, on 4, 104, 181n. 26
theology, on 175–6
truth, view of 34–6, 100, 113n.
113
Uexküll, Jakob von, and 233
Zeuge 29n. 21, 291, 294, 297, 301
Hermann, Ruth 87
hermeneutics (hermeneutic
phenomenology) 5n. 6, 35,
44, 51–5, 100, 109n. 102, 210,
228, 233, 291–2
Herwig, Malte 241
Hölderlin, Friedrich 4, 6, 94, 109n.
102, 244, 300
holy, the 4, 7, 106, 146, 173, 221n.
16, 263, 275
Hugo, Victor 119, 137
Hume, David 2–3, 16
Husserl, Edmund
Cartesian Meditations 11, 28, 38,
40, 43, 46n. 56, 47–51
dualism, and 1–2, 37–8, 46–51
empathy 47–51, 55, 184
Heidegger, and 11n. 18, 29n. 21,
33n. 29, 40, 43, 217, 291, 301
intentionality 33, 38, 55
Kant, and 27–31, 218–19

Lebenswelt (life-world) 11n. 18,
18n. 5, 27–31, 33, 37–40, 42,
44–7, 51n. 69, 55, 218, 220
Merleau-Ponty, and 27, 29, 38,
43, 218–19
natural attitude 11n. 18, 31–3, 37,
40–2, 171n. 1, 212, 217–18
objectifying thought, critique of
18–19, 31
objectness 29n. 21, 46, 49–50,
217–20, 291
ontology 33–4
Other, perception (constitution)
of the human 11, 40–4,
46–51, 54–5
phenomenological attitude 33,
40, 171n. 1, 218
phenomenological reduction
31–4, 216–18
Rilke, and 9, 174, 189n. 48,
216–19, 232, 254–5 *see also*
Hamburger, Käte
Scheler, and 27, 43
transcendental idealism 27–30,
37–8, 219
transcendental subjectivism 34,
38
Wesensschau 189, 216, 219, 254–5

idealism 3n. 1, 6, 16, 18n. 4, 24–5,
21n. 29, 27, 37–8, 88, 95, 180,
219, 301
imagination 10, 28, 61, 69, 71,
94, 204n. 70, 209, 213, 216,
221–7, 228n. 32, 229, 236–8,
240–1, 245, 248, 251–2, 260,
263, 265–7, 273, 275–6, 278,
282, 284–6, 292, 296–8,
300–1
Imagism 189n. 46, 219n. 11, 225
Imdahl, Max 165–6
individuation *see* haecceity
inspiration 10, 55, 74, 88–9n. 36,
102n. 76, 113–14, 119–20,

124n. 143, 178, 185, 207–12, 221, 271–2
intentionality
  counter-intentionality 56, 180
  reversal in directionality of 55, 67, 179–80, 186, 193–4, 198, 201, 252, 290
    see also intentionality under Husserl
  intermedial connections see Rilke under Rodin; Rilke under Cézanne

Jackson, Frank 23n. 11
Jamme, Christoph 8–9n. 12, 154n. 228, 167–8
Jephcott, E. F. N. 183
Johnson, Galen A. 218n. 7

Kandinsky, Wassily 154n. 228
Kant, Immanuel 2–5, 16–18, 26–31, 37–8, 88, 107, 180–1, 212, 219, 221, 238n. 61, 247
Kassner, Rudolf 73n. 10, 74, 176–7, 204n. 70
Keats, John 184, 244
Klee, Paul 127n. 149, 153, 195n. 57
Klieneberger, H. R. 90
Köhnen, Ralph 135n. 70, 142n. 188, 154n. 228, 161n. 245, 165n. 257
Krießbach-Thomasberger, Martina 136

language
  conceptual and poetic, differences between 209–11, 225–7, 285–6, 300–2, 305
  imagination, and 209, 213, 216, 221–7, 228n. 32, 236–7, 240, 245, 260, 263, 265–7, 275, 282, 284–6, 292, 296–7, 300–1
  synaesthetic 258, 274–5, 284–5

Leib 36, 43, 56–61, 65–6n. 86, 109n. 102, 118, 128, 136 see also Other, human; body, human
Levinas, Emmanuel 43
Locke, John 26–7, 30

Magnússon, Gísli 172n. 2, 232–3n. 41
Makkreel, Rudolf 50–1
Mallarmé, Stéphane 154n. 228
Man, Paul de 135n. 170
Marc, Franz 72n. 4, 127–8n. 149
Marion, Jean-Luc 33n. 29, 49, 83, 153, 174–5, 179–80, 217, 219
materialism 11, 16, 23–5, 53, 175
Mayer, Gerhart 73n. 10
meaning
  excess 83, 87, 89, 174, 181, 212–13, 219, 225–6, 244, 265
  irreducibility of 51–3, 212–13, 233, 244, 302
Merchant, Carolyn 19n. 6, 91n. 51, 180n. 22
Merleau-Ponty, Maurice
  active-passivity 37, 174, 187
  Cézanne, on 75, 99–100, 117, 148, 151, 154n. 228, 156, 162–3, 166–8, 217–18
  chiasm 7, 29n. 21, 59, 65, 174, 187n. 41, 195n. 57, 218–21, 256, 282
  dualism, response to 22n. 9, 36–9, 41, 56, 65, 148, 162–3, 166, 174, 187, 219–21, 233, 255–6 see also chiasm; flesh
  Empiricism, contrast to 26–7, 36, 53, 56, 65
  flesh 22n. 9, 37, 174, 233
  Heidegger, and 7–9, 11, 29n. 21, 99, 100, 151, 167–8, 233
  human Other, perception of 43, 53, 56–9, 63, 65
  Husserl, and 27, 29, 38, 43, 218–19

Kant, and 29, 39, 219
painting 7, 12, 36, 41, 58, 99–100, 117n. 122, 130, 151, 156, 162–3, 217–18
perception 7, 9–10, 22n. 9, 36–7, 41, 58, 65, 148, 168, 217–18, 255
phenomenology, on 7, 9–12, 26, 29n. 21, 30n. 25, 36–8, 41, 65
Rilke, and 7, 9–10, 12, 41, 75, 99–100, 117, 130, 150–68, 174, 187, 195n. 57, 217–21, 233, 255–6 see also chiasm
Rodin, on 129–30
Uexküll, Jakob von, and 233
visible and the invisible, the 10, 36–7, 130, 220–1, 255
metaphor 140, 173, 185, 197, 226–7, 230–1, 247–8, 267, 271, 274–5, 278, 283, 288
metaphysics
end of 1–6, 16, 206, 221, 300
Heidegger on 2–6, 16, 24, 206, 221, 300
objectifying, as 16–19, 23, 32–4, 65n. 85, 121, 175–6
phenomenology, and 1–7, 16, 25–39, 47–50, 99–100, 104, 167–8, 171, 175–6, 199, 205–6, 217, 218, 220–1, 231, 263, 273, 300
Meyer, Hermann 72n. 7, 114, 127–8n. 149, 162n. 247, 163, 182, 199n. 65
Mislin, Hans 238–41
modelé see *modelé* under Rilke; *modelé* under Rodin
models *see* models, use of *under* Rilke; models *under* Rodin
Modersohn, Otto 71, 74n. 13
Modersohn-Becker, Paula 71
Monet, Claude 154n. 228
monism
experiential 70, 83–4, 200, 206, 231–2, 239, 256 see also *Weltinnenraum*
idealist 11, 16, 24–5
materialist 11, 16, 23–5
moods *see* dispositions; atmospheres
Müller, Wolfgang 9, 189n. 46, 216–20, 225n. 25, 227, 231n. 37, 242, 246, 253–63, 267, 290
music 35, 45, 58, 66, 114, 123, 154, 184, 188, 210–11, 226, 229, 234, 236, 244–5, 249, 263, 281, 286
mysticism 7, 42, 67, 85, 103–5, 172, 174–7, 196–9, 202, 206, 219n. 11, 228, 299, 232, 273–5, 299–301 *see also* epiphany; esotericism; holy, the
mythology 5–6, 70n. 3, 126, 204n. 70, 215, 238–40, 244–6

Nature
art, relation to 76, 90, 103, 127n. 149, 128–9, 129n. 152, 138, 140, 146–69, 151n. 216, 158, 166n. 258, 178–9, 229–30
Book of 146, 164–5
concept of 67, 70n. 3, 117–18, 128–9, 145, 164, 203–5
disclosure of 71, 74, 77, 86, 88–90, 94, 97, 102–4, 106, 112, 122, 145–6, 163, 171, 174, 177–81, 197 203, 211, 229, 231–75
domination of 78, 180–1
estrangement from 71, 75–8, 84, 94, 99, 102
life 77, 102, 112, 116–17, 147
mechanism 37, 93–4, 231, 233, 239, 241
natura naturans and *natura naturata* 68, 78, 164, 166
organicism 37, 79n. 21, 94–5, 150, 157, 233–6
physis 35, 163, 296

science, and 68, 94–5, 120, 176, 180–1, 231, 239–40, 244
technology, and 104, 180–1
see also Nature under Cézanne; Nature under Rodin; Nature under Rilke
Nietzsche, Friedrich 2, 6, 16, 35
non-dualism see twofold under seeing; Weltinnenraum
Nostitz, Helene 118n. 126
Novalis [Friedrich von Hardenberg] 90, 94–6, 172, 221–2, 305–6
numinous, the see epiphany; God, gods, goddesses; mysticism

objectifying thinking see objectifying, as under metaphysics
objectivity, discussion of the term 33, 94n. 48, 95–6, 111n. 107, 121–3, 143, 152–4, 167–9, 172, 208, 255n. 92, 275 see also exactitude (detail); objectness under Husserl; reductionism
Olzien, Otto H. 292, 295
ontology 4, 7, 10, 15–18, 22–5, 31–4, 37–8, 40, 99, 117–18, 152–3, 162–4, 167–8, 187n. 41, 190–2, 226–30, 233, 235, 239–41, 252, 291, 294
Oppert, Kurt 227
Other, human 11–12, 39–44, 46–68, 70, 76–7, 87–8, 183, 285, 299

painting 7, 52, 57, 75–6, 84, 87, 92–4, 97n. 61, 98–100, 106–7, 116, 130, 133, 137, 141–2, 144–69, 177–8, 182, 186, 208, 210, 217–18, 286 see also Cézanne
perception see seeing
Petzet, Heinrich Wiegand 145–6, 153, 168

Phelan, Anthony 135n. 170, 228n. 32
phenomenology
  chiasmic 7, 29n. 21, 59–60, 65, 174, 187–9, 195n. 57, 213, 218–20, 227, 256, 282
  epiphanic 7, 39, 105n. 88, 145–50, 171, 173–4, 189n. 147, 195–8, 201–4, 219–20, 246–56, 260–3, 272–5, 289, 300–1
  everyday, and the 11, 33, 40–2, 67, 70–1, 171, 174–5, 177, 188, 202, 218, 290, 299–301
  exceptional, of the 12n. 19, 39, 41–2, 67, 71, 84, 145, 158, 171–7, 185, 196, 218–20, 226, 231, 238, 243, 262, 265, 299–301
  exceptionality of 25–40
phenomenological attitude 33, 40, 171n. 1, 218
phenomenological reduction 31–4, 144, 216–18
poetry, and 4–5, 207–10, 215–21, 227–8, 228–9n. 33, 232, 250–5, 260–4, 291–2, 300–3
see also Böhme; Heidegger; hermeneutics (hermeneutic phenomenology); Husserl; Marion; Merleau-Ponty; Scheler
philosophy
  end of 2–6, 16, 206, 221, 300
  poetry, and 4–5, 8–10, 209–10, 218, 220–8, 285–6, 300–3, 305–6
  transformation of 1, 4–6, 95, 221, 285n. 140, 301–3
  see also Heidegger; Husserl; Merleau–Ponty, language; metaphysics; phenomenology
Pissarro, Camille 161n. 245
Plumwood, Val 15n. 1, 39

poem
  criticism of 19, 99, 213–14, 225–6, 287, 302
  form of 211–14, 230, 242–3, 246, 249, 270, 282, 284–90, 297
  truth disclosing, as 212, 224, 259n. 102, 262
  see also Rilke; language
poet *see* Rilke; artist
poetry
  extending philosophy, as 5–7, 13, 221, 225n. 24, 300–3, 305–6 *see also* poetic *under* thinking
  mysticism, and 7, 42, 172–3, 175–7, 202, 228, 273–4, 301 *see also* mysticism *under* Rilke
  nature, and 76, 90, 99, 103, 127n. 149, 128–9, 129n. 152, 138, 140, 146–69, 151n. 216, 158, 166n. 258, 178–9, 229–69
  and philosophy as mutually beneficial 104n. 85, 302–3, 305–6
  see also language; poem; Rilke
portraiture 75–6, 124, 126, 128, 131–3, 135–6, 141, 143, 148–52, 156, 160–1, 186, 273
post-modernism 43, 98–9, 301
Pound, Ezra 210, 249, 261n. 103
Prel, Carl du 232
Pre-Socratics 4–6, 19, 35, 244

réalisation, la 146n. 207, 150–8, 162, 217, 242, 252, 275–6, 285, 298
reductionism 6, 24–5, 56, 120–3, 147, 181, 220, 244
Rigby, Kate 99, 129n. 152, 230n. 36
Rilke, Rainer Maria
  Capri 114, 143, 188, 197–8, 200, 204–5, 273–4
  Cézanne

  influence of 74–5, 97–100, 113–14, 123, 127n. 149, 141–3, 177–8, 199, 208
  intermedial connections (between painting and poetry) 9–10, 74–5, 94, 97–100, 110n. 104, 127–8n. 149, 146n. 207, 152–5, 154n. 228, 185, 188, 208–9, 215, 216–18, 227, 229, 237, 242, 252–3, 275–6, 284–5, 297–8, 300
  seeing, similarities in manner of 75, 110, 113, 123, 143–6, 177–8, 185, 217–18
  see also *Briefe über Cézanne under* works; *sachliches Sagen*; *réalisation, la*
  childhood, view of 78–92, 270–1, 281–2 *see also* childlikeness *under* dispositions
  Ding and *Kunst-Ding* 123–41, 178–82, 227–30 *see also* models, use of
  Dinggedicht, discussion of the term 10, 72, 94n. 48, 95, 124n. 140, 210, 215–16, 221–2, 224–5, 227–31, 236, 242–3, 252–3, 255–6, 273, 275, 279–80, 291, 293, 297–8, 300
  dualism, problem of
    approach to 1–2, 9–10, 15n. 1, 21, 39, 41–3, 67, 69–78, 92, 171–4, 191, 198–206, 215, 221–2, 231, 299–303
    developmental conception of 78–91, 271
  epiphany (epiphanic disclosure) 39, 41, 145–6, 171–2, 174, 187, 189n. 49, 195–6, 198, 201–2, 204, 219–20, 246, 249, 253–4, 256–7, 260, 262–3, 272–5, 282, 289, 301

Gadamer, and 8–9n. 12, 175n. 8, 290, 291–7
Gelassenheit see Gelassenheit under dispositions
Heidegger, and 2, 7–9, 12n. 19, 75, 99–100, 102–13, 150–68, 174–6, 181n. 26, 206, 207–11, 216–18, 221, 223, 226n. 27, 228, 230n. 36, 233, 280–1, 291–7, 300–3
Husserl, and 9, 171n. 1, 174, 184, 189n. 48, 216–21, 232, 253–6, 291, 300–1
impartiality *see* impartiality *under* dispositions
Kassner, Rudolf, and 73n. 10, 74, 176–7, 204n. 70
Merleau-Ponty, and 7, 9–10, 12, 41, 75, 99–100, 117, 130, 150–68, 174, 187, 195n. 57, 217–21, 233, 255–6 *see also* chiasm
middle period compared to late period 8n. 12, 70–3, 198–201, 205, 215 see also *Weltinnenraum*
modelé 115–17, 120, 124–7, 289
models, use of 182–4, 188, 285, 291 *see also* Rodin
mysticism 40–2, 67–8, 103–6, 172–7, 196–202, 206, 219n. 11, 228, 232, 273–4, 299–301 *see also* epiphany (epiphanic disclosure)
Nature
animals 12, 70–2, 79, 127–8n. 149, 143, 178–98, 200, 202–6, 209, 212, 216, 230n. 36, 231–53, 267, 275–6, 290
flowers 179, 181–2, 188, 193–5, 253–67
landscape 41, 70, 75–7, 98, 142, 145–6, 177–8, 182, 188, 199, 272–5

non–dualism *see* seeing, twofold (non–dualistic); *Weltinnenraum*
Paris 75n. 14, 101n. 72, 110n. 104, 140, 178, 184, 199, 228, 236–7, 276, 280, 289
poverty *see* poverty *under* dispositions
Rodin
influence of 9–10, 71, 74–5, 96–113, 115–46, 171, 178–9, 213, 286
intermedial connections (between sculpture and poetry) 182–3, 213, 215, 227–30, 237, 241, 275, 284–6, 289
seeing, similarities in manner of 75, 113–14, 178–9, 182–8, 227, 230, 237, 240–1, 275, 285–6, 289
Romanticism, and 70n. 3, 84, 90–6, 100, 103, 129n. 152, 169, 171, 211, 225, 230n. 36, 233, 244, 256–7
sachliches Sagen 207–10, 216–17, 223, 231, 237, 244, 255n. 92, 256, 292n. 157, 300 *see also* Cézanne
seeing, twofold (non–dualistic) learning 96–7, 137, 177–8, 181–2, 195 *see also* Rilke *under* Rodin; Rilke *under* Cézanne
poetry, imaginative articulation in 9–10, 69, 71, 209, 215–98, 300–1
praxis of 9–10, 12, 41–3, 67–8, 171–214, 299–301
Sehen (Anschauen, Einsehen, Schauen) see seeing, twofold (non–dualistic)
Spain 198–200, 202, 204, 273, 283
Uexküll, Jakob von, and 111n.

107, 186, 192–3, 232–42,
  246–50
Verwandlung (transformation)
  72–3, 96, 156n. 232, 204n. 70,
  206–7
Weltinnenraum 198–207, 239, 256,
  258, 270n. 116, 298
Werk des Gesichts, discussion of
  the expression 73, 88, 96,
  113
works
  "*Ach, nicht getrennt sein…*" 21
  Auguste Rodin 74–5, 101–3,
    105–6, 112, 115–41, 213n. 91
  Briefe an einen jungen Dichter
    (*Letters to a Young Poet*)
    110–11
  Briefe über Cézanne (*Letters on
    Cézanne*) 74–5, 93n. 46, 98,
    105–6, 133–4, 141–6, 153–8,
    160–2, 177–8, 208
  *Briefwechsel mit Magda von
    Hattingberg "Benvenuta"*
    (*Correspondence with Magda
    von Hattingberg "Benvenuta"*)
    190–3, 195–6
  Das Buch der Bilder (*The Book of
    Images*) 277n. 125
  Das Stundenbuch (*The Book of
    Hours*) 93n. 46, 177
  *Die Aufzeichnungen des Malte
    Laurids Brigge* (*The Notebooks
    of Malte Laurids Brigge*) 81,
    86, 94, 96–7, 103, 110, 120,
    153, 172, 181–2, 196, 199,
    212, 237, 261, 276
  Die Sonette an Orpheus (*The
    Sonnets to Orpheus*) 8–9,
    70–2, 180–1n. 25, 204n. 70,
    215, 244n. 73, 259–60n. 102
  Duineser Elegien (*Duino Elegies*)
    8–9, 71–3, 182, 204n. 70,
    206–7, 215, 305n. 2
  "Erlebnis (I & II)" 197–205
  "*Es winkt zu Fühlung…*"
    ["Weltinnenraum–Gedicht"]
    202–6
  Neue Gedichte (*New Poems*)
    "Archaïscher Torso
      Apollos" 138–41, 215, 271,
      286–91
    "Begegnung in der
      Kastanien–Allee" 189n.
      47, 290n. 150
    "Béguinage" 281
    "Blaue Hortensie" 217–19,
      253–63
    "Das Einhorn" 242
    "Das Karussell" 279–82
    "Das Rosen-Innere" 253,
      257–8, 260
    "Der Ball" 228, 291–7
    "Der Blinde" 228, 276–8
    "Der Gefangene" 242
    "Der Panther" 178, 182,
      190–2, 213, 215, 228,
      236–43, 245–6
    "Der Schwan" 228, 246–50,
      276
    "Die Erblindende" 276–8
    "Die Erwachsene" 84–6,
      89, 92
    "Die Fensterrose" 290
    "Die Gazelle" 184–8, 191–2,
      208–9, 213, 242–6
    "Die Rosenschale" 228, 253,
      258, 263–5
    "Früher Apollo" 102n. 77,
      138, 139n. 183, 244, 271–2,
      286, 288
    "Kindheit" 79–82
    "Landschaft" 272–5
    "Mädchen-Klage" 81–4
    "Persisches Heliotrop" 258
    "Quai du Rosaire" 281
    "Rosa Hortensie" 253,
      256–60, 262
    "Schlaf-Mohn" 265–7

Index

"Schlangen-Beschwörer" 252n. 86
"Schwarze Katze" 194–5, 250–2, 290
"Spanische Tänzerin" 254, 276, 282–6
"Todes-Erfahrung" 262
"Vor dem Sommerregen" 262, 267–71
"Wendung" 73, 88, 193
Worpswede 74–90, 92–5, 102, 142, 169, 171
Rilke-Westhoff, Clara 71, 74–5, 97, 102, 115, 134, 142, 153–5, 177, 182, 184–5, 187–8, 273–4
Rodin, Auguste
  artistic disposition 100–5, 110n. 104, 112, 119–20, 179
  Cézanne, and 74–5, 96–100, 110n. 104, 114–15, 105, 113, 139, 127n. 149, 137, 141–5, 146n. 206, 148, 150–1, 155–6, 159–61, 169, 171, 173, 229, 275, 284–5
  Ding and *Kunst-Ding* 123–41, 179, 227, 229–30
  fragments and torsi 120, 122, 124, 130, 136–41, 286, 289
  life 101–2, 112, 116–17, 122–3, 131, 137–8
  Merleau-Ponty on 129–30
  modelé 115–17, 120, 124–7, 289
  models 118–20, 123–5, 127, 182–8
  movement (dynamism) 115–23, 129–32, 229, 241
  Nature 100–5, 112, 116–18, 122, 128–9, 138, 178–9
  physiognomic vision 115–23, 131–2, 141 *see also* Rilke *under* Rodin
  portraiture 124, 126–8, 131–3, 135–6, 148, 150
Rilke
  influence on 9–10, 71, 74–5, 96–113, 115–46, 171, 178–9, 213, 286
  intermedial connections (between sculpture and poetry) 182–3, 213, 215, 227–30, 237, 241, 275, 284–6, 289
  seeing, similarities in manner of 75, 113–14, 178–9, 182–8, 227, 230, 237, 240–1, 275, 285–6, 289
Romanticism 6, 70n. 3, 84, 90–6, 100, 103, 129n. 152, 166n. 258, 169, 171, 211, 225, 230n. 36, 233, 244, 256
Rumi 172
Runge, Philipp Otto 84, 88, 92–4, 169
Ryan, Judith 229n. 33, 231n. 37
Ryan, Lawrence 215n. 1, 278n. 127

sachliches Sagen see *sachliches Sagen under* Cézanne; Rilke
Scheler, Max 27, 36, 43, 53–5, 68, 79n. 21, 112–13n. 113, 175n. 8, 183–4, 281
Schiller, Friedrich 6
Schlegel, Friedrich 95
Schleiermacher, Friedrich 50–1, 59
Schmidt–Pauli, Elisabeth von 292n. 157
Schmitz, Hermann 107, 109n. 102
Schmoll gen. Eisenwerth, J. A. 118n. 126, 136, 141n. 185, 289
Schnell, Werner 136, 141n. 186
seeing
  chiasmic 7, 29n. 21, 59–60, 65, 174, 187–9, 195n. 57, 213, 218–20, 227, 256, 282
  epiphanic 41, 105n. 88, 145–50, 171–2, 174, 189n. 49, 195–6, 198, 201–2, 204, 219–20, 246, 249, 253–4, 256–7, 260, 262–3, 272–5, 282, 289, 301

hermeneutic character of 46,
51–4, 60–4, 228 *see also*
hermeneutics (hermeneutic
phenomenology)
participative 84, 86, 119, 122,
141–50, 187–92, 195–8
physiognomic 114–23, 132, 141,
145, 184, 188, 198, 209, 227,
240–1, 245, 247, 250–3, 265,
275
twofold 11–12, 68–71, 76–7,
88, 99, 118, 123, 129, 166,
172–215, 220–7, 229, 252–3,
264, 275, 298, 300–1
see also Cézanne; Rilke; Rodin
Seubold, Günter 154n. 228, 159–60,
167
Shaw, George Bernard 131
Shiff, Richard 156
solipsism 44, 47n. 57, 64, 66, 183–4,
232
Steinbock, Anthony J. 40n. 50, 47n.
57, 105n. 88, 175–6
Steiner, Rudolf 112–13n. 113,
232–3n. 42
subjectivism 17, 27, 30–1, 34, 38,
199, 220, 231–2, 237, 239 *see
also* anthropomorphism;
solipsism
sympathy 43, 50n. 63, 82–3, 183–4,
212 *see also* empathy
synaesthesia 158, 258, 274–5, 284–5

Tagore, Rabindranath 268–9
theology 173–6, 245
thinking
  conceptual 1–2, 5–6, 10, 212–14,
  224n. 24, 225, 285–6, 300–2
  imaginative 28, 209, 213, 222–5,
  227, 238, 241–2, 245, 251–3,
  275, 278, 284–7, 296–8,
  300–1 *see also* imagination;

imagination, and *under*
language
philosophical *see* conceptual
poetic 35–6, 225–7, 285–6, 300–2,
305
scientific 18–19, 26–9, 31, 121–2,
144, 181, 217–18, 220, 225,
238–40, 244
see also language
truth (as unconcealment) *see* truth
under Heidegger; truth
disclosing, as *under* poem
twofold vision *see* seeing

Uexküll, Jakob von 111n. 107, 186,
192–3, 232–41, 248
Uexküll, Thure von 234–5
Umwelt 183, 185, 192, 195, 233–6,
239–42, 246–50
understanding 33–5, 50–5, 59–68,
100, 299

Valéry, Paul 210–11

Waldenfels, Bernhard 47n. 57, 49,
68n. 87
Waters, William 228–9n. 33, 247n.
77, 252n. 86
Weltinnenraum 198–207, 239, 256,
258, 270n. 116, 298
Werk des Gesichts, discussion of the
expression 73, 88, 96, 113
Wesensschau 189, 191, 216, 219,
254–5
Wordsworth, William 90–2, 94
Worpswede artists 71, 74–5, 84,
88–9

Yeats, W. B. 90, 172–3, 285

Zahavi, Dan 49n. 28
Zweig, Stefan 228–9n. 33

www.ingramcontent.com/pod-product-compliance
Lightning Source LLC
Chambersburg PA
CBHW071759300426
44116CB00009B/1136